The
Complete
Gardener

Monty Don

The Complete Gardener

Monty Don

For Sarah

Contents

Introduction

In January 2002 I found myself, for the first time in twelve years, with no television project lined up for the year ahead. So I set out to write what I thought would be my definitive work on organic gardening.

The book, which until a month before publication had the working title of *Completely Organic*, would cover every aspect of this garden that was then in its tenth year, and it was to be my final horticultural will and testament. Once it was published I would never write another gardening book because there would be no more to be said. I could give it all my time and attention and when it was done, I would devote myself to writing about landscape and perhaps novels, and garden just for myself and my family.

But, as ever, things did not go quite to plan. Throughout spring I worked away, the photographer Ari Ashley came weekly and photographed every aspect of my garden life, and the book steadily accrued in the laborious way that all books do.

But at the beginning of June I received a phone call from the BBC asking if I would like to take over the helm of *Gardeners' World*. Although I had made many gardening programmes for ITV and Channel 4 and had also worked a great deal with the BBC over the years, I had never previously had any connection or contact with *Gardeners' World*, had no idea that the job was vacant and had no designs or plans in that direction, so I was a little surprised. However it was, and is, the country's flagship gardening programme, arguably the most influential and important of its kind in the world, and it took me all of one second to accept.

This changed a number of things, some in ways I had not remotely considered. For a start it imposed a deadline on what had hitherto been a steady writing progress, influenced as much by the weather as anything else. When it was sunny, I gardened and when it rained I wrote. That had to be replaced by a more rigorous writing regime in order to have the book finished, edited and ready for publication before I began work on *Gardeners' World* at the beginning of the year. It also meant that the underlying fundamentals of the book – organic gardening – would come under much closer scrutiny. I realised that this was an opportunity to stand up and be counted and spread the organic word to a much wider audience than I had access to when I started to write the book. So the organic aspects were paramount.

Back in 2002 organic gardening was still seen as a slightly subversive activity by many in the horticultural establishment, and especially by the trade whose income derived hugely from the use and sale of pesticides, fungicides and herbicides, as well as from the almost universal commercial use of peat. But over and above the practical aspects, there was a cultural attitude that nature was the gardener's enemy. Good gardening involved conquering and subduing nature so that it would not spoil a lovely garden.

I am glad to say that now, in 2020 as I write this, only the very cynical, very stupid or very ignorant seriously believe these things. All of us are aware, through the evidence of climate change, the extinction of and decline in so many species, the increase in atmospheric pollution, the effects of plastics on the oceans, the rise in allergies and asthma in children, and so many other signs and signals, that we are starting to pay the price for mistreating this planet. Gardening (although sadly not farming) organically and holistically is now mainstream and the militant anti-organic gardeners are a diminishing minority.

I took a break from *Gardeners' World* in 2007 after suffering a minor stroke. Over the previous eighteen months I had travelled the world visiting gardens for a series and book, *Around the World in 80 Gardens*, and was exhausted. I recuperated in this garden, pottering gently and re-establishing a connection that had become stretched thin by other commitments. I realised that gardening had most meaning for me from a personal, subjective viewpoint and decided that if I ever returned to practical television gardening, it would have to be from here, in this deeply personal garden.

However, I returned to work with enthusiasm, made television series about Italian gardens, smallholding and crafts, and wrote a couple of gardening books as well as a second cookbook with my wife Sarah. I was enjoying the liberation from a weekly, instructive television series. Then I had another phone call from the BBC. Would I return to *Gardeners' World*? This time I thought long and hard. In the end I agreed, but only if it was filmed here, in this garden – which it has been since February 2011.

This has inevitably changed the garden a lot. We are now a very private garden which millions of people visit most weeks – even if few ever set foot in it.

We have had to smarten up. Until we started filming here every week, we would usually have at least one part of the garden that was not at its best or even lying fallow. We would get round to fixing it in our own sweet time and it was extremely rare for all the parts of the garden to be looking good all at the same moment. That does not work for filming. Television has an insatiable appetite for content and every corner of my two-acre plot is potential filming material every week – so it all has to look good all the time.

To that end I started to employ two full-time helpers and, with various personnel changes over the years, this is still the case. It means that we now garden as a team, dancing to the demands of television as much as according to our own whims, but it has brought opportunities to do and grow more. I have also had to dramatically increase

We are now a very private garden, which millions of people visit most weeks – even if few ever set foot in it

the range and variety of both the plants we grow and the different gardens within the garden. Only the Spring Garden, the Dry Garden, the Jewel Garden and the Coppice have remained more or less unchanged. Over the past ten years I have added the Cottage Garden, a large pond in the Damp Garden, the Grass Borders, the Mound, the Orchard Beds, the Soft Fruit Garden, the Writing Garden, the Paradise Garden and the Wildlife Garden. I have also moved the vegetables to a new location, made a completely new Herb Garden, added a new greenhouse and dramatically changed the Cricket Pitch. Box blight has meant ripping out the box balls and many of our hedges – and many more will have to go shortly.

Twenty years has added a huge amount of growth to all our trees and deciduous hedges and as a result we have much more dramatic and splendid specimens but rather less light. I had not foreseen this or at least not thought it through, and quite a lot of our planting has to change as a result. Also, 20 years of heavy mulching means that our soil is now a joy to work with. Heavy, intractable clay has become a rich, crumbly loam.

Where my children once rode their bikes, my grandson now toddles. Five dogs that were, in turn, at my side as I gardened are now buried in the Coppice. My knees remind me unkindly of the extra 20 years of use every morning as I stumble out of bed.

So it feels timely to bring this book up to date and to share all these changes, with new pictures of the garden by the wonderful Marsha Arnold, and to share

Our gardens are more important than ever as places of refuge and solace, and for physical and mental wellbeing

the extra experience and knowledge that I have acquired over the past two decades. In that time I have not only gardened here, but travelled the world extensively, visiting gardens of all kinds. This has inevitably informed and changed the way that I garden so although the techniques and processes that I used 20 years ago remain largely unchanged, the context, both private and public, is completely different.

In the public realm climate change, pandemics, flailing governments and constant destruction in pursuit of cheap, unsustainable food have made the world a more threatened and fragile place. Our gardens have become more important than ever as places of refuge and solace as well as bringing a much greater awareness of their role in achieving and maintaining physical and mental wellbeing.

But for all the passing of time and the glare of television publicity, the essence of this garden remains the same. If no longer wholly private, it is still personal, a family home made and shared with love. And that is the secret of good gardening. There is no one true way. If it works for you, then you are doing it right. If you have respect for the natural world, try and leave the lightest footprint possible and garden for your children and grandchildren, perhaps as yet unborn. Then you are doing right by the world.

Evolution of the garden

Looking from the centre of the Jewel Garden between the two halves of the Coppice, down along the length of the Cricket Pitch. The first picture was taken about 1993 and the second 20 years later.

Looking out over the box balls (now the Herb Garden) and the Cottage Garden. The picture on the left was taken in November 1991 and the one on the right about 20 years later, before box blight struck.

The Writing Garden – before and after. In fact very little changed other than all the turf was removed to make borders. The brick path follows exactly the line of the originally mown grass path.

A view of the garden taken in March 2011 from a huge crane brought in by the BBC when we began to film *Gardeners' World* in the garden. There have been many changes since then but the structure remains the same.

The Damp Garden just before and a few months after the pond was made. I placed the rope all over the garden, trying out different areas before choosing this site.

The Dry Garden was for many years our yard for dumping and storing building materials but although it was an unpromising site, it has made a lovely garden with its own distinct character.

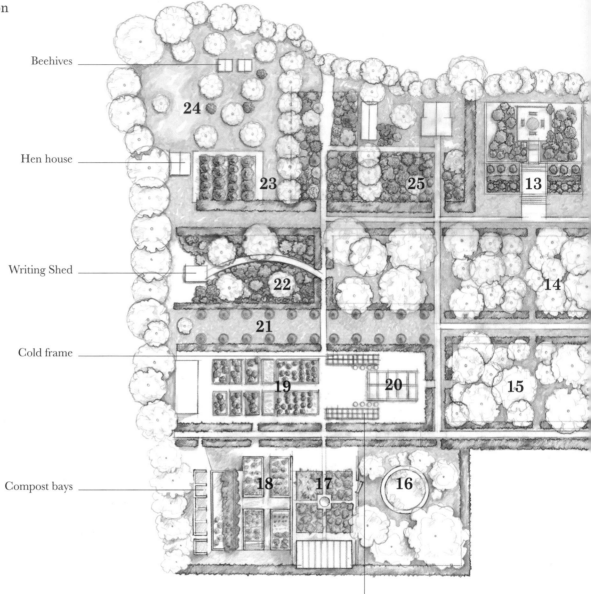

Beehives

Hen house

Writing Shed

Cold frame

Compost bays

Cold frame

The Longmeadow garden

A garden is never a fixed entity but always a process and although the structure of my garden stays largely the same, the planting is in a constant state of change and reinvention.

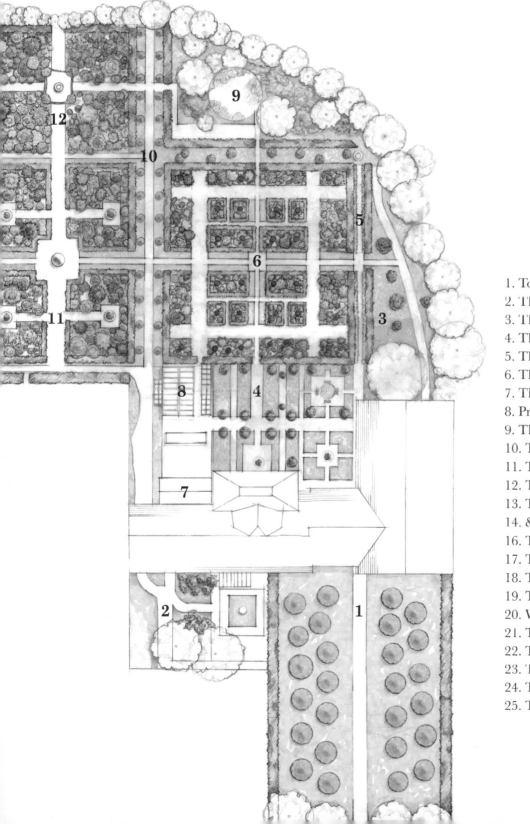

1. Topiary yew cones
2. The Dry Garden
3. The Spring Garden
4. The Herb Garden
5. The Lime Walk
6. The Cottage Garden
7. The Potting Shed
8. Propagating (bottom) greenhouse
9. The Damp Garden
10. The Long Walk
11. The Jewel Garden
12. The Grass Borders
13. The Mound
14. & 15. The Coppice
16. The Wildlife Garden
17. The Paradise Garden
18. The New Vegetable Garden
19. The Vegetable Garden
20. Wooden (top) greenhouse
21. The Cricket Pitch
22. The Writing Garden
23. The Soft Fruit Garden
24. The Orchard
25. The Orchard Beds

Wildlife

One of the biggest developments over the past 20-odd years is the huge growth in interest in the wildlife that we share our gardens with.

Opposite page, clockwise from top left: Some of our prunings are used as firewood but the stack provides good cover and protection for a wide range of wildlife, especially over winter.

A peacock butterfly feasting on nectar from *Verbena bonariensis*.

Teasels look good all winter and their seeds are loved by goldfinches.

Growing a wide range of open, accessible plants rich in pollen and nectar is the best way to attract pollinating insects to any garden.

Fifty years ago almost all living creatures that were not pets or producing eggs or meat were grouped as 'pests' and a measure of a gardener's skill was how effectively he or she killed them off. The concept of a holistic, integrated garden was at best eccentric and, much more commonly, viewed as incompetent.

In truth, I like to think of every little bit of this garden attracting as wide and varied a range of creatures as possible. I accept that some of them do not have my best horticultural interests at heart and others do not exist solely for my own entertainment or delight. In return, I hope they tolerate my presence as another bit of wildlife sharing the same space.

A few years ago I converted a corner into a specifically designated 'wildlife garden' – a kind of exemplar of how to attract a wide range of creatures – but in fact I have carefully contrived as rich and varied a habitat as I can for my fellow creatures right across every part of the garden. Create the right environment and animals will come.

To attract birds you need cover both for protection and nesting, and deciduous hedges and small garden trees are ideal for this. Add in the other essential ingredients of a certain lack of tidiness (of which more later), water and long grass, and the garden – any garden – becomes the perfect home for songbirds.

Piles of sticks and logs also make excellent shelter and cover, and marginal planting, both in and outside a pond, serves the same purpose. Any roots that spread or plants that fall should be left. Cover of all kinds is good even if it looks messy to the fastidious horticultural eye, so don't worry about algae, duckweed or keeping your pond clean and clear. Even a stagnant puddle is a rich resource for wildlife and far better than no water at all. Apart from anything else, water tends to self-regulate and respond to weather and the seasons without any human help. In fact, tidiness in general will always do more harm than good. Become the passive but fascinated observer rather than the busy gardener.

But bear in mind that all those hungry predators need prey, so a certain balance has to be struck in order not to eliminate all slugs and snails (chance would be a fine thing) or aphids, whitefly or whatever. Leave enough so that your garden can cope with their slight depredations but the predators – be they songbirds, hedgehogs, toads or beetles – have sufficient to eat. In turn, this means that you have a high number of predators to eat the so-called 'pests', which are nearly always a

Every wildlife pond should have a shallow 'beach' so small creatures of all kinds can easily get in and out of the water.

symptom rather than the disease. Instead of trying to get rid of them, work out what you are doing to make them so welcome to your garden. Almost certainly you have upset the restraining, self-regulating balance. It can be regained – but not by isolating and zapping pests.

But that balance does not happen without the helping hand of a gardener. A healthy garden is one where every action has a commensurate reaction, securing the balance rather than dislodging it. Much of a gardener's skill is best applied to maintaining and setting up this balance. Of course a natural balance of sorts will be struck over time – and there is a fascinating and very long-term rewilding experiment under way in the Netherlands at the Oostvaardersplassen, north of Amsterdam, instigated by the ecologist Frans Vera, to observe what really happens when man does not intervene at all – but that is not gardening. As with all definitions of a garden, it has to involve a gardener, however natural or rich with wildlife you wish it to be.

I have spent the past 25 years in the creation of this garden, trying to provide the best conditions for that balance to establish itself and flourish in the face of all seasons, weathers and circumstances. Some of this has been specific in terms of habitats such as long grass, woodland and ponds, and the rest more a set of attitudes and approaches to how I manage and run the garden.

Some long grass, be it a sweep of wildflower meadow or a straggly uncut corner, is essential

If you want to share your garden with beautiful and fascinating birds, reptiles insects and mammals, then you must start by not using pesticides, herbicides or fungicides. Stop killing wildlife in the name of neatness or a very selective version of 'health'. Chemicals are not selective. Although there are occasions when the caterpillars munching through your brassicas or the slug that has devastated your hostas might simply be classed as 'the enemy', in almost all circumstances they are part of a much bigger, much richer picture. Live and let live.

Then you can take a few simple but very effective proactive measures.

Any water in the garden – and we now have two ponds, one in the Damp Garden and the other, smaller one, in the Wildlife Garden – will immediately bring in dragonflies, grass snakes, frogs and toads, as well as increased bird and bat activity. If the water is planted with plenty of marginals that will provide cover, and has stones or logs that stick out of it for perching on (and frogs love the floating log in our wildlife pond), as well as having a section of shallow 'beach' so mammals such as hedgehogs can safely drink, then so much the better.

Some long grass, be it a sweep of wildflower meadow or a straggly uncut corner, is essential. We have a number of areas that have long grass, including the Orchard and Coppice, and the Cricket Pitch whose grass is left uncut from October through to July. This provides cover for insects but also for small mammals, invertebrates and reptiles. Ideally you would have grass of varying

lengths to provide a wide range of habitats, but a metre square of long grass will make all the difference.

As well as grass, the most active predatory insects, such as lacewings, hoverflies, ladybirds and parasitic wasps, that will keep your damaging insects under control far better than any insecticide, can be encouraged by planting a few essentials such as dill, angelica, marigolds, calendula and cosmos. All are good and potentially beautiful plants that can be enjoyed by you as much as by the insects.

After the indiscriminate use of pesticides, nothing is more detrimental to wildlife than officious tidiness. Leave long grass, fallen leaves, windfall fruit, rotting wood, patches of weeds, grass growing in the cracks, moss on the stone. These are all important habitats for wildlife and there is no reason why they cannot be gently tweaked to look beautiful as well as be useful. I keep any logs from larger

branches that I am increasingly pruning as the Longmeadow trees become ever more mature, and stack them in the Coppice to very slowly rot down – not so much a bug hotel as a complete wildlife city that will accommodate a range of beings as diverse as fungi and field mice.

There is evidence that butterfly numbers are dropping, albeit with annual fluctuations, but butterflies, like honeybees, can be encouraged by specific planting. This will include plants for their young – i.e. caterpillars (more 'pests') – as well as for the adults. Nettles, ivy, holly and long grass are all sites chosen by different butterflies to lay their eggs.

The adult butterflies will want nectar-filled and scented plants (especially, for some reason, vanilla-scented, which seems to be the most irresistible fragrance for butterflies), for example buddleja, honeysuckle, sedums, lavender, Michaelmas daisies and valerian.

Above left: A narrow mown path is the only grass in the Orchard that is cut until late summer, by which time the foliage of the bulbs has died back and the wild flowers set seed.

Above: A scythe is still one of the best ways to cut a small area of long grass and certainly the most satisfying, as well as being quiet, cheap and environmentally friendly.

For bees and pollinators

Annuals, biennials and perennials
- *Alcea*
- *Agastache*
- *Allium*
- *Asteraceae*
- *Campanula*
- *Centaurea cyanus*
- *Cosmos*
- *Geranium*
- *Geum*
- *Malva sylvestris*
- *Oenothera biennis*
- *Salvia verbenaca*
- *Scabiosa*

Shrubs
- *Buddleja*
- *Ceanothus*
- *Cotoneaster*
- *Mahonia*
- *Rosa* (shrub)
- *Syringa*

Trees
- *Castanea sativa*
- *Corylus*
- *Crataegus*
- Fruit trees (all)
- *Prunus avium*
- *Prunus spinosa*

Bees and other pollinators

I have two beehives in the Orchard. One is a top bar type and the other a more conventional WBC kind. From dawn to dusk there is now a constant procession of bees going out to forage in the garden and others returning laden with nectar. I have been mentored in this by a wise and charming local beekeeper who will watch over me for the next year or so until I have learned my bee-keeping ropes.

The planting for the bees is based upon the knowledge that honeybees will always exhaust a supply of preferred nectar before moving to another source – whereas bumblebees are more likely to graze, moving from plant to plant. So the key for bees is to supplement their fruit-blossom or heather supplies that arrive en masse for a few weeks, during which time the bees will gorge themselves almost exclusively upon them before they disappear for a year. So plants with a long flowering period and a succession of blooms are better for bees than a short, spectacular harvest. Such plants may be simple and very common – oxeye daisies, cornflowers and all forms of scabious are firm bee favourites – but

are essential and, critically, increasingly rare in the agricultural landscape. This means that gardens are becoming the most important habitat for bees as they are for so many forms of hitherto abundant wildlife.

Bear in mind that bees do not see red at all – so a purely red flower will be ignored by them unless it has blotches or stripes that lead the bee to the pollen and nectar. Blue, pink, green and yellow plants will always be the most attractive.

Bees also love all fruit trees – in fact any flowering trees – and all legumes such as peas, beans, clover and sweet peas, as well as dandelions, blackberries, asters, ivy and willow. It is always better to have simple flowers with an open, saucer shape that is easier for the bees' relatively short tongues to dip into than the more complex and inaccessible – to the human eye at least – flower heads of spectacular hybridised varieties.

Wildlife essentials
- Water
- Cover (including fallen leaves, bundles of sticks, old logs, etc.)
- Weeds
- Long grass
- A range of flowers with open and accessible shapes and as long a flowering season as possible
- Avoidance of all pesticides, herbicides and fungicides

Bumblebees have longer tongues than honeybees and gorge on nectar from plants such as this knapweed.

Weather

Gardeners have to be on intimate terms with the weather.
It is a language that we have to be fluent in because it
invariably contains information over and above its immediate
sensory experience that we must heed.

Rain, for example, has many horticultural meanings. Frost tells a story that may take weeks or even seasons to play out. Temperature is critical but subtle – and affects plants in very different ways to humans.

All gardeners quickly learn – usually the hard way and at a cost – that every wind comes brandishing a different weapon and that every garden has its vulnerabilities depending on planting and aspect. So in this garden, southerly winds are generally welcome because they quickly dry everything out – but it means we scurry round staking because they also buffet. Westerlies invariably bring rain and sometimes storms, northerlies carry snow and the easterlies are devastating in their coldness and ability to cut through everything – including the walls of the house.

Gardeners also know – or should know – the detailed variations within their own back yards. Microclimates really matter within all but the tiniest gardens. There are always bits of an otherwise seamless lawn that crunch underfoot with frost whilst the rest is still soft. Two identical plants within 1m (3ft) of each other fare completely differently because one just catches the wind that is funnelled through a gap in a hedge the other side of the garden. My melianthus will cope with any amount of winter chill but a cold snap in April – that east wind again – devastates it. And so on with a thousand variations on this theme.

But there is a kind of weather hysteria in almost inverse proportion to the lack of interest in climate change. The latter is arguably the greatest crisis that mankind has ever faced and desperately needs urgent attention – something that so far politicians, businesses and consumers seem blindly reluctant to acknowledge. But weather is variable, cyclical and on the whole pretty reliable. Summers often contain hot, dry spells and winters can bring snow and ice. It can be windy and wet in autumn. So it has always been.

However, for the first time in history more people now live in towns and cities than in the countryside. In the UK this has been the case for more than a hundred years but we have been part of the same global urbanising trend. If you live in the country – and especially if you garden in the country – you notice the weather with every glance out of the window and every step outside. Your weather antennae are

Every wind comes brandishing a different weapon and every garden has its vulnerabilities

acute and constantly active. But in modern cities weather hardly affects or moderates your life at all from one season to the next.

When, on the rare occasions that the weather does put its foot in your door and forces you to pay attention – like the rare heatwave, flood or sharp frost – then it becomes a big event rather than a full-throated expression of the season.

But weather is what happens from day to day. As far as the garden is concerned, weather is neither particularly good nor bad. It just is. Plants adapt and nearly always recover from a rough time. Most survive anything if they are planted in the right place. The gardener cannot always get out and do the jobs exactly as planned but usually, it really does not matter that much. Be flexible. Pay great attention to the weather and respect it but be patient. Adapt. Bend to the weather rather than rail against it.

However, the climate is changing and has changed noticeably since I wrote the first edition of this book 20 years ago. Our winters are steadily becoming wetter and warmer, our springs are coming earlier and tend to be warmer, and summers are warmer and drier but, rather counter-intuitively, less sunny and stormier. My experience is that spring is now arriving five days earlier than two decades ago and we are having at least a week less of freezing weather in winter.

But the main impact has been the dramatic increase in winter rain. Flooding is now a regular event between October and March, with perhaps eight weeks of that period with some part of the garden under water. The impact is rather like a heavy fall of snow. It is in turn slightly alarming, beautiful for a day or two and then just a nuisance, making everything wet and difficult to move around. The knock-on effect is that fungal problems have become much more prevalent through a combination of increased days of warmth and humidity, and the lack of both hot and dry and cold and dry weather to kill off the fungal spores. The box blight (see page 61), for example, that has devastated our box hedges and radically changed the garden in the past ten years, is a direct result of this change in the weather.

However, all in all, the weather here on the western edge of England, 80km (50 miles) west of Birmingham and with the hills on the Welsh border in sight from upstairs windows, is about as good and easy for gardening as anywhere in the world. Our weather can, and often does, change from hour to hour and is never predictable for more than a day or two at a time, but it is rarely very hot or very cold. Spring and autumn are both long and gentle, and rainfall, apart from the increase in flooding, mostly steady or light without torrential or damaging downpours. Strong winds are increasingly becoming a feature as a result of climate change but by and large, the damage they cause is superficial.

So on a micro level, climate change has not made gardening worse for us, just different. But on a macro level, we are acutely aware of the very real changes in climate and the implications for the world at large. Our gardens, for all their comfortable relationship with our mostly benign weather, are the first and most direct relationship we have with climate change.

Opposite page, clockwise from top left: The garden is low-lying and next to a river so has always flooded. Climate change is making the floods more frequent and higher.

Despite milder, wetter winters, we still have some sharp frosts. Horticultural fleece provides temporary protection.

Over our garden hedge wheat bales stand in the sun but in winter this view can be under water for weeks.

Increasing summer drought means we have to water our pots almost daily in hot weather.

Structure

Planning the design

The way that I have designed my garden is, as a friend of mine only half-jokingly described it, 'like a series of allotments'. It means that there are a number of different areas, all quite separate and usually hidden from the rest.

I make no apologies for this and enjoy the surprises and sense of enclosure that it brings.

Inevitably this means that different sections of the garden have their own character. We also try to treat each separate area as though it were the only garden that we had. This means that each section has to stand up to the strictest scrutiny and aesthetic standards. Having said this, one of the reasons for having many different compartments to a garden is that whilst it is very hard, if not impossible, to make an entire garden look wonderful year round, it is much more achievable to have at least one section looking good at any given time. By the same token, some of the different 'rooms' can rest for part of the year or even shut down completely for a while. This gives the opportunity to indulge in favourites that might have a short flowering season or a group of plants that share the same conditions but which are at odds with much of the rest of the garden.

The gardens I like all have two distinct qualities above all else. The first is a strong sense of ownership. Gardens are a human construct and do not just happen, so I like to see the hands of their maker on everything. This gives the garden character, which is more important than any horticultural aspect.

The second is a good use of space. It is the spaces between plants and objects that make a garden interesting, not just the plants themselves. This can be quite a hard concept to grasp for the organised western mind but in

Opposite page: Clipped hawthorn hedges flanking the path leading to the Writing Garden and the Orchard. Although it responds well to clipping, hawthorn always has a slightly informal feel, which is why I have used it as the garden moves out towards the countryside.

truth it is simplicity itself. I think of it (slightly pretentiously) as 'sculpting air'. In practice, it means getting the proportions right with the space available, using paths, walls, hedges, trees and every kind of plant that one wishes to grow so that they make beautiful spaces.

These spaces do not have to be formal or geometrical but they must be considered. Sometimes they create themselves by accident – but if they are recognised then they can be included and relished. It might just be the way that a tree is pruned or how the curve of a path is cut into the long grass or the grouping of pots by a doorway – there is no recipe other than a constant awareness of the shape of the spaces between things. I can be just as pleased by a length of grass path between flanking green hedges as by a complex flower border. The box pebbles of the hop-kiln yard never failed to give

me pleasure, even though I walked through them thousands of times. Knowing how to keep things simple is probably the most important part of any garden.

In practice this has translated itself to this garden by a grid of straight lines marked out by hedges, paths and pleached trees. That has created blocks which have been filled by a variety of gardens. In summer, when everything is lush and fulsome the grid softens and becomes subordinate to the planting within it. In winter it provides a structural framework for what is otherwise a very grey and brown formless scene.

There is a tendency to only visualise a garden in its summer pomp. The unhappy truth is that for half the year it is either waxing or waning and here at Longmeadow, halfway up Britain, it is more often cloudy than clear, more often

Below left: The view into the Jewel Garden in spring reveals the structured, formal layout but very informal, loose planting – a dynamic I love and have used all over Longmeadow.

Below right: Mowing a path through long grass, does not take anything from the looseness and informality that is the essential charm of the Orchard.

wet than dry and the winter days are at best cold and short, and more often positively drab. The most effective way to counter this is with crisp edges and shapes and strong colours. Too much fuzzy planting simply becomes absorbed in the general haze. This is fine on a soft summer's evening but disastrous on a wet November afternoon.

Practical considerations

Over and above any aesthetic considerations there is a mass of practical problems that have to be dealt with when designing a garden. All gardens start at the building to which they are attached. The first thing to do is to establish a 'platform' around the house which is the direct link between building and garden. The size of this will be determined by the house and not the garden and, I think, so should the materials.

Every door and window should relate to the garden, both from the view looking out and looking back to the house. One of the first things that we did here was to make the Lime Walk path that leads from a door in the hall ... only for years after the path was made, the door just led to a narrow passage. But I knew that one day it would become an important link between house and garden so the path had to be in place ready for that time.

For the first four years our only access to the vast majority of the garden was either through the house or via a field that was often flooded or at least very muddy. The gate to this field was right up at the other end of the garden yet became our main service point and the

Orchard was planned entirely around its accessibility. Anything that could not be carried or wheeled easily through the house had to go round there when conditions made it possible and then wheeled to where it was needed in the garden. This meant that paths had to link the end of the garden back to the house rather than vice versa.

It is important to get the practical infrastructure in before any planting begins because it inevitably makes a mess and disruption, and hard paths provide dry access for wheelbarrows, rotovators and even small diggers.

I had the good sense to put a water pipe in the ground when the digger was

The Lime Walk is flanked by pleached limes and immediately draws you down and out into the garden. The bricks for the path were my 40th birthday present from my wife Sarah.

Every door and window should relate to the garden, both from the view looking out and looking back to the house

Opposite page:
Looking down
through the centre of
the Cottage Garden
and on to the Cricket
Pitch in midwinter
shows the structural
bones created by
hedges and trees.

putting in the septic tank, before the garden began. We now have over half a dozen standpipes dotted around – but I wish I had thought this through a little more carefully before planting began.

It is a good idea to get as much structural planting in as soon as possible. With a new garden you can easily cut into grass to make beds and borders at any stage but the hedges and trees need time to establish. I was lucky to buy a whole load of trees in one afternoon from a clearance sale by a tree nursery. This included many hedging plants and kick-started the framework of the planting, turning ideas on a page into three-dimensional reality.

A large ball of heavy duty twine and a bundle of canes are the best design tools in the garden. All the plans are drawn accurately or sketched out on paper but until they are transferred to the ground they remain ideas. Marking everything out with string and canes gives a feel of the spaces and their volumes. I have often found that a convenient 'paper' measurement – usually rounded up or down to the nearest foot – is not best on the ground. As a general rule borders can always be bigger and lawns smaller.

Hedges take 1m (3ft) of ground themselves and affect whatever is growing at their base for a further 1m (3ft) by taking moisture and light. Do you want a path to hurry the walker along – in which case make it straight and narrow – or a place to meander and chat? If the latter it needs to be at least 1.5m (5ft) wide.

Wheelbarrows have to get round corners so need a turning area that is wider than the path. Remember that people do not like to go round things to reach what they can see: either block off the line of sight or make access easier and quicker. All these things can be tested on the ground with the help of some string and canes.

Once I have marked my lines of borders, hedges or paths so that they seem to be exactly where I want them, I have often used hurdles, temporarily staked, to represent hedges and increase the stagecraft. I always live with the strings and canes for at least a week before taking any further action. It is better to live with the rough idea of something for a while before committing yourself than to rush in and regret it later.

Then, when you do plant your hedges, make your paths and dig your borders, I have learned – often painfully – that no amount of preparation or time spent doing the job properly is ever wasted.

Marking everything out with string and canes gives a feel of the spaces and I live with those markings for at least a week before taking any further action

Paths

One of the most marked and unexpected effects of weekly filming in the garden was the wear and tear caused by the extra footfall.

The *Gardeners' World* film crew consists of two cameramen, a sound recordist, director, researcher, runner, usually a producer, and occasionally an extra runner or cameraman. We film in all weathers and never for less than ten hours a day, and the extra six to nine pairs of feet walking, or even just standing, on the grass paths quickly reduce them to a muddy quagmire. If the weather is at all wet – and it usually is – the paths do not have time to recover before the next two-day shoot, and a bad situation gets steadily worse.

So it became imperative to make as many hard paths as possible. But these are expensive and need a lot of labour to make so we have mostly gone for strip paths, wide enough for a wheelbarrow and a pair of feet, down the centre of grass. The disadvantage of this is that if the paths get slippery – and they do when damp – then there is a tendency to deliberately avoid them and walk on the much more sure-footed grass on either side – which completely undoes the point of the brick path!

The Writing Garden path is one of the most successful, partly because it is gently curving (following the original mown line) and partly because we used bricks taken from the interior of an old outbuilding and they are very beautiful. In the Vegetable Garden we have used concrete slabs edged with brick and done the same in the Paradise Garden – to reduce costs rather than as an aesthetic choice. But both work well.

The second thing that I have learned from working with film crews is that paths need to be extra-wide to accommodate splayed tripods and cameras, recordists, monitors and occasional lights. What may be ample for the gardener with a simple wheelbarrow gives much too limited access for a film crew. So our paths get wider and wider. This has meant that the side paths in the Jewel Garden could no longer be edged with box as they had to be widened, and the raised beds in the Vegetable Garden are more widely spaced than necessary so the crew can get at them from every angle.

But, despite the hundreds of yards of hard paths we have laid and the elaborate lengths to accommodate the depredations of the weekly visit of a film crew, of all the paths in the garden my favourite remains the simple mown line through the long grass of the Orchard in spring.

The placement of paths

The primary function of any path is to take you from A to B, but its role can be so much more than that. Paths have a character in their own right and are the viewing platform from which we see and identify with the garden. In other words, careful placement and manipulation of paths will shape every aspect of how we observe and think about our garden.

If a path is the main route to the compost heap, herb bed or greenhouse, then it wants to be as direct as possible. It is an absolute rule that people will eventually work out the quickest route and use it, even if it means ignoring a beautifully made dry path and slicing diagonally across a muddy lawn or stepping through a flower bed. If you want the path to lead indirectly to its goal you must block off alternative routes with impenetrable planting or a more solid barrier. It is not just humans that this applies to – our dogs, rather weirdly, leave the straight path down to the front door and do a little curving diversion onto the grass, making a worn doggy groove in winter.

When we first started work on the garden in 1992, I believed that we could simply cut beds from the grass of the field, mow the bits in between and call them paths. It is not a bad policy if you have limited funds, and half our paths are still just mown field and need only a pass with a mower once a week to keep them that way. I especially like the paths made by cutting the Orchard grass at different lengths, with the mown, gently curving strip fringed by the tall meadow grasses. Dead simple but dead lovely.

But grass paths on our undrained, heavy soil are useless in the rainy season which, with the unstoppable roll of global warming, is at least six months of the year. You can scarcely walk on them without

For the first ten years, all our paths were simply grass, which cost nothing and were quick to mow once a week. But the biggest wear and tear in any garden is footfall and feet wear out grass paths very quickly. Especially since we started to film in the garden in 2011, we have had to gradually put in paved or brick paths all over the garden.

The choice of materials affects not just how the path looks but also how it works. The stone and cobble paving in the Dry Garden gives it an informal, soft atmosphere despite the paving's solidity, whereas the brick path in the Herb Garden (above, right) is more formal and linear – although somewhat softened by the basket-weave pattern.

creating muddy puddles in your wake like an oar dipping into water. If you try and push a barrowful of compost, it simply sinks up to the axle in the mud and gets stuck.

And even in summer, every time you set foot on the path, let alone wheel a heavy barrow on it, you are compacting the soil down, worsening the drainage and increasing the subsequent winter quagmire. In this garden, by mid-October, going outside to get a sprig of rosemary or to shut the chickens in means taking off your shoes and putting on wellingtons. Only frost brings sufficient hard dryness to walk unprotected. If a path is to be any use for most of the year it must be made of almost anything except grass.

Choosing materials

So over the years, as money and time have allowed, we have been converting our paths from grass to hard surfaces. The luxury of walking dry-shod is worth the work and expense. It also opens up a whole range of colours, textures and structure to the garden. A grass path can somehow hardly be called structural, whereas a brick path is a wall on edge.

It is important to use local, natural materials wherever possible. We have tried to recycle stone that has been dug up as the garden was made or any left over from building work. When we have bought stone flags, they have all come from locally reclaimed buildings. There was a brickworks in Leominster, our local town, that closed in the mid-nineteenth century, and where they made especially dense, large bricks. These were used for most of the brick parts of the house and are ideal for paths, and wherever possible, we have sought these out.

Choosing bricks that relate to those of the house or of existing walls is the most important aspect of any brick path. Reclaimed and local materials have the obvious advantage of reusing existing resources and reducing travel emissions but they also maintain the connection to local identity and place, linking the garden to its immediate surroundings.

All our hard paths have deep foundations. We started with a trench 30–45cm (12–18in) deep, half of which was filled with hardcore of broken bricks and stones, then a generous layer of scalpings tamped down very hard, then a thick layer of sand on which the pavers were laid. If you have very well-drained soil you won't need such elaborate measures to ensure drainage and lack of subsidence, but for us it is essential.

Our first brick paths were laid directly against the earth walls of the trenches but in time the earth moved and big gaps appeared between the bricks. Now we set the outside bricks in cement mortar and these act as an edging that contains the inner bricks which are laid on sand.

We also have a few short paths that are made from stone flags. These are always handsome and often beautiful but invariably expensive. They are often priced by weight and the thicker – and therefore heavier –they are, the better the path sits. However, laying a stone flag (and most of ours are made from a Welsh sandstone and not the ubiquitous York stone, which is beautiful but involves heavy transport, financial and environmental costs) is no more difficult than or different from laying a concrete slab or brick path.

Our final paths, in the Jewel Garden, are topped with a material called Redgra which comes from a quarry in the Forest of Dean some 50km (30 miles) south of us. This is a kind of pink sand with an element of clay that binds it solid when laid. You prepare the path with hardcore and a layer of scalpings, then spread a thin layer of this binding surface, which you bang in with a motorised whacker plate. It goes on almost as sand but after 24 hours it is pretty solid. It is much cheaper and easier to lay than paving or brick but if it doesn't have really sharp drainage, it can get almost muddy in very wet weather.

Paths have to be practical and on our very wet ground this primarily means dry and firm enough all the year round to take heavy garden wear and tear. The Jewel Garden paths are made from Redgra.

Trees

It is a strange thing. You plant small trees – saplings that can be easily carried in one hand, the trunk thinner than the stake that supports them – and long for them to grow and become what is generally accepted as the real thing, the proper, finished tree.

I planted these trees in 1993 when all were small enough to easily hold in one hand. Watching them grow has been one of the great pleasures of the garden.

But be careful what you wish for. Twenty years ago none of the trees in the garden were more than ten years old and had not created the windbreak and shelter that I originally wanted. Many were still young but a few were starting to take their recognisably mature shape and form. Now some are 15m (50ft) or 18m (60ft) tall. I love the fact that they have become so big and that the missing element of the original bare field –

mature trees – is now there in what seems an astonishingly short time.

But there has been a price. The afternoon and evening light have been radically reduced. The late afternoon and early evening used to be the golden hours and the Jewel Garden, in particular, glowed in that thicker, later light. This is now almost completely blocked by trees. I have tried selective thinning – about 20 have been cut down and many have had branches lopped off – but although this helps, it does not solve the problem.

Also, I planted the trees and hedges as windbreaks and they now do that job too successfully. There is a noticeably reduced airflow. Allied to the effects of climate change and its wetter, warmer weather, along with the lusher growth that this encourages, this has allowed fungi to proliferate more. I suspect that we would not have had box blight if we had not had high hedges and tall trees, and in a damp summer, mould of various kinds is our biggest problem in the borders and vegetable beds.

But I will take it. I am happy to trade some fungal problems for the pleasure of seeing magnificent trees grow. I have grown more knowledgeable, too. I have learned a lot about planting, planting

distances, thinning, limbing and managing trees in a garden. In fact, I have only one regret. I wish I had planted a walnut tree 30 years ago and that I could eat my own walnuts at breakfast time instead of buying them.

When we first came to this garden in November 1991, it was an empty field bounded by a scruffy, gappy hedge. In fact there were two trees – a hazel near the back door and a hawthorn, bent almost sideways by the wind. Both are still here, growing well, but now accompanied by hundreds of other trees, most of which now dwarf those two originals and most of which I bought almost by accident.

Back in April 1993, after much building work and planning of the garden, I was ready to start planting in earnest. The local paper advertised an auction of all trees growing at a local nursery, so I went along specifically to buy some yews for the front garden. I set my budget at a strict, non-negotiable £200 – because that was absolutely all we had in our bank account. So I duly bought some yews, had a little of my budget to spare and, to cut a long and deeply irresponsible story short, went on bidding into the afternoon. At the end of the day I found I had purchased 1100 trees and spent £1400!

These became the bones of my garden, providing hedging plants, pleached limes and an avenue, as well as standalone trees, and I confess I regard it as one of the best investments I have ever made. Not only did it make for ridiculously cheap trees but also for years and years of intense pleasure from watching them grow.

And the trees grew not just with the garden but also with my family. At first they were as spindly as broom handles but very quickly they created height and stature. Soon some were strong enough to take a hammock or a swing and it was a momentous day when the biggest tree was large enough for my son to climb. Eventually, after about ten years, one of those slender saplings became big enough for a treehouse.

Half the pleasure of planting any tree is seeing it grow rather than waiting for it to become a 'proper' tree. Real gardeners know that no such thing exists. Gardening is not about creating the perfect, finished, horticultural stage set but about growing things, nurturing them, sharing their slow evolution into maturity. In fact, over the past few years, we have been cutting down some of those early trees I planted to let more air and light into the rest of the garden. That is all part of the change – and every scrap of the felled trees is used, from logs for the fire to wood chip for paths.

Unless you are extremely rich or extremely impatient, it always makes sense to plant trees small. My basic rule is that bare-root trees should be small enough to be lifted by one strong man and containerised trees should be able to be carried by two men.

Trees come in all shapes and sizes and there is at least one for every garden.

We now have hundreds of trees as well as the two original ones, most of which I bought almost by accident

There are tiny yet exquisite Japanese maples and tall, yet slender fastigiate trees with upright growth that are especially useful in a smaller garden that cannot accommodate the full canopy of a large spreading tree. Trees can weep, spread sideways, have a dense tangle of branches or be pruned to perfect spare shapes where the spaces between branches sculpt the air. Trees can be pleached and coppiced, espaliered or cordoned and, if you have the space, left to grow gloriously as they wish to be. Trees can flower, carry edible fruit or nuts or decorative berries. Trees can have rich autumn colour or sparkling new spring foliage. Trees can drop their leaves each year or be evergreen.

In short, there is a tree for every garden and every person.

Blossom fills the branches of the fruit trees in the garden with flower – and none is more voluptuous or spectacular than that of the great white 'Tai Haiku' cherry during its all-too-brief flowering in the Damp Garden.

Opposite page: Pleached limes, as here in the Lime Walk, and flanking the Long Walk and right round the Cottage Garden, create an imposing structure without blocking all light or sight.

A garden without trees – planted deliberately as specimens to be enjoyed from the first day – is a garden unfulfilled. We tend to only measure our gardens across two dimensions but the third – up – is just as important and almost every garden can accommodate very tall plants indeed, however limited their ground area. I know that some people feel that their garden is too small to take a whopping great tree towering over their house, shading out all the other plants, the roots breaking all the drains and the whole thing just waiting to come crashing down on the house at the first hint of a wind. But the chance of any of these things ever happening is very remote and certainly not in the lifetime of you or your children. One of the basic rules of garden design is that large objects make a small space seem bigger and a large space smaller. So a small garden with a single medium-sized tree will actually seem bigger as a result.

Choosing the right tree for your garden can seem overwhelming. But as with all plants, you can make the process of selection simpler and more effective. First of all, look around your immediate neighbourhood and see if there are any trees that you particularly like the look of and which seem to be growing healthily (and if they look healthy, they almost certainly *are* healthy). This will inform you what is best adapted for your soil and area, and therefore what will thrive in your own garden.

Secondly, try and visit gardens with good trees. This might be a local park, a botanic garden, a National Trust garden

– anywhere that has a good selection of mature trees. Rarity is unimportant. Some of the most beautiful trees are the most common and easiest to grow. Deciduous trees provide leaves for leafmould, shelter from wind and shade for the range of lovely woodland flowers as well as for people. In this garden, trees also have the unexpected effect of soaking up lots of excess moisture as they grow, which is becoming increasingly useful on this very wet ground.

We all know that trees are vital to maintaining the balance between oxygen and carbon dioxide. Without the excess carbon dioxide in the atmosphere being absorbed by trees and oxygen being released, human life would cease to be viable. Politicians love to bandy about the goal of planting millions or even billions

PLEACHING THE LIMES

Apart from the couple of limes in the Spring Garden, all our lime trees are pleached.

Pleaching is the process whereby a chosen number of parallel stems above a clean trunk are trained horizontally to meet the stems of the adjacent tree, forming either a 'hedge-on-stilts' or a framework very similar to espaliered fruit trees. My limes fit the latter category and have to be pruned hard every year.

Limes are ideal for pleaching because they grow fast, respond enthusiastically to pruning and have very long, whippy new stems that are easy to bend and tie into position. The fresh young growth of limes also cuts in a particularly satisfying manner, soft yet resistant.

I look forward to the job every winter. It takes two or three days to do them all but these can be spread over a number of weeks in January or even February. I have a routine. I now do it from a Japanese tripod ladder of which we have a number of different sizes. Over the past ten years, these have revolutionised pruning and all tree and hedge work. They are very light, very strong, very stable and can get in almost anywhere.

The first thing is to reduce all shoots growing at right angles to the line of the pleaching, cutting right back to the base. I then cut back all vertical growth, leaving just spurs with a few healthy buds. On the top row, which receives most sunshine,

this can be as high as 1.8m (6ft). When this is done, all that should be left are the horizontal shoots between each tree. I have learned over the years to be absolutely ruthless and to cut away everything other than the three chosen lateral branches. The only exception is if I wish to train in a new lateral to replace one that is broken or unsuitable.

What is left is just the skeleton of the trees and looks shockingly reduced. But this harsh pruning stimulates new growth and by April it is sprouting new leaves from each knobbly cut, followed in May by the new stems, which we give a light trim in midsummer.

of trees but planting one tree in your garden is a meaningful, positive act to redress the process of climate change. Better a million gardeners adding one tree that engages and improves the lives of all than a politician making a sweeping political gesture. It is not much – but could change the world.

Finally, trees can have real meaning, connecting us to those we love in a lasting way. In autumn 1997 we went to a wedding where all the guests were given an oak sapling as a gift. The idea was that we all planted it as a lasting remembrance of the union. I purloined an extra one, easily fitted both into the boot of the car and planted them in the garden. The two are now magnificent but in very different ways. They have real, individual character, one tall and dead straight and the other shorter and with a broader sweep of its branches. Every time I look at them – at least three or four times a day – I think of my two friends and, now, their four sons. Both trees, I hope, will live for hundreds of years, long after my friends and I have been forgotten, but the connection will live on.

Opposite page: The British climate does not often lend itself to shades of orange and red in autumn but there is a moment before the leaves start to fall in earnest – usually in the first week of November – when the garden glows a buttery yellow from the leaves of the hedges and trees.

Trees and wildlife

A few years ago a huge and very old oak was blown down from the other side of our hedge and landed in our garden. Whilst it was stretched out like a toppled giant, it was fascinating to see just how many holes and hollows there were right up the trunk and throughout the larger branches. Each one of these would have been a potential home for birds or bats, let alone the mass of different insect and fungal life that live in and on the bark and the leaves.

But you do not have to plant an oak to add a huge range of wildlife to your garden. Any tree is at the very least cover for birds and insects as well as a potential nesting and roosting site. Treecreepers and nuthatches can be seen working their way up (treecreepers) and down (nuthatches), finding insects in crevices in the bark. Bats will roost in hollows and holes and, if you are lucky, dormice, too.

Flowering trees such as orchard fruits like apple, pear, quince or plum will both attract insects and be an invaluable supply of nectar. Their fruits will then host insects and, in autumn and winter, when lying on the ground, feed hedgehogs, foxes and birds.

Autumn colour

The autumnal coloration of leaves is dependent upon two different processes, one leading to yellows, the other to reds. The yellows are due to carotenoid pigments always present in leaves, which are usually masked by the chlorophyll which makes photosynthesis possible. When the temperature begins to drop and the daylight hours get shorter, the chlorophyll is not renewed and the yellow pigments become visible. What you see is not so much the yellowing of the leaves as the fading of summer's green party dress. The most brilliant yellow of all autumn foliage is on the elm – although British elms now rarely make more than 6m (20ft) before succumbing to Dutch elm disease.

Red pigmentation of leaves is created anew each autumn. It is closely related to carbohydrates (sugars) and is made most on warm, sunny days followed by cool (but not frosty) nights. The sugars go back down the tree as sap via the phloem, feed new wood cells and give energy to the roots. But in late summer and early autumn, the build-up of sugars is confined to the leaves by the cold nights, leading to the concentration of red pigmentation there. So the intensity of our autumn colour is determined by the weather in August and September. Mild temperatures and rain lead to poor coloration. This means that at home, rarely do we have anything like the brilliance of the autumnal colour found on the east coast of America, because the temperature variation in late summer is so comparatively limited.

The best time to plant any tree – but especially bare-root ones – is when they are dormant between October and March.

Planting trees

The biggest influence that you can have on any tree is to plant it really well.

The smaller it is when planted, the faster and healthier it will grow. If you are prepared to be patient for the first few years, a sapling 90cm (36in) tall will catch up and overtake one three times that size within a few years, and is likely to have a much better root system.

Before planting, always soak a tree in water for at least ten minutes. If it is bare-root – and bare-root trees tend to be cheaper and better quality – never let the

roots dry out even for a minute. I find a soaked hessian sack useful to cover the roots with.

Whatever the size of tree, dig a hole at least 90cm (36in) in diameter or twice the spread of the roots – whichever is the larger. Remove one spade's depth of soil and break up the next spit with a fork, getting rid of all stones. Do not add any compost or manure to the planting hole at this stage as the tree will extract all that it needs from the soil, and the quicker it adapts to the soil and grows out, away from the planting hole, the better.

Place the tree in the hole and spread the roots so that the base of the tree is 2.5–5cm (1–2in) above soil level – you may have to make a little cone of soil at the bottom of the planting hole to achieve this. It has been shown that trees planted on a slight mound develop much deeper, wider and stronger root systems than those planted in a slight basin, so they are much less likely to be blown over by strong winds.

Holding the tree upright and at the right height, gradually add soil back into the hole, covering the roots, firming in with your heel as you do so and keeping your heel around the edge of the hole facing in towards the trunk so that the firmed soil forms a slight cone with the tree at its centre.

When all the soil is back in, if the tree is more than 1.5m (5ft) tall or is in an exposed position, stake it by banging a stake in at 45 degrees to the trunk, with the stake angled directly into the prevailing wind so that the strongest support is provided against the greatest and most frequent pressure. Tie the tree to the stake with a tree tie and then water it very thoroughly. This means adding at least a large bucketful and if possible, leaving a hose on it until the water overflows onto the surrounding area. The tree will probably need watering once a month for the first year or so, especially if it is evergreen.

When the water has fully drained, add a thick mulch – at least 5cm (2in) deep and ideally two or three times that amount – of compost or bark chips. This will stop evaporation and will work into the top 15cm (6in) of soil, which is where most of any tree's feeding roots are. Top up the mulch every spring and keep it completely weed-free for a couple of years.

Remove the stake after three years, keep the weeds away from the area around the base and enjoy every stage of its subsequent growth.

Pruning and training

Almost all our trees are pruned or trained in some way. Those around the edge of the garden or floral areas are pruned so they do not cast too much shade whilst the freestanding ones, such as the field maples and ash trees in the Orchard and

Do not add compost or manure when planting as the quicker a newly planted tree adapts to the soil and grows out, away from the planting hole, the better

The pleached limes are pruned at the beginning of the year, with all new growth cut right back to the permanent framework. It is one of my favourite winter jobs.

the standards in the Coppice, are pruned so that their trunks are clean for as high as we can reach. We also prune any crossing or ungainly branches. Not only is this deliberate artifice based on subjective aesthetic judgement, but it also lets in more light and air to the trees themselves and to the garden beyond.

However, even when just pruning off lower branches to establish a clean trunk, it is important to remember that any kind of leaf removal reduces the plant's ability to feed itself, so will potentially slow down growth. It is therefore best to do it in the tree's dormant season unless you are deliberately pruning to restrict growth (as with a hedge).

I sometimes have to remind myself that a tree grows only from its perimeters. In other words, the lower branches never shift up the tree and the inner section never moves out! Therefore a good-looking, healthy branch in the wrong place always has to go, whilst a mere leafy sprout in the right place must be nurtured into the permanent branch it can become.

When cutting any substantial branch it is important to undercut it first, cutting about a third of the way upwards through the branch, close to the trunk. This will stop a tear forming on the bark of the trunk itself. Then cut down, 2.5cm (1in) or so further along the branch. Finally, when the branch is removed, clean up the wound with a sharp saw so that the wound angles slightly and rainwater cannot settle on it. Never seal a wound, however big, as this can only lock in potential fungi, viruses and moisture. Just let it heal and scar over naturally, which it will do in its own time.

The trees in my garden

Most of the trees in the garden were bought on that day in April 1993 at an auction where I spent far more than I could afford (see page 35). But, for all my irresponsibility, they provided the basic structure of the garden that is there today.

Oak (*Quercus*)

Oaks are the archetypal tree of the British landscape, a measure of wealth and security. This was literally the case as land was judged by the size and health of the oak trees that grew on it. In the countryside around my garden, oaks grow better than anywhere else in the land. The framework of my house is constructed from oak as are all the barns. As I type these words, with the computer on an oaken table, my feet rest on oak floorboards, there are books on oak bookcases and the doors and windows are made from oak. When oak is 'green' or freshly cut, it is fairly soft and easy to work. But as it ages and dries, it becomes unbreakably hard and strong. I have reused timbers in the fifteenth-century part of the house that are at least 700 years old and they are still superbly strong and undamaged.

Oak has an extraordinary ability to stay alive even though the majority of its branches and trunk might die back. A few miles down the road is an oak tree that is reckoned to be at least a thousand years old and is 10m (34ft) in girth at 90cm (36in) above the ground. It is hollow, has caught fire, but is still living.

No other plant contributes more to the sustenance of diversity in our landscape, including gardens, for an oak tree houses more living creatures than any other growing plant in Britain. All kinds of birds will nest in its branches. More will nest in its hollowed trunk and stems, as will bats. Hundreds of different kinds of invertebrates and insects live on or in some part of it.

Lime (*Tilia*)

We have lime trees in this garden almost by default. I had never grown a lime before we came here but in April 1993, I bought dozens of them as part of that job lot in a tree sale – smaller ones for as little as 50p and twenty 4.5m (15ft) trees for around £3 each. They were sold to me as *Tilia cordata*, the small-leafed lime, and would have been ideal for my purpose of making a pleached avenue as *T. cordata* do not grow too monstrous and do not drip honeydew from aphids in the summer as other limes, especially the common lime, *T.* x *europaea*, are prone to do. As it turned out, some were *T. platyphyllos* 'Rubra', others were *T. p.* 'Aurea' and none were *T. cordata*.

T. platyphyllos is the big-leafed lime and this does produce enormous leaves each spring, growing to the size of serving dishes. It also has the advantage of not creating the forest of suckers that bristle out from the common lime.

The new shoots of *T. p.* 'Rubra' are bright red, coming into their own after leaf-fall. On a frosty day, against the backdrop of a clean blue sky, they glow like a jewelled aura around the tree. The new growth of *T. p.* 'Aurea' is a sort of olivey green, also rather fetching. Both look very good on their own but when mixed at (unintentional) random, they present a slightly rakish harlequin aspect to the winter sun. Never mind. They fairly represent my haphazard approach to gardening, and they are now a distinctive part of this garden in winter.

I have a few limes planted in the Spring Garden, which are now tall but still relatively slim and will not reach full stature for another couple of hundred years. But given time, limes make one of the best parkland trees, growing upwards as a tower of branches and having real grandeur when mature.

Ash (*Fraxinus*)

One of the largest trees in the garden is a 'Raywood' ash (*Fraxinus angustifolia* 'Raywood') that I planted in the spring of 1993 and which now towers tall and wide. However, like so many ash trees across the country, it has suffered from ash dieback disease. As if ash dieback was not threat enough, the emerald ash borer beetle (*Agrilus planipennis*) looks to be inevitably coming to this country and its effect will almost certainly be as disastrous as that of the Dutch elm beetle. The future of British ash trees looks extremely grim.

However, different trees, even growing side by side, seem to react in different ways and to different extents. The latest research indicates that trees that are solitary, such as those in fields or hedgerow or in mixed woodland, are more likely to remain alive. The fungus cannot survive temperatures above 35°C (95°F), so hot summers are good for the trees.

Ash trees have grace and often elegance despite the wood being, in many ways, the toughest and most durable that there is. Their branches, although growing almost laterally on some of the old gnarled trees on the farm, invariably curl up at the tips – a final gesture of refinement.

I am a great fan of the common ash (*F. excelsior*) and it is one of the dominant trees of the Herefordshire landscape. Until about 50 years ago, huge old ashes were regularly pollarded every 20 years or so over a period of hundreds of years, providing timber for carts, tool handles and fuel, as well as being a prime source of poles for growing hops up before the modern wire structures took over. After pollarding, the new growth would emerge beyond the reach of grazing cattle whilst the trunk became gnarled and massively thick through the centuries.

Most are now uncut so the 3m (10ft) high trunks are topped by a characteristic mass of thick branches, quite unlike the tall, lean and dead-straight trees of woodland. They are often positioned at corners of fields and at bends in the road to mark boundaries. Both pollarding and coppicing increase the life of the tree enormously and there exist ash stools that are still coppiced that are over a thousand years old.

Until about 50 years ago, ashes were regularly pollarded, providing timber for carts, tool handles, fuel and poles for growing hops

There are people who criticise ash because its leaves are one of the last to arrive in spring and amongst the first to fall in autumn. But there is more to the ash than mere summer dress and it is too utilitarian and philistine to measure beauty in terms of longevity. Certainly a mature ash tree in midsummer is a lovely living thing. The pinnate leaves cast a particularly delicate shade so there is always a feathery light filtering through, which makes it especially suitable for woodland underplanting.

Before they come into leaf, the knobbly tips of the branches carry matt black buds, curiously inanimate and almost crustacean before they open out. The male flowers come next, frizzy and strange, like party streamers caught on the end of a stick, and then finally, after the rest of the arboreal world has had leaves out for weeks, the ash leaves emerge, floppy fronds that might be considered exotic on another, less determinedly common tree.

The outline of a common ash in a field is of a huge blowsy tree with generously sweeping branches. But as a young tree it does not mimic its maturity, starting out spindly and only slowly developing its promise, and this, I think, is why it has never really been absorbed into the gardening lexicon. But it has real garden potential. One of the most interesting aspects of the ash is the speed with which it regrows after cutting, and this made it useful for coppicing. Ash wood is straight-grained and strong, and the ease with which it splits makes it possible to harness that strength along the grain as well as making splitting it for firewood a joy.

Yew (*Taxus baccata*)

There are eight large Irish yews (*Taxus baccata* 'Fastigiata') that now dominate the Cottage Garden, especially in winter when their tall pillars of dark green have stature and dignity even in the grimmest midwinter weather. They grew slowly for the first ten or so years of their life and we moved them from the Jewel Garden, with each fitting into a wheelbarrow, just twelve years ago. Now you would need a large crane to move

The ash trees of the Coppice are the uncoppiced standards that are part of every coppice woodland. In fact I now prune the branches of these hard to let light into the Jewel Garden.

them. Like all yews, Irish yew can be clipped hard back to the bare wood if need be, so that it is the perfect evergreen tree for making a green pillar.

A few years ago, after we removed the box balls and remade that area as the Herb Garden (see page 194), I planted sixteen more Irish yews, bought at great expense from a nursery in Germany. My idea was to continue the theme of green pillars and the legacy of evergreen structure that the box balls had provided, albeit vertically rather than horizontally. They work well.

All Irish yews growing in the world originate from a single female tree found in 1780 on a hillside in County Fermanagh, Northern Ireland. This was propagated by cuttings and spread throughout the world, especially in northern Europe and the United States, providing the same kind of slim columnar shape in a cool, wet climate as the Italian cypress (*Cupressus sempervirens*) does in the Mediterranean region.

Willow (*Salix*)

One of the stupidest things I did when we moved here was to take a bundle of willow cuttings from an incredibly vigorous hybrid of the white willow (*Salix alba*) and stick them along the edge of our boundary where it butts onto the water meadow. Like all willows, they rooted in

The Irish yews in the Cottage Garden have been with us since 1995 but Sarah and I moved each one in a wheelbarrow from the Jewel Garden to their current position in 2008.

weeks and in the ideal wet conditions, grew monstrously. Cutting them back to the ground did no good at all as they responded by throwing up multiple stems with renewed vigour, making 1.8m (6ft) of growth a year. I have calculated that for a month or so in midsummer, these monsters grow an inch a day! This makes them superb material for biomass but hopeless for any kind of garden. The cover that they provided was always thin and now, nearly 30 years later, I have 15m (50ft) trees with trunks 1.5m (5ft) across and very extensive roots. So beware the casually planted willow!

Having said that, they are beautiful, especially in spring when the new leaves appear. They are also one of the few trees that are happiest in very wet ground.

Field maple (*Acer campestre*)

Field maple provides the best autumn colour in our garden, turning a brilliant yellow before tingeing to pink and orange, and then leaf-fall. I planted a number of them as very small immature trees in the Orchard, the Spring Garden and along the boundary of the Damp Garden, and they have all matured into fine small trees, giving shape and shade to an otherwise empty field. It seems to me that this is an undervalued indigenous garden plant and, rather like hawthorn, is still mainly considered as a 'wild' tree of the agricultural hedgerow. So it might be, but it is a waste to leave it out of the garden.

There are a few 'garden' varieties, none of which I have grown myself. *Acer campestre* 'Postelense' has pale yellow leaves when young, turning greener as the summer progresses and *A. c.* 'Schwerinii' is a purple-leafed version, which could potentially be very useful in a large border, given the maple's comfort with being cut back.

Cherry (*Prunus*)

When I first saw *Prunus* 'Tai Haiku' in full flower in a friend's garden, I immediately ordered one for here. On the end of each spindly shoot was a bundle of huge white blossom, hanging like delicate explosions caught and frozen in midair. There was not a leaf on the tree, just thousands of white flowers set against a stony white sky. My poor tree has had three homes before finding its current (and I hope final) resting place in the Damp Garden, where it too can learn to explode into white spring flowers.

The flowering of the 'Tai Haiku' does not last very long and can be ruined by heavy rain, and when it is over, the leaves are not much to look at. It is a brief performance. But it does more than enough. It shines so brightly that to ask anything else of it would be greedy.

I planted a couple of *P. avium*, or gean, which are not nearly so voluptuous as 'Tai Haiku' but will powder the edge of an entire wood with delicate white blossom in early April (they tend to prosper at the edges of woods because they need light to regenerate). These have grown remarkably quickly, are now the two

I planted this group of field maples intending them to be a little sheltering clump in the pony paddock – but the garden has grown around them.

The best autumn colour in the garden comes from the yellow, pink and orange of field maples

The two geans – wild cherries – that I planted as tiny saplings 30 years ago have become the biggest trees in the garden. They are fine trees but I regret planting them as they cast a heavy shade and very little grows beneath them. It is a tree that is only suitable for the largest gardens.

biggest trees in the garden and have created a very dry shade beneath which little grows. However, although this dry shade is something of a horticultural challenge – which we rose to with *Euphorbia amygdaloides*, wood anemones and dog's tooth violets – it has become the final resting place for five of our dogs and two cats. So Beaufort, Red, Poppy, Barry and Nigel, along with Blue and Stimpy, the Burmese cats, lie deep within that dry and safe shade.

If you must prune flowering cherries to shape (and they will not need pruning for their health), do so at the end of summer, so that the wounds heal before winter. They will bleed gum from the cut and may go on doing so until the tree dies. So do not cut them back unless absolutely necessary.

Holly (*Ilex*)

Holly casts a drier shade than any other tree and is the first place that animals (and people) will go for protection against rain. This might lead you to think that holly likes dry shade to grow in but it actually prefers moist, well-drained soil and – especially the variegated varieties – looks best in full sunshine.

I have a number of small variegated hollies growing for topiary in the Jewel Garden and some plain *Ilex aquifolium* in the Spring Garden. Like yew or box, holly regenerates from bare wood so will

recover from being pruned very hard.

Most holly trees are either male or female and to get berries, you must have a mate in your garden (although this need not be of the same variety) to fertilise the flowers. This task is made absurdly difficult by the names given to various of the most popular varieties. To wit: 'Golden Queen' is male and 'Golden King' is female, and 'Silver Queen' (also known as 'Silver King') is female and does not have berries. If you do get it right – and you might be saved by the presence of a holly of the right sex in a neighbouring garden – then you do not have to have your berries red. *I. a.* 'Bacciflava' has very bright yellow berries, is female and does well in the Spring Garden.

Even if a holly starts to look sickly to the point of almost complete defoliation, it has amazing powers of recovery. Everything about it is tough – the close-grained hard wood (which, by the by, used to be favoured especially for whips thanks to the wood's flexibility and durability), the leaves that almost seem to defy the process of decay, and its generally defiant air.

All this refers to the English holly (*I. aquifolium*) – characteristically spiky, with red berries, and can grow to 15m (50ft). But there are 400 different species and even more cultivars and hybrids, most of which seem to stem from *I. aquifolium*. Of course as soon as you move into the world of hybrids and cultivars, you step out of

The dry shade of the two geans has become the final resting place for five of our dogs and two cats

the woods and fields and into the garden.
I do not think that the garden can improve
on 'wild' holly, but it can accommodate it
without diminishing any of its beauty.

Crab apple (*Malus sylvestris*)

I have a crab apple 'Evereste' growing in
the centre of each of the four beds in the
Paradise Garden and four more crab trees
growing in the Cottage Garden, as well as
four others that I planted nearly 30 years
ago as part of our boundary hedge. Crabs
were not part of the Islamic gardening
tradition but the important thing was to
choose a small tree that bore fruit and had
wonderful blossom and superb fragrance,
and the crab came out top in all points.

There are nearly a thousand different
cultivars of crab apple. The majority have
green leaves although a number have rich
purple foliage. Most have pink blossom of
some shade, although there are many that
are either white or as white as dammit.
Some though, like 'Prairie Fire', have rich
red flowers.

The fruits that result from the blossom
run from the bright yellow of *Malus* x *zumi*
'Golden Hornet' or *M.* 'Butterball' to the
rich plum burgundy of 'Laura' or
'Roberts Crab', and through every shade
of orange and pink in between. As well as
'Evereste', I am a great fan of 'Comtesse
de Paris'. We have one of those in the
Cottage Garden that has now become
quite large but has superb blossom and
the golden apples stay on the tree into the
new year. If I could only choose one crab
apple for my garden, this would be it.

M. x *floribunda* was introduced into this
country from Japan in 1862. The flowers,
carried on especially long, arching
branches, open from deep pink buds and
start out pink but fade to white, and then
develop into tiny yellow fruits. It is a low
but wide-spreading tree and when
full-grown, it will be wider than it is tall.
This makes it very suitable to grow as a
multi-stemmed specimen, especially if
raised in a container.

M. sargentii is another Japanese species
that never grows beyond the size of a
large bush and has white flowers with gold
centres and bright red fruits. Its size and
growth habit make it ideal for a fruity
hedge that birds will love in autumn.

The Chinese crab (*M. hupehensis*) is one
of the very few crab trees that will grow
true from seed. It has rather stiff, upright
branches that carry a mass of white
blossom very late in spring. These then
evolve into deep red, small fruits.

There are four
'Evereste' crab
apples in the
Paradise Garden –
one in the centre of
each bed. In spring
they have wonderful
white blossom and in
autumn they are
smothered in bright
orange fruits.

Opposite page:
The fastigiate
hornbeam 'Frans
Fontaine' is planted
at the end of the
Cricket Pitch as
the focal point.
It chimes with
the flanking
hornbeam hedges.

Crabs can, like orchard apples, be grown on a variety of rootstocks (see page 402), from the very small, like M27, which are ideal for containers, to full standards grown on MM111 rootstocks. Crabs tend to make smallish trees anyway so I would suggest looking for MM111 or MM106 if they are to be planted into the garden so they can grow large enough to realise their full shape and size – which will never be overpowering for even a small garden. They also make ideal pollinators for culinary apples and, of course, the tiny fruits can be made into crab apple jelly, which is one of the great delicacies of life. Richly coloured red fruits will make a wine-coloured jelly whereas paler fruits make a beautifully delicate, translucent version.

Hornbeam (*Carpinus betulus*)

At the end of our Cricket Pitch we had a horse chestnut tree that was growing very well and getting quite large before, exactly fifteen years to the day that we planted it, it split in a spring snowstorm. The remains of the tree were unsafe so it had to be cut down.

But that site was then empty and, being right at the end of the garden and absolutely the focus of the main view, begged a replacement. However, I knew I did not want to replace the chestnut like for like. This was because, as it grew, the spreading branches badly shaded the flanking hornbeam hedges. I needed something much more upright and taking up less space, and yet which would also be dramatic. So I have planted a hornbeam but have chosen a fastigiate variety called

'Frans Fontaine' that naturally grows into a tall column. Hornbeam is unjustifiably overlooked in my opinion in favour of the rather less interesting beech. In fact, the two will very rarely be happy in the same garden or even landscape as hornbeam thrives on cold, heavy clay, which never suits beech.

Whereas the leaves of beech are glossy and almost silky, hornbeam's retain a more corrugated appearance. Both trees keep many of their old leaves throughout the winter months but whereas those of beech are a tawny colour, hornbeam's are paler, resembling milky coffee. These are then pushed off by the emerging new leaves in spring, which causes a second leaf-fall in April.

Fastigiate trees of all kinds have long been used both as dramatic columnar features and, when planted in a row, as a screen – almost an extra-tall hedge. They work well in any garden but are especially useful in a smaller garden that cannot accommodate the full canopy of a large, spreading tree.

The upright growth habit is caused by the tree's inability to develop normal side branches, which grow straight up instead of spreading sideways to get as much light as possible. In most trees this seems to be a chance and random development in some seedlings, but over the centuries, nurserymen have selected these natural variants and developed the fastigiate form in many otherwise spreading trees by grafting.

Hedges

Hedges define all the separate spaces and gardens within Longmeadow. Here in the Long Walk, with its lines of clipped box cones, hornbeam hedges grow beneath pleached limes. A 'window' is cut into the hedge at the far end to provide a borrowed landscape.

The words 'garden' and the American 'yard' both derive, via the French *jardin* and the Norse *garth*, from the Old English *geard*, meaning an enclosure as well as fence or hedge. A cultivated space enclosed by a fence or hedge is the perfect definition of a garden and a field.

So instead of thinking of the garden as a series of outdoor 'rooms', perhaps we should more helpfully see it as a jumble of small fields or enclosed meadows. There we crop contentment, beauty, privacy and some prized bits and pieces of food, and maintain that direct link to our own private countryside.

Hedges are superb for encouraging all kinds of wildlife in the garden but particularly birds. Songbirds such as blackbirds, robins and wrens love them both for nesting and providing cover. Bats use hedges as a kind of road map, following their lines as they hunt. Small mammals use the base of hedges as cover and insects of all kinds breed and feed on and in them. Research has shown that the bigger the volume of hedging, the more wildlife it will support, so rather than keeping hedges tightly clipped and controlled, let them grow as high and wide as possible.

High hedges make a garden seem bigger and more beautiful as well as more private

In fact, I think that most gardeners tend to be too restrained with their hedges. Maintaining them is not much work – certainly much less than a lawn or border – and even a very small garden can usually be improved by subdivision. Hedges do not have to be foursquare. A cloud hedge looks great and hedges can just as easily snake and bend as march in a straight line. The important thing is to get the height right in relation to the space that the hedge bounds. As a rule, most hedges are too low. Just as a high ceiling tends to improve the proportions of a room, so high hedges make a garden seem bigger and more beautiful as well as more private. And there is the added bonus that the higher and longer your hedges, the more bird life you will have in the garden.

Hedge cutting

Hedge cutting is simply a form of mass pruning and the laws of pruning apply. So cutting a deciduous hedge in winter will stimulate vigorous growth the following spring and summer, whereas trimming it in midsummer (August is the best month in Britain) will restrict vigour and maintain shape. If you have an overgrown but thin hedge that you wish to be denser, it follows that the best time to cut it back hard is midwinter. If, on the other hand, you have a hedge that is healthy but you simply want to reduce it in size, then this can be done in summer.

Straight-sided hedges (as opposed to rounded ones) are best with sides that gently slope out so that the base is wider than the top. This is called 'a batter'. If you cut the sides dead straight, then the top of the hedge will shade out the bottom. A batter lets light get at the bottom half of the hedge, which in turn means that it maintains its thickness and density right to the ground.

Trimming a hedge encourages dense, sprouting growth. Therefore the more you trim the sides of a young hedge, the denser it will grow. Leave the top until it has reached the height you want to keep it at and then trim it off. Try and keep young hedges narrow – it is all too easy to let a hedge become sprawling and not very thick.

Cutting the yew hedge at the end of the Jewel Garden. Yew grows much faster than people think but only needs an annual trim in late summer to stay crisp until the following spring.

My garden hedges

The choice of hedges that I have planted in my own garden was dictated partly by the soil and what would grow best, and partly by availability. I had little money so on the whole, took what I could get and made it work.

Hornbeam makes for most of our tall deciduous hedges and provides the main structural divisions for the flower gardens. As the garden moves towards the Orchard and the fields beyond, I used hawthorn and mostly keep these hedges lower. They work well but I admit that when I planted them, their main virtues were their cheapness as well as their affinity to the surrounding farmland. I have some tall field maple hedges, bought as part of that auction job lot (see page 35). Not the best horticultural reason, although they have worked out to make fine, tall hedges. We also have yew hedges, now superbly structural and established, especially in the front of the house, as well as holly and also a rosemary hedge in the Herb Garden. There are quite a few box hedges left but all are afflicted with blight (see page 61) to some degree.

HEDGE PLANTING

• Do not cut corners in preparation. All time, effort or money put into preparing the ground for a hedge will pay dividends in health and speed of growth.

• In my experience it is always better to plant deciduous hedges small, ideally between the middle of October and Christmas, but certainly by the end of March. Evergreen hedges are best planted in April in colder areas and in September in a mild, sheltered garden.

• Plant deep enough to cover the roots but do not bury too much of the stem. Planting distances vary but in general, a single row with adequate spacing will make a stronger hedge than one planted more thickly. A minimum of 45cm (18in) apart is a good rule of thumb for beech, hornbeam and holly, and 30cm (12in) for hawthorn and box. Yew should be at least 60cm (24in) apart. Firm in really well and water very thoroughly. The watering after planting is as much to move the soil round the roots as to provide moisture. Then mulch thickly. This is important as it will stop weeds competing for moisture and nutrients in the vital first two or three years. Any mulch will do as long as it is water-permeable and thick enough to stop any light getting through.

• Staking each plant will stop wind rock and help the hedge to grow faster and straighter, so whilst not necessary, it is a good idea, especially if the plants are anything more than about 60cm (24in) tall.

• There is some debate as to the merits and extent of cutting a hedge back after planting. Hawthorn definitely grows denser if cut back by 50 per cent immediately after planting and some say that all deciduous hedges should be reduced by about a third. I now do not cut back any young hedges other than to trim them lightly to a uniform height. I then leave them until they have reached the final height that I want before cutting them back by about 30cm (12in). They will then thicken up over a few years.

• Do not cut the leaders of evergreen hedges until they have reached their intended height but keep the sides cut well back to encourage thick lateral growth.

• Keep an eye on the hedge for its first year and water if there is no good rain for a week. As long as the drainage is good, drought is the biggest hindrance to a young hedge and other than watering, keeping it free of grass and weeds for a strip at least 60cm (24in) wide on either side is best.

Hornbeam (*Carpinus betulus*)

One of the oddities of British – as opposed to continental – gardeners is that they do not use hornbeam very widely as a hedge, preferring beech, which it superficially resembles. The leaves have serrated edges like little teeth, and veins divided by gentle, corrugated troughs, unlike the much smoother, glossy beech foliage. Both plants retain many of their leaves throughout winter although hornbeam's turn a paler colour – milky coffee to beech's strong tea.

Conventional gardening wisdom has it that beech only grows happily on chalky soil and that hornbeam needs heavy clay to thrive, but beech will grow perfectly well on acidic soil with a clay subsoil and hornbeam, whilst certainly very happy on a rich, clay soil, will also thrive on well-drained sand or gravel soils.

My own empirical observation is that hornbeam grows very fast indeed if it has plenty of moisture, particularly when young, and that it responds dramatically to a rich, well-dug planting ground. It will also grow well in heavy shade, albeit a little less luxuriantly than in open sunlight. The long and short of it is that I believe hornbeam to be the best deciduous hedging plant available to the gardener.

But a hedge, be it as an outdoor covered walkway, 'balancing on stilts' or merely defining a boundary, is only a line of trees planted closely together. Hornbeam is not a hedge but a tree (see page 50) and a good one. It was usually managed as wood pasture, meaning that the trees were pollarded for timber and cattle grazed around them. The timber is good for firewood and exceptional for charcoal and it is so hard that in the days before cast iron, it was highly valued for things like cogwheels in mills, piano keys and hammers, pulley blocks, butcher's blocks – anything that needed exceptionally hard-wearing surfaces.

One thing I have learned about hornbeam over the years is that once planted, they hate being moved. Far better to start again with fresh young plants than to try and recycle otherwise healthy hornbeam. If they survive the trauma –

Hornbeam makes a fine living green wall in summer and holds many of its leaves all winter.

Hornbeam grows very fast indeed if it has plenty of moisture, particularly when young

and many do not – they grow so slowly that a new young plant will quickly overtake it and be much healthier.

Hawthorn (*Crataegus*)

Nothing is so thrilling as the first realisation on a fine March evening that the hawthorn hedges are starting to dance with leaf. For the first week the new green hovers above the undressed shape of hedge, half-memory and half-botany. Then it seems to slowly settle down upon each plant, green layering on impossibly bright green. Just writing this makes me sick with longing.

I have used hawthorn in this garden to soften the gradation from formal to informal and from our tightly controlled domesticity to the surrounding agricultural landscape, so all the hedges around the Coppice and in the Orchard are of hawthorn. It is a wonderful hedging material, suitable for any soil, as tough as anything, will get denser the more it is cut and can be laid every 20 years or so to provide an impassably solid barrier. Hence the thousands of miles of it planted in the eighteenth and nineteenth centuries.

But it has never quite made the grade as a garden hedge or tree – mainly, I suspect because it is so common outside the garden and so firmly fixed as an agricultural feature. But don't overlook the humble field hawthorn (*Crataegus monogyna*). It will grow in almost any soil or position, has lovely flowers, cuts to any shape, is ideal cover for birds, has fabulous berries or haws and is about the cheapest tree that you can buy. It is also, in my opinion, the best wood for burning on an open fire.

To keep it looking really crisp it will need cutting at least twice a year, with a light trim in early June and a more fierce cut in August. If you have time and inclination, a trim in January, before any birds nest, sets it up well for spring.

Field maple (*Acer campestre*)

It seems to me that the field maple is an undervalued indigenous garden plant, and rather like hawthorn, is still mainly considered a 'wild' tree of the agricultural hedgerow. So it might be, but it is a waste to leave it out of the garden. It holds its shape very well as a large hedge, coming into leaf early and losing its leaves late, and it grows fast and very sturdy but only needs trimming once a year to look good.

We planted a long field maple hedge down one boundary with our neighbours and it has made a vigorous and attractive barrier despite the soil there being stony and poor. In winter it is rather open although in summer, the leaves make it appear completely solid.

Yew (*Taxus baccata*)

No other hedge creates a better backdrop for a border or so perfectly defines an outdoor space as yew. Evergreen, dense, retaining a clipped edge for eight to nine months of the year (it grows vigorously from late spring to late summer), it adds substance to any garden. If yews are shaded – and no tree casts a deeper, drier shade than a vigorous yew – then they grow scrawny and woody, although perfectly healthy. But if exposed to sunshine – even after hundreds of years in shade – they become wonderfully dense. It is, of course,

Opposite page: Hawthorn (on the left-hand side of the path) and field maple (on the right) make excellent informal hedges that can be clipped foursquare. Both are excellent for wildlife too.

that density that we exploit by clipping it and making into a hedge.

One of the myths about yew hedges is that they are very slow to grow. This is completely untrue. Given the right conditions of rich, very free-draining soil and plenty of water and sunlight, they will put on a steady 30cm (12in) a year and plants 45cm (18in) tall will make a solid 2.5m (8ft) hedge in ten years. However, it is true that they slow right down once they reach maturity and they will reach an incredible age. It is now believed that the largest churchyard yews predate the earliest churches by as much as 2000 years and that the oldest may be over 4000 years old. In other words, churches were built on sites where there were already huge yew trees that had been the oldest and biggest thing around for longer than any cultural memory. No wonder they built churches near them.

The common yew grows best in the 'wild' on chalky soil but for garden purposes you can plant it in any type of soil as long as it has good drainage. This drainage is absolutely essential – as I discovered to my cost. I planted yew hedges in the front of our house bounding the yew topiary cones. Everything was planted in a deep trench or hole half-filled with manure or compost and grew well for the first few years, putting on 15–30cm (6–12in) of growth a year. On one side of this front garden, the yew hedge flourished and has become agelessly monumental. But on the other side, I lost half a dozen quite large plants and another 20 or so became bronzed and ill. My theory is that they grew strongly through the topsoil and compost provided for them but then met the stone foundations of much earlier buildings. Abnormally high levels of autumn rain saturated the ground so the roots sat in puddles on the subterranean stone walls and the plants were literally drowning. With yew, regardless of soil type, drainage is everything. So I dug them all up, broke up the stone pan, added drainage material and replanted them, and now, 20 years on, they have made a fine hedge.

A few years ago I planted a yew hedge at the end of the Jewel Garden, replacing a blighted box hedge that had stood for a decade. Before planting I worked in a large amount of grit to the soil to

A yew hedge is the perfect backdrop to a border but it does not have to be monumental. This hedge at the bottom of the Jewel Garden is kept clipped to make a low green parapet.

improve the drainage and then planted the hedge on a ridge to improve drainage even further. This treatment seems to have worked well and it is now thick and very healthy, despite being clipped much shorter than I would formerly have thought was comfortable for a yew hedge.

Holly (*Ilex aquifolium*)

Holly makes a marvellous hedge, albeit one a little slow to establish. I planted one ten years ago with plants 1m (3ft) high which I cut back by half to encourage them to be bushy at the base. They bushed all right but didn't grow up much for the first couple of years although – rather curiously – every fourth plant or so has thrown up a tall leader twice the height of its neighbours. However, the hedge is now a good 1.8m (6ft) and thickening encouragingly. I am confident that the entire hedge will be evenly thick and tall within a few years, and impenetrable to all but the most determined invaders.

Peter the Great was one who was unable to resist the challenge of a holly hedge. He borrowed the house of the diarist John Evelyn, where there was a holly hedge which was 2.8m (9ft) high, 1.5m (5ft) wide and 120m (400ft) long, much loved by Evelyn. In between learning about ship building, Peter whiled away empty afternoons by being wheeled in a barrow by his retainers smack through the middle of the hedge. We know that Peter survived the experience and apparently the hedge did too, although the shock nearly did for poor Evelyn.

Peter the Great whiled away time by being wheeled in a barrow smack through John Evelyn's hedge

Box (*Buxus sempervirens*)

When I wrote the first edition of this book I was busy extending the box hedges in the garden at every opportunity. Back then, box hedging was one of my garden essentials.

If you are in an area where there is no box blight … yet … (see page 61) then box is still a wonderful plant for low hedging. No other plant makes such a good job of spanning that ambiguous gap between edging and hedge. For hedging, there are only two types of box to consider – the common box (*Buxus sempervirens*) and the dwarf box (*B. s.* 'Suffruticosa'). The latter grows much more slowly and to much smaller ultimate dimensions. Traditionally it was used as edging for borders, growing to no more than 45cm (18in) tall. It is more expensive than common box and you need more plants to make a hedge as they have to be planted as close as 15cm (6in) apart. I think that a dwarf form of *B. sempervirens* such as 'Latifolia Maculata' (which has very yellow young growth) does the job just as well, although when mature it might need clipping twice a year to keep its crisp edge.

Some varieties of *B. sempervirens* can be planted very widely and will grow into a thick hedge 1.8m (6ft) or more tall. There is an amazing example at Powis Castle that must be 6m (20ft) high. I

The two box hedges down the centre of the Cottage Garden were the very first hedges at Longmeadow to be planted and have provided thousands of cuttings. They are 'Handsworthiensis', a very robust variety which does seem to recover from box blight although is not immune to it.

planted *B. s.* 'Handsworthiensis' 60cm (24in) apart and within three years it had grown into a solid hedge 90cm (36in) high and 30cm (12in) thick. This is a particularly vigorous type with much larger leaves than normal, although new growth after clipping has denser, smaller leaves. Variegated box, with the leaves edged in either cream or yellow, is extremely common but the variegated effect is minimal. *B. s.* 'Elegantissima' is a compact form with white edging and 'Gold Tip' and 'Aureovariegata' have yellow edging.

Growing box is straightforward enough. It is long-lived so should be planted with good preparation, which

means a trench for a hedge, or a hole for a single plant, dug and with organic material added. The roots are shallow and spread laterally, creating a no-grow area along an established box hedge. This can be unappealing if you are using it to frame a bed or border and you want the effect of plants spilling over its frame. But you can chop the roots back with a spade every couple of years without damaging it at all.

Although it is so tough, it responds well to feeding and watering, especially when it is young. It is also essential to allow a young box hedge plenty of light and air as it can be smothered by rampant growth around it.

BOX CUTTINGS AND MAINTENANCE

Choose healthy shoots of this year's growth and cut them long enough to include some hard (brown) wood as well. This is not essential, but will help. I have taken box cuttings anywhere between 2.5cm (1in) and 30cm (12in) long, but about 15cm (6in) is best. Strip off the leaves from the bottom half of the stem, trimming the end just below a leaf node. Stick them in 15cm (6in) pots, five to a pot, in a potting compost mixed half and half with perlite or grit. Water lightly (the water is not to help them grow but to stop the leaves from desiccating). If you have a cold frame, it is ideal. I also put 15cm (6in) of the compost/perlite mixture in the bottom of the cold frame and root them directly into this, leaving the cuttings there for a full year before planting them out in rows in a nursery bed. They are then transplanted to their final growing position six months or a year later. If the site where they are to grow is very open, they can be transplanted directly once they have rooted.

Old box that has not been cut regularly will get 'leggy', which means that all the foliage will be on the top, carried by a few naked stems. If the plant is fairly big, cut it right back, leaving, where practicable, half of the plant unpruned, and new growth will emerge from seemingly bare wood. When this is growing strongly – usually the second or third year after the drastic cut-back – repeat the operation with the other half. Within five years you should have a really dense, good-sized bush.

The best time to clip an established box hedge is the first week of June, after the last frost has past. It might need another clip before the end of August. A young box hedge should have its sides trimmed in August, leaving the top until it has reached its desired height before trimming. If you cut it later than August, there is a danger of an early autumn frost following a warm September burning tender young regrowth.

Box blight and other problems

For around ten years, between about 2002 and 2012, our box hedges were the pride and joy of this garden. They held it together with a green grid, clipped and symmetrical, the skeleton that enabled the much looser flesh and blood of the flowers to flourish. Whilst in summer they stepped back and let colour take over, in winter they became the dominant, defining essence.

I loved them and by taking hundreds of cuttings every year, they extended until every path in the Cottage and Jewel Gardens, the Grass Borders, the Herb Garden and much else was flanked by box hedging. My 64 box balls grew larger by the year without losing their shape. All was well with my green, healthy world of *Buxus sempervirens*. They took days to cut, once in late spring and again in September, but it was worth it.

The constant green grid, present when the rest of the garden had succumbed to an inevitable winter drabness, became a source of real delight. Even on the grimmest December day, the garden still had a kind of self-respect based upon the clipped green box hedges.

Almost all the plants were raised from cuttings. This is astonishingly easy (see above) but needs about five years from taking the cutting to having a plant mature enough to blend into a hedge. And in its incremental, slow accumulation, the garden became mature and fixed. However, I should have known that the first rule of gardens is that nothing, ever, stays the same.

In September 2012 we noticed a small flare of brown, blotched leaves on an area of hedge at the bottom of the Long Walk. It spread fast and within a few days, the green foliage was turning grey and brown, and collapsing in a mouldy mess. Otherwise unaffected leaves were showing chocolate-coloured stains. There was no mistaking the symptoms. I knew at once that this was one of my worst nightmares – box blight.

There are two forms of box blight, *Volutella buxi* and *Cylindrocladium buxicola*, both fungi that cause the interior of box plants to die back. Both types of fungi need humid, warm conditions to thrive, and the effects of climate change have been perfect for their spread. *Volutella buxi* needs open wounds – like those created every time that box is clipped – to infect the host plant whereas *Cylindrocladium buxicola* can infect unwounded plants and is the more pernicious of the two, affecting quite woody stems as well as the foliage. Fortunately it is less common than *Volutella buxi*.

The worst damage appears in August and September, when the combination of warmth and humidity is at its highest, and when vegetative growth of all kinds is at its most voluminous and therefore limits airflow, although recently our mild, wet winters have meant that box blight can continue to appear until the new

The box blight fungus kills much of the plant but not all, leaving it threadbare. The box does regrow but the new growth is especially vulnerable to reinfection, setting up a vicious and ultimately disastrous cycle.

year. Hard frost and summer drought will kill and inhibit the fungi although the spores will continue to live in the soil for years.

The best solution is to cut out all affected growth – and burn it. Gather up all fallen leaves and remove the top layer of mulch or soil as this can harbour spores. Do not plant box in the same soil or near it. Improve ventilation as much as possible and do not trim the box bushes. This latter point is the key. I have planted box in the Spring Garden and left it as untrimmed bushes and they have been untouched by blight. This is because they neither have the open wounds that are so easily infected nor the tightly clipped lack of airflow that any hedge, by definition, has. But the whole virtue of box hedges is that they can be tightly clipped.

There are resistant strains – I use the very thick-leafed and rather coarse *Buxus sempervirens* 'Handsworthiensis', which does get affected but seems to recover, but it is very vigorous and will not make a low hedge. There are strains of *B. microphylla* that are apparently showing good signs of resistance, but so far none that are completely immune.

As if box blight was not bad enough, we now also have box tree caterpillars to contend with. These are the larvae of the *Cydalima perspectalis* moth that were first noticed about ten years ago and have been very active in London for the past five years. The caterpillars eat the leaves and then leave a white webbing around the pupae. There are various means of control being trialled, including nematodes, pheromene traps and

I think the days of box as a formally clipped, structural plant are numbered for all but historic gardens

pesticides. However, using powerful pesticides to kill one specific problem is always a crude weapon because of the inevitable collateral damage.

The time has come, after 400 years of using box as the plant of first choice for evergreen, low hedges, to rethink how we use it. The best corrective would be long hot summers, dry autumns and hard winters but climate change means that this is becoming the rare exception. As a rule, we are experiencing consistently warmer and wetter summers and winters alike – which the box blight fungi love. Box moth is probably the final nail in box's coffin. I think its days as a formally clipped, structural plant are numbered for all but historic gardens. It still provides a good evergreen backdrop in a border or under trees but the tightly clipped, bright green box hedge is going to become increasingly rare.

We could replace our low box hedges with a substitute evergreen plant like *Ilex crenata*, euonymus, pittosporum or myrtle. But none are as good as box so I am inclined to embrace the forced change as a creative opportunity. Better to do something different and exciting rather than the same thing less well. One door closes – with a slam – but, as ever in a garden, another opens.

Topiary

'Topiary' seems rather a grand word for what I do
in this garden but topiary is simply the art of clipping
and training a woody plant to a shape. Any shape.

It does not have to be figurative and some of the loveliest topiary I have seen was in Japan, where almost every tree and shrub is carefully clipped and trained according to the form that the topiarist (the art of topiary is known as *niwake* in Japanese) thinks most appropriate.

I have two kinds of topiary in my garden. Above all I have scores of yew and box cones of different sizes in various parts of the garden, and my one figurative piece, Topiary Nigel, which is the yew representation of my golden retriever Nigel.

Twenty years ago, the 64 large box balls in what is now the Herb Garden (they were actually pebbles or box blobs, each slightly different from each other and each most definitely not round) were my pride and joy, and set to remain in place for the foreseeable future. But I failed to anticipate the ravages of the box blight (see page 61) that ripped through

We have used topiary cones as a recurring theme throughout the garden, not least because 'Handsworthiensis' box, like this in the Long Walk, is very upright and lends itself to cones rather than round shapes.

this garden and reduced the balls to burned-out caricatures of their former selves, so a few years ago we cut our losses, dug them up and put them on the bonfire.

The box cones that I still have growing, both down the Long Walk and in pots on the Cricket Pitch, are made from the exceptionally vigorous and thick-leafed *Buxus sempervirens* 'Handsworthiensis' that seems to recover well from box blight if it gets it at all. The downside is that it never clips very tight and has extremely strong vertical growth so is only suitable for cones or columns.

The other cones I have are in yew and are growing in front of the house. These have been there since 1993 and are unchanged except for the fact that they are now monumental in scale. Topiary has a tendency to grow, however hard you cut it back and whilst, when the first edition of this book was published, the children could run and play in and around the cones, these are now almost touching – which makes mowing between them interesting. But in principle they have not changed at all and give as much pleasure as they always did, and seem to be perfectly healthy, needing just an annual trim every August.

Topiary Nigel demands a different kind of approach. For a start, he is made of four separate plants (essentially, one for each leg, although the vast majority of him comes from two plants) that were trained from the outset on a crude cane structure. Secondly, there is not a lot of room for improvisation, although I confess the likeness is notional, at best.

I often think that topiary is a good

metaphor for the whole business of gardening – growing, nurturing and carefully shaping plants to look exactly as we want them. It is wholly unnatural and controlled but ironically takes less time, skill and trouble than, for example, growing a wildflower meadow. And it is fun. Too often we become solemn about gardening but, if it fails to offer pleasure and delight, then it fails completely.

I love the yew cones in front of the house – half of which I grew from cuttings. They are the easiest part of the whole garden to tend – taking just one day a year to cut.

Once the children could run and play in and around the yew cones but now the cones are almost touching

Topiary tips

Topiary of any kind is best done with shears or a light electric hedge-cutter. Whatever you are cutting, always use a very sharp tool. This might seem obvious but it is astonishing how many people cut their hedges and topiary with old hedge-trimmers that have never been sharpened. Not only do sharp tools make it much easier for the cutter, but also it is much better for the plant. A blunt hedge-trimmer crushes and shreds the leaves as it goes through them, leaving a large surface area that is much more prone to infection and fungal attack, as well as a brown, burned, bruised residue. But really sharp blades slice cleanly, leaving a neat wound that will heal quickly.

I have become a convert to hand shears over petrol or electric hedge-trimmers for all but the largest topiary jobs. Cutting deciduous hedges is different, but a good pair of shears, kept sharp, makes light work of the controlled leaf removal that comprises most topiary, and a pair of secateurs on one's belt is all that is needed to cope with the odd thicker stem.

If you are using shears, a good tip is to hold one hand still and rather than using both hands like a bellows, 'work' only one handle. This gives much more precise control.

It is a good idea to have a bucket of water, perhaps with a dash of bleach in it, in which to regularly dip the shears. This will reduce the build up of gunk from the cut leaves and make clipping easier. Always clean and oil shears at the end of a session.

I have become a convert to hand shears over petrol or electric hedge-trimmers for all but the largest topiary jobs as they make light work of things

When making a figurative piece of any kind it is important to establish a strong framework of growth where needed before you start any serious shaping. This will take a few years. Tying shoots in will help a lot. Any growth tied in to the vertical will grow stronger as a result, whereas tying in growth down to the horizontal will slow it down.

Cutting back a leader will result in bushier sideshoots below the cut point and eventually, regular clipping will make what at first seems alarmingly flimsy become really solid, especially if you are topiarising yew.

Opposite page: Topiary Nigel started as a piece of fun but now is a living tribute to a much-loved friend.

Below: To maintain crisp topiary and to avoid tearing the leaves, it is important to keep all tools razor-sharp.

Lawns

Strictly speaking, I no longer have a lawn. However, I have had various areas of grass kept mown short over the years and the Cricket Pitch, once the long grass is cut, effectively becomes a lawn between August and the end of the year.

Opposite page: The Cricket Pitch was for years a carefully tended lawn where my sons and I played cricket. The name has stuck but now the grass is filled with flowers and allowed to grow long.

If you have children, an area of lawn is essential for them to play and sprawl – and even the most grown-up adult can enjoy a good sprawl on newly mown grass on a summer's day.

I know that some people (almost always men it seems) are extremely concerned that their lawns should be as near to perfect as possible but this has always struck me as a matter of supreme unimportance. All I am after is an even-ish area of green dominated by grass (although the lawn around the topiary yews in my front garden is becoming almost entirely moss and is lovely). A few daisies, clover, dandelions, bents or moss do not trouble me too much.

However it is important not to cut grass too short and certainly not too short too soon. Mowing robs each grass plant of the opportunity to photosynthesise, let alone set seed, so gradually weakens all but the toughest of grasses.

We all want grass to be dominant in our lawns but it is very rare for there only to be one type of grass. Let your lawn grow uncut and you will see that the different types of grass can vary a great deal when mature. A hard-wearing lawn, suitable for family rough-and-tumble and more casual care will be based upon ryegrass (along with some timothy grass, Chewing's fescue and meadow grass) but the perfect sward you find on bowling or golf greens will be mainly Chewing's fescue. This creates a finer, more velvety surface and can tolerate being cut very short indeed – but is not at all hard-wearing. A careful choice of seed or turf mix will help hugely in the years of maintenance to come.

Making a lawn

Preparation is the key to this. It is a simple equation – the better prepared the soil is beneath the grass, the better the grass will look. Dig it over just as you would a border, removing all stones and weeds, including every scrap of root.

Unless the ground is naturally free-draining I would always add 50 per cent sharp sand or grit to the topsoil as well as putting in whatever drainage was necessary but this is expensive and laborious. Spread the sand or grit as a layer over the soil and lightly fork it in.

Level it with a rake but do not attempt to get too fine a surface yet. Leave it for at least two weeks. This lets any weeds left a chance to grow so that they can be hoed off just before sowing the seed, and allows the grass to establish before they return.

Above left:
Turf has the
advantage of giving
an immediate green
surface although
it cannot be walked
on for a few weeks
and is much
more expensive
than seed.

Above right:
Whether using
seed or turf, the
ground must be
prepared equally
painstakingly as a
lawn is only as good
as the surface and
quality of the soil
beneath it.

Rake it again, getting it as level and fine as possible as the grass will reveal any dips and hollows, and it is much easier to get it properly level at this stage.

Tread over it with your heels, compressing the surface down, then rake it again in both directions. Now it is ready for sowing or turf.

Turf or seed?
- Seed is much cheaper. Turf gives an instant effect.
- Seed is easy to sow. Turf must be laid very carefully.
- Seed can be stored and sown when it suits you. Turf must be laid within a day or two of delivery.
- A sown lawn cannot be walked on for about six weeks. A turf lawn cannot be used for about four weeks.
- Seed needs watering in dry weather. Turf needs a daily soak.

- Seed is eaten by birds and scratched up by cats. Turf is not.
- The type of seed is controllable to suit the precise needs of your garden. Buying turf can be a lottery.

On balance I would plump for turf if you can get a good supply and your lawn is in an open, sunny site. If you have a larger area, the lawn is in shade or you are not certain about the quality of the turf, go for grass seed, buying a mix that meets your requirements.

Sowing seed
Scatter the seed evenly and resist the temptation to sow any thicker than directed. Rake the seed in and water it well except on rainy days. Do not worry if it seems to be growing patchily or thinly as it will thicken up very fast over the course of a few months.

Laying turf

Water the soil the night before laying the turf.

1 Start laying the turf at one corner and work across the site in a line. Use a plank to stand on to avoid spoiling the surface of the soil.

2 Butt the edges of the turfs tight together.

3 Start the next row, staggering the joins of the turfs like a course of bricks, keeping them tightly together and tamping them down flat with another plank. Use a plank to walk on the laid area to avoid treading directly on the turfs.

4 Keep all short pieces in the middle, trimming them to fit with a sharp knife, so that there are no small pieces at the edges.

5 Water the laid turf thoroughly and keep it watered every day until it starts to grow. Do not step on it at all for at least a month.

For the first season let the grass from both seed and turf grow longer than you would normally have it, not cutting it until it reaches about 5cm (2in), when it can be cut back to 2.5cm (1in) and maintained at that length for the remainder of the season.

The best time to sow seed or turf is September, which gives it time to grow before winter and makes the fact that it is a no-go area less inconvenient. By the following spring it should be established and ready for use. Otherwise sow or lay turf in spring.

Maintaining your lawn

- The most common problem with lawns is lack of drainage, followed by lack of sun. Grass likes very free drainage and sunshine to grow well. Drainage can be improved by spiking the lawn with a fork or mechanical aerator and spreading sharp sand over, brushing it into the holes.

- The next most common cause of problems in lawns comes from cutting them too short. Grass is much healthier when kept a little longer than the average lawn owner is used to. It is also better to trim a bit off each time rather than make one drastic cut.

- When you make the first few cuts of the year, collect the grass clippings. As the weather gets warmer and drier they can be left uncollected. Mulching mowers chop and spread the clippings automatically, which helps the grass in dry periods by feeding the nutrients back into the roots. However, always collect the clippings after the last cut of the autumn.

- Rake the lawn in spring and autumn with a wire rake to remove the thatch or dead grass and to aerate the soil.

The most common problem with lawns is
lack of drainage followed by lack of sun –
grass likes very free drainage and sunshine

Water features

Water always improves any garden. Whether as a fountain, rill, cascade or, more usually, a pond, some water will add light, texture, a particular range of plants and, perhaps most significantly, is the best way of increasing the variety of wildlife in your garden.

After years of resisting any water features through anxiety about safety with small children and the presence of regular flooding, I now have a large pond in the Damp Garden, a smaller one in the Wildlife Garden and ponds and a central bubbling water feature in the Paradise Garden. All give us huge pleasure and I now wish I had made them earlier.

No garden is too small for some kind of water feature although a pond is undoubtedly the one that gives most scope for a wide range of moisture-loving and aquatic plants and for attracting wildlife.

When digging out any pond that is to be planted, it is important to create ledges of different heights for different marginal and deepwater planting. Also take great care to make the edges of the pond level.

Making a pond

- Choose a site that gets direct sunlight for at least half the day. Try and avoid any overhanging trees if possible.
- A round shape or one with flowing curves is likely to look more natural than a square or rectangular one. Allow plenty of room around the pond for planting, and try and design a shape that fits in comfortably with existing features such as paths and hedges.
- You can buy rigid liners with a predetermined size and shape or use a flexible liner that will adapt to any size or shape. My preference is always for

a flexible liner for the adaptability they give you but rigid liners can work very well, especially in a restricted space. However, both types need exactly the same preparation, with very careful attention paid to establishing a level.

- Calculate the size of flexible liner needed by measuring the longest distances along the length and breadth of the pond and adding twice the maximum depth to both measurements. So a pond 3m x 1.8m (10ft x 6ft) at its widest points and 90cm (36in) at its deepest will need a liner at least 5m x 3.5m (16ft x 12ft).
- Invest in a thick butyl liner. They are expensive but they stretch and are tough so last a long time, and replacing a cheap liner is an expensive and messy business.
- Mark out the pond using string and canes, or a hosepipe. Allow for marginal plants by including shallow shelves around the perimeter. Make these at least 45cm (18in) wide and as level as you can. Aquatic plants such as water lilies need deeper water, so aim to include a section that is at least 90cm (36in) deep.
- Even a small hole takes quite a few barrowloads of soil to excavate, so plan what you will do with the waste soil – ideally, incorporate it into the garden.

- Check that the edges are all level. Use a spirit level because water will instantly expose any inaccuracy. If the site is sloping then you will have to build up one side. Avoid steep slopes falling down into or away from the edges of the pond.
- When you are satisfied with the shape and size of the hole, remove any stones or roots and firm and smooth the soil. If you are using a rigid liner this can then be fitted into the hole and the soil backfilled around the edges. If you are using a flexible liner, first cover the surface of the soil with a geotextile underlay or carpeting underfelt to prevent the liner from being punctured.
- Open the liner out and leave it in the sun for an hour. This will soften it up and make it easier to fit. Stretch it gently over the hole and let it ease itself into all the contours, gathering it into folds where possible to avoid creases. Do not start to add water until you are happy that it has as few wrinkles as possible. Weight the excess liner around the edges securely with bricks or stones.
- Fill with water, pulling any creases free. The water will stretch the liner as it fills, ensuring a tight fit.
- Finally, trim the liner, leaving at least 30cm (12in) excess all the way round. Add stones, soil and plants to hide the liner and create a natural-looking pond.

Marginal plants

Marginal plants like the kingcup (*Caltha palustris*) are surprisingly adaptable and flexible in how they manage their growing conditions – as long as they are wet. So most are happy submerged in a few inches of water (but always with their roots on the bottom rather than floating, and with most of the growth above water), squelching around in sloshy mud or even growing in the heavy soil of a damp border. Most will survive for months out of the water if there is drought as long as they do not dry out completely. This means that they are ideal to make the link from the water's edge to the soil on the margins and on out into the completely dry waterside planting.

Alongside the kingcup I have the pickerel weed (*Pontederia cordata*), so called because baby pike – pickerels – hide in amongst its growth, water plantain (*Alisma*

The pond in the Damp Garden is a perfect circle and has a paved area along one side but is planted very naturalistically.

No garden is too small for a water feature although a pond undoubtedly offers the greatest scope *plantago-aquatica*), flowering rush (*Butomus umbellatus*), arrowhead (*Sagittaria sagittifolia*) and striped bullrush (*Scirpus zebrinus*). Two irises, *Iris pseudocorus* and *I. ensata,* add to the display. Water mint (*Mentha aquatica*) spreads in amongst the stones and provides excellent cover for tadpoles and newts. In fact, one of the great virtues of marginal plants in a pond, as well as looking good, is that they are a very important source of cover for insects, smaller mammals and aquatic life.

Marginal plants should be planted in aquatic baskets (essentially, pots with mesh sides) and placed in shallow water so that the pot sits on the bottom but the surface is only just submerged. Pond water has almost all the nutrients that plants need so do not use potting compost but ordinary garden soil that is not enriched with compost of any kind, and if that proves impractical, use special aquatic compost which can be bought from any garden centre.

Adjust the size of pot to the depth of water but aim to have it no more than 2.5–7.5cm (1–3in) below the surface and use large baskets for tall plants like rushes, otherwise, unless they are rooted directly into mud, they become top-heavy and can blow over. Most marginal plants prefer still water so never put any beneath a fountain or mini waterfall.

I find skimming weed from the pond a pleasant enough process and the weed makes first-rate compost

Deep-water plants

Deep-water plants such as water lilies and water soldier (*Stratiotes aloides*) spend their lives submerged in water, with only the foliage and flowers appearing above or on the surface in summer, before dying back below the water in winter. They have evolved to root in the mud at the bottom of a pond so if you use a liner, they must be planted in pots which can then be lowered into the water.

Water lilies need at least 90cm (36in) of water in order to protect them from winter frost and to give them enough room to grow, so they need placing on some kind of support (I use bricks placed inside a large pot) which can then be lowered as the plants grow so that the leaves can readily sit on the surface of the water.

Let the water have its space and do not crowd it with plants. A few judicious water lilies, the waterlily-like frog bit (*Hydrocharis morsus-ranae*) and perhaps the water soldier, which rises to the surface in warm weather and has small white flowers in early summer, will be far more effective than a mat of plants that smothers the water.

Beware of invaders that will take over and swamp all your best intentions of refinement. The real weeds are parrot's feather (*Miriophyllum aquaticum*), floating pennywort (*Hydrocotyle ranunculoides),* or – worst of all – fairy fern (*Azolla*). These will all choke the life out of any pond.

Submerged aquatics such as hornwort (*Ceratophyllum demersum*) or the water violet (*Hottonia palustris*) are vital to keep the pond clean as they feed off the dissolved mineral salts on which algae thrive. And if algae do thrive, then you end up with the pond covered in green slime and all your dancing reflections of light are turned off. However careful you are, every pond suffers to a degree from blanket weed (which can cover the entire water during the course of a day if conditions are right) and it takes a while for the pond to sort its own balance out, but I find skimming weed a pleasant enough process – and the weed makes first-rate compost!

The Paradise Garden water feature

I originally wanted a rill emanating from a central fountain in the Paradise Garden but the limitations of budget meant that I eventually settled for something much more modest. However, it looks good and works well but is home-made and cobbled together from bits and pieces.

The basin is a fire bowl, bought on eBay, with a hole drilled in the bottom. A copper pipe fits through this which is connected to a piece of hose attached to a small electric pump installed by a qualified electrician who took the feed from the wooden greenhouse. The water is brought from an underground pipe connected to a nearby tap and a common-or-garden lavatory ballcock ensures it does not overflow.

All is housed in a concrete-block underground tank about 1 cubic metre (35 cubic feet) in size. I dug a hole about 50 per cent bigger than that, lined it with the thickest butyl liner I could find and then covered that with a protective soft layer of carpet underfelt to stop it puncturing. We then made a concrete pad about 10cm (4in) deep over the base, let it set and built the walls on that. The butyl was then raised

up around these walls before trimming. This belt-and-braces approach means that the concrete tank is effectively wrapped in butyl so if the concrete leaks – which it shouldn't – the water is still contained.

A metal grid covers the top of the tank, over which are placed limestone slabs which the bowl sits on, with sufficient gaps for the overflowing water to run back down into the tank and be pumped back up to the bubble.

We have found that in hot or windy weather there is quite a lot of evaporation and dispersal, but the solution is simple: we leave a hose running into the bowl for fifteen minutes once a week. In an age of computerised pumps and high-tech gadgets, my main advice would be to keep everything as low-tech as possible – then you will be able to fix any of the inevitable problems with a minimum of fuss or equipment.

The water feature at the centre of the Paradise Garden is as much about sound as sight. It creates a continuous gentle murmur as the water bubbles gently up and spills over the edge of the bowl, to be recycled back down and up again from the cistern below.

Gardening basics

Soil

The most significant element in any garden is the soil. It is the soil not the plants that should be fed, watered and tended, and if the soil is good, then the garden will be good.

For most of my life I have believed that 'improving' the soil was the holy grail of gardening. Lick your soil into shape and your garden will inevitably become better too.

I also believed that soil had moral as well as practical qualities and was a kind of qualitative measure of the gardener. Good, rich soil exemplified the work of a good, hard-working gardener.

But over the past few years I have changed my view on this. It is not completely wrong of course, but it is only part of the truth and also depended on a very one-sided relationship between gardeners and the ground that they cultivated.

I was firmly of the school that a good spade wielded freely and vigorously would solve most horticultural problems. I even fetishised a special spade that I had made for me 25 years ago as a symbol of all that was noble and pure about my relationship

with the earth – and by that I included the entire planet as well as my back yard. However, research over the past 25 years has made us realise two things.

The first is that soil is a very much more complex material than we had imagined. Its relationship to plants is dependent upon a chain of interactions so interwoven and far-reaching that it makes the average neural pathway look like an on/off switch. The second is that we know practically nothing about any of this. It has been said that we know more about the outer reaches of the universe than we do about the soil 15cm (6in) beneath our feet. One-third of all organisms on this planet live in the soil and yet we have so far only even identified about 1 per cent of them. To put that in context: every hectare (2.5 acres) of soil has organisms equivalent to the volume of 200 sheep living within the first 30cm (12in) below the surface – but 198 of those sheep-shaped animals are utterly unknown, phantasmagorical creatures. The phrase 'barely scratching the surface' does not do justice to our ignorance.

Types of soil

But every gardener stands to benefit from a little understanding of what has so far been discovered from looking at the ground that our gardens grow from.

The old received wisdom was that there were four basic types of soil – clay, chalk, sand and peat. The average garden was likely to be a composite of two of these but dominated by one characteristic which would determine the broad swathe of plants you could comfortably grow. This is still broadly true but only as an expression of pH rather than of the soil itself. It was a given that all four types of soil would be immeasurably improved by digging – preferably doubly so – and by adding large quantities of manure – preferably in a trench as you dug.

In fact it is now reckoned – and I stress that this science is nascent and new discoveries are being made almost daily – that there are over 50,000 different soil types around the world. Each one is a separate ecosystem with individual characteristics. Each one hosts countless organisms and biota that are all interacting as part of the life of the soil and the plants that grow in it.

Confused? Well, you might well be. In fact, if you are not floundering then you have not begun to grasp the complexity of this. Suddenly a bit of virtuous digging and a fresh load of manure do not quite cover all bases.

Soil loss

We are also losing our soil at an alarming rate. The population is rising and almost all of that new growth is being housed in towns and cities which, by definition, do not provide food for their populaces. Yet over the past 40 years, about 2 billion hectares (2.5 billion acres) of soil in the unurbanised remnant of the globe – equivalent to 15 per cent of the earth's land area – has been degraded and soil is being lost at between ten and 40 times the rate at which it can be naturally regenerated. This is entirely through human mismanagement, carelessness or sheer ignorance.

It takes about a thousand years to make 2.5cm (1in) of soil and were we to continue abusing and misusing our soil at the same rate, we would run out of it in a couple of generations. That will not happen because many people around the world are aware of the dangers, not least the intergovernmental technical panel on soils that is both mapping soil around the world and starting to work on how best to conserve and use it. And gardeners are a key part of this.

There is also the other factor that soil, and in particular peat, is a major store of carbon in the form of organic matter. Loss of organic matter is as detrimental to the quality of the soil as it is important for fertility, stability and water retention, and is a key indicator of soil health. But digging soil – let alone ploughing it and, heaven forfend, open-cast peat mining – releases carbon into the atmosphere. In fact it is estimated that agricultural tillage releases ten times more carbon to the atmosphere every year than all deforestation.

This points to adding large volumes of manure and compost as people did before but in fact, the best supply of organic matter comes from plant material, mainly in the form of roots. And the best manager of this is not the spade or the plough but the earthworm. There are 25 species of earthworm in this country – and over 3000 worldwide – and they are remarkably efficient at bringing in, digesting and incorporating organic material. The common earthworm can move 100–200 tonnes (100–200 tons) of soil a year per hectare (2.5 acres), which is as much as any plough can do.

In other words, the spade can be put away. There is no need to dig anything other than planting holes. As for improving the organic content of soil, the best way to do this is by adding just 2.5–5cm (1–2in) of compost to the surface, letting worms incorporate it and covering the soil with plants. Do not leave any bare soil anywhere. Grow in it, mulch it but resist cultivating it.

The right environment for soil improvement

Soil structure is almost as important as soil content. Get the 'pores' of the soil right and it permits best root development, drainage, water retention and bacterial and rhizomatous growth and interaction. You the gardener cannot make this happen any

more than you can make your brain process a taste. But you can help provide the environment. So adding organic material and perhaps extra grit, avoiding compaction from walking and cultivation, and using plants – even weeds – to open out the soil with their roots and add their biomass, will all help soil structure. If the structure is good, so too will be the fertility because your plants will be best able to take up available nutrients and moisture.

Soil is not a static, fixed thing any more than light is. Think of it as alive and breathing, a living entity working with your plants rather than an inert medium in which you raise them at your bidding.

Which brings us to the relationship between plants and bacteria and fungi in the soil. This is both complex and dynamic, and almost entirely beneficial. I receive thousands of letters every year enquiring how to cope with, defeat or get rid of fungi, worms, beetles and other visible denizens of the soil. If the writers could see bacteria, I am sure they would want to zap them too. But without this subterranean life there would be no gardens at all. This is why the whole concept of sterilising soil for propagation purposes seems to be a kind of arrogant madness. Rather than a dead, sterile medium you want soil that contains as much life as possible to interact with seedlings as early as possible.

It is important to realise that there is no one perfect soil and the recipe for such perfection will change with circumstance. In fact, to adapt the old adage about clothes and weather, there is no such thing as bad soil – just the wrong plants. If a plant is healthy and happy it will not, I am

afraid, be down to your tender loving care or extreme skill but simply because it has found the right soil in which to put down its roots. Look after the soil and you invariably look after the plant too.

Normal garden compost (see pages 104–107), that any gardener can make from any back garden or allotment, is the best thing to nurture your soil. Think of compost like sourdough starter. When you apply a 2.5cm (1in) mulch – 5cm (2in) at most – you are not 'feeding' the soil as such, but recharging it. Adding compost made largely from plants grown in your own soil will add an intense dose of bacteria and fungi back into the ground and stimulate the dynamic that is already there – even in soil that seems unpromising. Life is already in the soil. It knows what to do. As yet, we barely have an inkling of how it does it but that is the

great field of discovery for the next generation of soil scientists.

Thus, after half a century of believing that digging was at the heart of all good garden cultivation, I have amended my views. In order to get the best from our soil – whatever type it seems to be – we should nurture a healthy worm population. Make compost and add it thinly as a booster for the life that is already busy at work in the ground. Cut right back on the digging. Forget all notions of a 'perfect' soil but work at making yours as good as it might be. Choose your plants wisely so they interact well with your soil as it is and not as you wish it might be. A healthy plant will make the most of what the soil provides and will limit both its rate and ultimate size of growth to achieve that end. Plants will always work with the soil that they grow in. It makes sense for gardeners to do so too.

The Cottage Garden was our vegetable garden for 20 years so the soil is exceptionally rich and productive – whether growing cabbages or roses.

Cultivation

Much has altered in the 20 years since I first published this book. My soil has changed as a result of two more decades of adding good organic matter, my opinions have changed about the necessity of digging in its various forms, and most pertinent of all, my body has changed.

I used to pride myself on my digging endurance and technique. It was, slightly embarrassingly, a measure of manhood and I embraced the challenge. But time and tide spare no man and my knees will no longer let me dig other than the bare necessity for planting. This means that whereas for years I saw digging as a kind of virtuous ritual that was a necessary part of tending for both the land and my soul, I now restrict it to breaking up compacted soil only as and when necessary.

The 'no-dig' method of using raised beds that are regularly mulched and never cultivated has proven itself to be very effective and beneficial to sustaining good soil structure. However, we find that a winter of our heavy rainfall can seriously compact the soil so we do still work raised beds with a light forking and will run a rotovator over an open vegetable bed that has been walked on.

I have visited astonishingly good gardens in America made from cleared forest where the planting was all done into the virgin, uncultivated soil, with simply a planting hole excavated. It has inspired me to attempt the same in part of the Coppice which, superficially at least, is soil that is dry, compacted and riven with roots. I will report back on that experiment in due course!

But the extra years of mulching mean that all our flower beds now have an open, easy structure that is rich and moisture-retentive but never waterlogged or compacted. In early 2011 we did dig over the whole of the Jewel Garden – but to remove bindweed rather than specifically to cultivate the soil.

However, if you are taking on an allotment or cultivating beds and borders from a field, as I did, you will need to dig the ground initially. Assuming, unlike me, your knees are up to it, here is the digging technique that stood me in good stead for many years.

- Only dig when the ground is reasonably dry. If the soil is sticking to your boots, then it is probably too wet.
- Bend your knees as you dig, not your back.
- Use a good spade, preferably of stainless steel. This will cost more cash but save a lot of effort and should last a lifetime. My own spade is well worn from over 30 years of almost daily use and is on its third handle now. A good spade should be comfortable to use and cut easily into

any soil, lifting it out in thick slabs or loose blocks, according to its composition. Only use a fork if the ground has been previously dug with a spade and you wish to break it up. Nine times out of ten, a spade is better.

- Hold the spade upright so that the blade chops into the ground vertically. It helps to imagine that you are cutting the straight side of a trench. This converts most of the energy into the ground and strains the back less. It is also more efficient, enabling you to take up the most soil with the least effort.

- Keep the soil in clods as large as you can. This will mean that initially, more air gets into the ground. The clods can easily be broken down later by you or by the weather.

- Wear stout boots. Proper footwear will mean you can use your feet and legs to dig the spade into the ground, further reducing the strain on your back.

Digging grassland

If you are digging up grass to make newly cultivated areas you should strip the turf off cleanly in rows before you begin. If the ground has been uncultivated for a number of years, and there is a good growth of grass or mixed weeds and wildflowers, it will be a rich and balanced soil and will not need any extra compost or manure. Dig it as follows:

- Strip the turf.
- Take out an initial trench across the plot, one spit deep and one spit wide (a 'spit' has no fixed dimension but refers to the depth of the particular spade you are using). Barrow the soil from this first trench to the end.
- Lay the cut turf upside down along the bottom of the trench. Some people say it should be chopped up, but I just put it in and let it slowly decompose.
- Continue this process, and use the soil from the first trench to fill the last.

Cultivation means preparing the soil so whatever you are sowing or planting has the best prospect of growing well from the first day. Cultivation can vary hugely but in principle there is never any virtue in cultivating more than the minimum necessary.

A flourishing vegetable garden or allotment is always a picture of healthy soil.

• After you have planted into this virgin ground, be sure to use a thick mulch of compost to start the process of ensuring sustained natural cultivation.

An alternative to using the turf to add organic matter to the soil is to make a turf stack by stacking the cut turfs grass-face to grass-face in a square block. If left for a year, this will rot to a wonderful rich cake of soil that you cut vertically with a spade. The resulting loam is a bacterial gold mine to add to home-made potting compost or if you need some high-quality topsoil elsewhere in the garden.

Raised beds

Raised beds are ideal if you are limited with space or mobility and are also the best way of coping with very poor or thin soil. The soil from the paths between can be shovelled into the beds to increase the depth of topsoil or topsoil can be bought in if necessary. The greater depth of topsoil means better root run and improved drainage, and is noticeably quicker to warm up in spring.

You should be able to reach everything from the paths without ever having to stand on the bed itself, so every bit of the bed can be planted. This also means that once made, the beds need no further cultivation at all.

Heavy rain can cause compaction but the addition of compost will encourage earthworm activity, which is enough to keep the soil open. I always have a length of scaffolding board cut so it rests firmly on the outside edging boards of the beds so I can stand or kneel on that when planting, rather than on the soil. But most of the time you should be able to reach whatever you want from the paths.

Do not be tempted to make raised beds too wide. The maximum workable width is 1.5m (5ft) and it is best to keep them to less than 4.5m (15ft) long so that they are quick and easy to walk around.

Mark the beds out with string and dig the ground deeply, adding as much manure or compost as you can obtain. This will raise the surface of the soil.

For many years I had raised beds that were simple mounds of soil. They worked well but the soil did spill annoyingly onto the paths and I have found hard edging to be much better. Recycled scaffolding planks are cheap and work well although I have also used greenwood oak boards that are a little more expensive but last longer and look better.

It is easier to cultivate the ground, marked out by string, and then construct the edging around the cultivated beds rather than digging them once they are constructed. Use bark chippings, paving or grass for the paths between the beds but if you use grass, leave room for a mower. Finally, top-dress the beds with a generous layer of compost and repeat with a fresh layer of 2.5–5cm (1–2in) each time you make a harvest. This will recharge the soil and worm activity will quickly incorporate the compost into the soil of the raised bed.

Preparing a tilth

However beautifully and dutifully you have dug the ground, it will need further preparation to get it ready for planting or sowing. My aim is to prepare the soil so that I can sow and plant out seedlings using only my hands. This means the soil must be finely prepared and uncompacted, although I am aware that this is not really necessary for the successful growth of the plants, which will cope with a much less well-prepared surface if need be.

If you have light soil that you have dug in autumn and have left it in large clods until spring, it may just need a vigorous raking over. I find that on my heavy soil, unless we have a good number of days of hard frost, in which case even the largest, thickest clods of soil break easily into a lovely crumbly texture, I have to fork or rotovate it before raking to break it down sufficiently. A mechanised rotary tiller is ideal for this. I use a very small one which is light and can be lifted to cultivate small, localised areas, and if I am working a large site, I hire a larger machine for the job. But a fork or sharp rake can do the job perfectly well, especially for small areas, and at a time when we are all trying to reduce our carbon emissions, it is to be encouraged wherever practical.

Spread a layer of well-rotted compost about 2.5cm (1in) deep over the previously dug ground before forking or rotovating it well into the top 15cm (6in). Try to tread on the soil as little as possible as you do this. Then rake it well in one direction and again at right angles, getting the soil level and smooth, and removing all surface stones or large, hard clods of earth. It is now ready for planting.

Raised beds are ideal if you have limited space or mobility and are the best way of coping with poor soil

Plant propagation

Above left: The tray in the potting shed contains the seed potting mix. Patti is helping!

Above right: Pricking out red Cos seedlings into individual plugs. These will be grown on until large enough to plant out in the Vegetable Garden.

Like any gardener, I love buying plants, especially from small, independent nurseries but best of all, I like to grow my own, be it lettuce or oak tree. In fact I would go so far as to say that the process of propagation is the distillation of all gardening.

The vast majority of propagation starts with seed but also includes cuttings of all kinds, division, offsets, layering and even the occasional graft. However you go about it, the magic of 'making' plants never wanes.

There is no doubt that my lovely potting shed makes propagation a joy. In the summer months I can find myself longing for a rainy Saturday morning so I can justify spending a few hours in there, pottering happily and regularly crossing the yard to the greenhouse with yet more trays of seeds or cuttings.

But my potting shed did not just appear. It used to be a stable and the present potting arrangement has evolved over 20 years and is the summation of experience, opportunity and convenience. It suits me in the same way as a keen carpenter will have a workshop customised specifically for their needs and preferences. As well as all the various pots and seeds, I have two wooden bays made from marine ply, one containing a seed mix and the other a potting mix. The seed mix provides less nutrition but has a lighter, more open structure, whereas the basic potting mix has more substance in the shape of extra home-made compost and soil added to proprietary peat-free compost. The seed mix has vermiculite to open it out and I use grit or perlite (see page 88) to do the same job for the potting mix.

I have to hand several metal dustbins that hold, respectively, sieved garden compost, sieved home-made leafmould, prepared coir (which we buy in dehydrated, compressed bricks and have to soak for twelve hours) and vermiculite or perlite. Added to that is a permanent bucketful of horticultural grit and another of sieved loam from our loam stack. All that sieving is tedious but makes for good bad-weather work and also justifies buying a few lovely gardening sieves which add a level of joy to anyone's life.

So much for the perfect potting shed but for ten years in the 1980s, when we lived in London, I did all my propagation and potting on a trestle table in the garden. I used the area beneath the table to store bags of compost and pots, and the very sheltered side access to the house to protect delicate seedlings from the worst of the weather. Whilst a fully kitted-out potting shed was always a dream, this arrangement worked perfectly well.

Potting mixes

I do have precise recipes but they come with a warning: I nearly always ignore them and mix by intuition. The recipes are not definitive but simply what I have found work for me here. They may well change or be adapted yet more. In fact, I rather hope that they are because it means that I am still paying attention and learning as I go. I suggest that they are a good place to start but urge you to adapt and alter them to suit your own experience.

- **Seed mix** 50% coir, 10% garden compost, 25% leafmould, 10% vermiculite, 5% loam
- **Potting-on mix** 30% garden compost, 30% coir, 20% grit/perlite, 10% loam, 10% leafmould
- **Container mix** 30% garden compost, 25% loam, 25% leafmould, 20% grit
- **Mix for cuttings, bulbs and high-drainage shrubs** 40% leafmould, 40% grit/perlite, 20% garden compost
- **Ericaceous mix** I substitute composted bracken for garden compost

I stress that none of these is measured but all is done by eye. If, when I have made a batch it just feels wrong, I will unhesitatingly alter it until it feels right without really analysing why that might be so. In the end much of this is ritual. I relish that but do not be precious about it. Seeds tend to grow where they fall.

Peat

Man has been digging peat for fuel from moor and wetland since pre-history. When peat was dug by hand it was used at a sustainable level – and still is as fuel in many parts of Great Britain. But large-scale mechanical extraction has made a mockery of the delicate relationship between man and this particular kind of landscape. The peat itself takes many generations to return and the layers just 60–90cm (24–36in) below the surface are often many hundreds of years old. Digging them up is on a par with ripping out ancient hedgerows solely to make sawdust. Around 95 per cent of British peat bogs have been lost in the past 100 years. None will return in our lifetime and few within the lives of our grandchildren – if ever. This is eco-vandalism on a grand scale and it is entirely unnecessary.

The truth is that peat makes an excellent growing medium. It smells good, is pleasant to handle, is light enough to buy in large bags and has a satisfyingly rich, dark brown colour. It retains moisture well yet drains freely. It is 'open' so that young plants can easily establish a good root system. It is pretty much sterile so can be safely used without fear of diseases being spread by it. It contains very little nutrition so commercial growers can control plant food by adding it rather than guessing the compost's own nutritional qualities.

But none of this justifies ravaging fragile peat bogs. It is just environmentally completely unacceptable. My own belief is that it should either be made illegal or have a prohibitively high tax put on it so that if people insist on using it, they will at least be contributing handsomely to the public coffers.

To strip peat in order to make gardens is no more justifiable than it is to dig up rare plants from the wild in order to adorn your garden. Every time you use a peat-based compost in the garden you are deliberately participating in the destruction of a non-renewable environment that sustains some of our most beautiful plant and animal life. No garden on this earth is worth that.

Finally, there are excellent alternatives that make peat redundant as a horticultural growing medium. Proprietary bark composts are excellent. Coir is a waste product from coconuts and can be shipped compressed in vast bulk so the transportation becomes sustainable. Home-made leafmould (see page 110) is superb and easy to make. Composted bracken, on its own or in combination with other compost, offers a wonderful loose texture and is ericaceous. These make peat an irresponsible and unnecessary irrelevance.

Grit, perlite and vermiculite

Perlite is a volcanic glass that is mined, usually in open-cast mines, in a number of countries, with Armenia, Turkey, Greece and the United States the main producers, although it is found in many parts of the world. It is then heated at temperatures of 850–900°C (1500–1600°F) so that it expands to over ten times its original volume. The resulting white 'bobbles' are soft on the outside but have a hard interior and are very light. The soft coating holds some moisture but the hard interior stops the bobble becoming saturated. Perlite's role in a potting compost is to both open it out, allowing more oxygen to reach the roots, and to hold moisture whilst stopping waterlogging by improving drainage.

Vermiculite is also a mineral, being a kind of mica found mostly in South Africa but also in the United States, China and Zimbabwe. Like perlite, vermiculite is

Ravaging fragile peat bogs is unacceptable and should be made illegal or prohibitively taxed

heated until it expands hugely. Unlike perlite, it absorbs water freely and expands even further. This means that it is less suitable to aerate soil but better at holding water. I use vermiculite only as part of a seed mix and perlite mainly for cuttings or plants such as succulents that suffer badly from being too wet.

Horticultural grit is made from crushed rock and comes in various sizes from 2mm to 6mm and makes an excellent material for opening out potting mixes, improving drainage and providing an open root run. It is ideal as a major part of a potting mix for bulbs and tulips – I use 50 per cent grit to 50 per cent of my standard mix. It is also very good as a surface mulch on pots, stopping soil splashing on petals or too much moisture sitting around the base of a stem and rotting it.

All three materials take significant energy to extract, create, package and deliver, and thus have a carbon footprint, so should be used carefully and responsibly. However, that applies to any product of any sort that you buy, so should be considered as part of the wider balance of your overall consumption.

Raising plants from seed

On one level this is the simplest horticultural recipe there is. Take a seed and place in or on a growing medium of some kind, add water and heat, and a brand-new plant magically appears. Simple.

In practice there are many variations and refinements on this and I know that for many people eager to grow as much as possible from seed, but not perhaps wholly confident with the whole business, there is a sense that they could or should be doing it better or differently.

Setting aside the first and most important rule of all horticulture – if it works then you are doing it right (the second being, if you are not enjoying it

Vermiculite is a mineral that is heated so it expands hugely. It is useful both as a component in seed compost and as a layer covering seeds in a seed tray.

Above and opposite page: Although many plants that we raise from seed start life in the propagating greenhouse and are raised to sturdy young plants before being placed out into the ground, some, like peas, are better sown direct as soon as the soil is warm enough.

then you are doing it wrong) – I have found from my own experience over the years that there are a number of factors that will improve the chances of success with all kinds of seeds. If nothing else, what ensures the best return on your investment is the seeds themselves. Although seeds are certainly the cheapest way – by far – of stocking your garden with the widest possible range of plants, a year's supply of seeds can still add up to a sizeable sum. So you want as many as possible to grow well from the very start.

Begin with the seeds as they arrive. Once you have been through them, lay them all out on a table, make a note of what you have, fling them in a corner, make a spreadsheet or whatever it is that you do, and store them somewhere cool and dry. If in doubt, you cannot go wrong by keeping seeds in the fridge.

Then you need to decide what growing medium is best for you. There is no magic formula. The one thing I am not trying to do is provide much nutrition. I want the seedlings to grow steadily but not too fast,

especially when the light levels are still low. From the moment of germination, strong, steady growth is what I am looking for to establish strong, mature plants. I also plan to prick out seedlings well before they have exhausted the available nutrients in their seed compost.

Of course seeds sown direct into the garden need none of this tarrafiddle. You just sow and they just grow. But very few seeds other than perhaps peas and broad beans are worth sowing direct until the soil warms up – and that can mean waiting until late April or even May on cold, heavy soils.

I tend to use seed trays rather than modules and very rarely sow into pots unless the seeds, such as sweet peas or climbing beans, are especially robust or large. Seed trays are easy to handle and sowing in them is very quick. However, you must prick out the seedlings as soon as they are large enough to handle.

Larger, heavier seeds such as beetroot or French beans are best sown into modules or small pots as these can then be

transplanted directly to the garden. Occasionally I sow in clusters in modules – this works well for beetroot, rocket or other leafy greens – and only thin each cluster lightly, transplanting them outside in small clumps rather than as individual plants. But on the whole, my aim from the outset is to produce strong individual seedlings able to withstand all the affronts that life in the garden will accost them with.

I always sow thinly with as even a spread as possible, trying to resist the temptation to scatter the last few pinches of seed because they are there. I then gently cover most seeds with a finely sieved layer of compost or sprinkle vermiculite over them. This protects them from being moved by watering and provides the dark that many seeds need for germination. Some seeds, such as achillea, celery, petunias and tobacco plants, need light for germination so are best left uncovered (although often, enough light will penetrate a fine layer of vermiculite or compost). Other seeds, such as lettuce, calendulas or delphiniums, need darkness.

I always label every container with the species, variety and date before it leaves the potting shed. Pencil is easiest and best. This is absolutely vital as it is amazing how often varieties or even species of seeds get mixed up.

If the compost mix is at all dry (and compost used straight from a sack is often very damp, whereas it dries out fast on the potting shed bench), I place the seed tray in a shallow container of water for about ten minutes so the compost can absorb moisture. It will then not need watering from above for a few days. This is especially useful for those seeds placed on the surface so they are not all pushed to the edge of the seed tray by the spray from the watering can. Otherwise I place the seed trays on a heated bench in the greenhouse, water them and leave them to germinate.

Watering is something you have to judge on a daily basis. I inspect all seed trays at least twice a day. As spring progresses, the greenhouse can become much warmer than the outside air and the seeds may well need watering twice a day. But too much moisture can rot seeds before they germinate or lead to fungal problems such as damping off. If in doubt, bear in mind that more harm is usually done by overwatering than by holding back for twelve hours.

For germinating most seeds I strongly recommend heated capillary matting.

I always sow thinly, trying to resist the temptation to scatter the last few pinches of seed

Although this needs a power supply it is not expensive and provides gentle heat at the roots that will greatly increase the speed and rate of germination. I find the matting lasts for years too. It works best in a greenhouse or conservatory but a well-lit porch or wide windowsill is viable too. If you do not have any of these then consider making or buying a cold frame (see page 103). These are old-fashioned but brilliant, both for germinating seeds and raising seedlings, as well as for storing plants over winter. I cannot imagine gardening without them.

I like to take the seed trays off the heated matting as soon as the majority of seeds have germinated. This creates space for another batch of fresh seeds and the emerging seedlings go on to another area within the greenhouse where they are slightly less mollycoddled. If I have sown too thickly – and even now, I often still do – I thin cheap and cheerful plants like lettuce, tobacco plants or celery simply by plucking clumps of tiny seedlings to stop them crowding. It also improves ventilation.

Then, as soon as they have a true leaf and are large enough to handle, I prick them out either into plugs or at wider and regular spacing in another seed tray. The seeds have become plants. These then get put in a cold frame as part of their progress to the harsh world outside. But that is another part of the story.

Gently ease the plant from its pot and if the roots hold the soil but are not potbound, then it is ready to go out

Annuals from seed

It is essential that you get the timing right when growing annuals for planting out. Because their life cycle is so short, the delay of a couple of weeks can irreparably limit their growth and flowering. I speak from bitter and repeated experience! As a rule it is best to prick them out, pot them on and plant them out as soon as possible, provided that they have a decent root system at every stage and that they are properly hardened off for at least two weeks before putting out into the border. However rich the potting compost (and it should not be too rich), and however carefully they are watered and tended, miss planting them out by more than ten days and they will never realise their potential.

How do you know when this is? First, by gently easing the plant from its pot. If the root structure holds the soil yet is not potbound, then it is ready to go out. Second, by checking that it has vigorous, healthy-looking leaves. If it has started to produce flowers or is looking stunted or etiolated, then it is a sure sign that it should have already been planted out.

The corollary to this is not to be too eager to sow your seeds. It is no use having a mass of annuals waiting to go outside if the weather and soil are too cold. Annuals will always do better sown too late than too early.

I raise my annuals under cover because our soil is cold and wet and I have the cover to raise them under, but sowing direct is not a bad thing, especially if you live in a mild area or if your garden is reasonably sheltered and dry. For the new garden or gardener nothing is more satisfying than a few packets of annual seeds sown into soil that has been dug and raked to a fine tilth (see page 85). The best way is to sow in zig-zags, crosses, circles or lines to differentiate the growing seedlings from the weeds that cultivation will inevitably produce. Annuals grow best in a rich soil but do not feed the soil with extra manure as that will only produce lots of green growth without any extra flowers.

The only hard bit is to sow much more thinly than seems sensible and then be ruthless enough to further thin the seedlings so that each plant has room to enrich itself – as much as 15cm (6in) apart for most plants. This is another good reason to grow annuals indoors if possible, especially if the seeds are difficult to come by or hard to germinate. But poppies, nigella, cornflowers, helianthus, eschscholzia, phacelia, zinnias, nasturtiums or calendulas, amongst others, will all do well sown directly where they are to flower.

Taking cuttings

I have always sown seeds with insouciance and divided with abandon. But for a while I was rather wary of cuttings. It seemed to be a skill that required techniques and knowledge that I did not have – or at least did not feel that I had and had not been taught. It also seemed to be rather a faff, involving misters and polythene bags, hormone rooting powder, special compost mixes and last but not least, the rather alarming-sounding 'bottom heat'. It was all too much. I wanted to flow not fiddle. My garden was not, heaven forbid, a laboratory but a studio where creativity

and intuition always trumped precision and experiment.

However I noticed that my eldest brother – and I have two older brothers, both of whom, like me, were brought up to garden from a young age – was always raising lots of cuttings from a wide range of plants and whenever I visited him in his garden, he would give me a tray of plants that he had raised from cuttings. All were healthy, many would have taken a few years to reach the stage they were at if grown from seed, and he obviously had lots to spare otherwise he certainly would not have dished them out to his upstart little brother. For my part, competitive sibling rivalry kicked in and I reckoned that if he could do it then so could I.

This was about 30 years ago and since then I take cuttings whenever I possibly can. Some strike fast and easily whilst some are reluctant to root and if they do so at all, take their time about it. But for a whole range of plants, and in particular shrubs of all kinds, it is the easiest and best way to propagate them. Cuttings also have the great advantage of replicating the parent exactly whereas seeds will always combine the qualities and not always the best ones – of both parents. So if you have a much-loved plant or if a friend would like one exactly like yours, cuttings will provide the replicas quickly and completely reliably.

All the advice that follows will merely help maximise your chances of success but it is important not to be precious about it. See how it goes. There will be failures but so too will there certainly be successes, and once you get into the swing

Above and opposite page: Taking cuttings is easy and guarantees an exact replica of the parent plant – which no seed can do. Always choose healthy growth without a flower bud and remove all but a pair of leaves. I am using pure perlite, which is excellent for any quick-rooting cuttings such as these from *Cosmos atrosanguineus*. They will root and be ready to be potted into compost in a matter of a few weeks.

of it you realise that there is a huge range of plants that will take from cuttings – from delphiniums and oriental poppies to yews and roses. Some are outrageously simple, like willow, which roots almost perversely quickly. I once cut down an overhanging branch of a crack willow, sawed it into thick logs and left them on the ground for a couple of weeks after which all had rooted where they made contact with the soil. Most cuttings need a little more care but once you demystify the process it really is not hard.

But you need to understand the process. From the second you remove a section of the plant from the parent plant it starts to die. It is then a race to encourage it to grow new roots quickly enough to sustain it. If the roots grow quickly, the top section will need little mollycoddling because this top section contains a small reserve of moisture. If the cutting is slow to root or the plant material is very new and fragile, then it will wilt irreversibly faster than the roots can form and you have lost it.

So foliage that is thicker or more mature will always last longer without roots than will fresh new leaves. However, it will mostly take longer to root. Tender foliage can be very delicate and temperamental but can also root very fast. This leads to cuttings being grouped into four broad divisions – soft, semi-ripe, hard and root. They all have pros and cons.

Softwood cuttings are taken from fresh growth that is, as the name suggests, still flexible, so easily damaged. They can be taken at any time but the best material is usually found in spring and early summer when growth is most vigorous. The cut material can often be rather short and very tender but if it roots, it does so very quickly – but it can also quickly die, so needs the greatest care and protection. Softwood cuttings are best for plants like fuchsias, clematis and pelargoniums that produce plenty of new growth in spring.

Semi-ripe cuttings made from the current season's new growth later in the season – any time from midsummer

through to October, when they have had a chance to mature a little and become more robust are probably the easiest of all but still need some protection and humidity control. Almost any shrub can be propagated by semi-ripe cuttings and I have made thousands of these over the years, particularly at the end of summer in August and September. These will form roots by autumn or, like box, not show any sign of doing so until the following spring but then grow very fast. The vast majority of cuttings that most gardeners will take from shrubs of all kinds can be classed as semi-ripe, although some are more semi and some more ripe than others.

Hardwood cuttings are taken from current season's growth that has matured sufficiently to develop a strong woody section at the base. These tend therefore to be longer and are always taken in autumn and winter, and often after the leaves have fallen. They are slow to form roots but very slow to die, so mostly need no protection at all other than good

drainage, and can be placed directly outside into a slit trench with some sand or grit in the bottom to improve drainage. They are ideal for soft fruit, roses, yew and indeed almost any tree.

Root cuttings are taken from sections of root rather than stem. Obviously these have no foliage but are treated in much the same way. Lift the parent plant – such as an oriental poppy clean the roots and cut off a section of strong, healthy root. Divide this into lengths about 5–7.5cm (2–3in) long, being careful to remember which is top and bottom. Bury the roots vertically in compost so the top part of the cutting is just at soil level. Because there is not the same race against time with the top section dying before roots are formed, root cuttings are much hardier and easier than stem cuttings, but they do better with a little warmth and must not dry out.

Whatever type of cutting you take there are a few ground rules that will make them much more successful.

- Always choose healthy, vigorous, straight growth without any flower buds. These will form roots the quickest.
- Try to take cuttings in the morning – the earlier the better – whilst they are still turgid.
- Always use a sharp pair of secateurs or knife so you have a clean cut.
- Always put any cut material straight into a polythene bag. This will reduce evaporation and delay wilting.
- Once you have taken the cut material you want from a plant, process and pot up the cuttings and place them where they are to root as quickly as you can. I always think of it as accident

procedure: this patient is gravely injured and dying so we need to work calmly and accurately – but above all, fast.

Once you have your material, you need somewhere where you can clean each cutting and pot it up. A wooden surface, glass or piece of slate is really useful to cut onto. Have a straight-edged knife and hone it to razor sharpness as a clean cut will root much easier. Ideally you must have a knife that is dedicated to cutting so is not blunted by day-to-day general use.

Take each piece of plant and cut the end cleanly. For most plants (except for any that are 'internodal' like clematis, that produce their roots from the stem between sets of leaves) it is best to cut just below a leaf node (the bit on the stem where leaves grow from).

Cleanly cut off all the leaves except the top two. If these are large it is a good idea to cut them in half across their width. The aim is to leave enough to enable transpiration but the greater the leaf surface, the quicker the cutting will lose moisture and wither. But this is not an exact science and there are many other factors such as humidity, temperature and the condition of each cutting. Trial and error is the best teacher.

Gardeners used to swear by dipping the cut stems into hormone rooting powder but I stopped doing that about 20 years ago and have not seen any reduction in

strike rates. However, it will do no harm, so if you feel inclined, have a jar of water that you dip the stems into before dipping them into the rooting powder.

Always use a very free-draining compost for cuttings. Half-perlite, grit or vermiculite with half peat-free seed compost works well and I often use pure perlite. The cutting does not need any nutrition, just oxygen and water, so the medium must be loose and open to allow oxygen but not so free-draining that it immediately dries out. Bury the stem as deeply as it will go in the pot, ensuring the remaining foliage is not touching the surface of the compost mix. Obviously, little softwood cuttings have little stems and a hardwood cutting like a rose needs a deep pot – although hardwood cuttings can be placed directly into soil outside.

Any container will do, although whatever you use, placing the cuttings around the edge of the pot also seems to help reduce drying out.

Water the cuttings in and thereafter the compost should not be allowed to dry out but does not need to be kept soaked as initially the plant is not taking up any moisture at all. But the more humid you can keep the air around the foliage, the slower the cutting will wilt and the greater the chance of roots growing before the cutting dies. This is why some cuttings are placed in a propagator or polythene bag as this retains atmospheric moisture around the cuttings. A mist propagator that automatically sprays very fine mist into the air once humidity drops below a certain level is a professional version of this. I bought my mist propagator

The more humid you can keep the air, the slower the cutting will wilt and the greater the chance of roots growing

seventeen years ago and regard it as the best investment I ever made in the garden. It has paid for itself a hundredfold. But a hand mister used a couple of times a day is more than adequate for most cuttings and ideal for cuttings raised indoors as opposed to in a greenhouse.

Cuttings strike much faster in warmth but hot direct sunlight will dry the foliage out too quickly, so gentle heat from below (the dreaded 'bottom heat') is best. Heated capillary matting is perfect and not expensive but a west- or east-facing windowsill (not south – too hot) with a radiator below it also works well.

You will know when the cutting has 'struck' – i.e. formed new roots – when you see healthy new growth. At this point gently separate the cuttings – by this stage some plants will have made a tangle of roots and some just one or two alarmingly small ones – and pot them up individually in potting compost to grow on. When the roots are filling this last container, the cuttings can either be planted out into the garden or repotted again to grow bigger until such a time as you are ready to set them into the garden.

Division

Many herbaceous plants and grasses can be propagated by division. In its simplest terms, this just means cutting or pulling apart the roots into a number of sections, each with at least one visible bud or shoot, and either directly replanting or potting them up to grow on before planting out. It is a good idea to do this to all herbaceous perennials every few years to reinvigorate their growth as well as to create more plants.

Some plants can very easily be used as parents for a number of new, very small plants and it is a very good – and cheap – way of creating a lot of plants, each with exactly the qualities of the parent. I do this with hardy geraniums, primulas, geums and many others. Either dig up or buy the largest specimen of the parent that you can get. Cut all the top-growth right back. Then systematically break the plant up so that you have as many sections as possible with roots and a growth point. Pot each of these up individually and put them in a cold frame or sheltered spot to grow on. They will take months rather than weeks and I often do this in late summer and plant the new plants out the following spring when they have a good root system. They will quickly grow bigger as the days warm up.

Containers and seed beds

When I was a boy working in my parents' garden, we had hundreds of terracotta pots and scores of wooden seed boxes. Both worked well. But the wooden boxes were very heavy and needed replacing often, and the pots were very fragile. However, both were very cheap. If you can get these things then all well and good but nowadays terracotta is expensive and wooden seed trays hard to find, tricky for many of us to make and not cheap. The alternative is plastic.

We all use too much plastic in our lives. All of it – every scrap of plastic any of us has ever used – is still out there filling holes in the ground or clogging up the oceans. However, in the short term, until either a genuinely biodegradable or fully recyclable

You and I do not 'recycle' plastic – we give it to someone else who gives it to a third party

plastic appears, or until a really viable alternative is widely available, the best way of cutting down our plastic consumption is by using the plastic that we already have as much as possible. We should treasure it, keep it safe, preferably out of the light, and use it again and again. The very worst thing to do is to 'dispose' of it or 'recycle' it. (You and I do not 'recycle' any plastic ever because we do not know how to do so. We give it to someone else to recycle and they give it to a third party and so it goes. So keep it and reuse it.)

There are two schools of thought about the best container to grow seeds in. The first swears by square plastic pots, which can be tightly fitted together for storing and are easily handled as well as holding a manageable amount of seed. The second prefers the bulk and simplicity of handling of seed trays, which come in full- and half-sizes. I tend towards seed trays (especially the half-size ones, which are much more difficult to get hold of) but only if they are rigid. The flimsy ones are a nightmare, invariably kinking and depositing their contents on the ground when you want to carry one in each hand, which you always do. Plugs are very useful too and soil blocks have great potential for avoiding excessive use of plastic – although are frankly a bit of a fiddle.

Whatever container I use gets placed in the greenhouse but any light, warm place is fine like a windowsill, porch or – that much underused bit of garden kit – a cold frame (see page 103).

If you don't have the facilities or space for sowing seeds under cover you can still raise an entire garden by preparing a couple of square metres as a seed bed and sowing short rows of seeds. You might have to work around the weather but you can be sure that your plants will all be tough, healthy and well adapted to your particular garden. A fleece screen 30–60cm (12–24in) high wrapped around a cane in each corner would provide a huge amount of protection and some polythene over the top would make it into a temporary cold frame.

Above and opposite page: This is the engine room of the garden and in spring it becomes a very crowded place, with plants jostling to go out into the garden. Once seedlings are pricked out, they go from the greenhouse into the cold frames and then are hardened off in the standing-out bay next to the greenhouse.

Greenhouses

Our propagating greenhouse, a few steps from the potting shed, is the same one that we had installed in 1998 and it is still going strong. Its main purpose is to provide a protective start for all the thousands of seedlings and cuttings that we produce every year.

The 'top' or wooden greenhouse with chillies and aubergines growing in pots beneath the vine – whose growth and fruit are inside but whose roots are planted outside in the soil.

It is heated by an electric blow heater operated by a thermostat that is set to come on when the temperature drops below 7°C (45°F). There is a small section at the far end that can be closed off and which houses the heated propagating bench with its mist propagator. In summer I squeeze in melons and cucumbers so they can take advantage of the extra heat and humidity at a time when we are raising few seeds.

I have had to replace the mist propagator once and have added heated capillary matting but very little has altered in the past 20 years, either in structure or how we use the greenhouse. We have the same cold frames just outside it and our basic system of sowing seeds has served us well for nearly quarter of a century. We start them in the potting shed, germinate them on the heated bench, move them to an unheated bench to grow on, prick them out in the potting shed, put them at the other end of the greenhouse for a week or two to get established, then put them into a cold frame to grow more. They then spend a week outdoors, to one side of the same greenhouse, to harden off before planting out. The system has its own growing and spatial logic and, because it spans between two and four months, is a very easy progression.

For years we had what we called the 'top' greenhouse, which was unheated and used primarily for growing tomatoes. This was moved in 2003 to the site where the Paradise Garden now is but was

decommissioned in 2017 when deemed unsafe. The tunnel, which occupied the site where the Vegetable Garden now is, was dismantled in 2008.

However, we acquired a new, wooden greenhouse in 2013 and we use this one as part-greenhouse, part-conservatory, growing tender flowering plants as well as edible ones. We also have a vine of 'Black Hamburg' grapes growing within the greenhouse, although the roots are planted outside and the stem passes through a hole in the brickwork. That way the grapes are protected from cold and bad weather but the roots can benefit from our rich soil and run as wide as they want. This greenhouse is also heated, albeit a little warmer than the other one – the thermostat kicks in when the temperature drops below 10°C (50°F) – and we store as many tender plants as we can there, such as the salvias, succulents, pelargoniums, streptocarpus and smaller citrus in the winter months.

There is one absolute law of greenhouses and that is that however much space you already have, you always want more and as I write I am preparing the groundwork for a new (second-hand) greenhouse to replace the one that we had for 25 years that occupied the site where the Paradise Garden now is.

But you do not need a large greenhouse to make a big difference. A small set-up, perhaps 3 x 1.5m (10 x 5ft) costs a few hundred pounds, is big enough to propagate seeds and cuttings and grow some tomato plants, can store tender plants in winter and would last at least ten years. It will also be a peaceful place to go – a glass shed, warm, protective and filled with light, and with a musky, sexy fragrance.

The 'bottom' or propagating greenhouse is made from aluminium and is mostly used for germinating seedlings and cuttings, except in midsummer when I grow yet more chillies there.

Insulate the greenhouse in autumn to give protection against frost and save on heating bills

Greenhouse practicalities

There are two main choices when it comes to buying a greenhouse: aluminium or wood. Wooden greenhouses are slower to heat up but hold their heat longer than aluminium. Almost all modern timber greenhouses are made from cedar, which should not be painted and therefore needs little attention, whereas a painted wooden one will need repainting regularly. Aluminium greenhouses are light so can buckle in very high winds, which can crack or break the glass. However, the weight of the glass is usually enough to prevent buckling in all but the fiercest storms. The aluminium framing collects condensation, so needs extra ventilation.

If you have a south-facing wall that is 3m (10ft) or more high, it will always be better to have a lean-to greenhouse built against it. Otherwise a freestanding one will give more options. Always get the biggest you can possibly afford and fit into your garden. You will find that every tiny bit will be used.

Ventilation is vital. The combination of warmth and water makes an ideal breeding ground for fungal growth, which, once established, is tricky to get rid of. Good ventilation is the best way to limit it. Most greenhouses now come with automatic hydraulic window vents, which I would consider an absolute necessity. Always open the doors wide except on the coldest days and fit as many side vents as

the manufacturer can supply. In winter it is a good idea to close the doors a few hours before sundown – by three o'clock here in midwinter – so the warm air inside the greenhouse does not cool down.

It is advisable to insulate the greenhouse in autumn with a layer of bubble wrap taped or tacked to the inside of the frame. This is a fiddle and does reduce light levels but is worth the trouble, gives sufficient protection against frost for all but the tenderest of plants and saves a lot on heating bills in really cold weather.

Overheating in summer is as much a problem as cold is in winter, and I know people who leave the bubble wrap on all year to insulate against heat as well as cold. A wash of distemper will do the job of shading well and can be washed off at the end of the summer, or you can use shading nets.

Finally, if at all possible, have water and electricity supplies laid on when you put the greenhouse in. You will need water from day one and a tap inside the greenhouse is best, although collect as much rainwater as possible – not least for those plants like citrus, carnivorous plants or blueberries for whom tap water is too alkaline. One of the more practical changes we have made to our greenhouses in recent years is to add large cattle drinking troughs to collect rainwater. These are easy and quick to dip watering cans into and relatively cheap from any farm supplies store. The electricity is for under-soil cables, the mist propagator, electric fan heating and lights, all of which are highly desirable extras that can be added at a later date.

Patti lending a
helping hand with
the cold frames.

Cold frames

In some ways cold frames are more useful
than a greenhouse. I have two sorts. The
main ones are home-made from brick,
built against a west-facing wall and glazed
with polycarbonate lights (safer, cheaper
and lighter than glass) that are opened
and closed by ropes on a pulley. The base
is made from a thick layer of grit
Everything that is propagated in the
greenhouse goes into the cold frame as
part of the hardening-off process.

The other cold frames are made
entirely from glass and in winter we use
these for the scores of pots planted with
spring bulbs and for Mediterranean plants
like lavender, tulbaghia and cuttings of
herbs like thyme and sage, which are
completely hardy yet will suffer from too
much rain. The tops are kept covered
with glass yet the sides are opened in all

but freezing weather. In summer we use
them to harden off annuals we have raised
like tithonias, zinnias and sunflowers, so
they can have maximum sunshine as well
as some protection from cold nights.

Both kinds of cold frame have their
virtues but on balance, one with brick or
wooden sides is more robust and useful.

One of the beauties of cold frames is
that you can regulate the level of
protection they offer, from almost total
exposure – good for hardening off on
warm days – to extreme insulation. In
winter I insulate the inside with thick
polystyrene sheets and in the coldest
weather, I unroll thick bubble wrap over
the closed lids and hold it down with
bricks, thus even the tenderest seedling is
unharmed by frost which, despite our
ever-warming winters, can still dip on
occasion below -10°C (14°F).

Composting

Compost making is the paradigm of recycling. It is a wonderful alchemy – you take all the the waste from your garden and household and turn it into an elixir of health. Nothing else is so effective for keeping the soil and your plants healthy.

We mow or shred all our composting material, which greatly reduces its bulk and hugely speeds up the composting process.

It follows that every garden should have a compost heap and every gardener should do whatever they can to make as much good compost as possible.

Good compost smells pleasantly of damp earth or of a woodland floor, should be pleasant to handle with bare hands, and of a texture that enables you to shovel it as well as use a fork. In other words, it is not too wet, has no unpleasant odours and is neither too coarse nor slimy.

Garden compost can be made from anything that has lived and has decomposed to humus. However, the word 'decomposed' suggests a rotting process – but that is not what happens in your compost heap. In fact, the transformation of odds and ends of kitchen waste, dried stems, deadheaded flowers and the thousand other possible components from wood chips to grass cuttings, is done mostly by digestion.

The entire contents of your compost heap will eventually pass through the digestive tracts of an unimaginable number of living creatures. Most of these are bacteria but nematodes, protozoa and fungi also play a major role, along with the much more visible worms, known as brandlings (*Eisenia foetida*) that appear whenever a compost heap gets established. These distinctive red worms do not live in soil and can only survive and multiply if their environment is not too wet, not too dry, has air, enough carbon in the form of straw, cardboard or any dry material, and is warm enough. They cease their composting activity and breeding if the temperature falls below 5°C (41°F) and die if they freeze – which is highly unlikely in the heart of a compost heap. They also need an alkaline environment, which is why I do not include much highly acidic material like citrus waste.

One perfectly good way to make compost is to heap up all your composting material in a mound and leave it alone for all these trillions of organisms to quietly digest. In about eighteen months to two years, the compost will be ready without you having to lift a finger. The down side to this 'slow' method is that it takes up time and space. We have a 'slow' heap at the end of the Orchard and use it for things like hellebore leaves that are evergreen and slow to compost, or any weeds that have a lot of soil on their roots. After a year or so, the interior invariably has become lovely, crumbly compost.

The much faster method is to accumulate at least 1 cubic metre (35 cubic feet) of material at a time (and ideally about three to four times that amount). When you have sufficient bulk, turn it into another bay. This will create space for more new material as well as adding oxygen to the original heap.

The oxygen is essential for the bacteria that are hard at work digesting your waste. When the heap gets really hot, turn it again – and go on doing so until it has become sweet-smelling, brown, crumbly material that no longer heats up when you turn it. You will have to turn your compost at least twice and usually three or four times. But the whole process from kitchen or garden waste to perfect finished compost should take between ten and 25 weeks as opposed to the 75–100 weeks for a slow heap.

The heat in a compost heap is mainly created by the energy of the bacterial digestive systems. As the heap becomes warmer, successive waves of fungi and bacteria get in on the action. However, if it gets too hot to hold your hand in the heap, then it is becoming destructive to a range of important bacteria, so needs turning again. Do not waste your money on self-styled 'activators'. They do nothing that will not occur naturally. Assemble your ingredients with care and the compost will make itself – every time.

Once the compost is ready, it is best used as a mulch about 2.5–5cm (1–2in) thick on the surface of the ground. Earthworms will quickly incorporate it into the soil and all

Opposite page, right: Turning compost is hard work but introduces air into a compost heap, which reinvigorates bacterial action and thus speeds up the composting process by about a year.

Oxygen in the compost heap is essential for the bacteria that are hard at work digesting your waste

those innumerable life forms that are essential for really healthy soil can be recharged. It really is the best way to creating a garden filled with healthy plants.

Making good compost

1 Aim at a minimum volume of 1 cubic metre (35 cubic feet). If you only have small, incremental amounts of waste material, gather it up in a bucket or plastic trug before adding it to the heap.

2 Shredding, mowing or chopping up waste increases its surface area and dramatically speeds up the composting process as well as using less space. I highly recommend getting hold of an old mower for this purpose. Spread the compost material on the ground, mow it well and then rake it up, mix thoroughly and put in the bin.

3 Compost is primarily composed of nitrogen and carbon. Nitrogen typically comes from lush, green material and carbon from dry or woody stems. Too much carbon and the composting process will be very slow, whereas too much nitrogen (as with fresh grass cuttings), and it becomes anaerobic and an evil-smelling sludge. So for every load of freshly cut grass you should add the same volume of straw, cardboard, sawdust or shredded dry garden waste such as old flower stems. Do not put the different materials into layers but mix them up well as you go along, preferably after shredding or mowing them (as described left) into smaller pieces. Incidentally, comfrey plants have almost the perfect balance of carbon to nitrogen and are worth growing simply for the way that they will invariably improve any compost heap.

4 Turning adds oxygen, which is the ingredient that bacteria depend on – and bacteria are the most important element in any compost heap. Turning once every three to four weeks is ideal. A closed container needs turning, too. When your bin is filled, tip it all out – which will turn it, add oxygen and stimulate bacterial activity to speed up the composting process – and refill it.

5 Be patient. There is no set time as to how long compost should take. Every batch is different but as a general rule allow three months in summer and six in winter. If a particular batch is claggy and evil-smelling, it is usually an indication that either there is not enough carbon – the 'brown' element' – or enough oxygen. So turn it again and add straw, dried stems or cardboard. Then cover it and it will dry out. If it is too dry at any stage, remove the cover and water it.

When ready, garden compost is soft, crumbly and sweet-smelling, and is the best soil conditioner that any gardener can use, as well as being a model of recycling and sustainability.

We find that nine batches out of ten come good – although all are different and some definitely better than others. Do not worry if you have an explosion of fruit flies when you open the lid or cover – they are occasionally part of the process and are harmless.

What to include

In theory, anything that has lived, from an oak tree to an old woollen jersey, will make compost although I exclude all meat, fat and anything that has been cooked as these will attract vermin. However, all uncooked kitchen waste, including eggshells and cardboard packaging and anything that has grown in the garden, can be added.

I compost the summer hedge cuttings but chip winter ones and any thicker branches, and use these to top up the bark paths. The top-growth of weeds can go into the heap but the roots of bindweed, couch grass or ground elder are best burned and the ashes added to the main heap.

We make a separate heap for the long grass from the Orchard because it adds too much dry 'brown' material in one go. That grass heap slowly breaks down and then, after a year, is added to the rest of the compost.

Cardboard makes excellent compost, although it should be scrumpled up and mixed in equally with the normal vegetable waste to allow plenty of air to get in, rather than placed in lasagne-like layers.

The containers

If you have a small garden, then proprietary top-loading compost bins work well. However you will need at least

two and ideally, three. You turn the material by moving it from bin to bin, although simply emptying a bin and then refilling it with the emptied material is also a good method of turning.

If you are constructing your own storage bays, then I have found that recycled pallets work extremely well. Using three pallets is ideal, one for each side of an open-fronted bay. In my time I have used corrugated iron, chestnut paling, pig and chicken wire, scaffolding planks and straw bales, and all have worked equally well.

Three bays are a workable minimum but if you have room, four or even five make managing and storing compost much easier. Whatever you use, it is best to have clear soil for the base so that the worms and bacteria in the ground can easily start work on the heap.

Every scrap of plant material from the garden, plus uncooked kitchen waste and cardboard packaging, goes into the Longmeadow compost heap and ends up enriching the garden a few months later.

Mulch

Mulch is a layer of organic material spread over bare ground in flower borders and vegetable beds. It is not dug or worked into the soil but left as a surface blanket.

In a border, a mulch has three distinct functions that it performs miraculously well without any assistance from the gardener. The first is to suppress weeds and thus radically reduce the labour of weeding for the rest of the year. It does this by denying weed seedlings light so some, like groundsel or shepherd's purse seedlings that need light to trigger germination, will simply not grow and others might germinate but will not have enough light to survive. Perennial weeds such as nettles or couch grass will be dramatically weakened and those that do make it through the mulch are much easier to pull out.

Its second function is to retain ground moisture. Drought works as a vicious cycle with most plants because the majority of feeding roots are near the surface and this is, of course, the part of the soil that dries out the quickest in hot, dry weather. As a response, the plant will push its roots even closer to the surface to try and get what moisture it can but if the drought persists, the roots dry out even quicker. Mulching breaks this cycle. The mulch itself may dry out but the soil beneath it remains moist. As a result, the plant has access to more water and also grows its roots deeper because there is no need for emergency root action. The thicker the mulch, the more effectively the plant resists drought.

Finally, a mulch of organic material will be worked into the soil by earthworms, moles and a myriad other burrowing creatures, and will improve the soil structure as well as its fertility.

So what is the best mulch? There is no one answer to this but over the years I have found that three, often used in rotation around the garden, work best for me on my clay soil. The first is home-made garden compost (see pages 106–107). In one sense this is absolutely the perfect mulch because it not only recycles garden waste and is free

We mulch the Jewel Garden in winter with mushroom compost before the first growth of the bulbs appears.

but also reinjects your own very specific soil bacteria back into the ground. The one major hitch is that however scrupulously you recycle all waste material, no garden can ever make enough compost to mulch everything. So you have to either use it on a rotation, mulching about a third of the garden each year or, as I do, keep your home-made compost for vegetables and potting compost.

The second mulch is woody waste. I shred all our woody waste – mostly from winter pruning – and use that to mulch trees, shrubs and hedges. I also buy in pine-bark chips which I use to mulch the grass borders every other year as it is slightly ericaceous and low in nutrients, and the grasses like that. Bark is an excellent weed suppressor and retains moisture well but is slow to break down into the soil – however once it does, it is excellent, particularly on heavy clay.

Finally, there is mushroom compost – and I use this most of all. Mushroom compost is made from cattle manure mixed with lime, which helps break it down very fast. The mushrooms are then grown in this mixture but once it is exhausted – which happens quite quickly – a fresh mix is needed. So inevitably, mushroom growers accumulate vast piles of waste compost and are very happy to get rid of it for mulch. It is clean, easy to handle, does not smell and is very effective in every respect. I have used hundreds of tonnes of it over the years and my soil is a delight as a result. Its only major drawback is that it is alkaline so not suitable for ericaceous plants like rhododendrons, camellias, blueberries or raspberries. I would also stress that, despite its many virtues, it is not a substitute for home-made compost which is always best if you can make it in any quantity.

But whatever mulch you use, ladle it on generously. To be effective it should be thick and dense enough to block light from the earth beneath and to slow down evaporation. In my experience – in flower borders at least – this means a layer at least 5cm (2in) and ideally, 10cm (4in) deep. It is better to do half the garden properly than spread it too thinly.

Mulching the Writing Garden. Whatever you use to mulch, it is important to spread it thickly – at least 5cm (2in) deep and preferably twice that to suppress weeds and retain moisture.

Leafmould

We treat fallen leaves as a rich harvest and gather every leaf that we can to make leafmould.

Leafmould is one of the few things that money cannot buy. For some reason no one has ever commercialised it, although it is much easier to gather leaves and make leafmould than rip up and destroy rare peat bogs to market the peat.

Leafmould makes an ideal soil improver, lightening heavy soils and adding gentle body to very light ones, and because it is nutritionally less rich than garden compost, is very useful as part of home-made potting compost.

The process by which fallen leaves are converted to crumbly, sweet-smelling leafmould is almost entirely down to

fungi. Because the decomposition process is fungal, it needs moisture but not heat so unlike garden compost, the leaves do not have to be turned at all. This means that you only need one storage bay to hold the leaves and a whole lot less work.

We take our leaf gathering very seriously. We set aside some leaves as cover for invertebrates and small mammals over winter and leave some in borders around shrubs, where they form a natural mulch, but otherwise we treat them as a harvest that we try to gather as assiduously as possible. My own technique is to use a combination of brush, rake and mower. If the ground is dry enough, raking the leaves into lines and then gathering them into the grass box by mowing is an excellent idea because it chops them as it collects, so they rot down faster. In fact, it is so useful that I often gather the leaves and spread them on a brick path, and then mow them on the path.

The bulk of the leaves come from the pleached limes and hornbeam hedges, with a good deal of hazel and field maple thrown in. After being mown they go into a large chicken-wire bay and are kept wet. The latter is hardly a problem in this wet part of the world but in a dry year it means putting the hose onto each 30cm (12in) layer as we add the leaves. The wetter they are the quicker they will break down.

Different leaves break down at different rates – hornbeam, field maple, ash, apple and hawthorn are very quick whereas oak takes longer – but we always have perfect leafmould by the following October. Then the container is emptied into old compost bags, it is ready for use and the wire bay is empty and waiting for the new batch of leaves.

A job for a wet winter's day is to sieve a supply of leafmould for potting compost. Whilst this is tedious in itself, the result is joyful – the most perfect, finely graded black gold, which makes the ideal structure for growing roots as well as adding to the fungal element of potting compost. But it is the structure that is most important.

Leafmould is also slightly acidic so is good for rhododendrons, camellias, blueberries and other ericaceous plants. Any unsieved leafmould is used to mulch the woodland beds such as the Spring Garden and the Orchard Beds.

We take our leaf gathering very seriously, setting aside some leaves as cover for invertebrates and small mammals over winter

If your garden is not big enough to have a large, permanent wire bay for leaves, the answer is to put them in a black plastic bin bag, leaving the top turned but not tied. Make sure the leaves are really wet and punch a few holes in the bag to drain excess water. They will rot down very well like this and can be stored behind a shed or tucked away in any corner until ready for use next year.

Another way of using leaves, especially in a new garden, is to gather them and spread them directly over any bare soil 15cm (6in) deep. Then, using a rotovator (which can be hired by the day), mix them into the earth. Unlike green matter, leaves use up very little nitrogen as they rot into the soil, so do not rob the ground of valuable nutrients. This method, combined with regular additions of garden compost, will help create usable topsoil out of the poorest subsoil.

Green manure

The principle of green manure is simple enough. You sow a crop that will cover the ground so weeds have no space or light to grow, the roots take up available goodness from the soil and then, when you are ready, you harvest excess top-growth to the compost heap.

What is left of the top-growth, along with the roots, can be worked into the soil where it will improve the fertility and structure for subsequent crops. This adds another weapon into the armoury of a healthy, fertile garden and is especially useful if you cannot get hold of animal manure or do not have the room to make large quantities of compost.

Almost any crop will make green manure, including weeds. In fact, every crop we grow in the Vegetable Garden, from broad beans to lettuce, acts as a green manure by virtue of the roots' residue that we dig in rather than dig up.

However, certain crops have been harnessed over the years to act in a pretty specific way and at particular stages of the year. So legumes such as crimson red clover, field beans or vetch will fix nitrogen from the atmosphere via the plants' relationship with a soil bacteria called rhizobia. These enter the roots of the legumes, causing nodules which are transformed to the point at which they can fix nitrogen. Some of this is left in the soil ready for subsequent crops in the rotation. So any heavy-feeding leafy crop such as spinach or cabbage will benefit from a preceding leguminous green manure.

A green manure like this will boost fertility but not change the organic matter in the soil very much. However, a carbon-rich green manure, such as ryegrass, buckwheat or phacelia, will release its nitrogen much slower and build up much more humus in the soil for a slower, longer-term effect. These kinds of green manure are often referred to as 'lifters' – they mop up available nitrogen in the soil and then return it to the soil after they are dug in.

Some green manures can stay in the ground for months or even longer. Ryegrass is best sown in August or September and dug in up to nine months later (although always before the seedheads appear). On the other hand, mustard and phacelia can be sown, grown and dug in within eight weeks so are good to use in spring whilst waiting to plant out a tender crop or to fill what would otherwise be an empty plot.

Good management and timing mean that no patch of soil need be empty or unproductive – even if the production is just material for compost and an investment in future soil structure and fertility. In fact, salad crops such as mizuna or rocket make very good green manures, and the seeds are relatively cheap and can

Crops such as crimson red clover, field beans or vetch fix nitrogen in the soil ready for subsequent crops in the rotation

easily be collected from mature plants, so they are harvestable at every level.

The key is not to leave ground 'empty' any more than necessary. There are two main reasons for this. The first is that many more nutrients are leached away from bare soil than are lost to any crop, so sowing a green manure will, at the very least, absorb nutrients that can be returned to the soil, even if the green manure crop is killed back by cold weather. The second is more applicable to the summer months and familiar to every allotment holder or veg gardener, which is that nature abhors a vacuum. Leave a patch of bare ground for more than a few days and weeds will soon fill it. Far better to use the ground deliberately, even if it is only to make material for the compost heap.

Green manures cover the ground and stop weeds taking over. They then can be dug into the soil, where the vegetative material will break down and enrich the soil for subsequent crops. In practice any annual plant can be used, even weeds, as long as you do not let them seed.

Liquid feeds

As a rule, an annual mulch of 5–7.5cm (2–3in) of garden compost is sufficient to replace the nutrients used up by most plants and it will improve the soil structure at the same time.

However, anything grown in a container for more than about five weeks will use up available nutrients and need a regular feed.

Traditionally, plant food is made from the three ingredients NPK – nitrogen, phosphorus and potassium – although trace minerals are vital for the health of the plant and, if the plant is edible, for the health of humans. Very crudely, nitrogen encourages good green growth – the stems and leaves of plants – phosphorus aids good root growth, and potash or potassium, the production of flowers and fruits. Liquid seaweed is an excellent source of phosphorus, potassium and minerals and I use it extensively on all our container-grown plants. But you can also make your own liquid feeds from nettles and comfrey. I especially like the notion of plants taking up the special brew of each individual garden's nutrients, with all the garden's idiosyncratic and complicated mix of nutrients and ecology, and then releasing it back to plants also growing in this precise soil.

Nettles are an excellent source of nitrogen, especially early in the year. Cut enough nettles to fill a bucket and top them up with water. Leave them for a couple of weeks, then drain and sieve the liquid and use the concentrate mixed to about 20 parts nettle to one part water as a weekly feed. This is especially good for plants like chillies and tomatoes, to encourage strong growth before they start flower production.

The best all-round feed that you can make yourself is from comfrey. This has a long taproot – up to 3m (10ft) in deep soil – and is spectacularly efficient at sucking up available nutrients and storing them in its leaves. These break down very fast and so transfer back into the soil exceptionally quickly. Comfrey also has the highest level of protein in its leaf structure of any member of the vegetable kingdom.

Twenty years ago I planted a row of comfrey plants specifically for harvesting to make a feed. These were all salvaged from various plants self-seeded from the nearby river bank, along the length of what was then the site of a polytunnel, but they are now tucked under the high hornbeam hedge that protects the Vegetable Garden from north winds. These plants are still going strong and I harvest them regularly, although we have scores

By using home-made liquid feeds you make available the nutrients that the nettles or comfrey have in their leaves

of others self-seeded around the garden that are all excellent additions to the compost heap as well as being excellent for bees. If you cut comfrey hard back to the ground, each plant should provide between three and five 'crops' a year.

To make the feed I fill a bucket with as many comfrey leaves as it will contain and then top it up with water. The leaves soon turn into a sludge that smells appalling. This stench means that the proteins – that make up 3.5 per cent of the comfrey – are breaking down. After two to three weeks, the mixture will be a greeny brown soup and ready for use. A ratio of one part comfrey to ten parts water is about right although if the liquid is a rich, dark brown, you could increase that up to 1:20.

You need not measure this but use your eye and common sense, but you do not get better results by increasing the richness beyond this kind of proportions. It can be used either as a foliar feed sprayed onto the leaves or fed as a drench directly to the roots. Home-made nettle and comfrey feeds will keep in sealed containers for a year although we find we use them up long before that.

The results are not spectacular, nor should they be. All you are doing is making available to plants in a greenhouse or container the nutrients that are already there in the ground and which the nettles or comfrey have stored in their leaves. As with everything in the garden, it is a balancing act.

Far left: Comfrey is incredibly useful to make an extremely effective home-made feed, especially for promoting flowers and fruit. It is an easy-to-grow perennial, liking deep, damp soil.

Left: Nettles make a good nitrogen-rich feed for spring that promotes healthy foliage.

Weeds

My mother had an obsession with keeping the bonfire going, often for weeks at a time. The last thing that she wanted to see was a bright blaze because that meant that it would quickly burn out.

What she delighted in was a thin trickle of smoke snaking up into the still air, with no risk of a breeze to fan the flames and yet enough of a core to keep burning unattended for half a day at a time. She would then wander out into the garden and gently sift a forkful onto the fire from the pile that was always heaped next to it.

The pile next to the bonfire consisted entirely of weeds and mostly of couch grass. As we dug the garden of my childhood, we would throw every bit of weed into a barrow. When the barrow was full it would be wheeled to the bonfire and tipped out next to it. This was the heap that was gradually burned. Of course there was a great deal of soil attached to the roots and over the years, the bonfire became a great mound of earth and ash. That was 50 years ago and there is a house on that bonfire site now.

Today I burn very few of my weeds. All the annual ones go on the compost heap and perennials like nettles, docks and thistles also compost very well. The only weeds that I do burn are those that can regenerate from a scrap of root, such as couch grass, bindweed, celandine or ground elder. Even then, I cut off the top-growth and compost it, and put the ashes of the roots on the compost heap.

This is because weeds are superb adapters and consumers. They always make the most of whatever nutrients are available in the soil and are always very quick to establish a good relationship with the myriad living entities in the soil that all interrelate to create healthy plants. If you compost them then some of that goodness will be recycled back into the soil – and the plants which you choose to grow can benefit from it.

Weeds can be beautiful too. After all, the cliche that a weed is merely a plant in the wrong place, holds true. There is nothing inherently bad or wrong with weeds. Were it not for their tendency to rampage and overrun given the slightest chance, then many would be prized as garden specimens and shown at Chelsea and garlanded with medals. Lesser hogweed can stand proud beside ammi or orleya until it seeds and horribly overstays its welcome. Lesser celandine would be treasured, shining like yellow stars as it covers the ground – if it did not go on and on and on covering. Ground elder would be a perfect low-level white froth in a border – as well being an excellent vegetable – if only it could restrain its invasive tendencies. The white flowers of bindweed are a joy twining elegantly up a specified support – but not swamping and ravaging through every damn thing in the border. Bracken is beautiful and if it did not cover hillsides by the square mile, would be planted alongside polypodium, dryopteris and asplenium with equal billing.

And of course every gardener knows that Japanese knotweed was introduced in 1850 as a fine garden-worthy plant. But I like the irony that every single knotweed growing in this country derives from that one initial introduction. Britain's most ineradicable and feared weed cannot reproduce from seed and is thus uniquely vulnerable to attack by disease or predation because it has no evolutionary wiggle room to escape from attack. In other words, its days as an all-conquering weed are certainly numbered.

My own love/hate relationships are serial but regular. Some have become fixtures – couch grass in the Jewel Garden and ground elder in the Walled Garden (and also in the Jewel Garden and the Grass Borders), lesser hogweed in the Writing Garden and Orchard, lesser celandine in the Spring and Cottage Gardens and duckweed in the pond.

But I welcome some weeds with open arms. Cow parsley is brought in by the floods and sweeps through the Spring Garden every year like a glorious frothy tide, and long may it do so. The delicate yellow flowers of *Corydalis flexuosa* were a well-established accompaniment to our box balls, establishing such a strong foothold that the spaces between the 64 box plants were completely filled for months on end by their delicate and delightful yellow flowers and glaucous foliage. It now grows eagerly in the bricks

There is nothing inherently wrong with weeds were it not for their tendency to go on the rampage

Many weed flowers are important as food sources for predators such as wasps and hoverflies

and cobbles along the margins of the new Herb Garden. Many years ago we carefully planted wild strawberries under our hedges and within months they had made themselves so at home that now they are a widespread 'weed'. But not only do they act as groundcover, inhibiting more annoying weeds, but they also bear delicious, albeit tiny, fruit.

All over this garden I have creeping buttercup, burdock, greater and lesser celandine, couch grass, bindweed, docks and nettles, and those are just the perennials. I can also count on annual weeds showing up year after year, like the great rafts of goosegrass, wavy bittercress, shepherd's purse, caper spurge, dead-nettle, groundsel, sow thistle and chickweed. But many weed flowers are important as food sources for predators such as wasps and hoverflies that in turn feed off pests such as aphids. Vast tracts of agricultural land are now plagued by insects that would have otherwise been naturally controlled by predators, simply because so many weedkillers have been used for so long that there are not the host plants to attract the predators. This inevitably promotes a vicious cycle whereby there is an increase in the insecticides used. The same loss of balance is created in the garden when you use weedkillers. A healthy garden has a number of flowering weeds as an important part of its self-sustaining biodiversity.

The greater the fecundity of your weed population, the healthier and better-conditioned your soil. So if you take on a new garden and it is filled with weeds, be thankful. The soil that they are growing in is good. Secondly, the greater the diversity and range of weed types that you have growing uninvited, the greater the range of plants of your choice that you will eventually be able to grow.

The type and limitations of the weeds growing are also a useful indicator of the nature and condition of your soil. Very acidic soil will produce lots of sorrel and plantain but no charlock or poppy, which thrive on lime. Chickweed is a good indicator of a neutral pH. Nettles, ground elder, fat hen and chickweed point to a soil high in nitrogen. Silverweed and greater plantain will grow on very compacted soil where other plants will not penetrate. Creeping buttercup, horsetail and silverweed (again) point to a wet soil with poor drainage. Lastly, some weeds are very good to eat. I like nettle soup very much, using just the freshest new growth, which makes a very good substitute for spinach and is equally rich in iron. Dandelion leaves are an excellent addition to a salad, ground elder was originally grown as a vegetable crop, wild sorrel makes a good sauce and horseradish, which can be one of the most intrusive and difficult of all weeds, is as essential to a rib of beef as marmalade is to breakfast toast.

Some deep-rooted weeds are extremely good at accumulating minerals. If you harvest their leaves and add them to the compost heap you will, in time, recycle these minerals back into the soil via the

Wild strawberries have become an ineradicable – and delicious – weed running along the base of many of our hedges.

compost. Most gardeners know that comfrey leaves contain high levels of potassium, but nettles and horsetail contain silica; chickweed contains copper, iron, manganese, nitrogen and potassium; dandelion leaves are high in nitrogen, calcium and copper; fat hen has calcium, iron, nitrogen, phosphorus and potassium. If you cannot remove these weeds you might be able to keep cutting them back to stop them seeding, adding the leaves and stems to your compost heap.

In practical terms there are two types of weed the gardener needs to know about – annual and perennial.

- **Annual weeds** grow from seed and survive only one growing season. On the whole, a thick crop of annual weeds is no problem and can even be seen as a good thing as they indicate that the soil is fertile. They are easy to pull up and add to the compost heap. If you cannot pull them up completely, hoeing or cutting them before they seed will stop them spreading. It is very common for a mulch of manure to be followed by a rash of annual weeds, the seeds of which have passed through the animal and have been quietly waiting in the manure until light triggers germination. The most common annual weeds in a garden are groundsel, chickweed, fat hen and annual meadow grass. When sowing any new crop, from a new lawn to a row of radish, it is always a good idea to prepare the ground and then leave it fallow for a few weeks. Inevitably, annual seeds in the ground will germinate. These can be hoed off and raked away, leaving the soil clear

for your sown seeds to germinate and establish without competition for water and nutrients before they are established.

- **Perennial weeds** survive for more than two growing seasons – sometimes for very much longer. Dock seeds can apparently lie dormant in the soil for up to 90 years, waiting for the soil to be disturbed before germinating. I like the thought that there are docks emerging from a century-old sleep, conceived in an age before aeroplanes, television and computers. Other common perennial weeds are nettles, bindweed, ground elder, couch grass and thistles.

In the Wildlife Garden we do very little weeding at all, allowing the weeds to provide food and cover for insects and birds. Weeds look fine too.

There is only one foolproof method of dealing with perennial weeds – remove the plant before it seeds, dig every last scrap of root from the ground and burn the lot. But there are also weeds like horsetail, horseradish and Japanese knotweed with roots of enormous depth and resilience. Horsetail can go down 2.5m (8ft) and knotweed be as tough as steel hawsers. Certain weeds like ground elder, bindweed and couch grass have a habit of winding in amongst the roots of plants you wish to keep, which provides them with a safe haven from the most diligent of weeding. The way to deal with this is to dig up the infested plant and wash the roots thoroughly under a tap or power hose, blasting out every scrap of weed root. Before you replant it, dig over the planting site with obsessive meticulousness to remove every tiny scrap of root.

One of the most effective ways of suppressing weeds is with a thick layer of organic mulch that will also retain moisture and feed the soil.

Weed control

There is no one easy solution, but a combination of the following should get your weeds under control. Focus your mulch and hand-weeding in areas like mixed borders where weeds are hardest to eradicate, and use a hoe regularly on open soil, as in the vegetable garden.

- **Mulch** Cover every piece of bare soil with a light-excluding but moisture-permeable layer of mulch. I use a lot of mushroom and garden compost, and cocoa shells. Well-rotted horse or cattle manure are good but cattle manure can include a lot of weed seeds if it is not very well rotted. If you are prepared to forgo aesthetics (which I am not), anything will do the job, including straw, hay, shredded bark, permeable plastic or old carpet. If you are using an organic mulch (i.e. one that will rot down into the soil), make it at least 5cm (2in) thick. A 10cm (4in) mulch is better. This will completely suppress annual weeds and although it will not stop perennial weeds growing through, it will make them much easier to pull up. Obviously an organic mulch that will increase the fertility and improve the structure of the soil as well as suppress weeds is infinitely preferable to one that works as a weed suppressant alone, but I do use a water-permeable proprietary black plastic mulch for some paths. This is not beautiful but extremely effective, especially as a temporary measure.
- **Hoe** There are lots of hoes available but only two basic principles to their use – you either push or you pull. I find I use a Dutch hoe most of the time, which, if kept sharp, slices through the

roots of any weeds just below the surface of the soil. I have one very old hoe that is much smaller than most and can get right in amongst young plants without damaging them. The secret of hoeing – like all weeding – is to do it little and often. Old gardeners used to say that if you could see that it was time to hoe, then you had left it too late. If you have a very weed-infested bit of ground you want to cultivate (and remember, weed infestation implies good healthy soil) and the weeds have not yet gone to seed, then a good tip is to hoe them off with a mattock or large draw or field hoe, let the weeds wilt for a day in the sun and then dig the whole thing over, weeds and all. This will not get rid of the perennial weeds but will increase soil fertility and allow you to grow a crop of fast-growing and weed-suppressing vegetables like potatoes, beans or squashes.

- **Hand-weed** Hand-weeding means getting down on your knees and carefully removing every scrap of weed with your fingers and a hand fork. But, unlikely as it initially may seem, hand-weeding is one of the most enjoyable aspects of gardening. I love it, especially in early spring just as everything is starting to grow and the weeds have not become depressingly rampant. You really get to know your soil, your plants and the seedlings and herbaceous perennials coming through, and you improve an area dramatically without major surgery. It is deeply satisfying work.

- **Careful timing** It is essential to try and stop weeds of any kind spreading their seed. Cut, hoe, mow or strim them, but do not let them go forth and multiply. There is a saying that 'One year's seeding is seven years' weeding' and there is a lot of truth in this. Trials have shown that, even if weeds are never allowed to set seed again, it takes about seven years for all one season's crop of seeds to stop germinating.

For the vegetable grower the most useful and effective way to control weeds is to hoe. It is best to hoe in the morning on dry days and to leave the hoed weeds to dry in the sun before taking them to the compost heap.

Pests

Umbellifers, like this fennel in the Jewel Garden, are superb magnet species for attracting predatory insects like hoverflies and lacewings that feed on aphids.

I dislike the term 'pests'. It is too sweeping and too lazily selective. It contains the inference that anything and everything that in any way interferes with our concept of horticultural purity and perfection is bad and can therefore be eliminated.

A truly healthy garden is one in which all living things co-exist in balance – if not in harmony – with one another. You and I and our precious plants are just some of those living things and the onus is on us to find that harmony – not to try and eradicate anything that challenges our narrow concept of the world.

But gardens are completely artificial. A lot of gardening is stopping plants and animals doing what they instinctively want to do and what we would find completely acceptable anywhere save in our back yard. To complain about slugs eating lettuce is as irrational as trying to stop blackbirds eating berries.

The urge to order and steer the natural world to make harmonious and useful spaces for mankind to enjoy is almost universal. But what begins as gentle coercion can easily slide into brutal dominance. However, all research, all scientific discoveries, all wisdom show that everything connects with everything else in ways that our fathers could scarcely imagine. No garden is an island.

My own garden suffers very little damage from the depredations of slugs, snails, caterpillars, aphids or insects of any kind. Yes, the odd slug occasionally gets medieval with a tray of seedlings but we never seem to lose anything we cannot spare and, in the scheme of things, that is no loss at all. Pigeons eat the brassicas, rabbits are partial to crocuses and *Ammi majus* in March, and the larvae of cabbage white butterflies can do a good job on young brassicas in summer, but by and large, none of this is a serious problem, or at least not one that we cannot easily control with barriers and good timing.

The secret lies in having a wide enough range of predators so that no one creature becomes an overwhelming problem. For this to happen you need lots of cover, some water, long grass, seeds and a diverse range of plants, as well the humility to accept that your garden is not necessarily more important than anything else.

The other thing you need and one which many people forget, are the pests. I know that this will seem perverse to many gardeners but if you have zero pests, you will very quickly lose predators as they move on to find another source of food. A healthy garden has a rich ecosystem that will include a food chain for all creatures, from the bacteria in the soil to the hawks taking beautiful song thrushes. Intervene clumsily and the chain is broken and very quickly the garden will suffer. Much of the whole ethos of organic gardening is based upon preserving and feeding this balance – often by not doing things rather than by jumping in with both feet.

A plant's ability to resist and heal from damage or disease, not the absence of such problems, indicates health

All things being equal (which they never are) the chain is inevitable. Song thrushes eat snails, ground beetles eat the eggs of root flies, rove beetles eat aphids, as do hoverfly and lacewing larvae and damsel bugs eat caterpillars. The numbers will reach saturation point within a year or two and then fluctuate according to weather and the type of plants you grow. A predatory balance will be established.

It means that you will lose some plants but your garden will be essentially healthy, rich with a diverse chain of animals ranging from bacteria in the soil and tiny insects to birds of prey and large mammals like foxes and badgers.

Healthy plants will cope with and recover from a certain degree of damage, attack or even disease. I think of this like the minor cuts, abrasions and viruses that the human body is constantly fighting and healing itself from. It is a plant's ability to resist and heal from damage or disease that indicates health, not the absence of such problems.

Occasionally there is a plague of pests, either because of circumstances beyond the garden, like exceptional rain or drought, or because of the life cycle of a particular animal, like that of the field vole, and then there can be a huge increase in one particular problem. Beyond short-term expediency, I tend not to take this personally and accept that it is beyond my control. Think of all the creatures in your garden – including slugs, vine weevils or whatever conventional 'pest' is particularly bothersome at any given moment – as a wildlife park that you are privileged to share and control and shape to your whim alongside your fellow creatures and not despite them.

Living with pests

1 Do everything you can to grow healthy plants. A robust plant will not be weakened by the odd nibble by a slug or caterpillar or by having sap sucked by an aphid. It will heal itself faster than the predator can cause permanent damage.

2 Never force any plant into growing quickly. This causes fast, sappy growth that provides choice 'pest' food and is weak to recover. That is why plants that are naturally fast-growing and sappy, like lettuce or the initial vigorous growth of young French beans, are the first to be attacked. The healthiest plant is not necessarily the biggest or most floriferous but the one that is best adapted to its precise situation and prevailing conditions.

3 Feed the soil, not the plant. If your soil is in good heart the plant will grow at the rate it can cope with. So on poorer soil it will grow smaller and slower than on rich soil but potentially be just as healthy.

4 Keep your housekeeping up to scratch. By this I mean basic horticultural practices such as:

• Pruning properly at the right time so that there is good ventilation
• Gathering up debris so slugs and insects cannot hide amongst it
• Tying climbers securely so that they do not get weakened by rocking and fraying against other branches
• Not leaving anything too long in a container so that it gets rootbound and grows weakly
• Keeping on top of the watering and weeding, so plants receive a steady supply of water and are not having to compete with weeds for nutrition
• Removing any diseased or weakened plants that will attract predators.
This is all common sense but makes a big contribution to a healthy garden.

5 Avoid monoculture wherever possible. The greater the variety of plants, the less chance of a visiting pest finding a host. In a small garden this is not so much of a problem, particularly if you have neighbours on either side with their own diverse mix of plants, but even within small areas of the garden, it is a good idea to break up blocks of plants, including alternating rows of unrelated vegetables.

6 Use companion plants to attract predators. My vegetable garden is full of self-seeded poppies, forget-me-nots, evening primroses and violas that attract hoverflies whose larvae eat aphids. I only remove them – individually – if they are competing too closely with a vegetable. They look good too. All umbellifers (dill, fennel, cow parsley) also attract hoverflies so I always have some dill growing in the Vegetable Garden as well as in the Herb Garden. In addition, I use annual companion plants amongst my soft fruit.

7 Never force anything to grow where it does not want to. You could argue that much of all horticulture over the past

200 years has been the process of doing just that, but it is not, to my mind, good gardening. Accept the limitations of your soil, climate and aspect.

8 Grow as many indigenous plants as possible. These will have evolved defence mechanisms against local pests as well as being an integral part of the local micro food chain.

9 Never rush the season. It is a temptation to push right up against the edge of hardiness in a plant in spring, putting it outside as soon as possible in the hope that it will flower or crop a few weeks early, but by and large it is better to be a bit too late than too early. Here at Longmeadow we often have very cold nights in April and May and over the years I have found that all but the hardiest plants are better sown or planted only when the nights have warmed up. Extreme fluctuations in temperature – which we can have in May, with daytime figures of 25°C (77°F) dropping to zero (32°F) at night – will weaken any young plant and make it more susceptible to damage by predation. Be patient. It is a long game.

Just a simple area of long grass is very effective at providing food and cover for predators of all kinds. These will keep your garden in a sustainable balance between predator and prey. The long grass looks good too.

The healthiest plant is the one that is best adapted to its precise situation and prevailing conditions

Watering

Watering the pots on the Mound. We have scores of pots all over the garden and every one gets a soak every Friday – although in hot weather some will need watering almost daily.

Back in 2002, climate change was already very apparent within the garden, affecting what we could grow and how, as well as our own relationship with the seasons.

Winters were starting to become warmer and wetter, and summers drier, albeit often overcast. Since then this trend has continued, although with a couple of extremely cold winters thrown into the mix as if to emphasise that the change is a gradual trend rather than the daily or even seasonal manifestation of weather. The main effect of this is that we now reliably have too much water for half the year and too little for the other half.

This is a wet part of a wet country. Real drought is never a serious consideration although our clay soil does get very hard and dry by late summer. However, we rarely have more than ten consecutive rain-free days and when this does happen, the advantages for human activity, such as relishing the luxury of being dry-shod, outweigh any extra watering that we have to do. This means that the garden remains green and lush all summer long.

However, we try and keep our watering regime to the bare minimum. We never water mature plants in a border. Everything is watered-in well when planted and as a rule that is it. We certainly never use a sprinkler and just occasionally I might give a canna or banana a burst from the hose whilst watering pots but in principle, mature plants have to fend for themselves.

However, all containers – and we have around 50 large and hundreds of smaller ones – must be watered at least once a week. We have institutionalised this into 'Feeding Friday'. Everything growing in a container of any kind gets a liquid feed and a good soak on a Friday and, except in the hottest weather, this suffices.

Young plants, from emerging seedlings to those hardening off and ready to plant out, must be watered daily and if it is warm, plants in the greenhouse are watered twice or even three times a day.

This can add up to a lot of time spent watering and a lot of water used. Whilst we have an overabundance of water across the year, summers are getting drier and in general, humanity has to learn to conserve and be careful with its water resources.

The following are all effective in helping to conserve water and to use it wisely.

Enrich the soil and mulch Adding plenty of compost or other organic material will help the soil retain water as well as provide a good medium for strong and healthy root development – enabling the plant to reach for water deeper in the soil. Enriching the soil also brings the

One of the wonders of compost is that it produces soil that drains well whilst simultaneously retaining enough moisture for the plants

advantage in the winter wet season of the soil being able to store a water reserve for summer use that the deep roots can reach. The miraculous combination of soil that drains well whilst simultaneously retaining enough moisture for plants to draw upon is one of the wonders of compost.

One word of caution though; do not add a large amount of compost to any planting hole. This will result in the growing roots being reluctant to leave the hole and spread out into the wider soil, and therefore make them more prone to being affected by drought. The aim is to encourage plants to have as wide and deep a root run as possible so as to reach maximum nutrients and water.

Mixing organic matter into the soil well and then topping it up at least once a year in the form of a good mulch will reduce evaporation as well as increase soil fertility and improve its structure.

Plant sensibly Use your common sense. Do not plant moisture-loving plants in a sunny, well-drained, exposed position and then spend great amounts of time, energy and resources watering them. Use the prevailing conditions to your advantage. Plant to suit the aspect, soil and drainage or – more drastically – alter these conditions to suit your planting.

Above left: A good way of watering seeds in a seed tray is to soak it in a shallow trough of water. This stops small seeds from being scattered by a spray of water.

Above right: I water everything in well when I plant and then rarely water again, which encourages the roots to go deep in search of moisture.

Water the soil not the plant A wet plant is not watered but a plant in wet soil is. Setting a sprinkler to run on a border in summer is wasteful and extremely inefficient as most of the water will fall on the foliage and evaporate before it can reach the soil and be taken up by the roots. Direct all water at the soil around the base of a plant so that it will work down into the ground where the roots can reach it.

Soak don't sprinkle It is far better to water very thoroughly once a week than to give a sprinkle every day. This is because the roots will go where the water is. A light watering never permeates much below the first few inches of the topsoil, so this is where the strongest root formation will be. As long as that water supply is constant, the plant will be fine. But if it is irregular – and this can be caused by extra sun and, especially, wind, as much as by a break in the water

supply – then the roots at the surface will be the first to dry out. And as these are the main feeding root system, the plant will suffer immediately.

If, however, you water very thoroughly every week, the ground will get really wet to a depth of 60–120cm (24–36in). The roots will then grow downwards to this water source and if the water dries up, they will not be affected so quickly.

Time your watering to be most effective Water everything when you plant it – even in wet weather. This will get the roots growing strongly so they can then go and find their own water in the soil. Some vegetable crops – like celery, leeks and fennel – are very sensitive to water stress and will bolt weeks later, so must not be allowed to dry out. But having watered them in when planted, many vegetables are most effectively watered after thinning and when they are in flower.

Mulch all bare soil This will dramatically reduce evaporation. Any porous material can be used and stones and gravel can mulch as effectively as an organic material, but it does seem better to kill two birds with one pile of compost, and mulch thickly every spring to both feed and protect the soil.

Create windbreaks Wind dries up plants quicker than sunshine and a strong, dry wind places a huge strain on the transpiration system of a young, leafy plant. If you can make barriers and fences whilst your garden is young, plants will grow much faster and develop root systems that will be able to reach much larger reserves of water. As hedges and trees grow, they can absorb the wind without drying out too much themselves, although never underestimate how much moisture a hedge will use when you are planning your planting in its shade.

Collecting water The best place to store water for the garden is in the soil. Whilst this may sound facetious, what it means is that a healthy soil, rich in humus, will hold long-lasting reserves of water far greater than any amount that you might store in tanks or water butts. But it also makes sense to attach a water butt to every downpipe from your house, shed and greenhouse. In fact, we use cattle troughs rather than butts as they are cheap and come in a wide variety of sizes and, by dipping a watering can into them, the cans are much quicker to fill than using a tap on a water butt.

The problem with collecting rainwater is that when it rains, the storage tanks fill far quicker than we can use them, and when the weather is dry, we use the water far quicker than they refill. However, mains water contains chlorine and aluminium, and in a limestone area will be too alkaline for acid-loving plants such as citrus, camellias, rhododendrons and blueberries, so try and collect what you can for that non-rainy day.

Grey water We discard huge amounts of grey water when we wash our bodies, our clothes and our eating and cooking implements. In the northern hemisphere it is not necessary to conserve this on a regular basis because for at least half the year we have more water than we could possibly want. But at times of water shortage it makes sense to recycle your grey water to your plants, especially shrubs, hedges and trees, although never use grey water that has had bleach in it.

Setting a sprinkler to run on a border in summer is wasteful and extremely inefficient, as most of the water will fall on the foliage and evaporate before it can reach the soil and be taken up by the roots

Tools

Trowels and hand forks ready for use. All my garden tools have a place they are returned to at the end of each day.

I am writing this in my converted hop-kiln workroom and below me is the tool shed where the tools wait in the dark, all roughly in their right place, not as clean or recently oiled as they might be, but ready.

I know their places and can walk in there in the dark, reach out and know exactly where to find every one of them. I have used them all and know how they all feel in the hand. This is the main thing about any kind of hand tool – it has to feel right in the hand. You can have ten identical spades or trowels, but only one will feel right.

I have accrued spades across the years with a compulsion verging on obsession. I love them. There is a stainless-steel border spade, small and precise and useful for moving plants in a busy border. I have digging spades with wide treads and long straps extending halfway up the handle, trenching, or Irish, spades with extra-long handles and tapering blades, spades with YD grips, T-handles or straight handles beautifully shaped to bulb out slightly at the end so that the handle instinctively seeks and finds the most comfortable, ergonomic position. I also have spades practically unused because they look fine but just feel wrong, as well as spades worn by many generations of gardeners to a lopsided shaving of their original selves.

All have ash handles, although American hickory is good too. Most have YD handles, where the end of the ash shaft is split and steamed open to create a

Y-shape which is then closed by a tubular ash bar. I would not dream of using a spade with a plastic handle, partly because wood, worn shiny smooth with use, feels so much nicer, but also because plastic will give you blisters much faster. How many people, when buying a spade from a garden centre, ask what wood the handle is from? But it makes all the difference. Would you buy a kitchen knife with a superb blade and a cheap plastic handle? No. Any hand tool works from the hand outwards. The point of contact has to be right or else the whole thing is wrong.

All my spades are sufficiently different to get an outing every now and then but only one spade has my heart. This is stainless steel and was made at the Wigan foundry of Bulldog Tools on 22 November 1990. The date is clearly blazoned into my memory. It also happened to be the day that Margaret Thatcher resigned, which was announced on the foundry tannoy as I watched my spade being made, from pouring the molten metal to sanding the handle.

It weighs exactly 2.25kg (5lb) and it balances perfectly cradled on my index finger. The blade, set on a swan neck of forged steel drawn from the same ingot as the haft is pressed from, is gently curved in cross-section, the curve diminishing as it opens towards the edge. That edge is sharp enough to cut string and chop through tree roots like a chisel. It is, after all, no more than a blade. But it is a miracle of sophisticated design, as perfectly evolved for its function as a wheel is for revolving. Its angles are subtle and yet precise. It cost about £90 in 1990 and I regard it as one of the best buys I ever made. It now has its third handle and I would not exchange it for any other spade in the world or indeed any amount of money. I let no one else use it. This is a spade taken very seriously.

But every gardener should take their tools seriously, just as chefs will take their knives seriously or musicians their instruments. Good tools don't make a good gardener but they do add enormously to the pleasure of gardening. Every single time I use my spade, I enjoy the experience. It introduces a pure aesthetic element to a task above and beyond its success. Digging a rich loam becomes one of life's great sensual pleasures. Good soil plus good spade equals good time spent.

Whilst there is a lot of truth in the saying 'a bad workman blames his tools', and whilst a good gardener will make a lovely garden with whatever is to hand, it is also absolutely true that good tools foster a kind of respect and sensuous pleasure that inevitably improve both the experience of gardening and the garden.

It goes without saying that I like hand tools best, and simple, refined combinations of steel and wood best of all. Most modern attempts at improving or redesigning garden tools look as though they have fallen out of a cracker.

For all that I love the scores of gardening tools I have collected over the years, you actually need very few to garden well. You need a good spade – perhaps two, with

The spade that has my heart was made on 22 November 1990, the day that Margaret Thatcher resigned

I prefer Japanese secateurs to all others as they hold a razor-sharp edge and are light and comfortable in the hand

the second smaller and more convenient for planting in the confines of a border.

You also need a fork. I prefer square tines (as opposed to round or flat ones), not too long, not too curved, of stainless steel and robust enough to serve arduous use. A small border fork is also useful for lifting a plant without damaging its neighbours. It is worth stressing that digging is always best done with a spade. Keep the fork for breaking up the soil once dug or for lifting plants.

One rake will do but three is a counsel of perfection. For general preparation of a seed bed, a round-tined flathead rake is best. A spring-tine rake doubles as a scratching grass and leaf collector, and rubber rakes are invaluable for gathering up leaves from borders without damaging plants and seedlings.

If you grow vegetables you must have a hoe. The design of a hoe depends upon whether you push the cutting edge through the soil or pull it back towards you. I think that for smaller annual weeds it is best to push, cutting through the roots of weeds just below the surface of the soil. Keep it sharp and keep it small. It is a big mistake to try and save time by using a big-bladed hoe. A small one is twice as useful. Bigger weeds are best chopped out with a swan-neck or draw hoe. If you find a good mattock, it can be very useful for rough digging as well as weeding.

You do need a good trowel or two for planting – one big and one small. A word of caution: cheap trowels just do not last, so go for quality of manufacture and steel, and the same goes for the final essential parts of gardening kit – good secateurs and a pocket knife. I have lots of both but prefer Japanese secateurs to all others. They will hold a razor-sharp edge and are light and comfortable in the hand. At last count I had about 30 pocket knives although I have never deliberately collected them. I use them on a whim, liking one or another for a week and then perhaps not using it for months. But if you have only one, it should have a straight blade for taking cuttings. As with any cutting tools, they are only as good as the steel that the blades are made from. The shape, colour or detail of design is a matter of subjective taste but high-quality steel holds an edge for much longer.

Finally, I love really good shears. As it happens, these are mostly Japanese – simply because Japanese steel is the best in the world. But whatever kind you choose, razor-sharp, comfortable shears make hedge trimming or topiary a delight as well as being very effective.

And that is really the secret to all good gardening tools. They should make your work easier and more pleasurable, and they should look good too. Just like your garden.

Machines

We have a powerful rotary mower that cuts the long grass as well as chopping up compost, and two mowers – one that is battery driven and another petrol. When I wrote the first edition of this book in 2002, the prospect of a battery-powered

mower was science fiction but they are now powerful, quiet and obviously much better for the environment than petrol-driven ones. We do not have a lawn of any kind, only mow once a week, and have systematically reduced the short grass wherever possible, replacing it with long meadow grass mixed with bulbs and wild flowers, with just paths mown through them.

We also use battery strimmers, one of which works off a backpack power pack that lasts for eight hours and can be recharged overnight. This has revolutionised our garden maintenance. It is quiet and effective, and we use it mainly to strim the brick paths once a week to keep the weeds down. We also use the power pack to operate a hedge-cutter and again, this is very quiet and very effective.

We use a tiller to mix in compost and to break up soil that has been previously dug. We rarely use a rotovator as this only

cultivates the ground to the depth of a few inches and creates a hard pan unless the ground has been well dug first. Over the years I have found it better to have a small machine that can be lifted on and off raised beds rather than a bigger, heavier one that is a struggle to move around the place. It might mean more time and labour but in the end, a machine is only as useful as the ease with which it can be handled. Otherwise it will not get used.

We also have a mechanical shredder for the compost. In principle, shredders are really useful for making good compost but in practice it is hard to find the right one at the right price. To be good enough to handle any large volume, it will be very expensive – certainly thousands rather than hundreds of pounds. Also, some are good at shredding softer material for compost, others are essentially chippers that are excellent for dealing with harder prunings. Very few indeed will do both jobs well.

Above left:
A shredder is incredibly useful for reducing prunings to wood chip for paths and for shredding compost to reduce the volume and increase the speed of compost making.

Above right: I love all good hand tools and especially tools that cut. Here I am using a scythe to cut the long grass in the Orchard.

The gardens

The Spring Garden

The Spring Garden has changed very little since it was made nearly 30 years ago, let alone since the first edition of this book appeared some ten years later.

It is where I go and dip my toe as we emerge from winter. It is where the first flowers peek through frost, snow and flood – snowdrops, aconites, hellebores – and where, as the days roll thrillingly into spring, the daffodils, fritillaries, tulips, pulmonaria, Solomon's seal, forget-me-nots, tiarella, brunnera, euphorbia, the first Species roses and the cow parsley all expand out into weeks of heady glory before subsiding into summer dormancy.

In recent years I have added *Smilacina racemosa*, the fragrant cousin of Solomon's seal, and have grown more tiarella from seed. *Tellima grandiflora* is another plant that I have increased greatly – although arguably not greatly enough. I must sow more. The tulips 'West Point', 'Spring Green' and 'Yellow Spring Green' do well and chionodoxa is spreading its delicate white flowers – touched with the palest blue – underneath the big hazel. I have

There are now thousands of snowdrops that reappear in the Spring Garden every January and all of them come from one small bunch wrapped in newspaper and given to us by a friend 30 years ago.

In mid-May the Spring Garden is taken over by a white froth of cow parsley whose seeds are spread by the annual winter floods.

planted *Actaea cordifolia* and *Aruncus dioicus* for their plumes of flower, and both tolerate the winter flooding.

The Spring Garden is still the first part of the garden to flood in winter and in late 2019 and early 2020, more than half of it was under water for weeks on end, but nothing seemed to suffer at all.

However, time has inevitably crept up on it and change has manifested itself simply as growth. The trees I planted as slips that I could hold in one hand in the spring of 1993 are now 15m (50ft) tall and more.

This means that light levels in the borders beneath them have progressively got lower, so a couple of years ago we

radically pruned the trees back – not to reduce the height but to take off any side branches we could reach with ladders and long-arm saws.

The other great change was a result of starting to film *Gardeners' World* each week from the garden. In 1995 we planted a hornbeam hedge beneath the pleached limes of the Lime Walk and by 2002, when the last edition of this book was originally photographed, this was well established beneath the parallel rows of the limes and formed a green wall bounding the west side of the Spring Garden. But as well as greatly increasing the shade, the hornbeam also made access

for the camera very difficult, so in 2013 I removed it. This meant the crew could film the Spring Garden from the path of the Lime Walk. It also added much more light and a whole new view of the garden.

Before, the Spring Garden was a narrowing corridor that became almost completely hidden and shaded as the spring leaves opened fully. This meant that all vision, all sensation, was narrowed, too, tunnelling perception into a linear experience that was either a single, long vista or else a process that meant moving down the very narrow path.

Taking out the hedge changed all this at a stroke. It is like taking the side off a building. The entire Spring Garden is now revealed in one cast of the eye. In fact, the rhythm of the pleached lime stems, acting like colonnades, introduces a rhythm that I cannot claim to have intended or even expected. The effect is that now, as you look between the trunks of the pleached limes through into the Spring Garden, it is like passing by a woodland glade filled with flower.

Above left: The door into the Spring Garden from the back yard.

Above: Crocuses and hellebores surround the large hazel, which was one of only two trees in the whole garden when we arrived in 1991.

The Jewel Garden

The Jewel Garden remains the heart of our entire garden, the physical and conceptual hub around which all other parts revolve.

In many ways it has not changed much at all in the last 20 years, as the basic concept is still to use jewel colours throughout the seasons in as rich and opulent a display as possible.

It is a big, difficult space to keep looking good, so we have invested an awful lot of thought, time and effort into it. Whereas there are times when most of the other sections of the garden seem to be like an engine that just needs a bit of maintenance here and the odd part repaired or replaced there, the Jewel Garden is very high-maintenance and demanding. Not so much a well oiled machine as a distinctly temperamental thoroughbred.

Like a lot of things in life, it was never really planned. That part of the garden was to be a circular lawn and was just that for a couple of years. Because I had cleared it from a tussocky mix of grass and brambles, I had made the assumption that lawn was an 'improvement' – a kind of horticultural award that I was bestowing on it. But – not for the first or last time – soil brought me to my senses. I ringed that circle with yew hedges and could not help relish the richness of the clay loam I was digging into. Grass was not going to be good enough for it. So out came the yews, off came the grass and we started planning a range of borders.

This phase of the Jewel Garden grew and thrived for about eight years. It took a lot of work to maintain, with hundreds of annuals grown and added each season, mulching each spring with 20 tons of mushroom compost that took endless barrows to shift from the drive where it was dumped, and almost constant weeding and cutting back. But that is gardening. It is what we all love and it looked fantastic and gave us huge pleasure.

But no border stays the same from year to year, let alone decade to decade. To keep things as they are, you have to change all the time. The mistake that we made with the Jewel Garden in this 1999–2008 incarnation was that we had become complacent. It was almost institutionalised in our minds and in our domestic life. It looked the way it did because that was the way it looked. Then the husband-and-wife team who had come in three days a week for the previous five years to help in the garden decided to retire and I began filming *Around the World in 80 Gardens* and was away a huge amount. Then I had a bit of a health blip and what with one thing and another, the garden took a back seat, the weeds romped happily and the lack of intensive maintenance meant that certain plants were allowed to be thuggish and others collapsed under their assault.

Opposite page:
The Jewel Garden is filled with rich, jewel-like hues from every kind of plant, and in summer is an intense wall of colour and foliage.

The Jewel Garden is the physical and spiritual heart of Longmeadow and represents a huge amount of planting and work. It is labour-intensive and very demanding – but worth it.

By 2010, some of the beds had become infested with bindweed and so at the end of that year, we took out every single plant, washed the roots clean of all traces of the spaghetti-like bindweed roots and potted up the plants or lined them out in the Vegetable Garden whilst we removed every last scrap of bindweed we could find. It was boring and took ages but was worth the trouble.

The small trees that were an important part of the Jewel Garden's original planting

– a laburnum, two weeping pears (*Pyrus salicifolia* 'Pendula'), a robinia, four crab apples 'Golden Hornet' – have all blown over, died or been so damaged by snow or wind that they have long gone. We had eight Irish yews for a few years but they were moved to the Cottage Garden, where they are now very large and established. Currently the only trees in the borders are four purple hazels (*Corylus maxima* 'Purpurea') that are coppiced back to the ground every five years or so, by which time they become a large cluster of stems with rich, purple foliage. This, if left, casts too much shade and is too dominant, so coppicing solves that problem perfectly.

I added to the structure with shrubs such as *Buddleja* 'Black Knight' and *B. globosa*, and with the elders that do so well for us, such as the golden *Sambucus racemosa* 'Plumosa Aurea' and the almost black *S. nigra* f. *porphyrophylla* 'Guincho Purple'. I have also added quite a few roses such as 'William Shakespeare' and 'Falstaff', and I let the tree peonies, *Paeonia lutea* and *P. daurica* subsp. *mlokosewitchii*, grow large to add structure around which more temporary planting can shift and evolve.

The *Allium hollandicum* 'Purple Sensation' has spread exponentially and is now a glorious thug whose bulbs we dig up and remove by the barrowload every year. If ever there was an example of 'be careful what you wish for', then that is it.

We now have many more dahlias and cannas as the touchstone of our late-summer display. Two enormous bananas with rich burgundy leaves (*Ensete ventricosum* 'Maurelii') dominate their respective areas and we grow masses of clematis up hazel wigwams. All the grasses have been moved to the Grass Borders and I can now no longer grow a decent leonotis – formerly a stalwart of the garden – to save my life. I put this down to climate change rather than ineptitude, but perhaps I have lost my touch. We still grow hundreds of zinnias, tithonias, sunflowers, cosmos, antirrhinums, scabious and many other annuals, and the driving motive and direction of the garden remains unchanged.

The trick is to have a foundation of large groups of perennials and then to allow yourself room and the mindset to play, adding in annuals and individual purchases or gifts as and when they occur and where they seem to suit. Otherwise there is a danger that the garden becomes a planting exercise executed to a plan but still-born. The Jewel Garden should always be a dance, not a static tableau, however glorious.

As well as a wide range of hardy shrubs, perennials and bulbs, we use a lot of tender plants in the Jewel Garden, both perennial and annual, that have to be raised every year or lifted and stored over winter.

The Cottage Garden

Opposite page:
The Cottage Garden
is a soft muddle
of pastel shades,
dominated by roses,
clematis, sweet peas
and the structure
of the columnar
Irish yews.

When I first designed this garden, back in 1992, I intended for there to be a square lawn near the house, bounded by pleached limes and hornbeam hedges.

It would be a cool green space where the children could play, secluded, safe, within earshot and yet free.

It never happened. A local farmer came with his reversible plough and ploughed all the areas that were not to be path, and as the soil was exposed on the site of the proposed lawn, I saw that it was the most wonderful, rich loam. This, I thought, is wasted on a lawn. So that area, still bounded by hornbeam hedges and pleached limes, became our vegetable garden and this is how it remained for the next 20 years, including the period when I wrote the first edition of this book.

Over the years it became increasingly formal, with clipped box hedges replacing the original low, woven-hazel fencing around 24 beds and eight large Irish yews – originally planted in the Jewel Garden and each moved in a wheelbarrow by Sarah and me in 2008 – adding structure. It was architectural and ornate, and more potager than allotment. But in 2013, it began the gradual transition to a cottage garden, where flowers, fruit and vegetables traditionally grew side by side in a lovely carefree jumble.

Cottage gardens evolved around the homes of the rural poor, living in tied cottages with a scrap of land where they could supplement their meagre incomes by growing some vegetables. Occasionally a flower was allowed to enter into this utilitarian mix, partly because you cannot bury the human spirit and partly because poverty does not in any way remove a love of flowers nor the skill in growing them.

However, what has filtered down into popular gardening culture is something much softer and more carefree, a loose, informal style of gardening that has become identified with rural charm, innocence and a sense of harmonious abandon.

One of the features of cottage gardens was that they grew organically. They were never planned or designed. It seems to me that this is the most useful inheritance from the cottage-garden tradition for the modern gardener. If you can let the garden grow up around you organically, then you will tap into a much looser, freer form of creativity. You plant according to the dictates of surrounding plants and your own intuition. You can mix shrubs, flowers, herbs, fruit and vegetables in an entirely unstructured way. This takes quite a lot of confidence and courage, but the results are both truly modern and much more like old-fashioned cottage gardening. It is also absolutely in line with modern organic theory. By planting the garden as a happy jumble, you are avoiding the concentration of pests and diseases that monoculture encourages.

Cottage gardens demand a certain softness of tone, so we have focussed on pinks, lemon-yellows, lavender, mauve and pale blues. This means that there is a real contrast with the Jewel Garden, which enables the two areas to play off each other. However, in the spirit of true cottage-garden style, there are no rules and whilst pastels dominate, the occasional flare of bright and brash colour muscles to the fore.

Our Cottage Garden has taken a number of years to evolve and that process has not ended, but the big change came when I began to replace vegetables with roses. Up until then, the mixture of vegetables, annuals, biennials – even herbaceous perennials – was flexible enough to change year on year. But a rose bush is a statement of intent. It is planted for a future that lasts at least ten years and I have roses growing and flowering as I write this that I bought 30 years ago. During the course of a couple of years, I planted over 40 different rose varieties in the beds and for a glorious few weeks in June, they dominate this garden. Most are Old or Classic roses and most are a shade of pink. Gallicas, Damasks, Albas, Bourbons, Centifolias and Moss roses are all represented, along with some Modern English roses.

As these became established, they increasingly edged out the lettuces, cabbages and carrots, and after a few years, all vegetables were kept to the two veg plots at the other end of the garden.

However, I still have fruit in the Cottage Garden, with gooseberries, rhubarb, apples, pears, medlars and crab apples growing in the borders. We have two beds dedicated to cut flowers and these have made a big difference, giving us the space to grow a good range of flowers that can be gathered to decorate the house without depleting the borders. Years of manuring for vegetables has meant that they grow especially lustily and well.

I grow lots of sweet peas up wigwams in the borders and a dozen different clematis, too, all in rather paler tones than those of the Jewel Garden. We also add annual climbers, such as *Cobaea scandens*, *Eccremocarpus scaber* and Spanish flag as the fancy takes us from year to year.

As well as the structure created by the climbers and shrubs, the temporary infusion of colour from annuals and biennials is terribly important for this kind of gardening. They are cheap – dozens for just the price of a packet of seed – invariably grow fast, have vivid flowers and can be used to fill gaps to maintain the intense level of planting that is necessary. So we grow biennial wallflowers, foxgloves, pansies, forget-me-nots, Canterbury bells, hollyhocks and sweet Williams.

Hardy annuals are ideal because they can be sown directly, avoiding all the expense of raising seedlings under cover. To capture the appropriate cottage-garden tone, these should include sweet peas, marigolds, poppies, nigella, alyssum, cornflowers, larkspur and lavatera.

Box blight (see page 61) has ravaged the box hedges that I grew from cuttings 20-odd years ago and by the time you read this, they should have all been pulled out and burned. But then I have been threatening to do that for the past few years and they are still there, hanging on with their bare bones.

Opposite page: We allow annuals and biennials to seed themselves freely in the borders and hedges of the Cottage Garden, and they add to the sense of the garden overflowing with flowers.

The Damp Garden

When the first edition of this book went to the printers in the first months of 2003, the Damp Garden was newly formed and only just taking shape as the place where we grew all the damp-loving plants.

Scooping fallen quince blossom from the pond in the Damp Garden in spring with the camassias in full flower.

Before that it was rather an unresolved space, tucked behind tall hornbeam hedges and often too wet to garden as I wanted. But then I saw sense and realised that this wetness was a potential benefit, so I moved all the hostas, ligularias, rodgersias, shuttlecock ferns, cornuses and quinces that had hitherto been spread across various parts of the garden into this one space. They immediately made themselves at home in each other's company, all relishing the dampness of the soil.

The dampness that gives this small section of the garden its name is down to its vicinity to the river. It is always the first bit of the garden to flood and is often

under water when everywhere else is dry. Flooding happens mostly in winter but even in summer drought – bearing in mind that our concept of drought would be considered the rainy season in many other parts of Britain, let alone in the world – the soil has a deep reservoir of moisture that plants can access.

For ten years it thrived and, within the limitations of site, soil and design, seemed set in its comfortable, established ways. But then the pond came along.

I resisted water of any kind in this garden until then. It seems an extraordinary omission to me now, but my reasons seemed valid enough at the time. The first, as already mentioned, was that when we came here we had small children. Friends of my parents had a two-year-old daughter who drowned in their small garden pond, so it was drummed into me from an early age that small children and ponds did not mix. In fact, my previous house had quite a large pond that was very beautiful, but one of the first things I did was to fence it off. No pond, I decided, until the youngest can swim unaided.

The time went by, the garden became more established, the youngest learned to swim like a fish, but water still did not officially feature in any way in the garden. But at least twice a year – and sometimes for weeks on end – the water pouring down from the Welsh hills burst the banks of the river just yards from our boundary and turned the surrounding landscape into a 200 hectare (500 acre) lake that lapped right to the edge of – and quite often inside – the garden. The children swam in the river and the fact that we lived in a very

wet, watery place fulfilled – we thought – all our horticultural watery needs.

But we were wrong. When the first series of *Gardeners' World* to be shot in this garden was coming to a close in October 2011, the producer said that I ought to have a pond. 'Just wait a little and one will come along,' I said. After all, the Damp Garden was called that because it often flooded. But I was persuaded to make a pond there in the winter of 2012, and by the end of April it looked as though it had always been there, with the hostas, ligularias, rodgersias, matteuccia ferns and primulas replanted around the margins.

From the outset I had decided that this was to be a natural-looking wildlife pond rather than a formal expanse of water illuminated with a few choice plants. It is a circle, edged with beautiful mossy stone and dug to create ledges at varying depths to accommodate a full range of marginal plants like the flowering rush (*Butomus umbellatus*), the water plantain (*Alisma plantago-aquatica*), the lovely porcupine-like striped bullrush (*Scirpus zebrinus*) and arrowhead (*Sagittaria sagittifolia*), as well as *Iris ensata* and the native flag (*I. pseudocorus*), all of which have evolved to have their roots in wet mud that is often covered by water.

There is also a central area that is 1.2m (4ft) deep, which allows me to grow largish water lilies that need deeper water. I have not added any fish because I know that

The dampness that gives this small section of the garden its name is down to its vicinity to the river

our local herons would eat them and because fish are not really compatible with a good range of aquatic plants. However, frogs, newts, water beetles and other aquatic insects quickly became established. In fact, one of the wonders of making any kind of pond in any garden is seeing how quickly the range of wildlife expands and takes up home there – as well as the bird and bat population benefitting hugely because ponds also attract lots of insects.

I put in a pipe connected to the large water butt outside the potting shed, which in turn collects all the rainwater from the roofs of that part of the house. When the water reaches the overflow point in the butt, it runs down to the pond to refresh and top it up.

One aspect of having a pond I had completely underrated was the quality of light that water brings into play. At different times of day, the light reflects in different ways off the water as it is thrown back up to the surrounding trees – three quinces, the cherry 'Tai-haku' and a *Viburnum plicatum* f. *tomentosum* 'Mariesii'. And when the setting sun falls exactly through a gap in the Long Walk's hornbeam hedge, it creates a shining line of light on the surface of the water.

We paved the area between the hedge and water and I often sit there. Here I am hidden from the rest of the garden, drinking deep of the peace and sense of harmony with the natural world that a pond, surrounded by plants that are all at home either in or at the water's edge, seems to impart more than any other area of a garden.

By midsummer there is a lot of plant cover around the border edges as well as in the margins and deeper water of the pond. All this contributes to improving the range of wildlife in the Damp Garden and Longmeadow as a whole.

The Lime Walk

It is curious how we assume the aspects of our gardens, their fronts, backs and sides, and from those assumptions our daily relationship is created.

The crew use a side entrance and come into the garden via the potting-shed yard. Almost always they turn left and gravitate to the Jewel Garden. It is their entrance, their starting point from which they radiate out.

But I always enter the garden from the door that opens out at one end of the Lime Walk. It is my entrance to the garden and everything else unfolds from that point. It gives me a rather different relationship with the garden than the one portrayed on television – and a different one from anyone who does not enter the garden via the house. It is a bit like knowing someone in uniform, through their job, and then meeting them in civilian clothes. Same person – but somehow very different.

So the Lime Walk has real significance for me and feels like the line from which the rest of the garden is measured and set. It is a 36m (40 yard) avenue of pleached limes that runs across the width of the garden, flanking one side of the Cottage Garden (the Long Walk runs parallel on the other side) and creating the Spring Garden from the long slither of land between the other side and the garden boundary.

The limes are now solid pillars and have had exactly the same regime – pruned back hard in early spring and otherwise left to their own devices for the rest of the year – since they were planted as broomstick-sized saplings in 1993. Even 20 years ago the shade they cast was becoming too much for most flowers and for the past decade they have been underplanted with the ferns *Dryopteris filix-mas* and *Dryopteris affinis*, with *Alchemilla mollis* and pink *Cyclamen hederifolium*, and in spring, taking advantage of the sunlight before the foliage of the limes appears, with the white tulip 'Triumphator' and the creamy 'Nicholas Heyek'.

At the far end there used to be a green door but a few years ago we moved it to the potting-shed yard and now we have a large Cretan pot that is the focal point both for the Lime Walk and for one of the three long paths that run right up the length of the garden.

The Lime Walk does not *do* very much. Yet I think it beautiful in its rhythmic balance and poise. More than that, it is our entrance into the garden from the house and the first part of the garden I greet every morning.

The Lime Walk is my entrance to the garden and everything else unfolds from that point

The Long Walk

I had completely forgotten – until I looked at the original edition of this book for the first time in years – that we used to call the Long Walk the Long Garden.

Either our plans for it changed or we have become more modest in our approach, but it is an interlude, a buffer zone, rather than a full-blown garden space and, running as it does the other side of the Cottage Garden from the Lime Walk, the two Walks have a parallel identity. However, whatever its name, it works well and has become satisfyingly simple over the past few years.

But it took quite a while to reach this point. Over the years it has hosted cardoons, sweet peas, giant alliums, pumpkins – all grown either side of this narrow path that cuts across the width of the garden and separates the Cottage Garden from the Jewel Garden and, at its far end, the Damp Garden from the Grass Borders.

The big change came when we edged the path with box, planting a succession of box plants up its length that, in time, became large topiary cones. They were intended originally to be box balls, but I used cuttings from a variety called 'Handsworthiensis', which is very vigorous and has an exceptionally large leaf. It also invariably wants to grow vertically, thus rendering it completely unsuitable for a clipped round shape. So the balls became what they always were desperate to be – cones.

With the pleached limes on either side, underplanted with hornbeam hedges and the clipped box hedges, and tulips and daffodils in spring followed by *Acanthus spinosus* planted between the cones, the Walk had a formal symmetricality that was a moment of ordered simplicity between the horticulturally hectic planting of the Cottage Garden and the Jewel Garden. I cut a window in the hornbeam hedge at the far end that offers a glimpse of the fields beyond. All seemed to be in place and we planned that it would continue so for any foreseeable future.

But if you want to make God laugh – tell him your plans. Just as everything was really established, box blight (see page 61) struck and the very first signs of it were in the Long Walk. The relative lack of air circulation meant that conditions were perfect for the fungus to thrive and spread, and it quickly went from one plant down at the far end to affect all the hedge and most of the cones.

After struggling for a couple of years, we took out the hedging plants and burned them, and left the cones uncut for three years, and they all recovered as a result. The blight is still chronic in the garden but 'Handsworthiensis' has thick enough leaves to recover and if it is really bad in any one year, we leave all the box uncut. This stops the spread and allows time for healthy regrowth.

I planted *Alchemilla mollis* as an edging plant where the box hedge had been. It looked pretty and we accepted the enforced change. But then we had a storm one July and the alchemilla – that had grown extraordinarily lustily in the rich soil – was flattened and spread completely across the path. The acanthus too was a bit battered, but attractively so, leaning in drunkenly. The effect was twofold. The first was to make the path completely unusable and the second was that it looked wonderful. I loved it.

So for the past few years this has been the pattern. The bulbs run down the whole length in spring, then the walk becomes leafy and linear for a few weeks before the first rainstorm spreads the alchemilla again and the Long Walk becomes an anarchic river of fluffy yellow and lime-green flower running right across the path, with lurching acanthus stems above.

When the flower heads of the alchemilla start to brown, we cut it right back to the knuckle, support the acanthus flower heads so they are upright, clip the box cones, cut the hedges and restore the status quo of the orderly, symmetrical path again.

The Long Walk is a simple corridor of clipped box and pleached limes that runs right across the width of the garden. As well as being a satisfying vista in its own right, it is a moment of pause between the floral intensity of the Cottage and Jewel Gardens.

The Mound

The Mound, like so much in this garden, has evolved slowly, going through a number of incarnations over the years until arriving at what feels like its natural, fully formed self.

The Mound is made from what was the dumping ground for a quarter of a century of spoil accumulated from bonfires, subsoil from digging paths and rubble from building work. We then shaped this into two terraces and chose plants with good fragrance and a predominantly white, pale yellow and blue colour scheme.

It was created exactly at the time that I wrote the first edition of this book. Before that, for the first ten years that we were here, it was the site of our spoil heap, comprised of all the waste material from the garden over the past quarter of a century. Every time we made a hard path, paved an area or did any kind of landscaping, we piled the subsoil, stones and debris on this spot. For years it also housed the bonfire where all our diseased plant material and non-compostable

paper were burned, and gradually ash and charcoal added to the increasingly untidy heap.

Then, in the spring of 2002, I hired a digger and a driver, who turned this unsightly, weed-covered, rubbish dump into a square plateau with gently sloping sides. I sowed it with grass seed and within weeks it became a smooth grassy knoll, where we instinctively gravitated to lie and look at the clouds or the stars. Then the children's trampoline moved there, later

For the first ten years that we were here, the Mound was the site of our spoil heap

replaced by a high-sided swimming pool that left a circle of bare soil. Gradually the tightly mown grass became shaggy and filled with a fine collection of thistles.

So we hired a digger again – although this time my son, having graduated from trampoline and paddling pool via university and adulthood, operated it and made it into two terraces with the sides somewhat steeper. We built a retaining wall between the top and bottom terraces and I planted a lavender hedge behind it – on a trench almost entirely filled with deep gravel to ensure good drainage. That lavender hedge now tops and spills over the wall and is humming with bees and butterflies in midsummer. The wall is also a good place to set smaller pots, according to what is flowering and looking good.

Brick steps lead up from the rest of the garden, on up to the top terrace, and a brick path takes you to a paved seating area beneath a simple wooden cube frame made from four large chestnut posts and the recycled trunks of hornbeams taken out to widen gaps in the hedges – mirroring the pergola made from four limes in the Grass Borders. We have planted *Rosa* 'Malvern Hills' and a white wisteria in opposite corners of the cube and they are now beginning to wind and twist their way towards clothing the structure.

In summer the steps are flanked with pots of agapanthus – although that could change. The beauty of having lots of plants growing in pots is that they can be moved around according to whim and fancy.

Around the outside of both terraces I moved some espaliered pears which, poor things, I had relocated twice before.

At the rear of the top terrace is a little brick square with a table and a fine view of the rest of the garden and the landscape beyond.

Nevertheless, they survived the trauma and produce very good pears, as well as creating a perfect structural balance of openness and containment.

We are on an absolutely flat floodplain so the Mound is the only spot where you can look down and survey the rest of the garden but, because of the screening trees of the Coppice, it is itself completely private and un-overlooked.

We decided that the flowers on the Mound should be selected to conform to two parameters. The first was their colour, which should be either pale yellow, pale blue or white. The second was that as many as possible should be fragrant. We wanted it to be a place where, as you climbed the steps, you would bathe in a swirl of heady scents. We have chosen to focus mainly on those plants that smell best in the evening because that is when we are most likely to sit and enjoy them.

On the top level I planted the Shrub roses 'Madame Legras de St. Germain', 'Alba Semi-Plena' and 'Madame Hardy'. All are Albas, white-flowered and gloriously scented, and make robust shrubs. They only flower once but I don't mind that. The *Paeonia lactiflora* 'Madame Lemoine' is big and blousy and smells divine, so she is in the mix, too, as are the two varieties of mock orange, *Philadelphus* 'Belle Étoile' and *P.* 'Manteau d'Hermine'. The latter is a bit smaller so better suited to a small garden. White foxgloves, fennel, *Nicotiana sylvestris* and white echinacea add to the mix.

Initially, the lower level was paved and filled with pots of scented-leaf pelargoniums, chocolate cosmos, citrus, lemon verbena and lilies that were then all

moved into a greenhouse in winter. But in 2019 I took up most of the paving and made two beds that are planted with 'Honky Tonk' and 'Lemon Snow' tulips and with wallflowers and forget-me-nots in spring, and with *Verbena bonariensis*, the rose 'Vanessa Bell', eryngium, daylilies, nepeta, evening primrose and tobacco plants in summer.

I added two small trees to the beds on the top terrace. One is *Ptelea trifoliata* 'Aurea' that grows delicate pale green foliage and a mass of small, yellow-green, beautifully scented flowers. The other was a gift from the students at Kew. It is the goat horn tree (*Carrierea calycina*), whose white, waxy flowers smell superb. The only downside is that they can take over 50 years to appear!

The banks that were tightly mown for many years are now underplanted with crocuses and wild daffodils, and the grass is allowed to grow long until the beginning of August, when we cut it short. Not only does this look good, but it has saved a lot of very awkward mowing.

The grass slopes of the Mound are underplanted with waves of crocuses, wild narcissi, wild garlic and then wild meadow flowers. Then in August it is all cut short and kept mown for the rest of the year.

Opposite page: The lower terrace was for a while paved but we never sat there, so lifted the paving and made a pair of beds. This is how our garden evolves – through constant tinkering!

The Orchard

When we came here in November 1991, the garden consisted of an open but abandoned field with two trees the only growing things that stood out above the uncut grass.

One was a hawthorn that remains as part of the Coppice and the other, the large hazel in the Spring Garden, right outside the back door. But there were two rotting trunks of damsons – one of which only toppled a year or two ago – and evidence of old, long-fallen apple trees submerged beneath the tangle of grass. In short, there had been a sizeable orchard on the site – probably for centuries, given the pattern of so many similar farmhouses nearby, so I wanted to plant an orchard here again, made up of mostly local varieties of apple.

For the first five years, this part of the garden was a field occupied by an extremely bad-tempered Shetland pony. He was given to me by a friend and I quickly found out why he had got rid of him, as Charley Farley was the worst-tempered little brute I have encountered. He bit everyone except those he chose to kick, and sometimes he bit those too for good measure. He reminded me of the Joe Pesci character in *Goodfellas* and I grew rather fond of Charley, admiring his extreme, unmoderated belligerence. But he had to go before he hurt someone badly and then his field was freed for the orchard I dreamed of making.

The Orchard was planted with 39 different varieties of apple in the winter of 1997–1998. Over the last 20 years the trees, that were mere stick-like saplings when planted, have grown vigorously and are acquiring the indefinite age of mature apples, heavy of bough and spreading wide, yet still with a freshness and vigour that will keep them growing bigger for another quarter of a century and living well for a couple of hundred years. We now have enough to supply us with stored apples for ten months of the year, plus hundreds of bottles of apple juice from windfalls, as well as leaving a large amount on the ground for the birds and small mammals to eat over the winter months.

Herefordshire is a county redolent of the cidery tang of apples. Until the mid- to late eighteenth century the majority of apple orchards were for cider, and there were also beautiful perry orchards filled with huge pear trees – a tiny few of which still magnificently remain. But the orchards filled with dessert and cooking apples, still more present here than in any other part of the country, are largely the result of a huge boom in apple breeding in the nineteenth century that all began just down the road from here with Thomas Andrew Knight at Downton Castle. He went on to be president of what was then the Horticultural Society, which nearly 30 years after his death, took on royal patronage and became the Royal Horticultural Society.

Opposite page: A mown path cuts between the apple trees and through the long grass of the Orchard. The grass is underplanted with bulbs and is in the process of being converted to a wildflower meadow.

When the apple
trees are all in
blossom, the Orchard
is my favourite part
of the garden.

So the vast range of today's apples (there
are more than 7500 known varieties) are
effectively modern, and apples were not
often eaten or valued raw as they were
considered hard to digest until cooked,
right up to the seventeenth century.

I am now working the Orchard here
back into a rather more complex version
that combines fruit, flowers, meadow
and, after 25 years of growth, the
substance and heft of what have now
become mature trees.

That maturity can only be created by
using standard or half-standard trees. The
development and mass adoption of bush,
spindle-bush, dwarf bush and dwarf
pyramid trees in the twentieth century
thwarts the whole concept of an orchard
as an area of the garden given over to the
production of fruit. It removes the magic
and reduces it to an open-air version of
a fruit cage. This is fine (up to a point) for
commercial purposes and obviously useful

for people with limited space, but can
never offer the majesty and wonder
of a full-scale orchard.

I prune the trees regularly (see pages
399–400), not to reduce them in size but to
keep them open to allow good airflow and
stop them becoming too top-heavy. Large
apple trees blow over easily, especially when
they are laden with fruit in autumn gales.

Some trees have fallen, others were
planted too close together and have been
selectively removed. The size of the
Orchard has contracted dramatically.
Originally it covered the whole of the top
of the garden and gradually it has been
cut into to make the Vegetable Garden,
Cricket Pitch, Writing Garden, Soft Fruit
Garden and Orchard Beds. Some trees
were relocated to achieve this and others
remain as part of these areas.

Of course an orchard does not have
to just contain apples or indeed any
apples at all. Any fruit that is produced

on a tree – apples, pears, plums, cherries, damsons, medlars, mulberries, apricots or peaches – can constitute an orchard. If I have chosen to focus on apples – and I do have a large perry pear tree, a 'Shropshire Prune' damson and a recently planted mulberry all growing as part of the mix – that is because it seems right for this particular place and anyway, I love apple trees and apples.

I have planted more apple trees on more dwarfing rootstocks (see page 402) in the Cottage Garden borders, as well as cordons around the Soft Fruit Garden and step-over ones in the Vegetable Garden. In all there are now over 40 different apple varieties, five pears on 30 trees, damsons, a mulberry, four different plums, two medlars, two cherries, half a dozen fig trees and ten crab apples – all of which are classed as 'top fruit' but not all are in the Orchard, which is so much more than the sum of its individual trees.

Twenty years ago that young orchard was more a symbol of hope than anything else, and for the first few years a lot of imagination was required to get beyond the spindly trees that were slimmer than the stakes that supported them. One of the odd things about planting any new apple tree is that although the tree is a whisper of its mature self, its fruits are full-sized from year one. This is hardly surprising but of course it means that the fruits are dramatically large in comparison to the feeble branches that bear them. In the case of a few of my very large cooking apples, such as 'Glory of England', 'Newton Wonder' or even the very early 'Arthur Turner' that stews to a wonderful white froth, the weight of the fruit can snap the branches. There is nothing for it in this situation but to be tough and remove any fruit that might possibly cause damage until the tree is large enough to bear the fruit safely.

Despite this slow start, the Orchard has now become a rich and varied garden, with long borders flanking the main path through, and borders with what was formerly just long grass now a wildflower meadow, with two beehives at the far end and the chickens at the other.

Mistletoe grows in great balls from many of the branches, which is a measure of climate change – mistletoe thrives in mild, damp air – of the increase in winter-migrating blackcaps that eat the berries and spread them, and of the maturity of the trees that allows the required thickness of bark and cambium layer for the mistletoe roots to penetrate and grow well. I have planted Rambling roses up some of the trees – and picking apples has become something of a thorny business as a result – but the amazing swags and festoons of flower in June and July make up for that.

Over the years we have also kept pigs up there, looked after orphan lambs and always kept chickens, and all walks with the dogs begin from the Orchard. It is the link from garden to countryside beyond, which itself is rich with orchards old and new.

Although a new apple tree is a whisper of its mature self, its fruits are full-sized from year one

The Orchard Beds

Five years ago we dug up the Orchard. Not all you understand, but an ambitious chunk of it. It started as a simple idea – making a large bed under the apple trees with lots of shrubs – especially Species roses.

This evolved from two rather different situations. The first was the present of three piglets from my son in July 2011. These proceeded to charm us and devastate the Orchard in equal measure before, that autumn, evolving into delicious pork and home-cured bacon. But their earth-moving antics proved hard to repair and the livid scars remained amongst the apple trees.

At the same time I wanted to fulfil a long-held desire to plant clipped box and roses in between the apple trees. I think I had seen a picture of this in a garden in Normandy – great billowing shrubs spilling with roses and topped by the broad branches of mature apples – and I loved it. But box blight (see page 61) had made box too risky and our orchard is too small and the trees too close together to make the idea feasible. So we decided to dig up the areas the pigs had trashed and rather than plant between the trees across the whole orchard, we would just use one area. Anyway, that is how things work in this garden – an unplanned event provokes ideas, which spark action, which, in turn, leads to failure out of which something else interesting and more viable emerges.

The Orchard Beds, as they quickly became known, changed shape and size over the following year or so. Starting as a large square, they then took over the site of the old compost heap, wrapped themselves around Tom's Shed and, before we knew it, we had also added in a pair of long, flanking borders running right down to the edge of the garden. What had started life as one ambitious shrub border had become a whole garden with a cultivated area not much smaller than the Jewel Garden.

But unlike the Jewel Garden, we had to deal with shade from the apple trees, the physical presence of their roots and the way that they suck up a lot of the available moisture. The soil is very heavy – five years of mulching has lightened it a bit although it is still good old Herefordshire clay.

I ordered and planted roses first. Most of these were Species roses, such as *Rosa californica* 'Plena', *Rosa majalis* (syn. *R. cinnamomea*), *R.* 'Dupontii', *R. corymbifera* and *R.* x *alba*. These are tough, adaptable and able to handle light shade. I also

One word of warning about growing Ramblers into trees – be careful what you wish for

ordered Rambling roses to grow into the apple trees, including *R*. 'Ethel', *R*. 'Aimée Vibert', *R. multiflora* 'Carnea' and *R*. 'Climbing Cécile Brünner', along with about a dozen others. One word of warning about growing Ramblers into trees – be careful what you wish for. They are stunning and I have no regrets at all but now, five years on, most of the roses are bigger than the trees that support them so need pretty radical pruning annually or the tree suffers.

We then decided on a colour theme. We have done this with all parts of the garden, selecting a palette to work with and then choosing the plants to fulfil it rather than opting for certain plants and working the colours around them. I think this is because Sarah and I are fundamentally designers not plantspeople,

and always see the detail of individual plants working towards the bigger picture rather than creating a picture from an assembly of treasured individual plants. Both methods have their merits. There is no one way. Anyway, we wanted pinks, plums, blues and coppery-oranges with the odd touch of white to complement the apple blossom.

There are many kinds, intensities and manifestations of garden. Does it vary during the course of the day? Does it change during the seasons? Does it have dry shade or wet? How heavy is the shade at its heaviest and at its lightest? Does the front of the border experience the same shade as the back? With a pair of long borders such as the Orchard Beds, do the two borders get equal shade? Does the shade vary along their length?

The pair of long borders, filled with camassias in spring, flank the path down to the field gate at the edge of the Orchard. Until very recently this was just a mown path running through the long grass under the apple trees.

The Orchard Beds wrap around Tom's Shed – creating the largest borders in the garden – and flow in and amongst the fruit trees.

Then you can plant with a sophisticated depth of information to hand. For example, many spring-flowering perennials and bulbs need as much sun as they can get but because they flower before the leaves of the trees open fully, they have flowered and set seed before the shade becomes more intense. Others are remarkably adaptable as long as they get a few hours of sun a day – and it does not terribly matter if this is in the morning or afternoon.

We planted tellima, tiarella, Solomon's seal, *Euphorbia amygdaloides*, brunnera, epimediums, wood anemones, *Iris foetida*, foxgloves, thalictrum and lots of ferns in the shadiest bits – all of which either flower early or prefer shade. We created rhythm with peonies, both tree and herbaceous, planted along the length of the top half of the twin borders which is the sunniest half. Hybrid Perpetual and Rugosa roses also provide structure and amelanchier blossoms in early April before the apples come into leaf. *Cornus kousa* seems to be happy – our soil is not perhaps as acidic as it would prefer but it has not visibly

complained about that yet – whilst hydrangeas such as the lacecap *Hydrangea macrophylla* 'Lanarth White' and *H. arborescens* 'Annabelle' prefer shade but do not like to be too dry, so in a dry summer we have to remember to water them.

Viburnum plicatum f. *tomentosum* 'Mariesii' is wonderful at establishing body and yet remaining open and balanced with its surrounding planting, and the white flowers of spiraea shine out of the shade.

I planted a mass (500) of the fabulous pink-and-caramel tulip 'Bruine Wimpel' in the first autumn and they made a stupendous display in the spring of 2017 but have receded since then and I have not been able to get more bulbs to top them up. We planted camassia quamash to give a hit of spring blue and, like the tulips, in their first year they were terrific. The balance between the tulips and the camassias in the dappled shade of the blossom from the apple trees was a huge success and we patted ourselves on the back for our brilliance. But whilst the tulips declined noticeably in their second year, the camassias thrived and now, four years on, they have doubled both in individual plant size and quantity, and completely overshadow the accompanying tulips. It is another case of being careful what you wish for. In principle I would suggest that camassias are best planted into grass rather than as part of a mixed border because though they are a plant of open prairie meadow, even in shade they are too dominant.

Later in the year when the shade has deepened and the sun is higher, *Dahlia* 'Rothesay Reveller' is a star, flowering consistently for months, with its big raspberry-ripple deep crimson-and-white blooms held high on extra-long stems, seemingly unaffected by being in some degree of shade all day. The Rambling roses are a fantastic success and I have learned that they are part of the borders rather than an embellishment of the trees – so they should be chosen with that in mind.

Foxgloves are a delight and *Digitalis purpurea* 'Sutton's Apricot' is a favourite along with *D. p.* 'Dalmatian Peach'. Tobacco plants grow well – both *Nicotiana sylvestris* and *N.* 'Lime Green' – as do penstemons, alchemilla, hardy geraniums, lilies and the lovely thistle, *Cirsium rivulare* 'Atropurpureum', which flowers first in May and then again in late summer, and in the deepest, darkest shade. Acanthus makes a glossy green backdrop – although it is another thug so should be reserved for those places where little else will grow.

There are two lessons that I have learned from making these large borders under trees, although they are still an ongoing experiment and no doubt there will be many more lessons to come. The first is that if a plant can get two or three hours of light a day, then it will tolerate much more shade than might be imagined. The second is that the shadier a border is, the more important it is to enrich the soil so that it can retain moisture. Dry shade is really tricky and I had not realised quite how much moisture the apple trees suck up. So if you are planting under and around trees, be sure to mulch and to keep mulching every year – forever.

Rosa multiflora 'Carnea' scrambling and sprawling through the branches of an apple tree. Every standard tree in the Orchard now hosts a different Rambling rose.

The Writing Garden

The shed at the end of the Writing Garden was built by my son when he was twelve. It is set in a small self-contained area created by hawthorn hedges that I planted to line paths in the Orchard.

This rectangular area had five apple trees ('Worcester Pearmain', 'Lane's Prince Albert', 'Herefordshire Beefing', 'Rosemary Russet' and 'Laxton's Superb') and a mown path curving gently through long grass to the door of the shed.

But every May this grass was overtaken by cow parsley and it became a little garden of exquisite white umbellifers beneath the blossom of the apple trees. It was magical and as good as anything that my own horticultural efforts could conjure. I put a table and chair in the shed and began to use it to write in so, in a garden rapidly accumulating sheds of all kinds, it was called the 'Writing Shed'.

However, once the cow parsley was finished, the apple blossom had converted to fruit and the rains had flattened the long grass, it became a hedged-in little corner of scruffy orchard followed by mown grass. The magic was lost.

So in the winter of 2012–2013, we lifted all the turf, replaced the mown path with one made from recycled eighteenth-century bricks, and started planting specifically to try and sustain that May-time magic for as much of the year as possible. In effect, the garden is now one big border with a narrow path curving through it. And all the plants are white.

White gardens, inspired by Vita Sackville West's famous one at Sissinghurst, have been popular and occasionally highly fashionable for the past 70 years or so. But they are not easy to get right and that is because white is one of the more difficult colours to use well in a border. Too much white and it becomes rather blank and empty, and too little, and it ceases to be white.

I started with snowdrops and then moved to the lovely white daffodil 'Thalia' accompanied by the summer snowflake (*Leucojum aestivum*). The next most dominant plant is ammi. I use two types, *Ammi majus* and *A. visnaga*. The former has looser, more open umbels of white flowers and the latter has a tighter, more rounded dome. Both are absolutely lovely. *A. visnaga* is a better 'doer' insomuch as it lasts longer and flowers slightly later, but *A. majus* exactly hits the cow-parsley tone that I want. Both are easy to grow from seed, which is best sown in autumn with the young plants kept over winter in a cold frame then planted out in spring. However, there is one big problem with both – rabbits love ammi more than any other plant. I once put out a hundred plants I had carefully raised and the next morning all but eight were chewed-off stumps.

Opposite page: The Writing Garden was for many years part of the Orchard but is now essentially one large border divided by a curving brick path. It is a 'white' garden – which really means it is mostly green with white highlights.

The giant lily 'Casa Blanca' can reach over 2m (6ft) and flowers for six weeks in July and August.

The Writing Shed hosts the lovely Rambler 'Albéric Barbier' which flowers well in some shade.

Another superb annual umbellifer is *Orlaya grandiflora*, whose delicate white petals are carried in a graceful splayed umbel. I sow this in spring and plant it out in May. The rabbits seem to leave it alone.

I also added in the white tulips 'Spring Green' and 'Cheryl' as well as the early-flowering 'Lady Jane' that is pink when closed but opens in the sun to reveal a pure white inner face to its petals. I have the white *Allium stipitatum* 'Mount Everest', white foxgloves (*Digitalis purpurea* f. *albiflora*), *Nicotiana sylvestris*, the sweet white rocket (*Hesperis matronalis* var. *albiflora* 'Alba Plena'), *Dicentra spectabilis* 'Alba', white sweet peas – both annual and the everlasting *Lathyrus latifolius* 'Albus' – white *Cosmos bipinnatus* 'Purity', *Thalictrum delavayi* 'Album', macleayas, onopordums, astrantias, cardoons and white lupins. I have white buddleja, philadelphus, white hydrangeas and white roses – especially the lovely 'Blanche Double de Coubert'.

For height I have two white Rambling roses – 'Sander's White Rambler' and 'Wedding Day' – climbing the apple trees, and a few white clematis – *Clematis alpina* 'Albiflora', *C.* 'Alba Luxurians', *C. flammula*

Although we have fewer apples growing in this piece of garden, we have many more stored there because the Writing Shed is now the apple store

and *C*. 'Paul Farges'. Non-white flowers such as hellebores, foxgloves and *Alchemilla mollis* creep in and are either ruthlessly culled or ruefully accepted, according to my mood.

But a white garden is measured by the way that you use green. In fact, a white garden is really a green garden accompanied by white. By using all the different greens, from the darkness of yew or hellebore leaves through the silvery foliage of onopordums to the glaucous, almost blue-green of cardoons, you will add a world of depth to what otherwise can be rather flat white flowers. Even cow parsley is much more green than white.

Over the years the biggest problem has been shade. The flanking hornbeam hedge on the south side of the garden is very tall and cuts out a lot of light. But it also forms the north face of the Cricket Pitch, where its height is essential to create the right balance in that long alleyway. So I have removed two of the apple trees (the 'Lane's Prince Albert' and the 'Herefordshire Beefing'). This has reduced the shade and made more room, and in truth, we never liked the apples from either tree.

And although we have fewer apples growing in this piece of garden, we have many more stored there because the Writing Shed is now the apple store. I found that I was using the Writing Shed less and less and on the odd occasion when I did, the temptation to stop writing and start gardening was too great. So now, from September to June, when the last apple is eaten, the Writing Shed contains tray upon tray of carefully picked apples that I collect almost daily and take back to the house.

The Writing Garden was made to capture the spirit of cow parsley (*Anthriscus sylvestris*) and for a glorious week or so in May, it does just that.

The Paradise Garden

Looking through the tall stems of *Verbena bonariensis* to the Bus Shelter at the far end of the Paradise Garden. The Bus Shelter is very loosely derived from the pavilion at Chehel Sotun in Isfahan, Iran, rather than being a stop-off for the number 11 bus, but the name has stuck.

The Paradise Garden was made in 2018 after I had spent much of the previous year visiting Islamic gardens around the world for a television series.

After such a complete immersion in the various styles of Islamic gardens, ranging from the *pairidaeza* of Persia to the Mughal gardens of seventeenth-century India, wanted to make something that would be a memento of what had been a profoundly enlightening experience.

Islamic paradise gardens were created primarily as places of shelter from the burning sun and sources of the most precious commodity of all – water. But here, in the wet western fringes of Britain, in Herefordshire, we are long on rain and lush green but short on arid desert, so the

Islamic paradise gardens were created primarily as places of shelter from the burning sun and sources of the most precious commodity of all – water

Oranges and lemons in pots outside the Bus Shelter. These are taken in under cover over winter to protect them from too much rain as much as from the cold.

garden had to be adapted to the realities of our climate. It would need to be in our idiom and relate to our garden and world rather than be a show-garden pastiche.

The site was chosen because our 'top' (as in further from the house) greenhouse was not only unsafe beyond repair. It had to go. It had been moved to that site a year or two after I wrote the first edition of this book and had been moved five years before that, too. When it was cleared away it revealed – for the first time in fifteen years – a coherent space and a whole new area that would be ideal for our own Paradise Garden.

It was to be based upon the *charbagh*, the universal quadrilateral layout of the four-part *(chaha)* garden *(bagh)*, with four equal-sized beds centred around a water feature.

It had to be enclosed and secluded so that it acted as a peaceful retreat, and it had to have a building of sorts, both as a pleasant shelter and a place to store plants in winter.

The paradise-garden idiom dictated lots of fragrance as well as colour, and that the plants should be based primarily on fruits. In Islamic gardens the four fruits – olives, dates, figs and pomegranates –

In Islamic tradition, every paradise garden must have gently flowing water, so at the centre of ours is this bubble of water spilling over from a steel basin.

were essential and each had its own garden or section of the *charbagh*. Dates were not a viable option in Herefordshire but the other three grow well in pots.

Oranges and lemons arrived from India via the Silk Road by the eleventh century and were planted throughout Islamic gardens primarily for the fragrance and beauty of their flowers and fruit but also to provide bitter oil for cooking. Sweet oranges came much later. Flowers were grown beneath the fruit trees but not in borders as such. In any event, flowering was largely restricted to a brief spring explosion before the searing heat kicked in.

I have planted *Tulipa acuminata* in the four beds. These are the nearest modern tulip to the wonderfully long, slim tulips of the Ottoman dynasty in sixteenth-century Constantinople. They rise up through scores of the soft grass *Stipa tenuissima* – inspired by a garden I saw in Marrakech – and are followed by blue and burgundy cornflowers, *Verbena bonariensis*, *Gaura lindheimeri* and tulbaghia. There are roses at each corner and an 'Evereste' crab apple at the centre of each bed. As well as the oranges, lemons, olives and pomegranates growing in pots, I have madonna lilies that add their rich fragrance to the heavenly mix.

I suspected the garden should have had sunken beds, but this would have meant practical problems of soil removal – about 25 tons even from this very small area – as well as needing retaining walls, so I kept the beds at ground level. The water required a piped supply, a pump and electricity to power it. And it would all have to be done on the cheap. The glittering riches of the Mughal or Safavid empires were sadly lacking.

I seriously considered making a rill as they feature strongly throughout the world of Islam, but the budget stymied that (the Paradise Garden was made on a shoestring, costing about as much as the sandwich budget for the average Chelsea garden). In its place we have a very simple bubbling fountain set in a metal bowl – originally a fire bowl but with a hole drilled through it and a copper pipe passing down into a concrete-block tank below (see page 75 for details of how it was made).

Nothing could be simpler but it is mesmerising and immediately made the Paradise Garden a calm and reflective place. What began as an act of homage, almost an academic exercise, has become an important and much-loved part of the garden.

Above: In spring, *Tulipa acuminata* rise through the *Stipa tenuissima* grass. This tulip is the most similar now available to the tulips of the Ottoman court of the sixteenth and seventeenth centuries that so bewitched the Dutch and led to tulip mania in the 1630s.

The Wildlife Garden

I deliberately allow the Wildlife Garden to become as 'wild' as it can without losing what I consider to be its horticultural charm. These things are always subjective but above all, I have created it to be an inner haven at the heart of what is already a very wildlife-friendly garden.

It was made in 2015 primarily to show that you do not need a big area to attract a wide and rich range of wildlife to your garden, and also to demonstrate that a wildlife garden can be good for your fellow creatures as well as being beautiful and well gardened.

When the first edition of *The Complete Gardener* was published, this area contained a greenhouse, our soft fruit and two asparagus beds – amounting to the opposite of anyone's idea of being notably wildlife friendly. Then we moved them all to different parts of the garden and planted

Opposite page: The pond filled and planted in mid-spring. One of the beauties of making any pond is that it establishes and looks good astonishingly quickly.

Reshaping and enlarging the wildlife pond with the help of Nigel and Nellie.

hazels, an oak tree and a field maple in their place, all behind a high hawthorn hedge. Having done this we more or less left them alone to do their thing. As such, it truly was good for wildlife – but not very attractive in any conventional horticultural sense. So I set about seeing to what extent I could combine horticulture with a wildlife preserve.

The first thing I did was to make a pond. Any pond is good for attracting insects, birds and bats to your garden as well as the amphibians and reptiles that gravitate naturally to water. However, unlike with the pond in the Damp Garden (see page 149), I added a shallow beach made up of small stones, so birds and mammals could safely walk in and out of the water, plus a log floating on the surface that is ideal for beetles but which was also quickly used by basking birds and frogs.

I added marginal plants such as the flowering rush (*Butomus umbellatus*), the water plantain (*Alisma plantago-aquatica*) and the native flag (*Iris pseudacorus*), all moved from our existing pond. But crucially, over the following few years, I made no attempt to thin or clear any of these plants but let them sprawl, jostle and take over the pond. The water was still there but the cover dominated.

This was clearly doing good – frogs in particular loved it – but in 2020 I decided that the pond was too small and in the wrong place, so I moved it. I drained it, carefully rehoming all visible life and almost all the remaining water into the pond in the Damp Garden, and made it bigger and more central. I moved the path – made of shredded prunings from around the garden and topped up annually – so that it now skirts the extended pond and passes under the trees.

It still has the same virtues for wildlife – and it is astonishing how quickly it has been reoccupied – but not only does the pond look better, but the whole garden

Right: The native British flag iris *(Iris pseudacorus)* makes a superb marginal plant for any natural garden pond, looking spectacular as well providing excellent cover for a range of creatures.

The most important aspect of any wildlife garden is to have as much cover as possible. This can come from hedges, trees, marginal pond plants, weeds, long grass – but lots and lots of cover is the key.

seems more balanced and proportionate around it. It is now more than just an example of a wildlife sanctuary – it is also somewhere that we have been gravitating to sit in as the sun gently falls. This is especially pleasing because the intention was always to make a space that was as good for the gardener as for the rest of its occupants.

Neatness, selective pruning and weeding are out, and generous and varied cover are most definitely in.

I do not mind if the water becomes smothered in weed or algae as that is another form of cover, and if grasses seed

themselves in the margins, so much the better, as an area of long grass and nettles provides good cover as well as being caterpillar fodder for a range of butterflies such as red admirals, tortoiseshells, peacocks and commas.

Next to the pond I planted a border filled with plants chosen specifically to attract bees. In practice, it will also attract a range of other insects and pollinators, such as the many different wasps (over 230 different British species, of which more than 220 are solitary and entirely harmless), hoverflies and moths that our gardens depend upon. Recent

The blue globe heads of the echinops thistle are much loved by bees. We have planted a succession of nectar- and pollen-rich flowers for a year-round supply for bees and other pollinating insects.

research has concluded that it does not matter where a plant comes from in order to be suitable for bees, so there is no need to focus solely on native species, but how accessible its nectar is does make a big difference. Thus any plant that is open and simple, such as members of the daisy family or any that are set on a bobble, such as scabious and all members of the thistle family, are always going to be ideal for attracting honeybees. Bumblebees have longer tongues so are better adapted for plants that have more of a funnel shape, such as foxgloves.

I have also planted hazels and elders as well as an oak, weeping ash, hawthorn and field maple which, although still less than 20 years old, are large enough to provide a home for all kinds of nesting birds. Beneath them I encourage dense groundcover in the shape of lamium, geraniums, vinca and ivy. All these grow happily despite the dry shade and provide cover for insects and small mammals.

Although it looks very natural, the Wildlife Garden is as carefully planted and 'gardened' as any other part of Longmeadow.

Neatness and weeding are out, whilst varied cover is most definitely in

The Dry Garden

The Dry Garden was made in early 2004 from a yard in front of old stables we had used to store building materials over the previous decade. It had a tarmac covering, which I unpeeled with a shovel to reveal a solid bed of stone.

This is the old red sandstone that lies under the garden and is soft and, critically, very porous. Water flows through it and roots work their way down into it with surprising ease. We excavated 5–7.5cm (2–3in) of the stone – which was hard pick-and-shovel work – and added literally just a few inches of topsoil mixed with garden compost. The result was two beds flanking a curving path that were sheltered, sunny all day long and with a maximum depth of 10cm (4in) of soil before reaching the bedrock.

Of course, our Dry Garden gets no less rain than the Damp Garden and although we have never considered watering it, even in the driest periods, its dryness refers to the sharpness of drainage and paucity of organic material in its soil that will retain moisture rather than to the actual rain it receives.

I confess that I seriously doubted if anything would grow at all as the net effect was rather like raising plants in a shallow stone trough. I need not have worried. From the first, not only have the conventional dry-loving plants such as sedums, bearded irises, stipas and Mediterranean herbs loved it, but cardoons, foxtail lilies, miscanthus, cistus and even roses flourished.

Since then, it has been one of the least demanding parts of the garden, although it has had a couple of revamps, with all the plants lifted, the couch grass removed and everything replanted with judicious editing and revisions.

The choice of plants is both obvious and experimental. In the obvious group are included cistus, phlomis, santolina, figs, rosemary, artemisia, lavender, *Stachys byzantina*, irises, *Stipa gigantea* (stipas in general need really good drainage), alliums, tulips, foxtail lilies, opium

The rose 'Madame Caroline Testout' loves the south-facing wall of the Dry Garden and thrives despite the very shallow soil.

poppies, eschscholzia, *Euphorbia characias*, melianthus, mulleins and sedums.

In fact, sedums were the very first plants we originally planted there as in the Jewel Garden they flopped catastrophically in the over-rich soil, whereas on the poor fare of the Dry Garden they are half the size but upright, hardy and very, very happy. Likewise, *Knautia macedonica* is a floppy thug in the Jewel Garden but an upright, very well-behaved citizen in this shallow soil. Fennel seeds itself everywhere although never reaches the same stature as it does elsewhere, but what it lacks in size in the Dry Garden, it makes up for in quantity.

Achillea is half the size as the same plant elsewhere in the garden – but just as healthy and long-lasting when in flower. *Euphorbia characias* is happy in these meagre conditions in a way that it is nowhere else in the garden and the stachys has just the right balance between sturdiness and a charming inclination to be floppy. Lavender mostly struggles with our high rainfall, even when grown in pots made up with exceptionally gritty compost, yet is carefree and completely at home in the Dry Garden.

The experimental group never ceases to surprise me. Cardoons, teasels, roses and foxgloves love the conditions. There is a pear ('Concord') planted in 5cm (2in) of soil that not only bears a heavy crop each year but is the only one in the garden completely free from canker. The best guide is to see where plants seed themselves but it is always worth giving things a go. Rules are made to be broken.

What is certain however, is that on this sun-baked thin soil, plants have to be tough to survive. Yet the overall display is powerful and dramatic. The 'Madame Caroline Testout' rose flowers profusely against the walls of the barns and a large fig overhangs from the Walled Garden on the shady south side, with a much smaller (and much more productive) fig on the west-facing wall.

Everything grows tough in this spot and the combination of that necessary robustness and the extra-good drainage means that there is not a hint of trouble from any so-called pests or diseases. Fungal problems are also unknown and despite the relatively exotic provenance of some of these plants, cold does not seem to bother them down to about

-12°C (10°F), which can happen here, but only every four or five years. In fifteen years we have never watered, never mulched, never fed. We encourage self-seeding and like the tapestry veering towards jumble that inevitably follows this laissez-faire approach.

The contrast to the rest of the garden, with its rich, fat soil and overwhelming lushness, is so strong and so unexpected that it has expanded the range of the garden far beyond its actual layout. And there is the excitement of realising that, despite climate change and the baking heat and the lack of soil and the way that almost every rule is being broken, if you select the right plant for the right place, you can make lovely gardens almost anywhere.

The one part of the garden where we can grow bearded irises well is in the Dry Garden and for a few glorious weeks at the end of May, they are the richest, most voluptuous flowers in the entire garden.

The Coppice

I would swap my garden, or any garden ever made,
for a hundred acres of unspoiled deciduous woodland.
No habitat seems to me to be more congenial or rich in
sensuous experience.

It is partly the scale and relationship of objects to space, from the grandeur of a mature oak or beech to the intimacy of woodland flowers or even fallen leaves; partly the way that light constantly plays inside the trees, falling in beams and spangles or distant splashes; partly the sheer variety of flora and fauna that all coexist in a state of perpetual shifting poise; and partly the practicality and sustainability of the harvest.

Luckily the choice between my garden or a large wood is never likely to present itself – not least because it is perfectly possible to distil the essence of woodland within even a small garden. I set out to do this when I planted the Coppice back in 1995 from hazels that had self-seeded in the Spring Garden and which I had collected over a few years, potted up and grown on. It was initially a struggle to get the Coppice established as I was planting into grass and the young hazels were tiny little slips of tree. A mature coppice, dense with multi-stemmed hazels and a few standard trees towering over them, seemed a lifetime away.

Back in 2002 I wrote, 'My own coppice is not yet ready for cutting although it soon will be'. I actually made that first cut on a frosty February day in 2005, harvesting my own home-grown bean sticks for the first time, which was an experience every bit as satisfying as eating my home-grown beans.

The essence of coppice management – and as well as hazel, sweet chestnut, ash, oak, lime, beech, field maple, willow and alder all lend themselves to regular coppicing – is to cut all top-growth down to a stub or 'stool' on a regular cycle that will vary from species to species. The shortest cycle is just two or three years for willow, whilst oak is often cut only once every 25 or even 30 years. This winter pruning stimulates vigorous regrowth and does not significantly curtail root development, so you get bigger and bigger root systems that only have to support limited top-growth. As a result, the new growth is very fast and the tree can live for much longer than it otherwise would. Coppice lime or ash, for example, can live for over a thousand years, whereas an uncut tree is unlikely to live more than a third of that time.

It is perfectly possible to distil the essence of woodland within even a small garden

Above left: The hazels are cut tight to the ground leaving just a stool.

Above right: Coppicing involves clearing whole areas at a time rather than cutting a few stools each year, otherwise not enough light reaches the regrowth – or the emerging flowers.

Left: Once the hazels are cut, I clean off the tops and side shoots, which gives me clean sticks for climbing plants and plenty of 'brash' for pea sticks and for using in the borders.

Since then, the Coppice has been cut twice more, on a seven-year rotation, each time doubling the crop it produced as the hazels grew and their cut stools threw up ever more shoots. But however rewarding their generative process is, the resulting hundreds of bean sticks are only part of the story.

The standards – in this case all ash – have grown tall and I have pruned the lower branches back hard to let in more light to both the Coppice and the neighbouring Jewel Garden. With hindsight I would have planted fewer of them and probably substituted oak for ash. In my next life.

The cluster of now-mature hazels with their mass of straight shoots reaching 6m (20ft) tall creates a beautiful, half-lit space on the brightest day, but the floral understorey of primroses, wood anemones, bluebells, dog's tooth violets, stinking hellebores and *Euphorbia amygdaloides* is just as important. In fact, at the time of writing, I am planning to increase the planting significantly in one half of the Coppice to make it more 'gardened', whilst leaving the other half as natural as possible.

Coppice woodland is also a rich and idiosyncratic habitat for wildlife. Birds, butterflies, insects and mammals all use its cover, adapting and adjusting as it grows and then is cut back hard. In commercial woodland at any one time there will be areas at different stages of the coppice cycle so creatures can easily move to the exact amount of cover that suits em, whilst in a garden, it is always important to keep a good amount of cover even though part of the garden might be undergoing drastic pruning.

However, in a coppice, flowers have all evolved to accommodate a sudden influx of light, which allows them to germinate and grow, and then adapt as the light level reduces over the following years before the next coppice cut draws back the curtains to let the light flood back in again. So it is important to cut all growth or none rather than to prune selectively.

When the Coppice is all cut and tidied there are tall hazel rods for beans, clematis and any other climbers, bushy pea sticks bundled up at the back, and in the foreground, the rest tied up as faggots for the fire.

The Cricket Pitch

The path that runs right down the length of the garden, dividing it in two slightly uneven halves, runs from the Lime Walk, through the Cottage Garden, across the Long Walk, through the Jewel Garden, on between the two halves of the Coppice, and finally arrives to continue down the middle of the Cricket Pitch until it reaches the end of our plot.

Opposite page: The Cricket Pitch is the culmination of the path that runs right down the middle of the garden like a nave, transforming from a flower-filled meadow in spring to mown grass with formal topiary in late summer and autumn.

For half the year, between late February and August, this path down the Cricket Pitch is the width of a mower but then, after the grass is cut until early spring, it is mown weekly and the grass kept short. Running down either side are large pots – made in Italy for citrus trees but far too big to move indoors in winter, so holding much hardier, topiarised box. Bounding the whole thing are 3.5m (12ft) tall hornbeam hedges.

Although we call it the Cricket Pitch, no cricket ball has been bowled there for 20 years (although plenty of tennis balls have been chased by ball-obsessed golden retrievers). My children grew uninterested in sport, I hurt my shoulder so could not bowl and the cricket net became a protective barrier against pigeons eating the cabbages.

We transplanted a horse chestnut in the bucket of a digger when we reconfigured the Mound and this became a focal point.

It grew well and quickly became large until one exceptionally windy April day in 2017, when it split down the middle. So I took it down and have replaced it with a fastigiate hornbeam that stands as an upright candle of a tree at the end of this long strip.

Just after the original edition of this book was published, we replaced the apple trees of the Cricket Pitch (moving them to the Orchard) with the hornbeam hedges on either side – tiny back then but now great 4.5m (15ft) ramparts – and a few years later, decided to let the lawn grow out where the original cricket net was situated. We planted crocuses, wild daffodils and snake's head fritillaries into the grass, followed by *Camassia leichtlinii* and tulips, and nowadays an increasing amount of perennials – what the Americans call 'forbs'. So in a few years it was transformed from the strip of highly tended cricket wicket to become a long, thin meadow filled with flower. However, I like it best when the grass is newly cut and the hedges and box cones freshly trimmed, and for a week or so it stands as a cool, balanced space separating the planting intensity of the Vegetable Garden and Writing Garden, and leading to the floral business of the rest of the garden.

Although we call it the Cricket Pitch, no cricket ball has been bowled there for 20 years

The Grass Borders

When I wrote the first edition of this book, the Jewel Garden was about 30 per cent bigger than it is now.

Opposite page: By midsummer the borders have filled out and the grasses are tying the rest of the planting together.

In spring the grasses are just beginning to grow and the Grass Borders are dominated by the new green leaves and the purple heads of *Allium hollandicum* 'Purple Sensation'.

This was because the area that is now filled with grasses – which is slightly predictably known as the Grass Borders – was a continuation of the Jewel Garden, its beds filled with the same rich colours from the first tulip to the last brave showing of a dahlia. But when we started to film *Gardeners' World* here in 2011, we made the decision to lose some jewels and gain some grasses. So we converted this area into completely separate borders, with all the jewel flowers redistributed amongst the reduced Jewel Garden in return for the various grasses that had been scattered around the whole area.

I planted almost all the grasses in one session on a June evening after I came home from *Gardeners' World Live* clutching four heavy bags of miscanthus, stipas, calamagrostis, molinias and deschampsias. There have been additions, but surprisingly few, and almost no housekeeping needed at all.

Grasses add a delicacy and shimmering elegance to any border but when planted en masse, have a flowing energy that no other planting can replicate. Twenty years ago they were just becoming popular through the work of designers and growers such as Piet Oudolf, but over the past few decades they have become an accepted style, with 'prairie planting' being distinctly trendy – not least because it does need very little maintenance.

There are two ways of using grasses. The first is to have a few dominant grasses planted across a whole area, through which ornamental plants can weave and thread. This is usually known as 'matrix' planting. The second is to have a larger variety of types of grasses planted in groups, drifts and clumps, and to work other plants around them – and this is how I planted the Grass Borders.

In spring they are slow to grow and have little to show for themselves before May, but the new growth, when it does come, is a flush of vibrant greens that

By September the grasses have grown to their full size and throughout autumn and into winter, when much else of the garden has faded, they remain a rich tawny tapestry of upright stems and leaves.

steadily rise to a green crescendo in July. After that starts the slow transformation to the tapestry of autumn colours, all browns, golds, coppers and faded yellows touched with burgundy and purple, like the feathers of a tawny owl. Then they gently fade to their bleached winter guise, upright and shifting with every breeze, which gives them a soft but vibrant sibilance when the rest of the garden is bowed under the yoke of winter.

In fact, remnants of the old jewel planting remain in the guise of the intense *Allium hollandicum* 'Purple Sensation' and the bright orange tulip 'Ballerina', both of which used to fill this area and still obstinately cling to the territory. Two huge

Rosa moyesii are also still there at the back of the borders, spangled with bright red flowers in June and festooned with their distinctive orange, bottle-shaped hips in autumn. I added cardoons, onopordums, heleniums, rudbeckias, cirsiums, *Angelica gigas*, *Knautia macedonica*, coreopsis, tree dahlias, kniphophias, *Helianthus salicifolius*, inulas and macleayas in amongst the grasses, and encouraged thalictrum, *Verbena bonariensis*, asters and mulleins to self-seed, together with masses of fennel, both bronze and green.

In the centre of these borders is a paved square with a lime tree (*Tilia cordata*) planted in each corner. I have trained these to form a pleached pergola that we prune back to its bare skeleton every February. It is a very sunny site and the emerging growth provides just enough shade in summer to be pleasant but not so much as to curtail the growth of the plants – all of which do best in full sun.

Underneath this lime pergola is a large Cretan pot – one of a pair given to us by a friend. It acts as the focal point looking down from the Jewel Garden and its twin is situated so that it is the eye-catcher of both the Lime Walk and the long path that divides the Grass Borders from the Jewel Garden and the Cottage Garden from the Damp Garden.

Once planted, no other part of the garden has demanded less maintenance. All the top-growth is cleared away in March, with the deciduous grasses like miscanthus being cut right back to the ground and the evergreen ones, like stipas, having any dead growth combed out with fingers or a rake. After all the growth is cleared away to the compost heap, we plant, divide or move any herbaceous plants. Grasses should not be planted or divided until there is strong new growth, which can be as late as mid-May in a cold spring and is never before late April.

We mulch every other year with pine bark, which slightly raises the acidity that most grasses prefer but does not increase the fertility, as this results in growth that is too soft and sappy. The alternate non-mulched years give self-sown plants such as teasels, fennel, thalictrums and pheasant grass (*Anemanthele lessoniana*) the chance to establish.

Each of the four large beds was originally bounded by box hedges. I loved the contrast between the neat symmetry of the clipped box and the untrammelled looseness of the grasses, but we have had to rip out all the box hedges due to the depredations of box blight (see page 61). For the first half hour or so after doing this, it felt like amputation. But then I realised that it was liberation. The borders were freed. The box was lovely but these large areas of grasses are lovelier without them. It is as though they have become more like themselves.

This is partly structural. Thanks to the absence of a horizontal line around them, the strong vertical lines of the dried miscanthus and calamagrostis that dominate for half the year are much more. Also, the language and influence of the Jewel Garden, with its tightly defined spaces spilling over with flowers, has been removed, so taking out the box hedges made the Grass Borders much more of a separate area. In short, the Grass Borders had come into their own.

Remnants of the old planting remain in the guise of the intense *Allium hollandicum* 'Purple Sensation' and the bright orange tulip 'Ballerina'

The Herb Garden

The Herb Garden
has taken the place
of the 64 box balls
that were ruined by
box blight, and
although that
felt like a disaster
at the time, the
Herb Garden works
very well.

The current Herb Garden is the result of the most
dramatic forced change to the whole garden. This area
was a stony yard when we arrived, albeit one covered
in 1.8m (6ft) high nettles.

It is backed by the high brick walls of the
hop kilns to the south and a path runs
north into the Cottage Garden and on
down into the Damp Garden. Another
path crosses this, leading from the house
to the potting shed, and is the main route
from the house into the garden. We pass
through the Herb Garden scores of times
a day so it is much more than just a place
where we grow kitchen herbs.

For many years this space was occupied by
64 clipped box balls. When I originally
cleared it I found it almost solid stone,
so dug 64 pits, employed the excavated
cobbles as a surface and used existing box
plants and cuttings. Over the years these
became large, irregular balls – although
they were deliberately cobble-shaped and
not round. As they grew they acquired
individuality, like 64 characters in a play.

I loved the repeated simplicity of the design and the evergreen rhythm that ran through all the seasons. But disaster struck in the shape of box blight (see page 61).

We tried to save the box balls by using biochar, seaweed feed, not cutting, not feeding, but nothing worked. They became threadbare and looked awful. So, one January day in 2017, we dug them all up and burned them. For a day the empty space was desolate but it then became an exciting new opportunity.

I planted eighteen Irish yews – which were by far the most expensive plants I have ever bought – and used these to recreate the grid and repeated rhythm of evergreen plants that had been such an effective aspect of the box balls, but providing a vertical framework rather than a low horizontal one. The planting holes of the box in the sunniest part of the area have been kept and deliberately filled with poor, gritty soil for Mediterranean herbs like thyme and sage. The shadier side now has a brick seating area surrounded by beds. We replaced the brick paths that were crumbling badly and made them slightly wider.

The brick wall on the western side now supports two roses, 'Madame Alfred Carrière' that has already become rampant, and the rather shier 'Souvenir du Docteur Jamain' in the shadiest half. I planted more pleached limes to separate this new area from the longstanding herb beds near the house, now paved and surrounded by fragrant herbs and flowers.

Given the chance I would have my (healthy) 64 large clipped box boulders back again. But nothing in gardening ever

The path leading to the Cottage Garden is flanked by Irish yews and a rosemary hedge of 'Miss Jessop's Upright'. On either side, fennel grows tall and Mediterranean herbs such as thyme and oregano love the impoverished, stony ground.

stays the same. The box balls were so strong and such a powerfully simple design that it has taken a while for this completely new design to bed in and become a space in its own right. But it works.

The Vegetable Garden

Although the vegetables have shifted around the garden – starting in what is now the Cottage Garden, moving up where the top greenhouse is now, taking root where the tunnel used to be, and a second plot added in what was formerly a nursery area – essentially, the same crops are grown in the same way in the same soil.

The location within the garden does not dictate what we grow or how we grow it. However, wherever it is situated, the Vegetable Garden is always one of the central and busiest parts of the whole garden.

And it has changed in the way it looks, too. The first Vegetable Garden, that remained until 2011 and which is now the Cottage Garden, had 24 beds, initially edged with woven-hazel fences, which were then replaced by clipped box. This meant that it morphed in appearance from a Tudor-inspired plot to a much more formal potager, what with its pleached limes, espaliered pears and hundreds of metres of neatly clipped box hedges.

I then made a number of raised beds in a new area (where the wooden greenhouse now stands) and this meant that we could grow a much greater quantity of vegetables and to some extent, better quality, as raised beds meant better drainage and were earlier to warm up in spring.

But as I have already said, when we began filming *Gardeners' World* here in 2011, the paths were too narrow for the cameras to fit so I made new ones and a whole new vegetable plot with both raised and conventional beds. There is no doubt that raised beds (see page 84) are the most space-efficient way to grow vegetables domestically and, for our heavy soil and high rainfall, the best way of extending the season by improving drainage and warming the soil.

I added another plot a few years later as a kind of overspill – so we are a two-veg-garden household and yet I still feel short of space to grow the amount and diversity of vegetables that I would like. Perhaps like work and time, vegetables will always expand to fill the space allotted to them.

Opposite page: I have grown vegetables since I was a small boy and in many ways the vegetable plot will always be the beating heart of the garden for me.

I made a number of raised beds which meant we could grow a much greater quantity of vegetables

The plants

Herbaceous perennials

Our flower borders, in the various parts of the garden, include trees, shrubs, perennials, bulbs and annuals all grown together. These tend to be known as 'mixed' borders and are now completely standard.

But until the 1970s and 1980s it was still very common for gardens to have borders comprised entirely of herbaceous perennials and I remember in my childhood the herbaceous border being the main floral showpiece of my parents' garden.

Herbaceous perennials have evolved to survive harsh winter conditions by having no woody growth or permanent structure, with all their growth above ground dying back completely in autumn whilst the roots remain perfectly healthy, if largely dormant, below ground. They then put on vigorous new growth in spring – sometimes, as in a cardoon, to a phenomenal extent. The dead growth from the summer acts as insulation against the cold as well as rotting down to provide nourishment. Because a herbaceous perennial's season is so short, the plant has to grow with tremendous vigour in order to flower and set seed before autumn. Hence the dramatic transformation in the herbaceous borders in the months from April to the end of July.

There are other herbaceous plants that maintain their foliage over winter – such as hellebores – with new growth adding to it and the old leaves dying back over spring. In principle, a perennial goes on living from year to year but in practice, there is a huge range of life expectancy, from three or four years for the average lupin to a hundred years for a peony. However long-lived, most are extremely tolerant of being dug up, split, moved around and generally manhandled. This is what makes them so invaluable to any gardener.

Opposite page: Our borders are a mix of shrubs, perennials, bulbs, annuals and tender plants but herbaceous perennials are the constant that sets the tone and choice of all the surrounding plants.

Above left: Delphiniums are the archetypal English herbaceous perennial, sending up spires of blue flowers in June. When they have finished they should be cut back to the ground and they will reflower at the end of summer.

Above right: White lupins growing on the Mound. As well as performing in June, they flower again in late summer if cut back hard after that initial display.

In the wild, perennials have adapted to every different type of environment and climate as a means of competing with trees and shrubs and grazing animals. Spring perennials tend to originate from woodland and put on most growth and flower before the leaf canopy shades them out. In summer they are dormant and start growing again in early autumn as the leaves begin to fall. Some will grow high on mountainsides, where trees and shrubs cannot survive, and are well adapted to summer drought. Others come from grass plains where they avoid being grazed through their spines or unpalatability.

The great beauty of an herbaceous plant is the never-failing element of surprise that comes with its renewal each spring. It adds the electricity to a mixed border and the lushness that can only come with rapid growth. So however old-fashioned the true herbaceous border is, dying back to a bleak emptiness in winter, herbaceous plants will always be part of any garden. There is something wonderful about the sheer volume of growth an herbaceous plant can make in a season, and added to their vigour is their hardy longevity – some herbaceous plants last for decades and easily survive the worst weather that our climate can muster.

Growing perennials

Because herbaceous plants live a long time and grow so fast, they need a lot of nourishment.

This starts with the soil, and the better the soil, the better the plants will thrive. Good soil has lots of organic matter incorporated into it and before planting it is best to dig over a proposed perennial border, breaking up any compaction and adding lots of manure or compost.

Traditionally, all plants were taken out of herbaceous borders so the soil could be redug every three or four years, but there is no need for this. Once a border is planted, an annual mulch tops up the soil nutrition and structure as well as suppressing weeds and retaining moisture.

If you have a new garden with a new house, you are very likely to have compacted soil as a result of the builders driving over and over it with forklift trucks. In this case you must break through that compaction pan and dig the soil to at least a spade's depth. There is no easy solution to this and it will be horribly hard work. Get stuck in. Better still, persuade someone else to stick in for you. Either way, what you want is soil that has enough body to retain moisture but also enough drainage to stop it becoming waterlogged.

When herbaceous borders were redug every three or four years, the plants were all divided before replanting. This increased plant stock and, more importantly, renewed the plants' vigour and flowering performance. This is because most herbaceous plants tend to grow outwards from the centre. After a few years this leaves a 'doughnut' effect, with a hollow or weak centre producing few or no flowers and all the best flowering in the external ring of new growth.

It is still a good idea to regularly lift and divide most herbaceous perennials to refresh and reinvigorate their performance. The best thing is to take healthy sections from the outside, cutting it with a sharp spade or teasing the roots apart if these are fibrous, and ditching the interior. This regenerates the plant, gives you a chance to get any weeds out of the roots and also provides more healthy plants. It also means that you can redesign your borders periodically.

The best time to plant herbaceous perennials is either in autumn, when the soil is still warm enough for the roots to grow a little and get established, or in spring, just as there are signs of new growth above ground.

Some favourite herbaceous plants

- *Acanthus mollis;
  A. spinosa*
- *Aconitum* x *bicolor*
- *Alcea rosea*
- *Alchemilla mollis*
- *Anchusa azurea*
  'Loddon
  Royalist'
- *Anemone* x *hybrida*
- *Aquilegia vulgaris*
- *Astrantia major;
  A. maxima*
- *Avens*
- *Crocosmia*
  'Lucifer'
- *Cynara cardunculus*
- *Delphinium*
- *Echinops*
- *Euphorbia characias*
  subsp. *wulfenii*
- *Filipendula rubra*
  'Venusta'
- *Geranium endressii*
- *Hemerocallis*
- *Hosta*
- *Inula magnifica*
- *Kniphofia*
- *Ligularia
  przewalkskii;
  L. dentata*
- *Lupinus*
- *Macleaya cordata*
- *Monarda*
  'Cambridge
  Scarlet'
- *Nepeta*
- *Paeonia*
- *Papaver orientale*
- *Phlomis russeliana*
- *Rheum palmatum*
- *Rodgersia*
- *Rudbeckia*
- *Sedum*
- *Verbascum*
- *Verbena bonariensis*

Crocosmia 'Lucifer' never fails to blaze into dramatic flower year after year.

A border must be composed with all the care of a picture, paying attention to colour, shape, height and texture. You need height at the back, using plants such as *Macleaya cordata*, rudbeckias, filipendulas and inulas to give the border a sense of scale. These tall plants need to be planted in groups so that they do not look too spindly. Oriental poppies, lupins, phlox and plants with bare stems should go in the middle of the border, so the plants in front of them will hide their naked nether regions but not obscure their flowers. Plants such as sedums and *Alchemilla mollis* are ideal for the front, spilling over onto a path or lawn. And always plant in blocks and clumps rather than individual dots. This takes great discipline in a small garden as the temptation is to collect more and more different plants, but you must decide whether you want a beautiful garden or an impressive collection. It takes great expertise to make the two compatible.

Because they grow so fast, herbaceous plants are very soft and will bend, buckle and break in bad weather so they must be supported. The secret is to provide support before they need it and not as a salvage job after a storm. You can use bamboos, which are effective but ugly, proprietary metal supports, which are pricey, string stretched between inconspicuous uprights and around each clump of plants or, best of all, twigs and branches cut specially for the job the previous winter. These are stuck into the ground all around each clump and become hidden as the plants grow.

If you are starting anew, either with a border or a whole garden, buy your herbaceous perennials small and in bulk. This is much cheaper than large specimens from a garden centre and enables you to plant the whole area at once. The nature of herbaceous plants is to grow very fast, giving you a mature border in a couple of years. Also, because they do not mind being moved, you can rearrange them over the course of the coming few years in the light of their maturity.

Perennials for moist conditions

There are a lot of perennials that do well in the mild, moist conditions that feed their fast, lush growth.

In a normal year a border is too dry for these plants except in the heaviest of ground, and by August they are looking as exhausted and dehydrated as a runner crossing the marathon finish line. Of course there is a fine line between true bog plants – like gunneras and *Rheum palmatum* – and plants that merely do well when the ground is wetter than normal. A true bog never dries out and is really permanent mud, and whilst it certainly feels that way here for weeks on end, by the end of summer the ground may well

be very dry indeed. So the perennials that are likely to adapt best to the climatic shift towards wet winters and dry summers are those that are happiest with a substantial amount of wet locked into the soil but able to cope with a couple of months' real dryness each summer.

Astrantias love our rather heavy, damp soil and are an excellent plant for attracting pollinators.

Large perennials for moist conditions

- *Astilbe rivularis*
- *Campanula lactiflora*
- *Eupatorium purpureum*
- *Filipendula rubra*
- *Inula magnifica*
- *Ligularia przewalkskii;* *L. dentata*
- *Lythrum salicaria*
- *Phormium tenax*
- *Rheum palmatum*
- *Rodgersia*
- *Rudbeckia*
- *Thalictrum delavayi;* *T. speciosissimum*

Medium-sized perennials for moist conditions

- *Achillea*
- *Astilbe*
- *Astrantia major*
- *Cirsium rivulare*
- *Euphorbia palustris*
- *Helenium*
- *Hemerocallis*
- *Heuchera*
- *Hosta*
- *Iris sibirica;* *I. pseudacorus;* *I. laevigata*
- *Knautia macedonica*
- *Lobelia*
- *Lychnis chalcedonica*
- *Lysimachia*
- *Lythrum*
- *Rudbeckia fulgida*
- *Trollius*

Small perennials for moist conditions

- *Ajuga reptans*
- *Bellis perennis*
- *Geum* 'Borisii'
- *Primula*
- *Viola*

Perennials for dry soil

Fewer perennial plants like to be in truly dry, thin soil and as a rule, bulbs and some shrubs have evolved to cope with real heat and drought much better.

Below left: In the Dry Garden, fennel, *Euphorbia characias* and acanthus are all very happy in the shallow, fast-draining soil.

Below right: *Nepeta* 'Six Hills Giant' growing on the Mound. In dry soil it remains upright whereas if too wet, it flops everywhere.

However, there are some perennials that will do well and quite a few others cope.

The first thing to do before planting them is to dig in – or at least thickly mulch with – plenty of organic matter. This will improve moisture retention whilst simultaneously opening the soil out so roots can delve deeper, reach moisture further from the surface and therefore grow better. There is no need to worry if the top 5–7.5cm (2–3in) of the soil is bone dry if the roots are deep and can find moisture further down.

Then choose your plants wisely. There are certain outward signs that indicate that a plant is likely to cope well with drought. The first is a silvery colour. This comes from a coating of fine hairs on the leaf surface, giving a felted or woolly texture, as with lamb's ear (*Stachys byzantina*) or *Artemisia schmidtiana*. The coating reflects light and reduces moisture loss through transpiration. A bluish tinge to the leaf such as that found in *Artemisia* is often caused by a waxy protective coating.

Another clue to a plant's ability to withstand drought is the size of its leaves. As a rule, the bigger the leaf, the more water it needs. But even plants that survive drought well need watering when first planted and will benefit from a well-dug soil with lots of added organic material.

For most of these plants it is not dryness that they require but drainage. All of them hate sitting in water, especially when it is cold, so good drainage is essential.

Sedum spectabile in all its manifestations is ideal for dry conditions and its flowers are a magnet for late-summer butterflies and insects. Of the grasses, all stipas are happy with sun, dry soil and very sharp drainage and *Briza media* and *Pennisetum advena* 'Rubrum' are likewise drought-tolerant. Once established, *Crambe cordifolia* is very drought-resistant too, as are cardoons. Both these add real presence and structure. The giant fennel (*Ferula communis*) is another statuesque plant for dry conditions (although it also grows well in our not-very-dry Grass Borders).

Most euphorbias prefer hot, sunny, well-drained spots and nepeta loves them. *Verbena bonariensis* likes summer to be as hot as possible and *Leonotis leonurus* is only really happy in our rare blazing years.

Achillea copes well and eryngiums of all kinds are happy. White gaura (*Oenothera lindheimeri*) is best with sharp drainage although can be a little tender so I treat it as an annual or at best a very short-lived perennial. *Lychnis coronaria* and *Knautia macedonica* are much more upright in dry spots than the sprawling versions we have in our heavy soil, and oriental poppies adapt well.

Of the umbellifers, *Seseli libanotis* is the best for dry spots, although like the gaura, it has a habit of disappearing over winter in this garden. However, it is very easy to grow from seed. Tulbaghia has become one of my favourites and we grow it in the Paradise Garden and the Dry Garden. It will flower endlessly even in the harshest conditions.

Tulbaghia violacea is a rhizomatous perennial that I plant out into the Paradise Garden as well as grow in pots. It is not fully hardy – especially when wet – so I lift it and bring it into a cold frame in winter.

Even plants that survive drought well will benefit from well-dug soil with lots of organic material

Perennials for shade

The combination of shade cast by leaves and evolution has seen to it that many plants have adapted and learned to love the gloom. And of course, there is shade and shade.

There is dry shade, which is tricky and has fewest plants that actually want to be in its category, and wet shade, which produces a wide range of invariably lush, leafy plants.

The amount of light that makes up shade varies from a haze of cloud to total gloom. So the daylong dark in the lee of a high, north-facing wall is an altogether different class of shade from the dappled pebbles of shadow that a deciduous tree drops from its leaves in mid-spring.

The timing of shade, both during the diurnal cycle and the annual one, is also very relevant to the type of plants that will make best use of it, both for themselves and for your gardening pleasure. Deciduous woodland plants have learned to flower early, before the canopy of the trees shades out all light, and to put on healthy growth despite the shade overhead. They are ideal for a garden that only gets early-morning sun. From then

Below left: Pulmonaria vallarsae thrives in shade.

Below right: Japanese anemones will grow equally well in sun or shade.

Hellebores love the dappled shade of the Orchard Beds.

through to leaf-fall, these plants – like primroses, violets and bluebells – are under an umbrella of leaves and they hibernate throughout what is for them a long summer's night. These plants have also learned to love what they cannot avoid, and that is an annual dressing of falling leaves that rot down to create a soil that is almost pure leafmould – which is the perfect growing medium for all woodland plants.

Perennials for shade

- *Ajuga*
- *Alchemilla mollis*
- *Anemone* x *hybrida*
- *Aquilegia vulgaris*
- *Astrantia*
- *Brunnera*
- *Euphorbia amygdaloides* var. *robbiae*
- *Geranium phaeum*
- *Helleborus argutifolius; H. foetidus; H.* x *hybridus*
- *Hosta*
- *Lamium*
- *Lamprocapnos spectabilis*
- *Lysimachia*
- *Pulmonaria*

Annuals and biennials

Annuals have always been a key part of any garden's armoury. In an age of instant garden gratification and magic transformation, no flowers do more in less time than annuals.

A packet of seed, costing less than a small perennial plant, will make scores if not hundreds of flowering annuals, most of which grow easily and reliably.

An annual is any plant that germinates, grows, flowers and sets seed in the same growing season – usually between March and October in this country, although some annuals, like field poppies and corn marigolds, can string together a complete life cycle in around three months. Drought will speed up the cycle as they race to set seed before the lack of water kills them. In the wild most annuals are found in cornfields or on dry open slopes. They are rarely found in tightly packed places, interspersed with shrubs or in damp conditions – situations that are closer to the average back garden than to a cornfield. Most annuals prefer to be dry and in full sun when in flower, and a wet summer reduces many to soggy tissue.

It is astonishing how big a slice of plant sales is made up of bedding plants designed to make a bright but brief performance that adds an instant splash of colour. Hundreds of millions of them are sold each year, making up over a third of all plants sales by value.

I like bedding. It is cheerful and lifts our spirits after a long winter. Annual bedding plants can be used in containers, hanging baskets, mixed borders or as a display on their own. They are fun.

But there are some downsides to this. Bedding plants are almost all mass-produced by a small handful of large growers using unsustainable, environmentally unfriendly methods. And for the cost of a tray of bedding, you can buy up to half a dozen packets of seed, each one of which will give

Opposite page: Sweet peas in the Cottage Garden. These are climbing annuals, sown in autumn or spring, flowering from June to October and then setting seed to repeat the process next year.

you half a dozen trays of plants from a range of flowers.

Every year I grow from seed a wide selection including tobacco plants, tithonias, leonotis, sunflowers, nasturtiums, marigolds, salvias, cleome, cosmos, cornflowers, nigella, gauras, *Ammi majus*, *Orlaya grandiflora*, rudbeckias, *Cerinthe major*, sweet peas, poppies (Shirley, field, opium and Californian) and zinnias. I also grow biennials – wallflowers, foxgloves, sweet rocket and antirrhinums – and use them as bedding. Other gardeners will have a list just as long composed of entirely different plants.

Officially there are three kinds of annuals – hardy, half-hardy and tender, but to all intents and purposes these can be reduced to two – those that can withstand frost (hardy) and those that cannot (tender).

Hardy annuals are 'long day' plants, which come from the northern hemisphere and have their growth pattern triggered mainly through changing light levels. As the days lengthen in spring, the plants grow very quickly and then, as the days shorten after midsummer, there is an increasing urgency to flower and set seed before the onset of winter.

So plants such as cornflowers, poppies and nigella grow in response to light and can cope with cold – although none enjoys it. As a result it is often best to sow hardy annuals directly where they are to grow, knowing that the seedlings will survive a late cold snap.

Tender annuals are 'short day' plants, which come from closer to the equator and are less influenced by light than by heat and moisture. This is because the light on the equator is more or less constant throughout the year. As the days get shorter from 21 June, they also get warmer. Hardy annuals start their inevitable movement towards producing fewer flowers and more seed as a race against the dying light to provide new plants for next year, whereas tender annuals are doing the exact opposite. They start flowering in earnest and will stay flowering until the weather cools down, regardless of falling light levels.

Tender annuals like sunflowers, tithonias, zinnias or petunias cannot be safely planted outside in this garden until well into May although in a large city, frost is much less likely after mid-April. They also need heat in order to germinate so must be raised in a greenhouse or indoors on a windowsill. Having been mollycoddled through their first few months of growth, they also need acclimatising to the atmospheric conditions – hardening off – for at least a week and preferably two before planting out.

Annuals can be divided into two groups – those that can withstand frost (hardy) and those that cannot (tender)

Annuals for damp soil

Many annuals do not grow well in wet sites but there are some that will make the best of the damp.

Poached egg plants will grow anywhere, wet or dry, and can be broadcast on almost any soil surface, *Mimulus* spp. grow best in the wet and pot marigolds like moist soil. Sweet peas are a must for really rich, damp soil and sunflowers do surprisingly well in the wet, too. I tend to associate them with sun and heat and therefore dryness but this is not so. Do remember to stake sunflowers much more securely than you can possibly imagine being necessary, otherwise by late summer they blow all over the place. Evening primrose is not conventionally a moisture lover but it grows freely in the wettest parts of our garden. It is not fashionable but I am very fond of it and love the way it seeds itself everywhere.

Annuals for the wet

- *Atriplex hortensis*
- *Calendula officinalis*
- *Lathyrus odoratus*
- *Limnanthes douglasii*
- *Mimulus* spp.

Above: Red orache (*Atriplex hortensis* var. *rubra*) is a dramatic plant, growing 2.5m (8ft) tall but when young, the leaves are delicious to eat.

Right: Sweet peas respond to drought by setting seed, which reduces their flowering, so they are happiest in damp soil, where they flower more prolifically and for longer.

Climbing annuals

Sweet peas are the best of all the annual climbers. There is no point in growing a sweet pea that does not smell sweetly, so avoid most modern varieties and stick to reliably scented plants like the Spencer group.

Sweet peas grow very well up trellis or netting, or in a pot up a wigwam of canes. If planted at the base of a wall they will need lots of water. They also like the richest soil possible. If you keep picking the flowers, they will flower on into August.

Black-eyed Susan (*Thunbergia alata*) will grow to 3m (10ft) and has striking yellow or orange flowers with chocolate centres. Morning glory (*Ipomoea tricolor*) is easy if it is raised in warm, humid conditions and then planted in a very sunny spot and the canary creeper (*Tropaeolum peregrinum*) grows as fast as anything and has a mass of tiny yellow flowers.

The secret of keeping sweet peas from setting seed and therefore not flowering is to pick them regularly every 8–10 days. They will then flower into autumn.

ANNUALS FOR CUTTING

If you want some annuals for cutting – and who does not? – plan for it by:

- **making extra sure** of feeding them to encourage vigorous plants with large flowers and long stems

- **thinning them** slightly less than normal but cutting them selectively to thin them out throughout the flowering season

- **sowing two or three** successive 'crops', starting in March and ending at the end of May to give a supply right until the autumn.

Biennials

Biennials differ from annuals – which grow, flower and set seed all in one growing season – in that they grow fast from seed and develop strong roots and foliage in one season, and then flower in the next.

For most, this means that they germinate and grow without flowering in summer and autumn, remain dormant over winter, then have another burst of growth before flowering in spring and early summer. They then set seed and die. Some biennial vegetables, such as carrot, parsley or parsnip, clearly manifest this habit and if left in the ground in the spring following planting will grow superb umbellifer flowers.

The great advantage of biennials over annuals is that they are hardy enough to withstand a cold winter and quickly produce flowers in spring without having to wait for the plant to grow first.

One of the first spring biennials to appear in this garden is honesty (*Lunaria annua*). I planted a few individual plants about ten years ago and they have self-seeded prolifically ever since. Honesty germinates well from fresh seed when the

Forget-me-nots create a blue floral froth in the Cottage Garden borders (note the blighted box hedges).

Useful biennials

- *Alcea rosea*
- *Bellis perennis*
- *Campanula medium*
- *Dianthus*
- *Digitalis purpurea*
- *Erysimum cheiri*
- *Lunaria annua*
- *Matthiola incana*
- *Myosotis* spp.
- *Oenethera biennis*
- *Onopordum acanthium*
- *Papaver nudicaule*
- *Verbascum* spp.

Red campion has become a welcome weed, seeding itself throughout the garden in May and June.

lovely lunar discs dissolve, and it quickly makes clumpy rosettes of leaves. These will overwinter and start to grow again in February. The seeds do not spread far so they tend to mass in groups in a border and therefore need thinning every few years or will thuggishly crowd out less vigorous neighbours, and anyway, they perform much better if given room. The leaves are elegantly nettlish and the stems have what look like stings along them but they are an empty – if in evolutionary terms an effective – threat. The flowers are a characteristic mix of freshness and richness, often on the same stem, ranging from plum through to pale mauve. *L. a.* 'Atrococcinea' is very red and *L. a.* 'Munstead Purple' is decidedly purple. The white form, *L. a.* var. *albiflora* – which is less prolific for me but is mingled in amongst its purple kin – is very good and a blindingly pure white. The pods of the white flowers are a pure green whereas the purple flowers produce pods with a purplish wash over them. Both become silvery when dry. They make a lovely cut flower both when fresh and when the seed pods have formed.

Biennials provide most of what I call our 'welcome weeds' – plants that self-seed along the margins and edges of paths, borders and hedges all over the garden, and sometimes in borders too. They do much to add to the floral display and are nearly all treasured rather than removed.

Red campion (*Silene dioica*) has become one of the most prominent welcome weeds over the past few years, especially in the Grass Borders and Orchard Beds, where its very pink (not red at all) starry flowers shine out brightly.

Forget-me-nots (*Myosotis* spp.) need no growing regime of any kind because they too seed themselves by the thousand. Indeed I know people that ban them from their gardens as being too invasive. Not me. I love and welcome them but you do have to remove the majority of your plants to the compost heap each year if they are not to become a weed. When they get dry they quickly get a powdery mildew (see page 270) and that is the point at which I pull them up (they were one of the plants that loved 2019's wet spring and summer). I think that forget-me-nots should be blue although *M. sylvatica* 'Rosylva' is pink and there are white forms too. There are a number of blue varieties to buy but *M. s.* 'Royal Blue' is taller than most. Like all biennials you can 'lose' a season of forget-me-nots by over-vigorous weeding or mulching. I transplant seedlings in winter by the spadeful, lifting them like turf to break up over-large drifts and spreading them around a bit.

Perhaps the best welcome weed of the lot is the foxglove (*Digitalis*). We collect the seedlings and move them to select spots around the garden, ideally with light shade like the Orchard Beds, although, like all biennials, this must not be left to spring but should be done in the autumn or late winter at the latest. Leave it to spring and they never really recover. Although formally biennial, they often take more than a season to flower and behave as short-lived perennials.

The white form (*D. purpurea* f. *albiflora*) will create beautiful ghostly plants for a shady border but subsequent seedlings often revert to purple so it is best to sow fresh seed each year or weed out the offending purple ones by identifying the pink mid-ribs in young plants. Or just accept the natural mix and go joyfully with it. You can buy other colours such as 'Sutton's Apricot' or various yellow varieties, and all are good although to my mind none better than the natural purple or white. Sow them in spring and keep them in pots until autumn when they can be planted out 60cm (24in) apart.

Sweet rocket or dame's violet (*Hesperis matronalis*) arrives around the same time as the foxgloves, adding a lilac-pink leap into a border, and the two look very good growing side by side. It will produce white flowers too on *H. m.* var. *albiflora*, and the two crop up side by side in our Walled Garden where it seeds itself in very erratic quantities from year to year. This irregularity is one of the charms of self-sown plants. If you want strict order and control (as we do with our wallflowers – see below), then impose it yourself, weed out all self-sown seedlings and start afresh every year. Go with nature and leave them untouched, and you take pot luck. I have seen sweet rocket referred to as a short-lived perennial, but treat it as a biennial and you will not go wrong.

Wallflowers (*Erysimum cheiri*) are one of my favourite biennials. I grow 'Blood Red', 'Primrose Monarch' and 'Fire King', which make a dramatic display amongst the tulips. It is a perfect combination – a rich tapestry of colour. Wallflowers have a distinctly honeyed fragrance intensified by sun and if you grow them in a confined area, the scent can fill the whole space on a sunny day.

Wallflowers are very easy to grow although like all biennials, you do have to plan ahead. I sow the seeds in a seed tray or plugs in late May – the same week that I clear the current year's flowers away to the compost heap – prick them out when big enough to handle, then line them out in a corner of the Vegetable Garden to grow on until October when they can be planted in their final positions. They can be sown direct outside but will need thinning to at least 10cm (4in) apart if the plants are to develop strongly. They are members of the brassica family so are subject to flea beetle (see page 301), club root and attack by cabbage white butterfly

Planting wallflowers in a pot planted with tulip bulbs. They make a great combination, both flowering in April and May.

Foxgloves and red campion growing together on the Mound in late spring. Foxgloves are a great favourite and we grow hundreds from seed every year, as well as allowing many more to grow where they have self-seeded.

(see page 357), so do not line them out where cabbages have grown the previous year and watch out for caterpillars.

You can buy young plants in September and October but make sure that they have some soil attached to the roots – just because they are tough does not mean that they are improved by being neglected. They will grow in very poor soil although a bit of goodness gives the plants a leafy, full body which I like.

Teasels and the vast silvery thistle *Onopordum acanthium* spread themselves all over the place in my garden. Both these latter two plants have fabulous style and presence but can be a bit overwhelming if you let all their seedlings mature. Although their readiness to seed removes the job of sowing a new crop ahead of time, you will need to move the self-sown seedlings in the autumn or early spring to the position you want them to grow next spring. If you leave it until spring they will have developed a taproot and will not move easily.

Tall annuals and biennials

Any annual growing over 1.2m (4ft) can
be very useful at the back of a border
to stagger flowering heights but will need
some kind of support. Sunflowers
(*Helianthus annuus*) are not all giants and
not all sunny yellow. 'Velvet Queen' is
a glorious russet and 'Lemon Queen' is,
er, lemon. Both grow to about 1.5m (5ft).
Cosmos bipinnatis is a tall, delicately
branched plant with beautifully elegant
flowers. It needs deadheading daily to
prolong flowering. Try the white 'Purity'.

Scented annuals and biennials

Because annuals and biennials are so
desperate for pollination, scent is often an
important part of their armoury. Use it!

Just a few of my favourite scented
annuals and biennials are *Nicotiana
sylvestris*, night scented stock and
evening primrose.

Annuals and biennnials
for shade

Although most annuals and biennials
really need as much sun as possible,
some have adapted to grow in shade.
My favourite biennial is the white foxglove
(*Digitalis purpurea* f. *albiflora*) which will
gracefully grow in almost complete shade
and, like night scented stock, dry shade
at that, which is rare. Tobacco plants all
grow in shade (but do not necessarily prefer
it) whilst *Mimulus* spp. is completely happy
without direct light.

Nicotiana sylvestris is an annual
that flowers in late summer and
has the most exotic musty
fragrance of all.

Bulbs

What differentiates a bulb from a perennial plant is that the nourishment for the creation and growth of the flower is all stored within the bulb itself. This is why a bulb will begin to shoot whilst still unplanted, abandoned in the corner of a shed.

Not only the nourishment but all the memory needed to tell the shoot how big to grow and when to flower is stored within that little dry root. There is something miraculous about the way that a small grenade of dried-up tissue can explode into a complete flower. I love to think of plants growing underground, showing nothing above the abrasive knobbliness of frozen earth, but secretly pushing out tentative shoots and new roots, blind and mole-like but unstoppable.

When the flower has finished, the leaves are greedily converting sunlight and water into the nourishment for next year's flower and they – the leaves – feed from the bulb's roots. That is why you must never cut off the leaves from a bulb after it has flowered. Leave them until they die back of their own accord before tidying them up or else you may find that there will not be enough food stored to make next year's flower and the plant will be 'blind' in a year's time.

The rule of thumb when planting bulbs is to allow at least twice their own depth of soil above them and to put them pointy end up. That's it. Everything else is fine-tuning. However, in practice, the ground is often like rock and the dibber won't dib a proper hole. If you have a bulb planter, which removes a plug of soil that you can put back over the planted bulb, life is made easier, but if your soil is heavy it is a counsel of perfection to put a handful of grit or sharp sand into each hole first, as few spring-flowering bulbs react well to sitting in the wet.

Opposite page: We always have a display of bulbs on the table outside the potting shed from late January through to May and these irises, crocuses, hyacinths and scillas brighten the bleakest winter day.

Planting in grass is slow and repetitive. However, it is worth doing, even if it is on a modest scale amongst a few trees. Most people will be aware that once you plant bulbs in grass you must never cut the grass until the leaves of the bulbs have started to yellow and die down, which, for daffodils, is going to be late June or July. Nothing looks worse than mown grass around the pathetic leaves of flowered-out daffodils.

Some bulbs break the rule of early planting. Snowdrops can be tricky to establish if planted as dry bulbs and do much better if planted 'green' straight after flowering. Tulips should be left until November to avoid tulip fire disease (see page 232), which can reduce an emerging bulb to a mouldy wreck. It is caused by the fungus *Botrytis tulipae* that persists in the soil (or in infected bulbs, although not from a reputable dealer). Planting in winter reduces the chances of the fungus developing.

In early autumn I plant lots of bulbs in pots and keep them in an open-sided glass cold frame to protect them from the rain rather than the cold until the buds form in January or February.

Most bulbs come from mountainous, almost alpine conditions. This means that they have a very short growing season between winter and summer – which accounts for the early flowering – they get a summer baking, are very well drained, yet get plenty of water from melting snow in spring. Consequentially, cold is rarely a problem but dampness can be, except for winter aconites (*Eranthis hyemalis*), fritillaries, snowdrops, *Anemone blanda*, summer snowflakes (*Leucojum aestivum*), *Narcissus cyclamineus* and the species tulip (*Tulipa sylvestris*), so choose your plants for your conditions.

One way of growing bulbs that prefer dry conditions – such as crocuses, daffodils, tulips and scillas – in ground that is fundamentally wet, is to plant them around the roots of a deciduous tree or shrub, which will take up most of the available moisture in the ground.

Tulips should not be planted until November, to avoid tulip fire disease, which can reduce an emerging bulb to a mouldy wreck

WHAT IS A BULB?

We tend to call anything that is bulbous a 'bulb', whereas there are a number of bulbous roots that have different characteristics. A true bulb is only one of a number of different underground storage organs. All share the characteristic of making new plants by division.

Bulbs are made from concentric layers of fleshy leaves with a protective, dry outer layer, although some lilies and fritillaries have no protective skin and the scales (fleshy leaves) are separate and visible. A true bulb is a reduced root stem which grows fresh roots each year. Also, each year, a new stem is formed in the centre of the bulb, but, as well as creating new bulbs or bulbils that are tiny and may take a few years to become large enough to produce a flower, some bulbs, like daffodils, can last for a number of years whilst others, like tulips rot away once they have produced a flower. Corms are replaced by new corms every year and develop from the swollen base of the stem. Crocuses, gladioli and colchicums are all corms.

Tubers are the swollen roots that are used for food storage – unlike most roots which are solely a medium for conveying food to the plant. Tubers are found in some orchids, in dahlias, anemones, corydalis and in cyclamen species.

Rhizomes are swollen underground stems, usually horizontal. The best known examples are irises and lily-of-the-valley.

The grassy banks of the Mound are planted with thousands of wild daffodils (*Narcissus pseudonarcissus*) and crocuses, and are at their best in March. These will be followed by wildflowers in summer.

Spring bulbs

Spring bulbs are the most hopeful of all flowers. Once they arrive then, regardless of the weather, everything becomes possible. They celebrate the present whilst holding an entirely optimistic future in their cupped petals.

Spring bulbs have three different categories and roles to play in our garden. The first are those that we grow in the flower borders as part of the floral narrative that we try to stretch from January through to November. For the early months they play the star and central role and then, as spring gathers pace, are balanced by an increasing number of herbaceous perennials and flowering shrubs. By May they are often playing an incidental, complementary role. It can be tricky to balance their effect at this time of year when the Jewel Garden, for example, is in full-rigged sail with herbaceous growth and the relative sparseness of early spring has long gone. But in the Spring and Writing Gardens, and in woodland areas like the Coppice and the Wildlife Garden, it is much easier to imagine the effect that these dry little bulbs will have when flowering next March and April. The Writing Garden, for example, has hundreds

The big work table outside the potting shed is at its full early-spring glory by the end of February. The pots on the ground contain tulips that will start to flower in April.

of the glorious white *Narcissus* 'Thalia' as well as summer snowflakes that completely dominate this little garden for a few weeks, and we top these up each autumn to maintain that effect.

However, as I often say, you must be careful what you wish for. 'Thalia' is pretty robust and spreads well, so a bit of judicious thinning every few years replaces the annual topping up. But its spread is nothing like so voracious as that of the *Allium hollandicum* 'Purple Sensation' in the Jewel Garden. We initially planted a few hundred bulbs about 20 years ago and now there must be thousands. Every time we make a planting hole, we uncover dozens of bulbs. We dig up and throw away barrowloads every year but it is still present in great drifts. This is not to say that it is not spectacular – but it is slightly too much of a good thing.

The second category of bulbs are those that we plant into grass. These are increasing year on year and are now every bit as important a spring display as the border bulbs. We began by planting a hundred bulbs of wild daffodils (*Narcissus pseudonarcissus*) in the Orchard. There were only nine flowers in the first year and they were very slow to spread but now they are well established and the hundreds that delicately swathe in and amongst the apple trees have been joined by *Narcissus poeticus* var. *recurvus*, or old pheasant's eye, and by white *Camassia leichtlinii* 'Alba Plena' and *Allium nigrum*, all planted in September 2019, and then joined by the tulip 'Yellow Spring Green' added in November.

The Cricket Pitch is underplanted with thousands of crocuses which look

The bulbs in the grass have increased every year and are now as important a spring display as the border bulbs

spectacular in February – if the rabbits don't eat them – but are nearly always over by the time we start filming. However, we have also planted snake's head fritillaries, more wild daffodils, *Allium atropurpureum* and the delicate blue *Camassia cusickii*.

Most spring bulbs do best on well-drained soil but fritillaries, camassias, snowdrops and snowflakes will all thrive in damper soil and we grow these in the strip between the Damp and Cottage Gardens. Last year, this was a canal for weeks on end but none of the bulbs seemed to mind in the least and have all flowered well.

As I've already said, when growing any bulbs in grass it is essential that the grass is left uncut until the last piece of bulb foliage has died right back otherwise next year's flowers will be severely limited and in time disappear altogether. In practice, that usually means waiting until July or even early August. We then keep the grass short, which makes planting fresh bulbs in September a lot easier – although the September soil can be very dry and hard, and we sometimes leave the hose soaking into it for a few hours the day before to soften it up.

When planting bulbs in a border you can be specific and place them individually, although we often use the square metre system. This involves

I have found that investing in a high-quality long-handled bulb planter saves a lot of time and effort when planting bulbs in turf

dividing each border into metre squares marked out with canes, then allocating the same number of bulbs to each square. The bulbs are then planted around whatever else might be growing there. The result is an equal balance of bulbs but an irregular and natural spread as you plant around and amongst the herbaceous perennials and shrubs.

But in grass, the best method is to simply throw a handful of bulbs on the ground and plant wherever they land, otherwise you invariably end up with the flowers appearing in an awkwardly regimented, stiff arrangement. Just chuck them and go with wherever they fall.

I have found that investing in a high-quality long-handled bulb planter saves a lot of time and effort. It will take out a core of turf and soil, you pop the bulb in, make another hole which forces out the core that came from the first hole – which you use to refill the second hole – and so it goes on. This way you can plant hundreds of bulbs relatively quickly, easily and deeply, and the end result looks as though the turf had barely been disturbed.

Depth is important whenever you are planting bulbs and as a rule, the deeper you plant them the better.

If daffodils in grass start to grow seemingly healthy and vigorous foliage but few if any flowers, it is usually a sign of two problems. The first is over-congestion and this is remedied by digging them up in late spring, when you can see where they are, and replanting with their foliage at a wider spacing. The second is that they are too dry in September when the bulbs are starting to break into active growth underground. Watering very dry turf in early autumn where you know the bulbs are to appear can help a great deal.

The third category of bulbs we grow is those in containers. We have scores of these and they range from exquisite but minute irises in tiny terracotta pots to giant pots with three layers of different tulips and with 20 bulbs to each layer – topped by wallflowers. In between these two extremes of size, we grow lots of small daffodils in pots, like *Narcissus* 'Tête à Tête', *N.* 'W.P. Milner', *N.* 'Minnow' and *N.* 'Hawera', as well as fritillaries, muscari, scillas, chionodoxa and hyacinths. These are stored in a cold frame under glass to protect them from becoming sodden with a Longmeadow rain, but with the sides open and unheated so they are exposed to cold, which helps trigger flowering. As the shoots appear and flower buds form, we bring them out and display them en masse outside the potting shed and all over the garden as bright points of colour from late January through to mid-May.

When growing bulbs in pots it is really important to give them good drainage and the best way to do this is to buy a bag or

two of horticultural grit and mix it in equal measure in a peat-free compost. The only exceptions are fritillaries that like a more moisture-retentive compost and hyacinths that love a loose, open compost. This is best provided either with a quite coarse bark mix or by adding plenty of home-made leafmould.

But in the end, all bulb growing is remarkably easy. You make a hole in the ground and stick them in, preferably pointy side up, and then forget about them until they start to show their snouts of shoots early in the year. Then you know that they are soon going to explode into colour.

Aconites

Aconites (*Eranthis hyemalis*) are rhizomatous tubers that spread very fast once they are established but by seed rather than by bulbous increase. They like damp, light shade to do well and the base of deciduous trees is ideal. The flowers only open up in sunshine, which is perhaps why, as they are always associated with sunlight, we always think of them as being a particularly brilliant yellow. The sunshine can be accompanied by frost and icy snow, and still the flowers will open.

If you dig up a patch of ground and plant them as a group, they will gradually make their own colony. It is important to plant the rhizomes at the right depth, which is generally rather deeper than one might think, with the top of the roots about 7.5–10cm (3–4in) below the soil. They prefer an alkaline soil, so adding a mulch of mushroom compost will always make them happy.

Snowdrops

Snowdrops (*Galanthus nivalis*) are one of the few spring bulbs (fritillaries are another) that like to be damp and slightly shaded. Most spring bulbs, like crocuses, irises or tulips, do best in lots of sunshine with really sharp drainage, but snowdrops are flowers of the woodland edge and like to creep out from cover, be in shade for at least some of the day and never dry out save in midsummer, when dormant.

The essence of snowdrops in the garden is that they span the worlds of wildflowers and garden plants. No one seems to know whether they are a native or not. They certainly grow freely in the wild but equally certainly, nearly all 'wild' snowdrops are garden escapees. There is apparently no reference to snowdrops growing wild before 1770 and the first garden reference is as late as 1597.

They spring up in mid-winter, regardless of weather, with the freedom and abundance of bluebells, and yet can be cultivated and treasured both individually

Snowdrops are one of the few bulbs that do best in slightly shaded, damp conditions and start to appear in the Spring Garden in January.

in pots and as part of mixed planting in a border. And they will go on reliably reappearing year after year for generations – even centuries. Each year they spread a little more by seed and the clumps increase as they create new bulbs so, in time, they form the great white carpets that you can see in some of our country parks.

There are over 350 different species and cultivars and galanthophiles – collectors of the snowdrop – are obsessive about the variations between them, although the differences are likely to be measured in minute markings within the flower. *G. nivalis* is the commonest self-naturalising type, and I love the double *G. nivalis* f. *pleniflorus* 'Flore Pleno'. This is sterile but increases perfectly well from offsets and because it does not produce seed, the flowers last an extra-long time. *G. n.* 'S Arnott' is exceptionally successful, being tough, big and strong-scented.

The pollination of snowdrop seed depends upon two things – some sunny, mild weather and insects to spread the pollen. When the temperature rises to about 10°C (50°F), the three outer hanging petals react by lifting to the horizontal and acting as a funnel and halo to attract pollinators like the queen bumblebees that one sees bumbling around in the winter sun.

But you can speed up the spreading process. Lift a clump, divide it into three or four, replace one of these in the hole and then distribute the rest further afield. The ideal time to do that is in early spring, just after the flowers have faded but before the leaves begin to die back. All the snowdrops in my own garden have been spread this way from one original clump given to me by a friend from her garden 25 years ago.

Water them in well and they will immediately make themselves at home in their new position. Repeat this according to the amount of snowdrops that you already have. Not only can you can expect 100 per cent survival rate using this method but it will also give you a good idea of how they will look next year and enable you to plan other planting around them. The only thing to watch for is the ground getting too dry, especially in autumn when they start to grow again, albeit underground and out of sight for another few months.

Crocuses

I think a mass of crocuses in grass in early March sunshine is one of the memorable floral peaks. And, like snowdrops and daffodils, crocuses create a direct and meaningful connection between the back garden and the landscape at large, even if that is via a window box or a pot on a windowsill. In fact, crocuses grow very well in pots and look particularly good planted cheek by jowl in a shallow terracotta alpine pan. It is worth buying the species crocuses for containers – rather than the much brasher Dutch cultivars – because they are subtle and delicate and deserve close inspection.

Crocuses are corms which are really just short stems stuffed like hamster cheeks with sustenance. Inside the corm the flower is fully formed and the food supply is principally used to develop the roots and leaves, and is completely consumed by the process of flowering. The new leaves then store next year's food in a new

corm that is built up sitting on top of the old one. It dries out over summer and starts developing new roots sometime in autumn – which is why the best time to plant spring bulbs is at the end of summer, to give these new roots maximum time to get established.

Crocus laevigatus is usually the first to appear, pushing up lilac or white flowers in any mild period from Christmas on. This has two great advantages for the ordinary garden – unlike most crocuses it will grow well in dappled shade (in other words in the lee of a deciduous tree or shrub but not under an evergreen hedge) and it also seeds itself everywhere.

Other than their first wispy presence, crocuses seem to appear from the ground all flower. I think that this is what makes them seem an annual miracle as opposed to the seasonal ritual of daffodils or snowdrops. We planted ours in the Orchard by lifting turfs and placing them like woody marbles on the ground before covering them back over with the turf. The corms are tiny. You order a thousand crocuses to make a statement and they arrive in a bag about the size of a kilo (2¼lb) of sugar. A thousand crocuses are a mere dapple.

As ever with plants, the closer you can make their growing conditions to their original habitat, the happier they will be, and crocuses mainly come from Greece and the hot, thin soils of that part of the Mediterranean. They belong to the *Iridaceae*, or Iris family that includes, as well as irises and crocuses, gladioli, crocosmias and freesias. Give them good drainage and plenty of sunshine, and they will not worry too much about the quality of the soil.

The first bulbs to appear in the Cricket Pitch are crocuses. The hurdles are there to stop the dogs crashing through them!

Early irises

I remember filming at RHS Wisley for *Gardeners' World* on on a bitterly cold day in early April 2013. A cruel east wind was making the spring day arctic so I took refuge in the alpine house which, that exceptionally cold spring, was about the only place at Wisley that had some colour. And what colour! I was bewitched by the jewel-like intensity of the flowers, all growing in terracotta pots sunk into benches filled with sand.

And, amongst the species tulips and fritillaries, no flowers were more intense than the various irises that they had growing there. I had given up growing winter-flowering irises at that time because they really did not appreciate our combination of heavy clay and exceptionally damp winters, but I immediately resolved to try again and since then, irises have been a delight that has brightened up the late-winter days here.

Rather than force them to cope with conditions that they are never going to enjoy – all these alpine bulbs can cope with a lot of cold but absolutely hate sitting in damp soil – I grow my early irises in terracotta pots (that not only look good but drain better than plastic ones) filled with a compost mix that is fully half-grit so very, very free-draining. I plant them any time between the beginning of September and the end of November. They can be left outside as long as they do not get too wet but I put mine in a glass frame that is like an umbrella – open at the sides to the cold weather but shielded by a glass roof from the wet. The shoots appear about Christmas and they will flower from mid-January through to early March.

Iris danfordiae is bright yellow and one of the first irises to flower. It is compact so looks best in a shallow alpine pan. It is not expensive and tends to flower less well after the first year, so it is a good idea to buy fresh bulbs each year for the best display. *Iris reticulata* blazes in February with beautiful, deep indigo-purple petals flowering on short stems and looking like an especially glamorous crocus. I have *I. r.* 'Harmony' which has particularly deep blue flowers with a gold blaze on the lower 'fall'. The leaves remain quite stubby during flowering but then grow taller to reach 30cm (12in) or more at maturity. *I. r.* 'J. S. Dijt' is a rich burgundy colour and flowers later, so extends the iris season. *Iris histriodes* is a

I love the rich intensity of the jewel-like early irises like *Iris reticulata* 'Harmony'. Our soil is too wet for them so I only grow them in pots and bring them out like treasures in February and March.

member of the Reticulata group and 'George' is especially magnificent, with rich plum-purple flowers that are rather larger than most others in this group. *I. h.* 'Lady Beatrix Stanley' has lovely blue flowers with yellow markings in the centre of the petals carried on a short stem. Unlike some early irises, all cultivars of *I. histroides* flower strongly year after year.

Iris unguicularis has delicate violet-blue flowers about 20cm (8in) high and an untidy sprawl of foliage which should not be cut back but allowed to die back slowly. They are often planted outside in a border but as well as good drainage, like all these bulbs, they need exposure to summer sun – preferably hot sun at that – if they are to flower well next year. *I. u.* 'Mary Barnard' is a rich shade of mauve and *I. u.* 'Alba' is rather late-flowering and, as the name suggests, white.

Daffodils

The daffodils in my garden come in waves and flushes of yellow. They start as early as late February in the Spring Garden, with little clumps of *Narcissus* 'Tête à Tête' in amongst the last of the snowdrops and aconites. Then by mid-March – when the daffodils in the London parks are at their peak – the wild narcissi in the Orchard and Cricket Pitch start to get going. These are delicate little flowers, often just 15cm (6in) tall and nodding with every passing breath of wind. Although they are very far removed from the more common, robust, tall hybrids that we see right across the country in March, I think they are exceptionally beautiful and are the best daffs to plant in grass. The bulbs are very small, about the size of a marble and quick and easy to plant, so a massed effect is not hard to achieve. They gradually spread by seed.

Narcissus 'Thalia' in the Writing Garden. As well as being unusually and dramatically pure white, 'Thalia' is also deliciously fragrant.

Not far from my home, on the Herefordshire/Gloucestershire border near Ledbury, there are fields and woods covered with these lovely, delicate flowers seemingly spilling out by the hundreds of thousands from the shade of the woodland into open meadows. It is a fabulous sight but you can capture the essence of it in just a patch of grass in the back garden.

Of course, planting daffodil bulbs in grass in September (the ideal time) does commit you to not cutting that grass for the first six months of the year. This gives the leaves time to grow and the plant to flower and then, critically, the foliage to die back and feed the bulb, ensuring that next year's flower is formed. Cut the grass too soon and you will have few or no flowers next March.

I have daffodils in pots – *Narcissus* 'Tête à Tête' and *N.* 'Geranium', which is a tazetta type, with a tiny orange trumpet and delicate white petals. They have a lovely fragrance so are placed where we sit outside – although in early spring that is normally in the mornings with a cup of hot coffee rather than in the evenings, which are still chilly.

Daffodils grow well in pots as long as they have good drainage. They can be left to die back and then taken out, and the bulbs stored in a cool, dry place so the pot can be used for a summer display or left in place for a repeat performance next year. However, like daffodils growing in grass, do not be tempted to 'tidy' the leaves but let them die back slowly so they can feed the bulbs beneath the soil.

My final show of daffodils, *Narcissus poeticus* var. *recurvus*, flowers in the Orchard in May at the same time as the tulips. These are taller than the wild daffodils flowering six weeks earlier in the grass, and are out at the same time as the bluebells and cow parsley.

All daffodils, whenever they flower, grow fresh roots each year and the bulb is fed by the leaves after flowering. The flowers set seed which will spread the plant but in doing so, they reduce the stored energy in the bulb. So if you want bulbs to naturalise in long grass, leave the seedpods on, but if you have daffodils in a border or container, nip off the seedheads as soon as they form but keep the stems and leaves uncut until they have died right down. Established clumps that are flowering weakly can be rejuvenated by lifting and dividing immediately after the leaves have died back, but clumps that are flowering well should not be disturbed.

Tulips

It can seem as though the garden is slowly collapsing in on itself throughout November like a deflated balloon. But the highlight of the month is that it is tulip planting time and the thought of tulips lighting up next April and May is a beacon of hope carrying me through the grimmest of days.

The reason for delaying planting tulips until November is to avoid the risk of tulip fire, which initially manifests itself with small pin-prick-sized holes and lumps on the petals and some visible grey mould on the leaves. The holes are caused by spores being exposed to sunlight and the mould on the leaves is a sign of the rot that can totally reduce a tulip to a molten-

looking lump. By November the soil will be colder and therefore any fungal spores in the soil are much less likely to spread.

In fact, we plant our tulips to be grown in containers first and usually complete this by the end of October. We mainly use the terracotta pots that are occupied by dahlias in the summer, so until these are cut back and put into storage, the pots are inaccessible. We do sometimes plant tulip bulbs into plastic and then plunge these into the terracotta pots in spring, but they tend to flower better if planted direct.

This is because the deeper that you can plant tulips, the stronger and taller the stems tend to grow within the limitations of the tulip type. Ideally I like to plant them 15cm (6in) or more below the surface of a pot. However, if you are growing them in a border as part of mixed planting or as bedding, there is also an argument for burying them just 5–7.5cm (2–3in) below the surface where they can root into better soil. But this is only a good idea if these bulbs are all to be lifted after flowering. If you want strong growth and any kind of permanent planting, then deep is good and very deep best.

All tulips prefer really good drainage and as much sunshine as you can give them. Some buck this trend better than others but if in doubt, add masses of grit and keep them out of the shade. Extreme cold and heat will not bother them at all but the bulbs hate sitting in wet soil.

Unlike daffodils, tulip bulbs do not last after flowering. Instead, they form a new bulb as well as much smaller bulbils. The bulbs that you buy are carefully bred, selected and grown for maximum size. In a

good year, each plant will produce a couple of flowering bulbs although these will almost certainly be smaller than the parent and the resulting flower smaller, too. Leave tulips unreplaced in the ground year after year and the display will become increasingly erratic and comprise of multiple rather small flowers. So if you want maximum display, you are best to treat tulips as annuals and replace them every year. But that can become an expensive habit and I think that there is a compromise.

We order new bulbs each year for the containers and place these in pride of place for the best possible effect. Then after they have finished flowering and have started to die back, we lift them, foliage and all, and sort through them, carefully drying the biggest ones in a sunny, dry place until the foliage has completely withered. The very smallest we discard but the medium-sized bulbs we line out in the Vegetable Garden or in a spare spot in the nursery beds to

The lovely wispy *Tulipa acuminata* in the Paradise Garden glows bright in the sun.

The tulips 'Prinses Irene', 'Ronaldo' and 'Flaming Parrot' in the Jewel Garden. I plant 50 or more tulips in the large pots, putting the different varieties in layers.

grow on. If these flower next year, they are picked as cut flowers. After a year or two, these are lifted in turn and the bulbs planted out the following autumn in the borders to bulk out the tulip numbers there. Once this system has had a year or two to get established, you find that you have wonderful displays in pots, a supply of cut flowers and a constant topping-up of tulips in the borders. It works well.

We use tulips in different parts of the gardens to harmonise with both the colours of the flowers that precede and accompany them and – equally importantly – with the theme and tone of each particular area.

The first to emerge here are the species tulips, *Tulipa saxatilis* and *T. sylvestris*. These tend to flower earlier than most hybrids, all have floppy leaves and the lax-petalled flowers are often held on equally bendy

stems. *T. saxatilis* has mauve petals that open in sunshine to reveal a yellow centre. Those of *T. sylvestris* are bright yellow, opening into buttercup looseness with a little sun. There is something of the crocus about both these tulips and a delicacy that none of the hybrids can aspire to. But the real display comes from the more showy – not to say exhibitionist – cultivars.

'Negrita' is often the first to flower and has long stems on top of which are poised plum-purple flowers with single, satin petals. It is from the Triumph group, which was bred about a hundred years ago specifically for bedding and cutting. 'Abu Hassan' follows about a week later and is a burnished copper colour at the base of its petals, lightening to a rim of orange. It is one of my favourites. 'Prinses Irene' has a wonderful chocolate stem topped with orange petals flushed with pink and streaked with plum and a touch of green.

We can normally reckon on 'Queen of Sheba' being amongst the first to flower. She has a lovely curvy swell with the petals arching outwards, making each flower look like a cockbird in full mating rig frozen in display.

Parrot tulips are frilled ink stains that are almost embarrassingly voluptuous. We have 'Black Parrot', which is a deep purple, 'Blue Parrot', which is in fact pale mauve, 'Flaming Parrot', which has pale yellow flowers flamed garishly with a raspberry streak, and 'Texas Flame', which shares the same combination of colours but adds a flash of green. These are catwalk flowers in party frocks, flowers shamelessly flaunting themselves, and I love them for that.

At the other end of the orange scale there is 'Generaal de Wet', so simple and unfussy that it is almost like a species tulip. There is yet more orange with 'Ballerina' – a Lily-flowered type with real elegance – and the very late 'Orange Parrot', which is a pure and frilly orange. Last cold spring it was still going strong into June.

For years we had the pure white 'White Triumphator' flanking the Lime Walk but have recently added 'Nicolas Heyek', which has a touch of yellow to modify the whiteness and is a robust, long-standing flower.

In a good year we have tulips flowering from late March (usually *T. sylvestris*) until late May ('Queen of Night' is usually the last to leave). It is a breathtaking, glorious performance – and it is the memory of this that adds a spring to my November step.

'Queen of Sheba', 'Abu Hassan' and, in the foreground, 'Prinses Irene' flowering in the Jewel Garden amongst the foliage of the unopened *Allium hollandicum* 'Purple Sensation'.

MY CURRENT TULIP FAVOURITES

• **'Lady Jane':** I grow this in the Writing Garden beneath the apple trees to pick up on the apple blossom. It has delicate, pointed, alternately pink and white petals so that it seems striped like an awning, but opens wide in the sun to reveal a pure white interior before closing up again at night.

• **'Rococo':** Fully open, this is a crimson explosion, as subtle as a blow to the head and one of the earliest Parrots. I think I like it best before it opens, when the flower heads are fully formed but still closed, because this reveals the extraordinary crumpled, gathered, pinched and crimped base to the vermilion petals streaked with yellow, grey and green.

• **'West Point':** This is one of the most elegant of all flowers. It is a Lily-flowered tulip with pure lemon flowers that twist, the tips of each petal crossing each other as though held into a ballerina's arch. I grow it in the Spring Garden and will be planting a mass more this autumn.

• **T. acuminata:** This is a species tulip that flowers later than most, often not until May, and has wonderfully spidery, twisted petals of vermillion and yellow. We grow this in the Paradise Garden, being the nearest thing to the original spidery Ottoman tulips that instigated tulip mania at the beginning of the seventeenth century.

• **'Yellow Spring Green':** This does superbly well in the Spring Garden, as much for the mood that it captures and expresses as for any horticultural qualities. It is a delicate, pale primrose flushed with green.

• **'Indian Velvet':** This is a Single Late type with lovely plum-coloured petals and works very well with the darker flowers of 'Recreado' and the almost-black 'Queen of Night', creating a tapestry with real richness and depth.

Fritillaries

Fritillaria meleagris, the common snake's head fritillary, has a sinister, reptilian quality, especially before it opens out, its pointed flower head hooked over the straight stem with its evenly and sparsely spaced leaves – hardly more than thin, green grooves. Look at the chequered petals closely and you will see how they are a perfect combination of blocked precision and smudged expressionism – perfect because they are not predictable or measurable. I like their folk name of Sulky Ladies – it exactly catches their pouty appeal.

As ever, there is a lesson for the gardener to learn from observing how something grows best beyond the garden boundary. It is a bulbous wildflower that thrives in wet meadows that are allowed to grow for hay under the Lammas Land regime. The hay is cut and harvested between 1 July and 12 August (Lammas Day) and then grazed until 12 February. This exactly dovetails with the fritillary's growth pattern. The bulb goes dormant after June until August, when it grows new shoots that stop just below the surface, then these also go dormant in response to cooler night temperatures. As soon as the weather warms up in spring, the shoots start to grow fast from this poised position so that they can flower and set seed before the grass gets growing.

We grow the much larger crown imperial (*F. imperialis*) in the Jewel and Spring Gardens. Crown imperial fritillaries let you know of their presence weeks before they start to flower. From early March, when the leaves first appear, they fill the Spring Garden with their distinctive aroma of fox and tomcat. They stand about 90cm (36in) tall on curiously flattened, thick, chocolate stems, the bright terracotta-orange (*F. imperialis* 'Rubra') or yellow (*F. imperialis* 'Lutea') flowers hanging beneath a topknot of leaf, like a punk pineapple. In a season of growing subtlety dominated by the freshness of new green, they are louche, pantomime plants, smelly, tall, loud, proud and utterly magnificent.

They are the only plant in Britain to be pollinated by birds – specifically blue tits that stick their heads in the flowers to sip the nectar inside and get dusted with pollen in the process.

They should be planted in early autumn with the huge bulb, with its distinctive hole like a half-cored apple, as deep as possible and on its side. They make take a few years before flowering – but are well worth the wait.

Spring snowflakes

Although the spring snowflake (*Leucojum vernum*) can be mistaken for a large snowdrop – and is related to it – it is larger and usually flowers somewhat later, although the two often overlap. The best variety, *L. v.* var. *wagneri*, has a pair of wonderful, green-rimmed white flowers on each stem, each with six petals of equal length. It prefers a shaded but damp position amongst deciduous trees or shrubs, and is very happy both in The Writing Garden and growing in the grass of the strip between the Cottage and the Damp Gardens. It can be planted as a dry bulb in autumn and will spread slowly by seed but,

The snake's head fritillary is a bulb of water meadows and it grows very happily in the very damp grassy strip between the Cottage and Damp Gardens.

like snowdrops, the best way to propagate them is to lift plants after flowering but whilst the foliage is still green. Then divide them before replanting in separate clumps.

Camassias

Camassias come from wet meadows of the United States and unlike most bulbs, need wet or heavy ground in which to thrive. Given these conditions, they are just as happy in a border or in grass although, as with all spring bulbs, the grass must not be cut until the camassia leaves have died right back, so they are not suitable for a lawn nor, arguably, for a mixed border. We grow camassia quamash in the Orchard Beds and in the Damp Garden, and in both places they have become a bit of a thug. They grow much more strongly after a couple of years of getting established and, because the leaves take a long time to die back and are very dominant, they can – and do – mask and inhibit other less thuggish plants that are struggling to display their wares. Long grass is really their ideal home in a garden.

Camassia leichtlinii has flowers that run the whole tonal range of blue, from violet to white, and are at their best in early May. We grow the white version along the strip between the Damp Garden and the Cottage Garden and they look very good, as well as being happy in that strip which invariably floods in winter. *C. cusickii* is slightly smaller and the pale blue flowers appear some weeks earlier. We have this growing in the Cricket Pitch. Both should be planted in autumn, putting the bulbs a full 10cm (4in) deep and about 30cm (12in) apart.

Other spring bulbs

Wood anemones (*Anemone nemorosa*) now carpet the Coppice. If any plant can be compared to stars in a dark sky, it is the wood anemone in April. They grow from a rhizome that creeps underground and, like primroses, do best in areas that are only lightly shaded, surviving the last few years of the coppice growth but bursting out in the years following a cut, providing pollen and nectar for bumble- and honeybees as well as for voles and mice.

We also have erythroniums growing happily in the Coppice as well as in the Orchard Beds, and grow grape hyacinths and scillas in pots and alpine pans as part of the spring display that we set up on the long table outside the potting shed. When they have finished flowering and have died right back, we plant them out in the Spring Garden and buy fresh bulbs for the containers.

Camassia cusickii flowering in the Cricket Pitch.

Summer bulbs

Summer bulbs never really get the attention that they deserve but it is a pity not to explore the full range of bulbous possibilities in the summer months.

Allium hollandicum 'Purple Sensation' has become a barely controlled weed in the Jewel Garden and Grass Borders. We remove barrowloads every year to keep it in check – just! However, it is beautiful and dramatic.

Whereas most spring-flowering bulbs have evolved to cope with blazing summer heat and drought (with exceptions such as our native meadow fritillaries), summer-flowering bulbs have evolved to survive winter cold and drought, and they tend to come from parts of the globe where summers are warm and moist. Our idea of a moist summer in Britain is one of dampness but many bulbs such as lilies come from Asia, where the monsoon in all its torrential glory provides the water for the year, whilst gladioli and eucomis come from the Eastern Cape in South Africa that has summer rainfall. Knowing this, it makes sense to plant summer bulbs in spring as the soil begins to warm up, in tune with the rhythm of their growth. Plant them in autumn along with your spring bulbs, and you are effectively storing them in cold, wet soil – which for them is an unnatural state.

Alliums

Alliums start their display in early May, just as the last tulip is fading, and the last – *Allium sphaerocephalon* – flowers in July and will stay well into August. But their real function seems to be as the perfect practical and symbolic link from spring into summer.

Alliums are true bulbs and fully paid-up members of the onion family. Most will obligingly reappear year after year – often too obligingly as they will spread dramatically by seed as well as by new bulbs. They are all characterised by a straight (usually long) drumstick of a stem with a burst of florets balanced on top. The first in my garden is always 'Purple Sensation', which is a clone of *A. aflatunense* and has become almost a weed of the Jewel Garden, dominating it with a bobbly sea of purple in May. It has a tight ball of flower that can vary from nearly maroon to almost imperial-purple, according to light and strain.

A. christophii follows just days later. It is bigger, paler and the florets explode away more dramatically than 'Purple Sensation'. It lasts for ages and the dried flower heads make lovely winter decoration. *A. schubertii* is even better because it is bigger and more eccentric, almost chaotic, in shape, but the stem is much shorter so is best put at the front of a border, despite the size of the flower head. If you want huge flower heads on huge stems, then *A. giganteum* is your onion. The only problem with them is that the whopping great bulbs are expensive and prone to rot unless they have very good drainage. And the leaves are always well past their best by the time they flower, so they need some companionable hiding.

Lilies

The next major player in the summer bulb stakes is the lily. It is easiest to divide lilies into three groups – the species (such as *Lilium martagon*, *L. regale* and *L. candidum*), the Asiatic hybrids and the North American (mostly Oregon hybrids) lilies. All lilies have bulbs with open scales like a half-opened artichoke.

Most lilies grow better in slightly acidic soil although most are perfectly happy with a loose soil with lots of leafmould added to it plus an annual mulch of the same. The Madonna lily (*L. candidum*) is the one exception that does best in alkaline, sunny conditions, but lilies are essentially woodland plants and like a cool, loose root run and sun on their faces.

If this sounds complicated, lilies always do very well in pots as long as you add plenty of leafmould to the potting compost. The key thing about lilies in pots is to give them enough room. Don't try and cram half a dozen bulbs into a small container. Instead, plan for about three bulbs for a 5 litre (1.5 gallon) or bigger pot – and then they will grow strongly and produce masses of flowers over a longer period.

L. regale is perhaps the most voluptuous, both of flower and fragrance and is one of the easiest to grow although it is top-heavy and needs support. Its natural Chinese home has very hot summers and

The oriental lilies 'Casablanca' in the Writing Garden grow 1.8m (6ft) or more tall and flower for weeks from mid-July

Agapanthus flower best with lots of sun, good drainage and constricted roots, so I grow them in pots and keep them frost-free over winter.

equally cold winters so it is extremely hardy, although the leaves and buds can be nipped by late frosts. The only thing is to ensure that it has good drainage, as it can cope much better with drought than with being too wet.

Martagon lilies have a mass of small Turk's cap flowers and superb structure to their foliage. They are very happy in the shade and very good in amongst the shrubs of a mixed border. I am a fan of *L. henryi* which grows 2–2.5m (7–8ft) tall in our heavy, damp soil. Its bright orange flower is the sort that is wonderful in the right place but can easily look horribly awkward – like turning up in fancy dress to a formal dinner party.

These are 'true' lilies but there are other 'bastard' lilies that adorn summer. I adore the foxtail lily (*Eremurus*), but it is a fleshy-rooted perennial rather than a bulb, even in the broadest sense.

However, cardiocrinum is a true bulb if not a true lily and is as melodramatic a plant as any. *Cardiocrinum giganteum* will reach 4m (13ft) tall, with huge glossy leaves and a flower spike of white trumpets. It needs a moisture-retentive (but not wet) soil and – more difficult to control – a damp atmosphere. Hot, dry summers do not suit it at all and it is most likely to thrive in the same conditions that rhododendrons are happiest in. The bulbs die after flowering and the offsets may take another three or four years to produce a flower, so new bulbs should be planted each year, with the tips just below the surface.

Gladioli

I was brought up with a bed of gladioli grown each year alongside dahlias and chrysanthemums, specifically for cutting. All were in a range of 1950s lipstick-pinks, pastel yellows, mauves, lilacs, oranges and other hues of that ilk. But it is wrong to brand them exclusively with that palette because there are wonderful rich colours, too, especially in the species gladioli (of which there are nearly 200), like *Gladiolus communis* subsp. *byzantinus*, *G. cardinalis*, the white with deep interior markings of *G. callianthus* and some of the florist's varieties like 'Firestorm', 'Fidelio', 'Black Beauty' or the green 'Spring Green' (which exactly fits what my American friends would call 'chartroose') and 'Green Isle'. Most are tender and are best dug up each winter along with the dahlias. However, *G. communis* subsp. *byzantinus* is a hardy perennial that comes from the Mediterranean – unlike most gladioli, which are from South Africa – so does not need lifting after flowering.

Unlike the species, florist's gladioli need quite a lot of tending to get the best out of them. They must be staked individually, deadheaded, weeded, watered and fed if the tower of flower is to be at its best. They are also prone to the gladiolus thrip, which is a tiny black insect that feeds off both foliage and flowers, rasping the leaves and leaving the surfaces a glistening pale grey. The leaves then turn brown and dry out. They also have a go at the developing flowers so that the buds wither before they open.

Summer irises

There are bearded irises in the Dry and Jewel Gardens, flag irises rising out of the water of the pond and *Iris sibirica* in great clumps, also in the Jewel Garden. With their intense colours and gorgeously rich petals, they are the most sumptuous of flowers.

The bearded irises have the greatest range of colours available of almost any flower, from a purple like 'Dusky Dancer', so inky dark that it is almost black, to pure white via every blue, mauve, pink, burgundy, yellow and orange, and some voluptuous, velvety browns. The only shade missing from their palette is crimson. The petals are frilled and ruffled and waved, and carried on strong, straight stems up to 1.2m (4ft) tall, accompanied by beautifully sculptural, upright spears of glaucous foliage fanning out from the rhizome. Everything about them is upright and dramatic.

Bearded irises grow from rhizomes looking like pieces of fresh ginger that sit on top of the soil. The roots grow down from these and when planting, it is very important to leave the rhizomes on the surface with just the roots underground so that the rhizomes can become sun-baked. It is the intensity of the baking that the rhizomes get in July and August that will determine the quantity and quality of the flowers the following May and June – hence the need for the sunniest spot possible.

The best time to buy and plant irises is between midsummer and early autumn. If, like me, you live in a wet area and also have clay soil, then it is a good idea to plant them on a little mound with lots of added grit beneath them. They really do like good drainage and baking sun in order to perform their best.

Every three or four years it is advisable to dig up a clump of rhizome immediately after flowering and cut it into sections, being sure that each section has a visible bud. Replant these new divisions to make three or four new clumps planted 15–30cm (6–12in) apart. It is best to throw away the oldest part of the rhizome as it will have lost its vigour. Trim the leaves by half to stop them rocking in the wind before the roots have a chance to anchor them firmly.

No plant in my garden has richer or more voluptuous flowers than the bearded iris. I have long since lost the label to this beauty but it delights me year after year for a few magical weeks in May and June.

The opposite, in growing conditions at least, are the flag irises, *Iris pseudocorus*, which are happiest in a bog or in the muddy shallows of a pond. They can become a thicket so I divide mine every few years, breaking or cutting up the clumps and replanting at wider spacing. *I. versicolor*, from America, will also be very happy in these boggy conditions but will also grow in a border with rich soil. The Japanese iris, *I. laevigata*, is bright blue and is best grown submerged in shallow water. There is also a white variety, *I. l.* var. *alba*.

Last but by no means least in the roll call of irises in my own garden is *I. sibirica*, which has small blue flowers tinged with mauve and yellow, and orange 'tiger'

Crocosmia 'Lucifer' is a powerful force in the summer Jewel Garden, not just for its vermilion flowers but also its dramatic, upright, sword-shaped foliage.

stripes at the base of the falls. It has a freshness and clarity that few other flowers of any sort ever achieve. It will grow both in the damp margins of a pond or quite happily in a border as long as the soil is not too light and has plenty of organic matter added to it. The foliage is much slimmer and floppier than that of bearded irises and it does need supporting. *I. sibirica* is available in other colours such as 'Ruffled Velvet', which is amethyst, and the claret-coloured 'Showdown'. But I love the clear blue the best.

The clumps grow outwards and tend to thin out in the centre, so it is a good idea to lift the whole lot every few years, divide them up and replant in a number of new groups which will grow away all the more vigorously for this treatment.

Crocosmias

Crocosmias are a very important part of the high-summer garden, although their large, strap-like leaves give body and form for weeks before the flowers emerge.

The dominant crocosmia in the Jewel Garden is 'Lucifer'. It is a hybrid from *Crocosmia masonorum*, which is a brilliant orange-red flower from South Africa, and *C. paniculata*. The leaves of 'Lucifer' appear like blades from the corms, behaving like one of my least-favourite gardening bits of jargon – an 'architectural plant' (what *does* that mean?) – and I support them early on so that they do not flop too much over their neighbours. The flowering stems rise above the leaves to a good 1m (3ft) high, making incredibly fine splays of pleated bud before they open into an upright row of blooms

standing on each spray, with orange bases and petals of their familiar devilish red. Well, vermilion, actually. It is as tough as old boots and will take any amount of cold and wet in winter, and needs no feeding or watering in summer (although that might be a reflection of my heavy soil). After it has flowered (it has quite a short season), the seedheads are worth their place, starting out as a row of green peas flanking the flowering spine and turning ochre into autumn.

We also grow *C.* x *crocosmiiflora* 'Emily Mackenzie', which has intense orange flowers and rather darker leaves. In fact, as I write, the dozen or so 'Emily Mackenzies' that we have in the garden are small plants, bunched in groups of three. But crocosmias spread and grow very large and it is a good idea to lift large clumps in early spring and tease the corms apart, replanting them in smaller groups. They will respond with increased vigour and flowers.

Dahlias

I grew up with dahlias. They are part of the flora of my strange childhood. My mother grew the big Cactus-flowered sort, all pinks, yellows and shouty reds. They had their own bed next to the veg, relegated along with gladioli in a kind of apartheid cutting garden. Here the soil was bare and every plant was supported by a stout, square stake of a kind we used for nothing else in the garden and which lived bundled at the back of the shed for most of the year. These vibrant, garish flowers duly served their turn in vases and then

ended on the compost heap in a slump of bedraggled petals, the remnants of a party stained with regret.

But I grow dahlias now in my own garden with a fervour and love everything about them. We have them singly in pots, as part of big containers growing alongside cannas, cosmos, bidens, petunias and nasturtiums, and in borders. All add immeasurably to the pleasure and beauty of the garden and I cannot conceive of being without them.

Of course they have their season. The dahlia year begins in early March, when we take out all the stored tubers overwintered in bakers' trays in what was a purpose-built apple store but proved a little warm for apples and never really worked. But it is ideal for dahlias and cannas. They are inspected to see if any have rotted (too wet) or shrivelled (too dry) and then are potted into compost. A few are put onto the hot bench to be forced for cuttings and the rest set out in a cold frame to gently ease into growth. Too much too soon is counterproductive because they will not be able to be planted out until May at the earliest.

Cuttings are taken in March and April, potted on and grown in a container or in the cutting beds for flowering in early autumn. They take a year or two to bulk up but it is an extremely easy way to increase stock of favourite cultivars.

In late May, after the tulips have finished, we take them out of the 20-odd large terracotta pots they always occupy in the Jewel Garden, line them out in a spare bit of ground to provide cut flowers for next spring, and use the pots for the

Dahlias grow equally well in pots, as part of a mixed border or as cut flowers. But they must be constantly deadheaded or picked to keep them flowering.

Jewel Garden dahlias such as 'Chimborazo', 'Bishop of Llandaff', 'Grenadier', 'Tamburo', 'Arabian Knight' and 'David Howard'.

'Rothesay Reveller', which is hugely floriferous, producing a mass of rich plum-coloured flowers seated on a white background, goes into the Orchard Beds and the pink Cactus varieties such as 'Hillcrest Royal' and a yellow one whose name I never knew but have often taken cuttings from are destined for the Cottage Garden. Any whose labels are lost or are growing rather weakly are lined out in a cutting border where they grow strongly and bulk up well.

We deadhead our dahlias almost daily to stop them setting seed and to keep the new flowers coming. Sometimes it can be hard to tell a bud from a used flower but the easiest way is to look at the shape. An unopened bud is always round whereas a

spent flower is more or less conical. I always cut right back to the next bud or leaf on the stem – which can often be a fair way – otherwise you end up with the new flowers appearing amongst a bristle of dead stems like a blooming porcupine.

Eventually frost gets them all and blackens the leaves to rags. This is the point – and not before – to bring them in. It is a mistake to 'protect' them from frost as the tubers grow a lot in the early days of autumn and are not touched by light frost, so bringing them in too early is at the price of next year's display. Large, plump tubers mean a healthy plant with lots of flowers the following season.

If your soil is well drained then they can be left outside in the borders, protected by a generous mulch. But we have found that if we do this we lose too many plants, mostly rotting in the damp soil.

We also grow tree dahlias – *Dahlia imperialis* – in the Grass Borders. These will reach 4.5m (15ft) tall. They rarely flower as they need a long, hot summer – of distant but loving memory – to produce their mass of small white flowers. These giants are also cut to the ground in early November but are lifted and stored directly in large pots. They take up an absurd amount of winter space and grow into 1.8m (6ft) monsters before they are hardy enough to plant out, so they are a ridiculous cuckoo in our gardening nest, but I rather love them for it and would not be without them.

Other summer bulbs

As we move into late summer, there come the South African bulbs such as galtonias, eucomis and gladioli. The most exotic of the lot is eucomis, which I grow in containers so I can bring them in during the winter to keep them dry as much as to protect them from cold. They like to be bone dry all winter and to have plenty of moisture in summer. I like the purple-leafed and purple-flowered hybrids of *Eucomis comosa* and the species itself – all are the toughest of the eucomis.

Galtonia candicans with its racemes of white flower bells always looks good at the back of a mixed border, the stems reaching to 1.8m (6ft) in the rich soil of the Writing Garden. Galtonias are fairly hardy but if in doubt it is best to treat them like dahlias and plant the bulbs in pots in spring and grow them on before planting out when the soil has warmed up. Then lift them in November and store somewhere cool and dry.

Tamburo' is a superb deep burgundy dahlia that we grow in the cut-flower beds.

After the dahlias have been dug up or lifted from their pots, we cut them right back, leaving about 15cm (6in) of hollow stems, take off the soil from the tubers and turn them upside down, under cover, for a few days to drain properly. This is the point where it is essential to make sure that every clump has a label firmly attached because it is nigh on impossible to tell varieties just from their tubers and stems. They are then packed in separate varieties in scrumpled-up newspaper, old potting compost, leafmould, sand or vermiculite – anything to slightly protect them and which will hold a little moisture. Then they are put on dark, cool but frost-free shelves for the winter. It is worth checking every six weeks or so to make sure that they are not too dry and lightly watering them if they are. Moist but not wet is the goal. Then March comes around and the cycle starts again.

Climbers

Twenty years ago I began this section of the book with the words, 'This garden is noticeably devoid of climbers against any of our walls.'

I went on to say, 'Of the very limited range of Climbers that we do grow here, clematis and sweet peas dominate. We do have a couple of climbing roses ('Souvenir du Docteur Jamain' and the Rambler 'Paul's Himalayan Musk') and a handful of honeysuckles.'

But much has changed since then. We still grow a lot of sweet peas and clematis in the borders up wigwams made from hazel bean sticks, but we now have six good climbing roses growing up walls and another four climbing permanent wooden supports, as well as over 20 rambling roses growing up apple trees in the Orchard. We also grow a wider range of annual climbers such as *Cobaea scandens* and *Eccremocarpus*, and have a wisteria growing over the structure on the Mound that has just begun to flower as I write these words in May. In short, our repertoire and number of climbers has greatly increased.

A garden with lots of height is always much more interesting – and environmentally rich – than one that is spread out flat like a carpet. The best place to start when wishing to maximise the virtues of height in your garden is to look at the available vertical surfaces. Most houses have at least one face that can be planted against and most gardens have a wall or fence around the outside. These are all ideal for training climbers against.

You can also easily erect fences and walls within the garden, however small it might be, to immediately provide two more vertical planes to grow plants against. In fact, many small gardens have more vertical growing space than horizontal.

Opposite page: The rambling rose 'Apple Blossom' climbing, appropriately, into an apple tree by one of our garden sheds.

Choosing climbers

It is a truth that most plants will grow in most places but if you want to make the best of the resources you have, then you must choose those plants that will thrive rather than merely survive where you plant them.

The smaller the space available, the more it is worth taking trouble with your choice. Where you have room for six plants in a theme or colour, it hardly matters if one fails. Where space only permits one specimen and that goes pear-shaped, then it blows the whole garden apart.

If you are not certain of the points of the compass in relation to your garden, then shame on you and you must rectify that immediately. To have any chance of growing things with any success you really must know where the sun rises, where it is in the middle of the day and where it sets – for every week of the year.

A south-facing wall will, of course, be on the north side of the house or garden. It is going to get the full effect of the sun from mid-morning until early evening, which is 9am until 3pm in winter and 10am until about 7pm in summer. The cold winds from north and east will not touch it. It is not just bright but hot and dry. It is exposed to winds from the south, which are invariably warm and drying, and fairly protected from westerlies that bring rain. The base of any wall, even after quite heavy rain, is a dry place. Brick or stone walls suck up moisture from the ground as well as deflecting a lot of rain,

so any plant against a south wall needs extra irrigation and mulching. Whilst a south-facing wall might seem horticultural heaven, there are many plants that find it too bright and hot. Most clematis, for example, are much happier against a west-facing wall and many do surprisingly well on a shady north wall. Notable exceptions to this rule are *Clematis armandii* or *C. cirrhosa* var. *balearica*, both of which love as much early-spring sunshine as they can get.

Many roses on a south-facing wall will do well early in the year and at the end of summer but will not give of their best in midsummer – which is when most roses flower. However, tender roses like *Rosa banksiae* 'Lutea' really must have a south wall – and a sheltered one at that – to give of their best. Wisteria always love a south wall as will ceanothus, eccremocarpus, jasmine and trachelospermum.

For all the sunny virtues of a south-facing wall, in many ways one that is west-facing is the best of the lot. By the time the sun has moved round to the west, the light is carrying much more heat so that a west-facing wall will be much warmer than one facing east, and secondly, the light will be much 'thicker'

and more intense. Strong colours seem to absorb this quality and reflect it so that oranges, purples and deep crimsons always look best when facing west. Thus late-summer clematis like *C. viticella* or *C.* 'Jackmanii' are ideal, with their range of purple and plum colours. Almost all climbing roses love a west-facing wall as do all honeysuckles. Camellias fare well and all fruit will ripen well. Sweet peas can do very well against a west wall but it is a mistake to plant them facing south as this will be too hot and dry. Above all, sweet peas need moisture and it is better to sacrifice a little sun to ensure that they remain wet enough.

Planting and care

All climbers should be planted well away from any wall or fence, and ideally up to 1m (3ft) away. This might look very odd initially, but if angled back to the wall with a cane, they will soon start to grow vertically. This spacing will give the plant a chance to establish without competing with the wall for moisture, and will allow rain to reach the roots.

Almost any climber will need support. This is best either via a series of wires attached tautly to hooks at 30cm (12in) spacing or using a trellis screwed onto wooden blocks that hold it well away from the surface of the wall or fence so that the plant can have room to grow without being cramped.

Do not use plastic-coated wire ties for anything other than annual climbers or growth that is to be pruned away at the end of the season as although they are very convenient, they cut into the plant tissue. Instead, always use soft twine.

The very first flowers of the white Japanese *Wisteria floribunda* 'Alba' planted on the Mound.

Climbers for a sunny wall

A south-facing wall will get most of the available sun (although not a lot more than a west-facing wall) and, most pertinently, is the hottest and driest wall. It is ideal for the tenderest climbers, especially if it is well sheltered.

However, it is generally unsuitable for most clematis, honeysuckles and many roses as it can get very dry, so choose your south-facing climbers carefully, both to make the most of this precious heat and to ensure that they can cope with the dry conditions. Then, having chosen, be sure to mulch well every year to retain what moisture there is.

Spanish flag (*Ipomoea lobata*) is a tender climbing annual that grows very easily from seed and will flower profusely if given enough sun, so is ideal for a south-facing fence or wall.

PLANTS FOR SOUTH-FACING WALLS

Where plants appear twice, it indicates that they have more than one distinct quality. Unless otherwise stated, these are all summer-flowering.

• Evergreen
Ceanothus impressus
Clematis armandii
Magnolia grandiflora
Trachelospermum jasminoides

• Spring-flowering
Clematis armandii
Jasminum beesianum
Wisteria x *formosa* 'Caroline'

• Autumn-flowering
Ceanothus 'Autumnal Blue'
Eccremocarpus scaber
Jasminum officinale
Solanum crispum 'Glasnevin'

• Winter-flowering
Clematis cirrhosa
Chimonanthus praecox 'Luteus'

• Annual
Eccremocarpus scaber
Ipomoea
Passiflora caerulea
Thunbergia alata

• Fast-growing
Ceanothus (any evergreen)
Fallopia baldschuanica (very vigorous)
Passiflora caerulea
Wisteria sinensis (once it gets going)

• Good scent
Jasminum officinale
Jasminum x *stephanense*
Rosa banksiae 'Lutescens'
Rosa x *fortuniana*
Solanum laxum 'Album'
Wisteria sinensis var. *sinensis* f. *alba*

Climbers for a shady wall

The smaller your garden, the more important it is that you make the most of all the walls and fences that you have, including those facing north and east, which will be more or less shady. Shade is not necessarily a 'problem' for the gardener to overcome. It inevitably means protection from the wind and rain as well as from the sun. Most green looks better in shade and many white flowers have evolved to shine out in shade (or at night time) and so draw the eye in.

The shadiest wall is always one facing north. The only time a north-facing wall gets any direct sunlight is in the first and last few hours of the day at midsummer – assuming nothing is blocking the rays of the sun as it sinks to or rises from the horizon. Therefore it will never be somewhere that you choose to sit but there are a number of flowering climbers that do well in quite deep shade. They all tend to have white or very pale flowers for the obvious reason that this makes them more visible for would-be pollinators.

Clematis 'Moonlight' fades to practically tissue colour in full sun whereas it retains a strong white glow in shade. I have a *C. montana* that is perfectly happy on its north wall and the flowers of the ubiquitous 'Nelly Moser' retain their colour much better out of the glare of sun, although it is perhaps better on an east wall if there is a choice. One of my favourite spring-flowering clematis, *C. macropetala*, is very comfortable in the lee of a north wall, too. Also try *C.* 'Snowbird', which is white.

The roses 'Madame Grégoire Staechelin' and 'Madame Alfred Carrière' are both good for a mass of flower on a dark wall. 'Zéphirine Drouhin' is a beautiful pink climbing rose and shade-loving, as well as having the quality of being thornless, so is good for placing near a path or a door. Two white Alba roses, 'Madame Legras de St. Germain' and 'Madame Plantier' are deliciously scented, tough and guaranteed to flower in shade, although only for about

Rosa 'Madame Alfred Carrière' is a superb rose for almost any aspect and very happy on a north- or east-facing wall. It will flower from May through to Christmas and although vigorous, can be pruned hard every year.

six weeks in June and July. The practically evergreen rambling rose, 'Albéric Barbier', is more ivory than white and is especially good on a shaded wall if you have enough space for it to ramble over. But my favourite rose for a north wall is the ruby-red 'Souvenir du Docteur Jamain', which actively prefers the cool shade.

Honeysuckles are woodland plants that have evolved to grow in the shade of a tree and clamber up in search of light, so if you have a door opening in a north wall, a honeysuckle planted beside and over it will spill its delicious scent every time you go in and out. *Lonicera* x *americana*, which has creamy, beautifully scented flowers in summer, *L.* x *brownii* with its scarlet trumpets in late summer and *L. caprifolium* in early summer will all perform well on a north fence or wall.

The winter honeysuckle, *L. fragrantissima*, is not really a climber but it can be pruned tight against a wall and a dry, north-facing one would be ideal. It has, I think, as lovely a fragrance as any flower.

There are a few plants, all suitable for a north wall, that are self-clinging and need no support. The most important are ivy, climbing hydrangea (*Hydrangea anomala* subsp. *petiolaris*), *Euonymus fortunei* var. *radicans* and Virginia creeper (*Parthenocissus quinquefolia*), although the latter will have better autumn colour if given some sun. Of these, the hydrangea is the most handsome, with white flowers in mid- to late summer. It can be slow to get established but have patience and it will make good progress after two or three years.

The winter-flowering jasmine (*Jasminum nudiflorum*) will produce its buttery flowers on bare green stems in the deepest, driest shade. The same is true of the ornamental quinces (*Chaenomeles*), but an east-facing wall is also ideal for both of these early-spring flowering plants.

An east-facing wall gets a lot of light – but only until midday. In the afternoon and evening it is in shade. Morning sun can be very bright but also rather thin and is best suited to soft colours – all the pastels, yellows and whites, as well as the cooler blues look at their best planted so that they catch the first light.

The best-known rule about an east-facing wall is directly connected to the morning sunshine, and it is that such a wall is not a good place for any delicate early-flowering climbers. The reason is that in cold weather the wall will have been cooling since midday and is prone to any frost that is about. The frost itself will probably not damage any hardy flowers but a cold spring night is often followed by a bright morning. The first light will be intensified by the layer of ice around the flowers and will scorch them. By the time the much hotter sun reaches the west wall opposite – which might have been just as frosty – the frost will have melted and no damage will be done. Not all plants are afflicted (for

A honeysuckle planted beside a door in a north wall will spill its delicious scent every time you go in and out

example, ornamental quinces shrug off any combination of ice and sun) but camellias in particular are prone to this type of damage and should not be planted on an east wall except in the mildest areas, even though they will flower very well on it.

Many clematis – especially spring-flowering ones – do well on an east-facing wall although the lack of moisture against such a wall is a bigger problem for them than the lack of sun. Keep them well watered and mulch thickly every spring.

Clematis 'Étoile Violette' growing up a bean-stick wigwam in the Jewel Garden.

Shrubs

There was a time in my childhood when there was a trend to grow shrubs as a labour-saving device. All over England, in gardens larger than average, borders and vegetable gardens were put down to grass.

They were a kind of inverted reduction of a border, with individual shrubby specimens scattered across a grassed area that had formerly contained a number of intensely planted flower beds. The emergence of garden centres meant that you could go out on a Saturday morning, come back with half a dozen shrubs in flower and plant them on Sunday. Before then you would have had to order from a pictureless catalogue and wait six months for delivery of a bare-root specimen. Not so gratifying and not nearly so instant. In its own quiet way it was the beginning of a gardening revolution.

It is fashionable to be dismissive of this, but shrubs can be used creatively en masse to look beautiful as well as being incorporated into a border or within woodland. It is a question of choice and judgement and of using the basic structure that defines shrubby plants – with their mass of woody, permanent branches growing from the base – to best effect.

I grow many shrubs in my garden, from witch hazel, Species roses and azaleas in the Spring Garden through scores of glorious roses in the Cottage Garden, lilacs, buddleja and sambucus in the Jewel Garden, and hydrangeas, philadelphus and amelanchier in the Orchard Beds. No other type of plant gives the same range of width or graceful spread in relation to its height, and its woody structure means that its flowers and foliage are held more or less in space without needing support.

Shrubs are tough. Many resist cold, wind, rabbits and human neglect. Many respond gratefully to a modicum of care in the shape of a little pruning and weeding. They take very little from the gardener and give an awful lot back. Shrubberies may have a dank and gloomy Victorian image but there is no practical reason why they cannot brighten and enrich your garden throughout the year – and for many years to come.

Opposite page: The *Viburnum plicatum* f. *tomentosum* 'Mariesii' in the Damp Garden has tiers of white blossom in May – and then in autumn it has a second display, when the leaves turn an intense deep burgundy colour.

Planting shrubs

Plant shrubs as you would a tree, with a wide hole with a loosened, but not deeply dug base.

Shrubs for small gardens that can be pruned hard

- *Buddleija*
- *Cornus*
- *Corylus avellana*
- *Fuchsia* (hardy)
- *Rubus cockburnianus*
- *Sambucus*
- *Salix daphnoides*
- *Weigela*

Opposite page, clockwise from top left: Making a hole in our heavy clay in the Berry Border to plant a cornus; adding mycorrhizal powder to the roots to help them quickly establish and grow; setting the height so the plant is not too deep; back-filling and firming the shrub into position.

Do not add organic material to the planting hole unless the soil is very heavy, in which case some garden compost and horticultural grit or sharp sand will help open the soil out for the initial root growth, but always mulch thickly and widely with good compost. Water in very well, even on a wet winter's day and allow plenty of space for your young shrubs to grow – you can always infill with a temporary planting of bulbs, annuals or grasses if it looks too empty.

- When planting any shrub, it is a good idea to add mycorrhizal powder. This should be dusted directly onto the roots and the soil in the planting hole so the roots make direct contact with it. This is very helpful in aiding the shrub to establish quickly and take up all available nutrients. It can be bought from any garden centre.
- An established shrub will provide the best flowers, so pick sparingly for the first few years, letting the plant establish a strong root system that will then support repeated removal of foliage and flowers.
- All shrubs should be kept weed-free and mulched generously with garden compost or a thick layer of wood bark to suppress weeds and retain moisture.

PRUNING SHRUBS

- **The first rule** of all pruning is when in doubt, don't.

- **The second rule** is to always cut back to something, be it a leaf, bud or branch.

- **Notice** if the flowers are produced on the current year's fresh growth or on the previous year's. If the former, it is best to prune in early spring – as with buddleja – and if the latter, the time to do it is immediately after flowering – as with *Ribes*.

- **If you are growing a shrub for its leaves,** as I do with a cut-leaf golden elder, cut it back hard each spring and the new leaves will be both bigger and better coloured than if it is left unpruned.

- **Always prune** any woody plant using sharp secateurs and never risk leaving damaged wood by forcing the cut. If it will not cut easily it means that you need to use two-handed loppers.

- **Remember that pruning provokes growth,** so if you have a lopsided shrub, prune the weaker side back hard and leave the well-developed side alone. This will balance the shrub out.

Shrubs for lime soil

- *Berberis*
- *Brachyglottis*
- *Buxus*
- *Cistus*
- *Cotoneaster*
- *Daphne*
- *Deutzia*
- *Elaeagnus*
- *Escallonia*
- *Euonymus*
- *Forsythia*
- *Fuchsia*
- *Hebe*
- *Kerria*
- *Kolkwitzia*
- *Mahonia*
- *Osmanthus*
- *Paeonia*
- *Philadelphus*
- *Potentilla*
- *Pyracantha*
- *Ribes*
- *Romneya*
- *Rosemarinus*
- *Rubus*
- *Syringa*
- *Viburnum*
- *Weigela*

Shrubs for acidic soil

- *Azalea*
- *Calluna*
- *Camellia*
- *Clethra*
- *Erica*
- *Gaultheria*
- *Hydrangea macrophylla*
- *Kalmia*
- *Pernettya*
- *Pieris*
- *Rhododendron*

Flowering shrubs for cutting

Although the best known and best loved, roses are by no means the only shrubs that can provide wonderful cut flowers.

Lilacs are scruffy shrubs but the flowers are superb and look terrific either on their own or as part of a bigger arrangement. To ensure the very best and biggest lilac blooms, prune old stems right to the ground immediately after flowering, and water and mulch the shrub very generously. Next year's flowers will be bigger and more profuse as a result.

Hydrangeas are essential components of a good cut-flower border. *Hydrangea macrophylla* will flower pink on alkaline soil and blue if it is acidic, and these flowers last long into autumn. It flowers best on older

Roses make the best cut flowers of all and English roses like this 'Charles Darwin' will flower all summer if cut regularly.

wood, so leave any unpicked flower heads on until April and then remove with a short stem attached. If it gets too crowded, cut older branches right back to the ground.

H. paniculata 'Grandiflora' has magnificent white flowers in late summer that open from pale green buds – which are also good as part of an arrangement. It flowers on new growth so can be pruned hard each spring, making it ideal for limited space despite its dramatic flowers. *H. arborescens* 'Annabelle' has enormous pale green flowers that will regrow steadily throughout late summer and autumn if you keep picking them. Like *H. paniculata*, it flowers on new wood so can be pruned hard in spring. Buddlejas make wonderful cut flowers and by removing the blooms from the plant, you encourage more to replace them – so are not denying butterflies essential food. The species is a pale purple and earns a perfectly honourable place in almost any garden but the hybrids have been bred primarily to be more intense in colour and are therefore especially suited to the cutting garden. I particularly like 'Ellen's Blue', which is a plant that holds its spent flowers particularly well, *Buddleja davidii* 'Glasnevin Hybrid', which has quite small, silvery leaves and lavender flowers, *B. d.* 'Black Knight', which is an intense maroon and

Fuchsias look wonderful as part of a floral display, indoors and out, and can take repeated cutting.

B. d. 'Royal Red', which is a purple so iridescent red that it is almost magenta, especially when the tiny orange centres to each floret are visible to add to the effect. You can also get white buddlejas such as *B. d.* 'Peace', *B. d.* 'White Bouquet' and *B. d.* 'White Cloud'.

All buddlejas flowering after June produce their leaves on new shoots so need pruning back hard in March, leaving just a couple of strongly growing leaves below the cut. This can look drastic but will stimulate lots of new growth and as a result, lots of butterfly-enticing flowers.

Of course, shrubs do not just provide flowers but are also an invaluable source of foliage for flower arrangements. To some extent this can be taken from random shrubs growing all over the garden but it is worth especially growing *Cotinus* in the cutting garden for its spectacular purple leaves that turn crimson in autumn. There are a number of different *Cotinus* varieties

to choose from but *C.* 'Grace' is particularly good. Like all purple-leafed plants it does much better in full sun and needs rich but well-drained soil. You can let *Cotinus* grow into a large shrub but it also responds well to very hard pruning in spring, removing all growth save for two or three buds. It will respond to this drastic pruning by producing extra-large leaves.

The guelder rose (*Viburnum opulus*) serves both as a provider of white flowers in late spring and of scarlet foliage and bright red berries in autumn. Provided it has plenty of moisture, it is not fussy where it grows and is an incredibly useful cut-flower plant.

A flowering shrub for early-spring flowers is *Daphne odora* 'Aureomarginata'. The flowers – white delicately touched with pink – are not only beautiful in a small vase but also deliciously fragrant. It needs a little shade and will grow fairly easily although rather slowly. But worth the wait.

Shrubs with scented flowers

- *Buddleja*
- *Ceanothus* x *delileanus* 'Gloire de Versailles'
- *Choisya ternata*
- *Corylopsis*
- *Daphne*
- *Elaeagnus*
- *Hamamelis mollis*
- *Lonicera*
- *Magnolia*
- *Osmanthus*
- *Rosa*
- *Syringa*
- *Viburnum*

Winter shrubs

Winter-flowering shrubs tend to be fairly nondescript plants when compared to their more flamboyant spring or summer rivals but in the bleak midwinter, their flowers are carried like precious jewels and they make a really significant contribution to the garden. And most make excellent cut flowers with fragrance that can fill a room.

Perhaps my favourite is the winter-flowering honeysuckle (*Lonicera fragrantissima*) which manages to be both modest and glorious at the same time. It has tiny ivory flowers on its untidy scramble of bare, woody stems (although in mild areas it will be almost evergreen). The flowers would scarcely be noticed in the hurly burly of a May garden but earn pride of place in winter. However, the real point of these flowers is that they have a haunting and supremely sensuous fragrance that is as good as anything that grows in the garden at any time of year. It is a shrub that will grow perfectly happily in dry shade and does not need feeding or rich soil as this will only encourage a mass of foliage at the expense of flowers.

The winter-flowering honeysuckles are in the triangular slither of ground that we call the Spring Garden, which is really a tiny piece of deciduous woodland underplanted with bulbs, hellebores, early clematis, Species roses and early herbaceous perennials, all of which thrive in the period before the trees come fully into leaf.

We also used to have a witch hazel (*Hamamelis* x *intermedia*) planted there that presented us with intense lemon flowers each January, looking something between

confetti caught on the branches of the shrub and the tendrils of sea anemones. I planted it about eight years ago and although it flowered well enough, its growth was so slow as to be imperceptible. After eight years it had practically shrunk. At first I thought that the ground was too alkaline because witch hazel likes its soil to be slightly acidic and I had been mulching with mushroom compost, which tends to

Witch hazel has lovely confetti-like flowers in January and February.

make a soil more alkaline, but the soil there has a pH of about 6.5, which is fine. Slowly I worked out what was wrong. Witch hazel likes and needs sunshine and shelter. It does best at the edge of a shrubbery or woodland. I was giving it lots of shelter but by mid-May, the leaf canopy had closed over it and during its growing season – which is after the flowers have finished – it was receiving practically no light at all. So give your witch hazel light and air as well as shelter, and neutral to acidic soil, and it should flourish. The leaves turn a good autumnal colour, too, with most turning yellow but with, notably, *Hamamelis* x *intermedia* 'Diane' and *H.* x *intermedia* 'Ruby Glow' turning red in a good year.

Like the winter-flowering honeysuckle, wintersweet (*Chimonanthus praecox*) is a deciduous shrub that has tiny flowers that smell delicious carried on the bare branches. New growth can get hit by frost or cold winds, so it is a good idea to give it some shelter or a west- or south-facing wall or fence, but other shrubs around it would do the trick. Also, a sprinkling of wood ash in early autumn will help ripen the new wood before winter. The flowers are egg-yolk yellow, an impression heightened by the scarlet interior base to each petal. It grows best on well-drained soil and is very happy on chalk or limestone. I grow mine in a pot, which means I can give it the drainage it likes as well as move it to bask in summer sun and then to the shadier spot by the back door when it flowers, so we can make the most of its fragrance.

Another shrub that tends to thrive on chalky soil is daphne. There is the early-flowering *Daphne bholua*, whilst *D. mezereum*

var. *autumnalis* will also flower very early in the year. Like so many other very early flowers, they have an extraordinarily powerful scent from their dark pink, almost mauve, flowers – although there is a white-flowering form too. The pink flowers make red berries whereas the white forms have yellow berries.

Winter-flowering jasmine (*Jasminum nudiflorum*) grows in a green tangle covered with yellow flowers in almost any aspect or conditions, although it will flower better in whatever sunshine January and February have on offer. The secret of keeping it looking really good is to prune it back hard immediately after flowering. Like wintersweet, it can be used to cover a fence.

We associate the yellow of daffodils, primroses, catkins and cowslips with spring and then look to plant more yellow spring flowers to reinforce that association. However, *Viburnum* x *bodnantense* has white bobbles of flower and *V.* x *bodnantense* 'Dawn' has the same but in pink. 'Charles Lamont' is another variety with pink flowers whilst *V. tinus* is evergreen with white flowers that start out as pink buds.

Daphne bholua can be temperamental and hates being disturbed but is worth the trouble for its wonderfully fragrant winter flowers.

Shrubs for shade

- *Camellia*
- *Choisya ternata*
- *Daphne laureola*
- *Elaeagnus*
- *Fatsia*
- *Garrya elliptica*
- *Hypericum*
- *Kerria japonica*
- *Mahonia*
- *Osmanthus decorus*
- *Pyracantha*
- *Ribes alpinum*
- *Skimmia japonica*
- *Viburnum davidii*

Shrubs with coloured bark and stems

A number of barks shine with jewel-like brilliance in the depths of winter, especially in the month or two between the sap beginning to rise and the first leaf buds emerging.

They would be diminished by the brightness of spring, let alone the glare of summer, but are the brightest thing in the landscape on a grey or even wet January day. Cometh the hour, cometh the plant.

The best known is the dogwood (*Cornus alba*), which has brilliant stems in shades of crimson. It is the new growth that shines the most and if you coppice it back hard to a stool 5–7.5cm (2–3in) from the ground, the smooth, whippy stems grow up

thicket-thick like a haze of intense coral. The trick is to cut half of each shrub back each year. All the varieties of *C. alba* grow in almost all conditions (hence their invariable use in municipal and corporate planting), but they thrive in rich, slightly damp soil in full sun. *C. alba* 'Sibirica' (sometimes called *C.* 'Westonbirt') is the most common, principally, I suspect, because it does not get too big and therefore is better suited to small gardens,

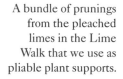

A bundle of prunings from the pleached limes in the Lime Walk that we use as pliable plant supports.

but there are a number of *C. alba* varieties, all with red shoots except *C. a.* 'Kesselringii', which has melodramatic purple-black stems.

The common dogwood (*C. sanguinea*) has richly coloured stems and wonderful deep purple autumn leaves (there are miles of dogwood hedges along the lanes around here), and the cultivated varieties *C. s.* 'Winter Beauty' and *C. s.* 'Magic Flame' have all the common dogwood's robustness and distinctly orangey stems. *C. stolonifera* 'Flamiravera' has wonderful shoots that are yellow ochre at the tips, maturing to a rich olive-green at their base. In this garden it seems to produce much denser growth than *C. alba* and shimmers rather than glows. These niceties matter on a bleak January afternoon.

There are some willows that have fabulously bright skins on their branches and can also be cut back hard every year to encourage more vigorous, especially vivid growth. One cannot overstress this point with these shrubs grown for their bark – the harder you cut them back, the more vigorous and dynamic the resulting growth and the more intense the colour between December and March.

Whilst the dogwoods will grow anywhere, willows have a distinct preference for damp soil and will struggle on chalk or sand. There is the golden willow (*Salix alba* var. *vitellina*), with yellow stems veering towards a yolky orange, the hybrid crack willow (*S.* x *rubens*) and the red willow (*S. a.* var. *vitellina* 'Britzensis'), which is more vermilion than scarlet. *S. daphnoides* has purple stems coated in cottony bloom.

Although willows and dogwoods look best in groups, there is hardly any need to buy them in bulk unless you are impatient, because they all take very easily as hardwood cuttings (see page 95), especially the willows. When I cut them back in early March, I always stick a group of 20cm (8in) cut stems in a row in a corner of the seed bed, perhaps adding some sharp sand to the narrow trench first. They can be planted out the following autumn.

A few of the ornamental brambles have stems that are covered in a white bloom over winter, which makes them starkly ornate. The problem with these ornate brambles is one of space. I grow *Rubus cockburnianus* 'Goldenvale', primarily for its lime-green foliage in spring and summer, but it also has wonderful winter stems, a pinky red dusted liberally with a white bloom. It also takes terribly easily from cuttings and I have found that it will quickly become invasive if you don't keep it cut back, as it roots wherever the arching stems touch the soil – as I suppose you might expect a bramble to do. However, prune it like another bramble, the autumn-fruiting raspberry, and cut the whole thing to the ground each spring, and this will stymie any incipient suckers and encourage vibrant new growth. The true *R. cockburnianus* seems to have a whiter bloom than 'Goldenvale' and is probably a better bet for a winter display.

Shrubs with purple foliage

- *Acer palmatum* 'Dissectum Atropurpureum'
- *Cercis canadensis* 'Forest Pansy'
- *Corylus maxima* 'Purpurea'
- *Cotinus coggygria* 'Royal Purple'
- *Malus* x *purpurea*; *M.* x *p.* 'Lemoinei'
- *Rosa rubrifolia*
- *Sambucus nigra* 'Guincho Purple'
- *Weigela florida* 'Foliis Purpureis'

Shrubs with berries

There are a number of flowering shrubs that have exceptional fruit, for that is all any berry is, edible or otherwise. To get fruit you must leave the flowers to fade into shaggy maturity. Deadhead your roses and you get no hips.

For many gardeners leaving the flowers goes against the puritanical grain of tidiness, unlike the more reasonable practice of cutting back faded flower heads to stimulate more flowers. The fruit need summer sun to ripen, so shrubs that flower in May and June tend to make better berriers than later-flowering plants. Also, shrubs that produce a mass of flowers (ideally high up, well out of tidiness's way) are always going to be a better bet for berries than those with a few choice 'blooms'.

The white berries of *Cornus alba* 'Sibirica' are in stark contrast to the blazing red stems.

The most obvious candidates for this harvest of neglect are roses. Not all roses produce hips (just berries by another name) but most do and some almost more spectacularly than they flower. In the main, the Species roses are more prolific and interesting hip-bearers than Hybrid roses. Hips have an unbreakable link for me with haws, the fruit of the hawthorn, whose blossom is best on untended hedges between fields rather than on all the neatly trimmed roadside ones. So anyone not near stretches of wild-hedged fields misses the beauty of haws turning a dark red as they ripen and become irresistibly delicious for the birds.

Hips and haws framed against bare twigs or yellowing leaves are part of the pleasant melancholy of autumn but the bright red of a berry against an evergreen leaf is a defiant stand against winter. Nothing else quite hits this button in the same way as holly. When people complain that their holly is failing to produce berries, it is usually for faults of gender rather than performance because for holly to have berries, it must be female with a male reasonably near to hand to pollinate with. Many of the variegated cultivars are male and will never bear berries. As I've already observed, the names hardly help: 'Golden

Far left: The berries of *Callicarpa bodinieri* var. *giraldii* are the most unusual in any garden with their purple, almost metallic, sheen.

Left: Birds love the massed berries of cotoneaster and the spreading branches provide excellent cover for wildlife too.

Queen' is a male as is 'Silver Queen', but 'Golden King' is female. All very confusing. Nor are all holly berries red. *Ilex aquifolium* 'Bacciflava' has masses of yellow fruits like tiny little lemons.

The oddest of berries are those of *Callicarpa bodinieri* var. *giraldii*, which have a metallic sheen to their purple shanks, as unvegetative as anything growing in the garden. It has taken years for the one bush here to get established and it is still small, although now growing healthily and smothered in small berries, which will stay on long after the leaves fall and will grow more metallic as autumn pushes in.

Pyracantha seems to be regarded as rather a lowly plant but I like it, both for its tiny white summer flowers that smell so intensely sweet and which bees love so much, and for its fabulous display of berries. I like its common name, firethorn, as it perfectly describes the way the berries blaze out from the unexceptional matt leaves. At a time of year when light and colour are at a premium, the firethorn more than earns its place in any garden. One should be as brash as possible with *Pyracantha* and 'Orange Glow' is as brash as they come although 'Navaho' or 'Golden Charmer' push it hard.

Cotoneaster is slightly more subtle and slightly less dramatic, but still jolly in the kind of way that is infra dig. But, like *Pyracantha*, it will grow in dry shade, trains well against a wall or fence, has lovely berries and there are hundreds of different species to choose from (although I realise that for most people that can be a daunting turn-off – a choice of five good ones would be enough). Most are completely unfussy about where you put them as long as it is not boggy, and they will tolerate dry shade. Prostrate cotoneasters like *Cotoneaster horizontalis* are not the most inspired of choices for groundcover, but they can be very useful to hide a septic tank or somesuch, especially in dry shade.

Roses

In my twenties, although a keen gardener, I had no real feeling for roses as plants. I liked them as flowers in the kind of knee-jerk way that most of us love sunsets or the song of a blackbird, and grew them almost because I felt that was what was required of anyone planting a 'proper' garden, not because they had any special meaning to me.

This all changed when I bought my mother-in-law a couple of roses for her birthday and became seduced by the names of the roses in the catalogue of a local nursery. They were all 'old' or 'classic' roses – Gallicas, Albas, Damasks, Mosses, Centifolias, Bourbons – not fashionable back then in the 1980s. Their names ran off my tongue like a floral charm, conjuring a velvety richness and fulsome sensuality that the Floribundas and Hybrid Teas of my youth had never even hinted at. I was hooked.

So I went and visited the nursery – Acton Beauchamp Roses – and ordered about 50 different ones, three of each at an absurdly cheap wholesale price of about a pound or so a rose. That summer the little stubby plants produced their first flowers and I savoured and tried each one as a wine buff tasting a new vintage. A lifelong passion had begun.

I bought and devoured Peter Beale's wonderful book *Classic Roses* – still the best on the subject – and visited his nursery in Suffolk. He became my wise rose guru and until his untimely death, my guiding rose spirit.

When we moved to this garden I dug up a few dozen of those first roses and took them with me. Then I became severely depressed and did very little for a year or so. They were dark days. But my wife would pick small bunches of roses from the pots I had not yet planted out and place them in vases before me – 'Tuscany', 'Charles De Mills', 'Alba Semi-Plena', 'Celestial', 'Chapeau de Napoléon', 'De Resht' – and those exquisite flowers lightened my deep darkness.

In time I planted them all out and some still remain, a quarter of a century later, still flowering. Since then I have acquired perhaps a couple of hundred different roses here – I have never counted – and love them all.

They begin with the yellow Species roses in the Spring Garden – *Rosa hugonis*, *R.* 'Cantabrigiensis' and *R. primula*. Each has its own individual charm but all share the same single, pale yellow flowers.

A few years ago I added 32 of my favourite roses to the Cottage Garden – one in each corner of the eight square beds – and now they are substantial shrubs frothing with every shade of pink flower for about six weeks from the end of May to mid-July.

You have to have faith in these shrub roses for a year or two. They should all be

Opposite page: The flowers of *Rosa* x *alba* 'Alba Maxima' are an exquisite muddle of slightly pink-flushed white petals.

Above: The very ancient Gallica rose flowers for just a few glorious weeks in June.

Above right: The modern English rose 'Crown Princess Margareta' will go on producing new flowers all summer long.

Opposite page: The climbing rose 'Madame Caroline Testout' trained against the south-facing wall backing the Dry Garden.

pruned hard on planting – which takes a bit of nerve – and for the first year or two, the new growth will be too small and too sappy to satisfactorily carry the flowers – which of course, like apples on a very young tree, are all full size from year one. But by year three there is sufficient permanent structure to hold the flowers high and proud.

I also have a couple of beds of yellow and apricot roses – 'Pilgrim', 'Crown Princess Margareta', 'Vanessa Bell', 'Roald Dahl' and 'Charles Darwin' – all David Austin English roses that flower profusely, whereas most of the Classic roses flower once for about a month, with the occasional second flurry later in summer. I have added English roses to the Mound and to the Paradise and Jewel Gardens too.

I love the simplicity and purity of Species roses and have a couple of dozen different ones now in various parts of the garden, but especially in the new Orchard Beds where I

want them to relate to the simplicity of the apple blossom. Some are very well known and straightforward such as *Rosa* 'Dupontii', *R. pimpinellifolia* or *R. glauca* whereas others, like *R. cinnammonea* or *R. corymbifera* are a bit more arcane, but all are entirely themselves, untouched by the guile of the breeder. The hand of man has never improved them. If they tangle and twist, then that is what they do. If they only flower for a few days, then that is unchangeable. This imbues them with a freshness and wildness that I love.

One of their great attractions for the gardener nervous about roses and the various problems they may have, from blackspot to powdery mildew or rust (see page 270), is that Species roses are amongst the toughest plants in the garden and will grow in almost any soil and any position. They hardly ever suffer from any of the afflictions that their more highly bred cousins suffer from.

I have had a pair of *R. moyesii* shrubs (to be honest two groups of three) at the back of the Grass Borders that I planted back in 1997. I replace the old growth every few years by pruning the woodiest stems down to the ground but they show no sign of diminishing their performance, with their glorious spangle of flowers evenly spread across the large shrub like a blood-red stellar display. They then go on to have a second performance as the flowers convert into dramatic, bottle-shaped orange hips hanging like artfully placed decoration as spectacular as any flowering.

As well as *R. moyesii*, many of the Species' flowers fruit into lovely, curvy hips. *R. rugosa* are like tomatoes, those of *R. pimpinellifolia* are a deep brown and those on *R. glauca* are bunched like grapes. *R.* 'Wintoniensis' has great clusters of flagon-shaped hips that have a curious purplish bloom.

If you want to make the most of these hips then you should not prune until late winter – and then only to remove dead or damaged wood or to restrict the size. But if you want to make the most of the flowers, the time to prune is immediately after flowering. But don't get in a state about it. it. Just cut out dead wood and take off any crossing or damaged stems or those that are becoming very old, taking them right back to ground level. Then let the shrub get on with what it does perfectly well without any help from even the most skilful gardener.

There are two types of climbing roses, Climbers and Ramblers. The major difference between the two is how and when they flower. Climbers – like Hybrid Teas and most Shrub roses – form their

flowers on new wood that grows in spring before flowering, whereas Ramblers – like most Species roses – do so on the growth that took place in the previous spring and summer. Ramblers such as *R. multiflora* 'Carnea', 'Ethel', 'Paul's Himalayan Musk', 'Alister Stella Grey', 'Cécile Brünner', 'Wedding Day' or 'Rambling Rector' make one gorgeous, frothy display of small flowers produced in clusters for just 4–6 weeks in summer.

Climbers – such as 'Madame Alfred Carrière', 'Souvenir de la Malmaison', 'Zéphirine Drouhin' or 'Climbing Madame Caroline Testout'– tend to have larger individual flowers that last for longer and many repeat-flower throughout much of summer. In general, Climbers are also much easier to train against a fence or wall whereas most Ramblers are happiest when left scrambling freely up a tree.

I have planted Climbers and Ramblers up most of the apple trees – including those in the Writing Garden and, like the roses in the Cottage Garden, this was the first year that they really started to perform. They can only get better and will see me out even if I live to 100 – which I fully intend to do, gardening to the end.

ROSE PROBLEMS

• **Balling** is the state where the bud almost opens but the outer petals form a carapace that stops it developing into a flower at the last moment. The result is a ball of petals that rots and eventually drops off. This can be salvaged if you tease apart the outer petals, literally freeing the rose from its bonds. It is caused by prolonged rain at the late-bud stage and is especially bad if the rain is followed by hot sun which dries the buds and forms a crust.

• **Blackspot** is a fungal disease made worse by too much atmospheric moisture – i.e. rain – and there is little that you can do about it. The best policy is to prune well in spring so that each plant has good ventilation, not to crowd the roses with too many leafy herbaceous plants (which is what we tend to do here and which stops air flow and holds water), and to collect up all fallen leaves and burn them so that the fungus does not linger in the soil at the base of the bush. There is some evidence that growing tomatoes near – and even twining through – roses helps ward off blackspot. But it sounds aesthetically challenged.

• **Powdery mildew,** which takes the form of a pale grey mould on shoots and leaves, is a problem exacerbated by the base of the plant being too dry. The rose gets weakened and becomes more prone to blackspot and other diseases. It often happens in apparently wet summer weather when the leaves are getting soaked in a lot of gentle moisture, but a combination of evaporation and the umbrella effect of the foliage means that very little moisture actually reaches the ground. Along with sunshine, plenty of water is what roses like, so give them a soak if the soil is very dry.

• **Rust** is another disease that thrives in wet, warm weather. It starts with small orange pustules on the underneath of leaves that can spread very quickly over the whole plant. These spores turn brown and eventually black, killing the leaves. Remove any leaf that has a trace of rust and burn it. As with all fungal diseases, clean up round the base of the plant scrupulously in autumn so that the spores cannot overwinter in the ground.

Planting and care

- Plant roses deep so that the stems – not just a central trunk – protrude from the soil.
- Always prune newly planted roses ruthlessly hard immediately after planting to encourage strong growth from the ground.
- Cut back weak stems in late winter to induce strong regrowth and trim over-long stems in autumn to stop the wind rocking the roots.
- Established Shrub roses do not really need pruning. Tests have shown that a trim with a hedge-cutter is as effective for health and flowering as careful and selective pruning.

- It is important to deadhead if you want to prolong flowering. Never just pull off the faded petals but cut back to the next leaf or bud with secateurs.
- Late-flowering clematis such as *Clematis viticella* or *C.* 'Jackmanii' are ideal for growing through a rose shrub, flowering just as the roses are coming to an end. The clematis is pruned back to the ground in early spring, so does not smother the roses. A good partnership.

Shrub roses need little pruning other than to remove old or damaged growth, leaving a sturdy framework to carry new growth.

The Climbers and Ramblers up most of the apple trees can only get better and will see me out even if I live to 100

Wildflower meadows, grasses and bamboos

One of the biggest changes to this garden over the past five years was the decision to have as little short grass as possible and to replace it with flower-filled long grass. The result is a series of small – some, mere strips along a hedgerow – wildflower meadows.

A large hayfield of dozens of different flower species dominating the grass is a glorious sight although vanishingly rare because in the UK, 98 per cent of all wildflower meadows have been lost to intensive agriculture since 1945. The sad truth is that it takes years to make a flower-filled meadow – and many have endured for hundreds of years – but they can be destroyed in one afternoon.

But gardeners can make meadows with all the same intrinsic qualities on a very small scale, and our enthusiasm for wildflowers in this garden is being taken up much more widely nowadays, with many people allowing some or all of their previously tightly mown lawns to grow free and run wild.

I suspect that the recent adoption of wildflowers in the garden is as much to do with a growing realisation that gardens are an important source of pollen and nectar for insects, as with a love of the wildflowers themselves. There is no need to discriminate or make a hierarchy of either – insects and flowers are yoked as close as birds and sky.

For 20 years this was a neatly mown strip of lawn but it was always rather wet, so in the past few years we have let the grass grow and planted snowdrops, fritillaries and camassias, which all thrive in the damp.

The management of meadows

Although technically there are variations on the theme, a meadow is essentially a grass field that is managed and mown for hay. This means that once the grass starts to grow in spring – usually in April – the field is 'shut up' and grazing stock kept out of it so that it can grow. It is then cut and all the hay taken away some time between mid-June and October, depending on weather and location, and the 'aftermath' – the regrowth following the hay harvest – is grazed throughout autumn and winter. Until World War Two this was practically the only way that animals could have enough fodder to survive over winter, and hay meadows

With the correct wildflower seed mix, you can have the right combination of grasses and flowers for any garden

were therefore found wherever cattle and sheep were kept. Pasture, on the other hand, is grassland that is grazed year round. It is possible to have an interesting pasture ecosystem but it will be different and usually much less diverse than that of a meadow.

The critical factor for the biodiversity of a meadow is the timing of the cut and that it is not fed except by the manure from the grazing animals, or perhaps with occasional manure spread

after the hay is cut. This ensures that the grasses do not overwhelm the accompanying annual and perennial plants. If you feed grass nitrogen, it will respond with rapid growth. The result is that almost immediately, many of the accompanying flowers cannot compete and ironically, the only ones that can, are the thugs like docks and thistles.

So although it can be cut, trampled upon, grazed, even reduced to a quagmire in winter, a meadow is delicate. Its balance and ecosystem are dependent upon the timing of its cut and the amount it is fed.

You can grow a meadow almost anywhere. One of the gardening myths of 'wildflower meadows' is that they will only thrive on poor, shallow soil. This is not true although, like all myths, it is based upon a grain of truth which is that grasses grow best in rich, deep, well-drained topsoil, and where grasses grow best, they tend to out-muscle most neighbouring plants. However, if you get your seed mix correct, then you can have the right combination of grasses and flowers for damp soil, shade, clay, chalk, peat, mountain – almost any conceivable garden situation.

Incidentally, mowing lawns is rather like farmers feeding their meadows nitrogen and cutting them for silage before any flowers have a chance to seed. It is a form of aggressive monoculture. That is not to say that lawns do not look nice but in general, it would make a world of difference to all forms of biodiversity if we mowed less grass and allowed more to grow long.

Making a wildflower meadow on grass

However, you cannot make a wildflower meadow simply by letting your lawn grow unmown. This will be highly beneficial to wildlife but is unlikely to result in a very varied mix of wildflowers because grass will always dominate at the expense of everything else. Grass is one of nature's winners. It takes over. It not only dominates but thrives on being cut and eaten and generally knocked about. This is what makes it so useful as a lawn or surface for sports. It is also fruitless to scatter wildflower seed onto a lawn because most seed needs contact with bare soil to germinate.

In practice, this means scalping the existing grass as short as possible and then scarifying it in an effort to rough it up and expose as much bare soil as possible. I have hired motorised scarifiers and they work well for larger areas but a small area can be easily and effectively done using a wire rake, taking all the accumulated moss and thatch to the compost heap and leaving the ground appearing wrecked – with more soil showing than grass. This might look alarming but is ideal and having scarified the lawn in autumn, it is the best time to sow wildflower seeds.

I did this most recently in the Orchard and then sowed a dedicated pollen-and-nectar mix with over 20 different flowers including orchids, yellow rattle, clover, scabious, bird's foot trefoil, plantain, meadowsweet, knapweed, buttercups and sorrel. These will provide pollen and nectar for bees, butterflies, hoverflies and other insects.

But one of those 20 flowers is infinitely more important than the other nineteen, at least to make this meadow work. That is *Rhinanthus minor*, or yellow rattle. It is semi-parasitic on grass, so the more it gets established, the weaker the grass becomes and as a result, the greater the chance of the other nineteen plants getting established and thriving. Without the yellow rattle, and especially on my rich clay loam, the grass will always return with a vengeance.

Yellow rattle is an annual, so if the flowers are cut before the seed has a chance to ripen, there will be no plants

It is essential to rake up and remove all cut hay so it does not rot down and enrich the grass at the expense of the wildflowers.

The hardest part of making any wildflower meadow is restricting the growth of the grass so it does not overwhelm the flowers – although long grass in late spring is very beautiful.

next year. On top of that, the seed has no dormancy and needs to be sown at the end of summer or certainly by mid-autumn – which happens naturally as it falls, is knocked or cut to the ground. It needs a period of about five months' vernalisation – i.e. cold weather – to trigger germination the following spring and, if all this were not enough, it must have sufficient rain in spring to trigger germination. A dry April and May is a disaster for it.

The good news is that, in my experience, it will unfailingly return each year if you follow the seasonal rhythms of the hayfield. Make sure the grass is as short as possible by the end of winter and do not cut it at all until at least July – preferably mid- to late August – so the flowers can all set and ripen their seed. Then gather up all the cut grass and compost it so it does not rot down where it falls and improve fertility, which would only encourage grass at the expense of flowers. However, once cut, the 'meadow' can be mown like a lawn for the rest of the summer and autumn – ensuring the return of a touch of late-summer respectability.

By mid-September the meadow has been cut and cleared and is kept very short right through to early spring so the first bulbs have no competition from the grass.

Making a wildflower meadow on bare soil

You can make a meadow from scratch into otherwise bare soil. Prepare the ground as for a lawn by digging over and raking, and removing all weeds and large stones. Leave it for a fortnight to three weeks to allow annual weeds to germinate and then hoe these off immediately before sowing.

Choose an appropriate seed mix. These are widely available in almost any permutation to cover every location, aspect, season and effect, so you can get butterfly mixes, mixes for pollinators, woodland mixes and mixes to grow along banks and hedgerows as well as in open meadows. We have used all of these in this garden with great success.

Sow as directed and in particular, resist the temptation to sow too thickly. There should be bare patches of soil after the first growing season to allow seeds to fall and germinate. Do not rake the seed in but roll or tread it into the surface. Keep it watered and if necessary, protected from birds. Be aware that this meadow-from-scratch will evolve and change as it adapts to your particular garden, and that this evolution is part of the fascination.

Ornamental grasses

Since we made the four Grass Borders in 2011, we grow fewer grasses in the rest of the garden, other than the Paradise Garden that relies on *Stipa tenuissima* as its basic matrix to hold the rest of the planting together.

As a result I confess that the Jewel Garden has lost a lightness of touch, an interwoven delicacy, that perhaps we should reinstate, but that the Grass Borders have gained a fullness and distinct tone and character by massing grasses into them.

Grasses undoubtedly look best between late August and winter, even wonderful in a bleached-out way right into spring. But I think it is a mistake to think of them only as late-season plants, as their first few months of growth, from early May through to July, have a distinctive green swell quite unlike any other planting, and make the perfect foil for a range of early-summer plants.

Their tardiness in growing makes grasses the ideal accompaniment for bulbs like tulips and alliums, and the early, feathery growth of fennel – so different from its later, vertical energy – adds a softness of touch.

By mid-June the new green growth of the grasses has a lusciousness to it. The cardoons are all glaucous foliage, spilling over themselves with leaf, and the stipa flower heads catch the late midsummer light like flaming brands. *Cirsium rivulare* floats amongst the green with highlights of rich pinky plum and any umbellifer – angelica, orlaya, *Ammi majus*, lesser hogweed (yes, the so-called weed, lesser hogweed – lovely plant) – catches exactly the right floating tone above the green waves. Foxgloves, *Actaea* and foxtail lilies stand sentinel.

By July these waves have become strong stands exploding skywards and the accompanying planting has to be very bold to hold its own. So be bold! Verbascums, valerian, eupatorium, rudbeckias and tree dahlias will match even the huge *Miscanthus sacchariflorus* that, by the end of summer, will grow fully 4.5m (15ft) tall.

October brings an amazing richness of colour, from the deep plum of the flower heads of *M. sinensis* 'Malepartus' to the gold of the fading foliage of all the grasses. At this point the grasses are, to my mind, the best and richest players in the garden. Winter becomes them well as they withstand almost all weather save for very heavy snow, and emerge upright and intact, albeit increasingly threadbare, until in March it is time to pull and cut all the old stems and foliage, and let the cycle begin again.

There are so many grasses to choose from you can always find exactly the right ones for the space available in your garden. They are not expensive and if you

grow them from seed, are ridiculously cheap. From a single packet of seed I raised over a hundred stipa plants for the Paradise Garden and after twelve months, each of those would have cost as much as two packets of seed, so I made a two-hundredfold saving. The greatest advantage of growing your own grasses from seed is that you can have the luxury of planting in drifts and in real quantity, which is usually how they look best – all for the price of a single mature plant from a garden centre. The downside is that you have to wait a year or so for your seedlings to come up to garden-centre size.

Most grasses – and especially all miscanthus – are incredibly tolerant of almost every growing situation but stipas really must be grown with good drainage

and full sun if they are to last. I do grow *Stipa gigantea* and *Anemanthele lessoniana* in the heavy clay of my Grass Borders, and *S. tenuissima* in the Paradise Garden, but I added a huge amount of sharp sand to the Paradise Garden borders before planting to improve the drainage.

Grasses add texture, sibilant sound and shimmering sensuality throughout the summer months as they grow and then, from mid-August right through to Christmas, their flowering and autumnal colours match anything else that the garden can offer for colour and drama.

I particularly love the flowering of the so-called 'warm season' grasses. They all have the habit of growing rather slowly and late in spring, so need accompanying planting to cover the gap between the

The Grass Borders in early summer, with their soft billow of textures and colour, are my favourite part of the garden.

removal of their old foliage in March and any reasonable display of their own, which can be as late as mid-June for some of the bigger miscanthus. But what they lose in their slow start, they more than make up for later in the year, with their flowering and long winter display. Grasses that fall into this category include miscanthus, molinias, cortaderias and pennisetums.

Grasses that grow sooner and faster in spring, and which produce their flowering display in midsummer, include stipas, deschampsias, carex and calamogrostis. By mixing the two groups in the same borders, you can have a display that starts in midsummer and lasts until the new year.

The flowers in autumn vary hugely from those plum tones of *M. sinensis*

'Malepartus' that then turn burnished gold, to the wonderfully zig-zagged silver plumes of *M. s.* 'Silberfeder'. Pennisetum has glorious bottle-brush plumes as wispy and delicate as thistledown, and *Deschampsia cespitosa* has perhaps my favourite flower heads of all, held on tall, straight stems high above the foliage. 'Goldtau' is perhaps the best garden variety. The only drawback to it is that it comes from damp, acidic woodland and will not tolerate chalk at all – but it grows well enough on my neutral clay.

Molinia, which also has lovely airy flower heads, is one of the few native grasses that crosses the line successfully from its natural damp, acidic habitat to ordinary garden soil, as long as it does

The Paradise Garden is planted with an underlying matrix of the soft grass *Stipa tenuissima* through which the rest of the planting grows. A friend calls this a 'tameflower meadow'.

not dry out too much. *Molinia caerulea* subsp. *arundinacea* 'Windspiel' has flower stems 1.8m (6ft) tall that move gently in the wind, catching the autumnal sun.

As we move into autumn, the foliage dominates. Really tall grasses like *Miscanthus sacchariflorus* rarely produce any flowers in the UK – and certainly not in my garden over the past five years – but the foliage turns a lovely tawny hue and looks good with the striped bands of *Miscanthus sinensis* 'Strictus'. On a day of hard frost, when the herbaceous plants crumple and fold in a blackened heap, grasses still stand upright in shades of straw, extending the garden season far beyond the reach of any flowers.

Do not be tempted to tidy, let alone cut back, any grasses before spring. Their fallen stems provide excellent cover for hedgehogs and other small mammals to hibernate in, so leave them well alone and enjoy their gentle fading as the year draws to a close.

The time to tidy border grasses is just as the new growth appears, which will be somewhere between late February and mid April, depending where you live. Deciduous grasses such as miscanthus or deschampsias can be cut back hard every spring but evergreen ones, like stipas or carex, should be cleaned up just by pulling away any old or dead growth. We mulch the Grass Borders every other year (see page 193) so any chance seedlings have the opportunity to grow and establish. When we do mulch we use pine bark, chosen because it is low in fertility and high in acidity. Our clay loam is more than fertile enough for all

grasses and a slightly acidic soil suits most of them best. The bark is slow to biodegrade but when it does, it opens out the clay soil very well, creating the loose, open root run that most grasses thrive in.

Never plant, move or divide grasses after mid-September at the latest. The best time to do this is from mid- to late spring – May in this garden – when the soil has warmed up, otherwise there is a real risk of the roots rotting off.

In winter the deciduous ornamental grasses such as miscanthus become sere and by March can all be cut to the ground.

Bamboos

Bamboos are true grasses with large (sometimes very, very large) woody culms or stems. ('Culm' is the name for a cane or stem of bamboo and means the jointed stalk of a grass, and as bamboos are grasses, you can see the derivation.)

I have two bamboos growing in the Grass Borders. One is *Phyllostachys aureosulcata aureocaulis* whose buttery golden culms shine as bright as anything in the February garden. The other is the black-stemmed *P. nigra*. This is very trendy nowadays and deservedly so, because the polished black culms are extraordinary. It is clump-forming, reaching perhaps 4m (13ft) tall and the same across, with arching, slender stems, green at first and changing to black in their second or third year. The more sun it gets, the quicker the culms will turn a rich black.

Other bamboos with good culm colours include *P. vivax* f. *aureocaulis*, which is a gold with a distinctive thin green stripe, *P. bambusoides* 'Sulphurea' which is a rich olive-green, *Himalayacalamus falconeri* 'Damarapa', which is a stripy mix of gold and green like medieval Florentine tights, and the glaucous green of *Thamnocalamus crassinodus* 'Kew Beauty'.

The *Phyllostachys* bamboos are perhaps the best to start with if you are a bamboo novice, partly because they have such wonderful colours but also because they do not present the risk of spreading uncontrollably as some bamboos do.

The *Sasa* bamboos do not grow upwards with anything like the same vigour but many of them will spread with unstoppable determination and are not really suitable for anything other than a large garden that can accommodate their thicket-like tendencies. Likewise, *Pleioblastus* 'Gauntlettii' and *P. pygmaeus* both spread very vigorously and can be almost impossible to get rid of. However, they can be mown as the new shoots are very soft, and this is a perfectly good way of constraining them. Bamboos are also very sensitive to fire, so a flame gun is effective at controlling invasive species as long as there are no neighbouring plants that you want to keep.

Growing bamboos

As a general rule, bamboos like damp – but not wet – soil and a sunny site that is sheltered from strong winds. The Chilean *Chusquea culeou* will tolerate more dryness than most, as will some of the *Sasa* bamboos.

As a general rule, bamboos like damp – but not wet – soil and a sunny site that is sheltered from strong winds

Bamboos will grow in containers but they are much happier in the ground than in a pot. The best time to plant them is as soon as you can prepare the ground in early spring. Always plant a little deeper than they are in the pot you bought them in, give them a thorough soaking and mulch thickly with compost or bark. If the plant is tall it will need staking for the first couple of years, and keep any bamboo well watered for this initial growing period.

Unlike other grasses, bamboos respond very well to feeding and should have an annual mulch of manure or garden compost. They are best watered regularly until they reach the size you want. However, they do not like seaweed, so do not use this as a liquid feed.

Prune by cutting out old culms at the base but do this sparingly as the starch stored in mature culms feeds the vigorous new growth in spring. Cut too much away and the new culms will be shorter and thinner as a result. As a rule, never remove more than a third of the plant in any one year. The best time to prune is in late summer. If it is garden canes you are after, *Pseudosasa japonica* is the one to choose. They are best cut in late summer when two to three years old and should be left flat on a rack to dry over winter.

The yellow-stemmed bamboo *Phyllostachys aureosulcata aureocaulis* growing at the back of the Grass Borders.

Food from
the garden

Why grow your own food?

We have all become dependent upon an endless supply of foods available from all around the world, every day of the year and practically every hour of every day.

The Vegetable Garden at Longmeadow looks good but it is above all practical. Its sole purpose is to grow organic, seasonal, fresh produce all the year round for the family to eat and enjoy.

We expect to have access to exactly the same food in the middle of winter as we do in summer, let alone all the subtle variations of season that play out across the year in any British garden. More and more people have grown up completely unaware that vegetables and fruits have seasons and meaning that are connected to the rhythm of life.

In itself this is nothing new. People of my age – sixties and above – are the last generation that can truly remember eating food that was only available at certain times of the year, whether it was oranges and Brussels sprouts at Christmas time, asparagus in May and June, strawberries in early summer, and apples and pears in autumn and winter. But having year-round, endless supplies of fresh food when, where and how we want it is not sustainable at any level. However, increasing numbers of us have been encouraged to grow our own vegetables and to look for local, seasonal supplies, with the result that more of us will

be eating and enjoying fresh produce in season that is not loaded with air or road miles. It will taste good, do us good and give the added satisfaction of having raised it all with our own hands – and that counts for a lot.

Before beginning to grow anything edible it is worth working out what you want from it. Few of us have the space, time or resources to be anything like self-sufficient but even a small plot of just a few raised beds, going right up to the luxury of a full-sized allotment, could supply you with a year-round contribution that can transform your kitchen and diet.

It might be that you focus on a few things you love so you can eat them at their very best. This is particularly true if you think of the many varieties of fruits and vegetables that are grown and sold more for their appearance and ability to travel well than for their taste. The range of strawberries that you can buy in a supermarket, for example, can be counted on the fingers of one hand with enough left over to play the piano, whereas there are a dozen exquisite varieties that are easy to grow but which store very badly, so you never find them for sale.

You might want to focus your efforts on bringing the produce to a crescendo for a few special occasions like a summer birthday or pumpkins for Hallowe'en. Perhaps – as I do – you want the freshness that salad leaves can give you for as much of the year as possible, and make that your priority. It really does not matter what your aim is. But by focussing it a little, you will maximise the potential of your space and time.

If you have never grown anything edible before, the secret is to keep it simple. It is not a competition and should not feel like a tyranny. You should never grow any thing edible that you do not like to eat.

Sprinkle some seeds onto the warming spring soil, thin them as the seedlings grow, keep them watered and weeded, and harvest them in their season to enjoy with family and friends. Nothing could be simpler. But few things in life give such lasting satisfaction.

Planting out red Cos lettuce. Most of our vegetables are raised under cover in plugs before hardening off and planting out. This way we avoid a lot of slug damage.

Many people are unaware that vegetables and fruits have seasons and meaning connected to life's rhythm

Introducing vegetable growing

You should treat your crops with the same degree of respect and even reverence as you do your own body and the wellbeing of your loved ones.

So it makes sense to grow all edible crops organically as part of a holistic organic garden where you do not use any herbicides, fungicides, pesticides or artificial fertilisers. In fact, I have a basic principle that I do not put anything into the soil or the plants I intend to eat that I would not put onto my plate.

First, choose your site carefully. Vegetables all need as much sun as possible so do what you can to avoid shade. This may not be entirely possible and some vegetables like lettuces, runner beans and root vegetables will cope with some shade, especially in the full glare of a hot summer, but an open, sunny site is ideal.

All goodness starts in the ground and the better your soil, the better your vegetables will be. However, 'better' is not an absolute term. No matter how much goodness you add and however carefully you tend it, you cannot change the nature of your soil. So heavy clay will always be heavy and a sandy free-draining soil will always have that character. Likewise if your ground is very acidic or alkaline, nothing you can do will change that.

However, what you can do is improve the structure of the soil. Adding lots of organic matter will make any soil moisture-retentive whilst simultaneously free-draining. Roots will be able to grow deep and yet have access to nutrients and water, and the soil will be easier to work. The simplest and most effective way to improve soil structure is to add a generous layer of compost (see page 104) as a mulch twice year and let the earthworms work it into the soil for you.

Opposite page: Once made, raised beds do not need digging as such, but I break up the surface compaction in between crops.

When and how to sow

There is a temptation to rush out into the garden on the first sunny day and sow masses of seeds in the full expectation of a marvellous harvest by mid-spring. It won't happen. Feel the soil. If it is cold to your touch then few seeds will germinate. Whilst there is no point in delaying things if the conditions are right, there is little to be gained by trying to cheat the seasons or the weather. A good rule of thumb is that if the weeds are not growing then it is too cold for your vegetable seeds. Instead, prepare the soil and leave it. When a flush of weeds starts to grow, hoe them off and sow your seeds. They will then avoid competition in their first vital weeks of growth.

When you sow outside you can make drills and sow the seed in rows, which means you can see the seedlings as soon as they emerge and avoid treading on them or confusing them with weeds. Alternatively, you can broadcast the seed. I use this latter technique for carrots or when I use a mixture of seed such as saladesi or saladini, which I broadcast and do not thin except to eat. Otherwise I stick to rows.

However you sow, always be careful to sow as thinly as possible. In an ideal world you would have the seeds twice as close together as the final desired spacing. This would provide for failed germination and the thinning out of any ailing seedlings, along with normal thinning. In practice, when sowing direct, just keep it thin!

The advantages of sowing thinly are that the roots of the plants are not disturbed more than they have to be and the plants require no potting compost, seed trays, plugs, greenhouses or paraphernalia

Chillies growing in terracotta pots in the greenhouse. I deliberately restrict the roots to provoke more fruiting.

of any kind. As long as the growing medium is well drained and quite rich – I always lightly rake in 2.5cm (1in) of fresh garden compost before sowing or planting out salad crops – they should grow well.

Even if it is miserably wet and cold outside and your soil is nowhere near ready for sowing, early spring is the perfect time to sow seeds under cover for planting outside once the soil has warmed up a little and – crucially – when there is more daylight.

However, this depends upon having some kind of well-lit protection. A greenhouse is best but cold frames are very good and a porch or spare windowsill or two perfectly workable. Even if you have a small yard and intend just to grow a few pots of salad leaves at any one time, a small cold frame is a really good idea.

When your seeds have germinated and reached reasonable-sized seedlings, put them outside to harden off for a week or two before planting them out at 23cm (9in) spacing when the soil is warm and they are big enough to withstand any kind of slug or snail attack.

You must have a water supply to grow vegetables. When I plant out young plants that I have raised from seed, I always soak them really well and many crops will need very little water thereafter. But some, like lettuce, spinach, rocket, leeks, Florence fennel, celery and celeriac, are quick to bolt – i.e. run to seed – if they are stressed by water shortage, so it is important to give them a steady water supply. As with all watering, it is much more effective to give something a really good soak once a week than a sprinkle every few days. A soak will encourage deep roots, which will, in turn, mean that they will be able to access more water. It is a virtuous circle.

Ideally you will have a standpipe connected to the mains as well as generous water butts or tanks for rainwater, but whatever you have should make watering easy rather than a chore. Collecting rainwater in an open tank makes filling a watering can much quicker and easier because you can dip into it rather than waiting for the can to fill via a small tap.

Growing in containers

I realise that if you live in a flat or have no garden, then the prospect of rows of potatoes or raised beds filled with carrots, lettuce and peas has to remain a dream. But you can grow some vegetables in containers on a balcony or roof, or in a small back yard as long as it has sun for half the day.

Some crops are better suited to containers than others. Salad crops of all kinds, including lettuce, radish and rocket, are ideal. Containers are best suited to cut-and-come-again crops like saladesi and saladini, or for crops like rocket, Oak-Leaf lettuces, spinach and corn salad, which can all be harvested by the leaf and which will regrow to provide second or even third cuttings. Accept that you have limited space and concentrate on growing a few healthy plants, which will always give a better harvest than masses of small, weedy ones.

You can even be more adventurous and grow some peas and beans in containers as well as root crops like carrot, beetroot and turnip. Remember

that many varieties of carrot have a long root so choose a variety like 'Early Nantes' that is very tasty but quite short. Chillies, tomatoes and cucumbers can also all be grown in a generous container, although they will not survive the first frost.

Even potatoes can be container-grown and do very well in a bin bag with holes added for drainage. Put two first or second early seed potatoes (I like 'Red Duke of York' and 'Charlotte') on 30cm (12in) of peat-free potting compost in the bottom of the bag and cover with more compost. As the shoots appear, keep adding compost until the bag is half-full.

Watering in the young celeriac. Most of our crops are watered well when planted out and only ever watered again if it is very dry, but some crops such as celeriac or celery, should never dry out.

The secret of keeping on top of weeds in a vegetable plot is a sharp hoe used little and often. Hoeing should always be done in dry weather so the hoed weeds left on the soil surface die, thus avoiding the risk of rerooting.

Water well and after flowering – about three months from planting – your bag should be full of delicious potatoes.

Whatever container you use must have good drainage. If you have your pots on a roof or balcony, they will have to be stood on a tray of sorts to collect the drips, but make sure that the pot itself is not standing in the water as this will negate the effects of the drainage. Raise it up on chocks of some kind.

Succession planting

Succession planting is the key to a steady supply of fresh vegetables for as long as possible. What this means is sowing batches of your favourite vegetables in two or three goes across the growing season, so that as one batch is coming to the end, another is just ready to be harvested, with perhaps a third being sown or grown on.

Obviously this takes a little organisation. Start with a small amount of fast-growing salad leaves raised indoors in plugs so they can be planted out as soon as the ground warms up, and follow these with regular additions, both raised in plugs and sown directly, right through to September.

Crops like peas and beans, chard, carrots and beetroot grow more slowly but can be spread over months to provide two or three overlapping waves of harvest.

Finally, there are the long, slow crops like most brassicas, chicory, garlic or celery that are going to tie up space for much of the growing year. I always interplant these with a catchcrop like radish or rocket that can be eaten before it starts to compete with the slow grower.

Crop rotation

You rotate crops primarily to avoid the build-up of disease in the soil. Rotation also helps break the cycle of certain pests that live in the soil and feed on particular types of vegetable. It also means that the different cultivation demands of different vegetables can be incorporated into an annual cycle. It is therefore a useful part of healthy vegetable growing. But my own approach is not to be hidebound by this. It is rarely the end of the world if a legume follows a legume or if you grow your onions in the same place for two consecutive years. But the principle is sound and should be adhered to as far as possible.

There are three main groups of vegetable in a rotation, the idea being that no member of any group follows another from the same group on the same piece of ground. By shuffling everything round at the same time, you get a minimum gap of three years between same-group crops.

The three groups are not actually fixed (and, just to confuse things, many people work on a four-group rotation) because plants in the same group may not have the same soil requirements. So carrots are related to celery yet need completely different soil preparation, so are included with legumes.

Legumes include all kinds of beans and peas. Tomatoes and peppers get included in this group, too – even though they belong to the same family as potatoes – as do celery, celeriac and squashes. The soil for this group needs plenty of added manure or compost.

Brassicas include all cabbages, cauliflowers, broccoli, kohlrabi, radish, mizuna, mibuna, land cress, swede, turnip, seakale and Chinese cabbages. These follow on from legumes and are usually planted without extra compost being added, and with the nitrogen left from the legumes taken up by the growing brassicas.

Roots include carrots, parsnips, beetroot, chard, spinach, salsify, scorzonera, onions, leeks, garlic and potatoes. Some people also include lettuce in this group although I divide lettuce between roots and legumes. In practice, this is the most diverse and confusing group. Carrots and parsnips, for example, grow best in soil that has had no added compost whereas it is important to top up the soil with compost for spinach, lettuce, chard and potatoes. Common sense prevails.

The important thing to try and maintain is the direction of the rotation, so a legume is followed by a brassica which, in turn, is followed by a root, and it is then back to a legume. Parts of the rotation might demand different cultivation but the balance between the crops and the soil is maintained. The solution is to plan it all well in advance so that you know exactly what you intend to grow in each plot, together with its subsequent winter crops. I work it all out on my computer and stick the plans up in the potting shed – but once the plans are made, they are there to be changed. You must be flexible.

In a vegetable rotation, no member of any group follows another from the same group on the same ground

Spring vegetables

From the new year, despite some of the coldest weather, the days slowly stretch until, on a great day at the end of March, the clocks change and we are blessed with an extra hour of daylight in the evenings.

That is the moment, regardless of the weather, when spring becomes undeniable. The days reach out into the light, birdsong is at its best and there is no other moment in the year – in life itself – that is so suffused with promise.

The temperature of the ground is the key and is much more significant at this time of year than the air temperature. Our soil can be cold and clammy on a beautifully warm, shirt-sleeve April day. However, climate change over the past 20 years has meant a trend to warmer spring weather so the tendency is to planting and sowing outdoors into the garden earlier and earlier.

But if the soil feels cold to you then it will to seeds as well and very few will germinate. Better always to wait until the soil is ready before sowing or planting seedlings in your veg plot, even if that means holding back until May. And if you don't trust your judgement with the temperature of the soil, then weeds are a good indicator. If they are not actively growing, it is probably too cold for your much less robust vegetable seedlings.

Some crops are less sensitive to cold than others. Broad beans can be sown as soon as the soil is workable, which is as early as February in some years, and this is true also of onion and shallot sets.

The rituals of spring include ordering favourite varieties as well as preparing the plot, and there is an inevitable tendency to grow things that you always grow – especially if you grow them well. But you should never grow anything edible that you do not like to eat. Horticulture should serve your taste buds and your stomach – not the other way round.

For many years I have raised anything that can be transplanted in seed trays or plugs, starting in the greenhouse in January and February with chillies, tomatoes and early salad crops, and moving them on to a cold frame and standing-out area before planting the young seedlings into their growing position. This germination and raising process normally takes 6–8 weeks, so I start sowing rocket and broad beans in mid-February for planting in April, along with Mediterranean crops like chillies and tomatoes that are destined for the greenhouse.

However, April is a good time to sow tender crops, especially if they are to be raised outdoors. But they should be sown as soon as possible and, critically, kept warm as the seedlings grow. The idea is not to force them in any way but to keep the growth steady. Aubergines, tomatoes

– and to an even greater extent chillies – produce most fruit on large plants, so the initial growing phase should be geared to encourage really robust, healthy plants before worrying about the fruits. This means regular water, food and, if necessary, potting on so the growing roots have a constant supply of growing medium and nutrition. There is no formula to this. In the end it is just a matter of paying attention to the plants and responding to their needs – which vary from year to year, variety to variety and place to place.

Many tender vegetables such as the whole cucurbit family, green beans, sweetcorn and fennel, and later-cropping ones like chicories and winter brassicas as well as all the root vegetables and celery and celeriac, do best with an April and May sowing so that they can germinate and grow steadily, ready to go out into the garden when the nights start to warm up – which at Longmeadow is not until June.

Seeds sown in February and March will germinate quickly indoors but the seedlings will be slower to develop than those sown in late spring or summer, and at the end of the growing season, anything sown after mid-August will start to slow right down again. So from February through to June I try and sow lettuce of various kinds in six-week waves. If you sow into seed trays or plugs, a pretty good rule of thumb is to sow your next batch of seeds at the same time as the previous batch is planted out into the garden.

One of the anomalies of spring is that just at the time when you are busiest in the garden sowing a huge range of edible crops, there is less produce than at any other time of year. The winter crops of

Staking peas immediately after sowing using hazel cut from the Coppice.

If weeds are not actively growing, it is probably too cold for your much less robust vegetable seedlings

cabbages, leeks, parsnips, chard and chicory are diminishing rapidly and there is very little growing sufficiently quickly outside to take its place. So our leanest months in the garden are April and May, although there are real treats like purple sprouting broccoli and asparagus, and since we have some cover, early salad crops.

Lettuces

Pricking out lettuce seedlings from a seed tray to individual plugs. They will grow on, protected from slugs, before being planted out when they have a good root system.

The more that I grow vegetables – and I have been doing so for over 50 years now – the more I value fresh salad crops. When I am at home I try and eat a salad from the garden at least once a day every day of the year. Salad can cover a multitude of things – and sins – but I am completely happy with a plate of just one kind of fresh lettuce dressed with good olive oil and a squeeze of lemon.

Lettuce varieties and types

The principles of growing lettuce are the same at any time of year, but in order to have a year-round supply you need to select varieties and kinds that are appropriate to the season – for example the large 'Lobjoit's' or 'Paris Island'. Cos varieties grow less well in spring than they do in summer, whereas 'Little Gem' or a red variety like 'Rouge D'Hiver' are very good early and late in the year – although all are Cos lettuces and share many of the same eating qualities.

I would recommend that every gardener experiments with different varieties until they find the ones that they

like but even then, they should take advantage of the choices available and grow three or four different types and varieties at any one time through the year.

The most old-fashioned and familiar variety to many people is the Butterhead which is the one with rosettes of soft, cabbage-like leaves. It has the virtue of growing well in cold weather so can provide fresh leaves in winter, and Butterheads like a good 'Tom Thumb' have a delicacy and freshness that is lovely. 'All Year Round' is, as the name implies, hardy and adaptable enough to crop most of the year and whilst not the best you can grow, is a lot better than almost anything you can buy, especially in that spring gap when there is precious little else in the garden. 'Valdor' is another overwintering Butterhead that I grow, sowing the seeds in August for harvesting from Christmas time onwards. Butterheads store badly so should be cut and eaten on the same day.

I love a good crisp Cos lettuce. 'Little Gem' will do well from an early sowing and certainly is always worth finding room for in the garden. A home-grown one will astonish you with its freshness and taste compared to the supermarket version. 'Lobjoit's Cos' is even better, much bigger, rather slower to develop and with a shorter season, but is one of my favourites. It does need plenty of water to heart up well and if allowed to become dry, the outer leaves will rot. 'Rouge D'Hiver' is a Cos that will grow in cooler conditions (although not really over winter) and 'Paris Island Cos' is another one that I grow and enjoy. 'Winter

Density' is a Cos hybrid which will stay small over the winter months and then grow in spring to provide an early harvest.

Cos are higher in vitamin C and beta-carotene than the ubiquitous Iceberg, the bought version of which has no taste of any kind and is grown solely for its admirable crispness – it fact it is usually the crispest part of any sandwich or burger that it adorns. 'Webb's Wonderful' is the best-known Crisphead, and 'Chou de Naples' is the parent of most modern Iceberg lettuces and has the great virtue of being slow to bolt.

Loose-leaf or Salad Bowl lettuce is nearly always good and has the great virtue that it can be picked leaf by leaf or cut flush with the ground and left to regrow for at least one and usually two

One of the great luxuries of growing your own vegetables is that you can harvest young lettuce like this Cos when they are especially delicious and tender.

Young red Cos lettuce growing in a raised bed.

LETTUCE PESTS AND DISEASES

• **Slugs and snails** love a juicy young lettuce more than anything else. The best organic defence against slugs is to grow the seeds in sheltered, slug-free conditions, harden them off for at least ten days and then plant out into their final growing postion 15–23cm (6–9in) apart. They then tend to grow strongly enough to resist slugs at the critical seedling stage. However, I wash summer lettuces carefully as they are always full of slugs.

• **Lettuce root aphids** attack lettuce later in the season, when they have been allowed to get too dry. The first sign is that the plants visibly wilt and then die. When pulled up, the roots have a white, powdery, waxy coating, which is discharged by little yellow aphids (*Pemphigus bursarius*) that eat the roots. After an attack, do not grow lettuces in the same soil for a full year.

• **Downy mildew** will turn outer leaves yellow and then pale brown, and the underside of the leaves develops a nasty downy growth. This is a fungal disease encouraged by very humid conditions. The only solution is to remove all affected leaves and thin to increase ventilation.

• **Lettuce grey mould** is another fungus (*Botrytis cinerea*), which produces fluffy grey mould on the leaves. Sometimes this is first noticeable as a slimy brown rot on the stem and the whole plant collapses. Good ventilation and growing healthy plants are the best correctives.

subsequent cuttings. I grow red and green Oak-Leaf or Salad Bowl varieties (they come with various proprietary names). Red lettuce grow slower than green ones and tend to be a little bitter – which I like. They are also less likely to be eaten by slugs than green leaves.

Growing lettuce

There are two ways to grow any type of lettuce. The first and traditional one is to sow them directly into the ground where they are to grow (including into any kind of container), in drills or broadcast. You then thin them carefully as soon as they are large enough to handle and thin again a few weeks later (eating the meltingly tender thinnings, roots and all) so that you are left with a row of maturing plants about 7.5–23cm (3–9in) apart. The advantage of sowing directly is that the

roots are not disturbed by transplanting. The disadvantage is that they are very susceptible to slugs and snails (see opposite), especially at the young seedling stage and especially at this time of year when growth can be slowed almost to a standstill by a bout of cold weather.

Nor is less handling required if you sow them in drills because the thinning process is fiddly but essential. They must also be kept watered and weed-free. I only sow direct when I use a mixture of seed such as saladesi or saladini, which I broadcast and do not thin except to eat.

I find it much more controllable to sow the seed in plugs or seed trays, grow them into reasonable-sized seedlings and then plant out at 23cm (9in) spacing in rows on open beds or in a grid on a raised bed. I use a home-made seed compost but any bought peat-free compost will do. This system depends upon having cover such as a greenhouse, cold frame or even a porch or windowsill.

Most lettuce take about six to ten weeks to grow sufficiently large to eat, depending on the time of year. To provide a constant supply of salad leaves, sow a few seeds every ten to fourteen days from mid-February through to early September, so as one small harvest is used up, another is ready to take its place. Or, as I do, sow a new batch of lettuce seed every time you plant young seedlings out into the beds.

I prefer to sow lettuce seed in plugs or seed trays, grow them into reasonable-sized seedlings and then plant them out

Lettuce germinate at surprisingly low temperatures and many will fail to germinate once the soil temperature rises above 25°C (77°F). Mature plants will respond to higher temperatures by producing flower stems – bolting – and running to seed. This makes the leaves bitter. There are ways around this. If you are sowing directly into the soil, water the drill before sowing to cool the soil down. Sow in the afternoon so that the vital germination phase coincides with the cool of night. Also sow into a shaded part of the midsummer vegetable garden.

If sowing in seed trays, put them in the shade and cover with glass or newspaper to keep them cool until the seedlings appear. If the seeds are showing no signs of life after a week, put them into the fridge for 24± hours.

Rocket

In April, when the vegetable plot has least to offer other than broccoli and perhaps some greenhouse-grown salad crops, rocket is at its peak. If you taste fresh rocket in spring at its best you will always be searching for that melting, spicy succulence that no other season can provide. Rocket is very happy growing in an unheated greenhouse in winter and although the taste of these leaves is twice as good as anything you can buy at that time, they are only half as good as their spring cousins.

Most of the rocket that is sold in supermarkets or dished up in a restaurant is wild rocket (*Diplotaxis*), a perennial with much slenderer, more finely indented leaves, which is good but nothing compared to well-grown sweet rocket (*Eruca sativa*).

We love rocket and happily eat it daily, as and when it is in season. But my parents would have viewed it with the same polite hostility as a sheep's eye or garlic. Edible, but only in extremis.

After radish – to which it is closely related – it is the easiest of all seeds to germinate. Chuck them out onto any old soil or compost and they will grow. But the crucial thing is to thin boldly and transplant them early. Rocket seeds are biggish and reasonably easy to handle so I now sprinkle two or three per plug, wait until at least two germinate successfully and then ruthlessly thin down to one healthy seedling. These can then be grown on and hardened off until they are about 5–7.5cm (2–3in) tall before planting out at 23cm (9in) spacing. You can easily sow them direct but they will still need fierce thinning. This will seem a ridiculously generous use of space but closer spacing does not result in any greater harvest, and as the widely spaced plants can enjoy lots of nutrition and water, they are much healthier and last longer.

I start picking leaves as soon as they are large enough to handle and expect to make three or four pickings from each plant over as many months. The leaves can vary hugely in size and shape, with some with no indentation other than an odd crinkle, and others scooped back to the stem. In my experience taste is not affected.

By the middle of May the plants are irresistibly drawn to flower, growing a thick hairy stem with much hotter leaves

that have lost their early spring succulence. This has to be literally nipped in the bud – I pinch out the first sign of a flowering stem. You cannot hold back the tide completely but this does delay it and gives one more harvest of good-sized leaves. The flowers, of course, are perfectly edible and the summer seeds provide all of next year's crop.

Slugs will nibble at very young seedlings but tend to leave them alone once they start growing vigorously. A much greater problem is the flea beetle which will pinprick each leaf with innumerable small holes, each one of which will create a scarring, toughening reaction. As a consequence, taste and all-round plant health suffer. But the life cycle of the flea beetle coincides with the

plant's most urgent desire to reproduce and set seed, so around the end of May I leave a few plants to set seed and pull up the rest, and we have our brief rocketless season over high summer.

But I sow another batch of seeds in July for planting out in early September, and as the days shorten and nights cool, they grow well and are almost as good as their spring-grown selves. In a greenhouse they will keep going all winter and a batch sown in late August will be big enough to plant into a greenhouse in October. Although they will not grow much over winter, as soon as the days lengthen in the new year, they will take off, ready for picking in February and March – by which time the January-sown outdoor crop will be ready to harvest.

Harvesting the last of the spring rocket before the warmer weather inevitably makes it bolt.

Radishes

Radishes have been grown and eaten for thousands of years. They were domesticated in the Mediterranean, cultivated by the Egyptians nearly 5000 years ago, and introduced to Britain by the Romans nearly 2000 years ago.

Their hot, peppery flavour is popular across all cultures but another reason for their ubiquity is that they are probably the easiest of all vegetables to grow. Just sprinkle the seed thinly in a shallow drill 1cm (½in) deep and they will appear within a week or so and be ready to start harvesting a few weeks later. It is important to thin them so that they are at least 2.5cm (1in) apart to allow each root to become juicy and swollen before they get woody. The thinnings can be eaten, leaves, roots and all, when they are the size of peas, although the perfect size for a radish is the circumference of a two-penny piece. Fresh radishes in early May, eaten with salted butter, are one of the seasonal treats of spring.

They will run to seed in warm or very dry weather so sow as soon as the soil is warm enough in spring and make a repeat sowing every two weeks thereafter. Water regularly, but too much moisture will only result in extra foliage and split roots.

Radishes are also a very useful indicator crop. I sow mine in with parsnips, on the ridge of potatoes and between slow-growing crops like cabbages. Radishes are a brassica and are prone to flea beetle attack (see page 301) which leaves holes in the leaves and weakens the plant, making it more likely to bolt. To minimise this, keep them very well watered, thin to 2.5cm (1in) spacing between each plant and pull them to eat whilst they are marble-sized.

My favourite varieties: 'Cherry Belle', 'Saxa', 'Scarlet Globe', 'Flamboyant' (long) and 'French Breakfast'

Broccoli

I love purple sprouting broccoli. I love the way that it becomes top-heavily laden with leaf – so much plant yet such a delicate harvest. I even like its slowness, steadily accruing all that growth from sowing in March to its first tentative picking – in my unforced garden at any rate – in February. To invest a year of growth, weeding and staking, and protecting from slugs, cabbage white butterflies and pigeons, has an unfashionable layer of trust built into the relationship between gardener and plant. Growing broccoli takes some imagination and confidence to surrender a slab of garden for a harvest tucked three seasons ahead.

Let me get one thing straight. The great bulbous green affairs that you buy in supermarkets or that are ubiquitously served with stolidly unchanging 'seasonal veg' are not purple sprouting broccoli but calabrese. Nothing wrong with calabrese on its day, but it is synonymous with healthy but dull eating, whereas broccoli is subtle, delicate and restricted to a season that starts in the new year and ends at the beginning of May – although in my own garden I am lucky to make a picking in February and by the end of April it is bolting faster than I can pick it.

Opposite page: Fresh radish, swished under a tap and eaten with salt and butter are an epicurean treat.

Purple sprouting broccoli grow into large plants so must be very firmly planted and given space. However, there is room for a catchcrop of lettuce that can be grown and harvested before the broccoli plants shade them out.

Broccoli arrived in Italy from the eastern Mediterranean, was introduced into France by Catherine de Medici in the 1560s and came across the Channel to us some time in the following hundred years. In 1724, Philip Miller, the curator of the Apothecaries' Garden at Chelsea (as Chelsea Physic Garden was then known) called it 'Italian asparagus'. The word 'broccoli' is derived from the Italian for a shoot. By the nineteenth century, its cultivation had become sophisticated to the extent that there were brown, red and cream varieties, as well as green, purple and white sprouting ones. 'Romanesco' has a lime-green colour to the florets and is very delicious and 'Broccoletto' is a fast-maturing variety with a single edible floret. Calabrese (simply meaning 'from Calabria') is really a mini green cauliflower, not bad to eat but matures quicker and has a longer season.

But I am happy with common or garden purple sprouting. I want a big, glaucous plant on a thick stalk with a mass of delicate little branching buds, rich purple, no bigger than a marble and some much smaller than that but each packed with a sweet – almost tender – cabbagey tang that demands ritual celebration.

Broccoli certainly requires lots of space but I always underplant it with lettuce for the first three months or so of its growing year. To this end, it is best to plant the seedlings out in a grid with each plant at least 1m (3ft) apart in any direction. There is always a temptation to sneak them closer than this but resist it. You gain no extra broccoli spears for your parsimony with space and you lose the chance to grow a good crop of lettuce (or radish, rocket or even spinach) before the lettuce gets crowded out by those lovely crinkled blue-green leaves.

The plants grow slowly, giving no sign of florets until spring, and even then they tease, taking weeks to be pickable. But when the spears do arrive, they arrive fast. The secret is to keep picking and they will respond by producing more and more spears until you are thoroughly sick of the damn stuff, and it's off to the compost heap with them. By which time, next year's crop is emerging as young plants ready to be potted on.

I sow mine just when the harvest of last year's sowing is hitting its stride, in mid-March. It is easiest to sow them in plugs, thinning to one seed per plug and then potting them on into a generous pot – at least 7.5cm (3in) – so they can develop a decent root system before planting them out in mid- to late May.

Nowadays I always add a good 2.5–5cm (1–2in) of compost to a brassica bed, working it in lightly so the plants grow strong and lusty. This seems to make a big difference to the way that they cope with cabbage white attack later in summer. I also add wood ash before planting out and if your soil is acidic, I would certainly lime the ground too – but do so at least a fortnight before adding the compost. Firm the young seedlings into the ground fiercely well – these will become big, robust plants – but early next spring, use their harvest like a treat rather than a worthy but dull health food.

Spring greens

Perhaps the nicest meal I have ever eaten in my life was at a friend's house some 20 years ago at Easter time. We had rib of beef, gravy made from the meat juices, plainly boiled potatoes and spring greens. There was also fresh horseradish sauce. That's it. No posturing chef ever produced anything more memorably delicious. I have been an ardent fan of spring greens ever since.

Spring greens are loose-leaf cabbage that help fill the Hungry Gap between Easter and Whitsun when the vegetable garden is filling up with seeds and seedlings but is pitifully short of edible produce. It seems that only in modern times – i.e. the past two or three hundred years – have they been refined into a deliberate seasonal crop. But for at least a thousand years before that – going back to Roman times – the stalks of headed winter cabbage would be left in the ground to resprout in spring and these loose fresh shoots would be eaten as a welcome second harvest.

They should be sown in mid- to late summer either in a seed bed or under cover in plugs, and planted out to their growing position in late September. They are extremely hardy and yet their taste is tender and subtle. I guess that their real

I always add a good layer of compost to a brassica bed, working it in lightly so the plants grow strong and lusty

attraction lies in their freshness and the immediacy and sense of urgency that goes with that – whereas a hearted cabbage, for all its virtues, can knock around at the bottom of a fridge for days and days and still perform – without ever scaling the same culinary heights.

By harvesting every other one in a row or block whilst they are still loose-leafed, the remainder have the chance to form small hearts that have exceptional flavour. These hearts have none of the packed tightness of a Savoy but will just about hold together when cooked. But that is a refinement. Not much can beat the loose leaves lightly boiled in early April and served with a dab of butter and salt and pepper.

Because they do not make hearts they can be planted much closer than normal cabbages – about 30cm (12in) is fine. I have found 'Greyhound' and 'Durham Early' to be reliably good and am told that 'Hispi', which I have always allowed to heart-up, can also be eaten whilst still loose. I have not grown it but 'Delaway' was a Northern Irish cabbage grown as a cut-and-come-again variety and was the variety used for colcannon – of which bubble and squeak is a bastardised British version.

'Collards' was the eighteenth-century name given to these loose-leaf cabbages, derived from the medieval 'colewort'. It is a good word, still retained in vernacular use by Americans, and we should use it more often too for all loose-leaf cabbages, be they kale or spring greens.

Spinach

The freshness of home-grown spinach in spring is tangible – no other vegetable *feels* so vibrantly fresh. And no other chemically grown vegetable contains such high residues of pesticides, coming just behind strawberries in an American Environmental Protection Agency report on the dietary effect of pesticide residues.

I love it raw in salads or cooked, although you need a surprising quantity of leaves for the latter. Fresh spinach and a fresh poached egg are an incomparably good combination. It is very rich in iron, has a higher protein content than any other leaf vegetable and is rich in vitamin A. Raw spinach also has twice the amount of carotenoids as raw carrots – although when cooked, its oxalic acid halts the absorption of calcium, so if your motive for eating spinach is entirely for your health, it is better to consume it raw. Oxalic acid is a poison, with a fatal dose

Spinach grows best in cool (but not cold) conditions, so I sow a crop in early spring and a second in late summer for autumn and winter harvests.

of around 1500mg, so in theory, a huge portion of spinach with a side order of chard or beetroot followed by an equally robust volume of rhubarb could kill you. But you would have to be very, very determined … In any event, 'Monnopa' and 'Viroflay' have less oxalic acid than most so are the most suitable for feeding to very young children.

Spinach is a cool-season crop and very quickly runs to seed when the temperature rises and the light increases. It is therefore one of the first seeds to be sown in spring, – which means mid-March here – and then grows well again in late summer and early autumn, so I make another sowing at the end of August. It will overwinter well with protection.

Spinach beet is more resistant to cold and longer-lasting than spinach, and although not quite so good as spinach, makes a perfectly good substitute in winter, as well as being attractively luxuriant.

You will see 'long-day' varieties that are bred to resist the plants' urge to run to seed as the days lengthen, and are therefore good for later sowings. I have grown spinach in plugs and transplanted it but the germination rate can be very poor inside a warm greenhouse. It is better to sow it in situ, thinning it to 15cm (6in) spacing.

The best spinach is young, so I always crop the whole plant, cutting it with a knife at ground level. It will then produce new leaves for another harvest, although as the days and nights warm up, all its instincts are to produce a thick flower stem rather than new leaves. It is also important to grow the varieties most suitable to the season to give yourself a chance of harvesting it before it

The best spinach is young, so I always crop the whole plant, cutting it with a knife at ground level

bolts. Whatever the variety, it needs really rich soil and lots of water. As a member of the beet family, it naturally grows alongside chard and beetroot but can be fitted in anywhere within the rotation (see page 293). It makes a good companion for legumes, celeriac, lettuces or even potatoes, grown as a catchcrop between the rows.
My favourite early season varieties: 'Monnopa', 'Tundra', 'Avanti' F1, 'Bloomsdale'
My favourite autumn and winter varieties: 'Giant Winter', 'Galaxy' F1, 'Norfolk'

Asparagus

Home-grown asparagus, eaten in season (mid-spring to midsummer) and harvested just minutes before cooking, is one of the most sensuous, delicious foods known to mankind.

Growing asparagus is not difficult once the plants are established but can involve quite a lot of work getting to that point, especially if your soil is heavy clay like my own. To thrive, asparagus must have full sun and good drainage and has always famously tended to be grown in areas like Evesham and Pershore, that have well-drained but fertile soil.

Asparagus is a member of the lily family and there are over 150 different species, of which only one, *Asparagus officinalis*, is edible. We know it was being grown by the

Asparagus needs very good drainage so I grow mine in a raised bed that has had a great deal of grit added before planting. The plants then should last and crop for decades.

1600s, and by the nineteenth century, Britain was growing more asparagus than any other country, with a reported 100 hectares (250 acres) in Battersea in London alone devoted to the crop.

You can grow asparagus from seed although it is more usual to buy 'crowns' – that is one-year-old plants. Although these are rarely available from a garden centre, they can easily be found online. Male plants are more productive than female ones, do not set seed and are less prone to fusarium wilt, which can do a lot of damage. There are many good varieties and 'Connovers Colossal' is a tried-and-tested favourite, although I currently grow 'Guelph Millennium'. If you have sandy soil or are growing asparagus in raised beds, I would suggest adding plenty of compost or well-rotted manure to the soil the winter before

planting, and perhaps extra horticultural grit to the raised bed, and working all this material in deeply. Plant the crowns in spring, spacing them in a grid about 45cm (18in) apart and making sure that they have 15cm (6in) of soil covering them. The tentacled roots that hang from the crown are very brittle so dig a generous hole and handle them carefully.

However, if you have heavy soil, then I suggest growing asparagus in trenches, which is how I grow it here. Dig a trench about 1.2m (4ft) wide and 30cm (12in) deep, piling the soil on either side. Then dig the bottom of the trench deeply, adding as much grit and compost as you can spare, and rotovate it all into the trench so it is mixed well and the soil is crumbly. The better you make the drainage, the better the asparagus will like it, so do not hold back on the grit!

Next make two parallel ridges along the length of the bottom of the trench and plant the crowns about 45cm (18in) apart with the roots draped over the ridges and hanging down the sides. Then carefully cover them over with the soil you have put to one side. The result will be a long, low raised bed. I have edged my current asparagus bed with boards – mainly to stop wheelbarrows and feet treading on it.

This is all hard work. But you will only have to do it once every 30 years or so and I find it deeply satisfying.

Do not cut any of the sprues in the first year but allow them to develop foliage that will feed back into the roots. In the second year only make one cutting, taking a maximum of two sprues from each plant. In the third year you can cut freely until 1 June and in the fourth year, eat to your heart's content until 1 July and then stop cutting and allow the sprues to grow tall and develop foliage. This, in turn, will feed the roots for next year's harvest. Asparagus will need support so they do not get damaged by heavy winds and I use string and canes, just like broad bean supports. I mulch the whole asparagus bed thickly with compost or well-rotted manure immediately after the last cut and then repeat the mulch after cutting the yellowed foliage back in November, as they respond well to lots of goodness. I repeat this every autumn.

Asparagus is one of those plants whose sugars convert very quickly to starch, so the spears should be cut and eaten within hours – if not minutes – to get the depth of flavour that no bought asparagus can match.

Summer vegetables

Summer slips into the vegetable garden without a fanfare. As May ends, spring is quietly shed and from the first minute of the first hour of June, summer is here. In practice there are two quite separate summer seasons, the beginning of June through to mid-July and then the end of July to mid-September.

Early summer is often coolish and wettish but filled with light, the days stretching from very early to very late, and the second half of the season often hotter, but carrying the whisper of autumn in the folds of its summer clothes. The first summer season is surprisingly short on crops to harvest whereas the second is a period of glut, where much of what is grown is gathered to be stored through the winter.

For the vegetable gardener this means that planning is important. It is a question of balancing resources and demands. So new potatoes are wonderful but they take up a lot of ground and lose much in storage, whereas lettuces are essential but can bolt very fast in a hot, dry spell, so need a constant succession. Peas and broad beans are important but only if you are prepared and able to keep picking them whilst still young. Plants like celeriac, parsnip, squashes and tomatoes will not provide anything for most of this time but must have a long growing season and take up space. So a plan is essential.

But however much you plan, there are bound to be problems to cope with involving some or all of slugs and snails, aphids, birds, fungal diseases and weather damage. My response to this is always the same: go with it. Gardening is not a war waged against nature. Any garden imposes a super-abundance of growth on a piece of land and the rest of the natural world responds very quickly to this. If I insist on growing 50 lettuces spaced 23cm (9in) from each other in a block, then I cannot complain if a thousand slugs join the feast! But I can ensure that each lettuce is growing strongly with a healthy root system before I expose it to the depredations of the slugs.

An important factor in keeping the cornucopia of the summer vegetable garden healthy is to keep weeds to a minimum so that plants can get the maximum available nutrition and moisture from the soil and therefore grow as well as the soil allows. This will vary from garden to garden and even within areas of the vegetable patch itself because no two areas of ground are exactly alike. Therefore the healthiest plant might be growing more

An important factor in keeping the cornucopia of summer vegetables healthy is to keep weeds to a minimum

slowly and be smaller than other, identical ones, growing faster and bigger but ultimately more prone to problems.

As ever, the best defence from attack comes from the plants themselves, not the gardener. Our job is to maximise the potential for each plant in each given situation. In return we will receive the biggest, healthiest, tastiest harvests from our vegetables.

Broad beans

Broad beans were an absolute staple of the ancient Mediterranean and northern medieval diet but their ability to be stored dry made fresh beans a rare treat. Perhaps that is how we should view them, although when I was a child we used to dutifully wade through weeks of leathery, bitter beans the size of pebbles until we could, thankfully, pull up the plants. There is no need for this. Broad beans are best eaten young, whilst they are still small and sweet, and will freeze very well in this youthful condition. If they do get large, they can be very successfully puréed.

To ensure young beans you need to make two or more sowings so that the harvest is spread across the summer. Growing them is easiness itself. Being hardy, they can be sown as early as October for a crop in May and June, or as late as June for September cropping. Autumn-sown beans are always a bit of a lottery in this garden as two years out of three they are ravaged by weather and slugs, and do not grow or crop as well as those sown in early spring. However, the one year in three when they do work well means that we can harvest our

first beans at the end of May, which is a treat, so I persevere with a row or two sown in October.

Whenever you sow, a double row, 30–45cm (12–18in) apart is best, with the beans planted 23cm (9in) apart down the rows. If sowing early in October or February, choose a variety like 'Aquadulce'. Don't worry if they seem to stop growing once they have germinated and appeared above ground. They will pick up as soon as the days start to lengthen and warm up, and will have a head start over later crops.

For mid- and late-spring sowings I grow 'Bunyards Exhibition' as a very reliable cropper, 'The Sutton' for its excellent taste and 'Red Epicure', which has wonderful garnet-coloured beans and vermilion flowers.

Broad beans are included to crop very heavily and produce a glut, so should be picked regularly, when they are big enough to pod but small enough to be deliciously tender.

The plants will need support once they are about 90cm (36in) tall and the easiest way to do this is to put a cane at the end of each row and halfway along, and then tie string between them, adding another layer of string every 60cm (24in) or so as the beans grow.

Broad beans have extraordinary long roots going down over 1.5m (5ft), so they open out a heavy soil, tapping into mineral resources that other, more shallow-rooted plants will not reach. These minerals then go back into the soil by way of the compost heap as the finished crop has a huge amount of top-growth. This is incredibly useful for bulking out and adding fibre to the compost heap at a time of year when it can be dominated by grass clippings.

Broad beans are notoriously prone to blackfly in late spring which can turn the top few inches of each shoot a sooty black due to the sheer number of the aphids feeding off the soft, sappy growing tip of the bean. If these tips are pinched out after the plants have set pods, it usually solves the problem and although it may look bad, blackfly rarely damage or limit the crop.

Bean chocolate spot is caused by a fungus called *Botrytis fabae* which manifests itself as brown splashes on the leaves. It can affect yields and even destroy the plant if the infection is bad. Like all fungal infections, it is encouraged by humid, warm weather and tends to afflict later crops rather than the earlier, overwintering ones.

Climbing beans are decorative and add height to the vegetable garden

Climbing beans

These are always superbly decorative with a choice of green, yellow or purple beans, and they add height to the vegetable garden. By the same token, they are ideal for very limited spaces and grow well in a large container. There are climbing beans that have distinct and delicious tastes so it is worth trialling different varieties to find out what suits you best. My favourite is 'Burro d'Ingegnoli' that has a curiously buttery texture when cooked, pod and all, and is delicious, especially as part of a ratatouille.

They need very rich, water-retentive soil, so I dig a pit or a trench and add plenty of organic material before covering it back over with soil. I then build a structure of strong hazel bean sticks lashed firmly together at the top to support what becomes a wall or pyramid (according to the support) of solid beans.

My favourite varieties:
'Burro d'Ingegnoli', 'Blue Lake', 'Hunter', 'Blauhilde'

French beans

French beans (which are not French at all, coming, as do runner beans, fromCentral and South America) are *Phaseolus vulgaris* and include haricot beans, kidney beans, dwarf, pole, yellow, green, purple and blotchy ones. Unlike broad beans or peas, French beans are tender and grow best in this garden between the middle of June and October. But they are very prolific and a few plants will give you a supply of beautiful fresh bean pods for months.

I make my first sowing in large plugs in the greenhouse at the beginning of May and harden them off carefully via the cold frames before planting them out in early June. I sow another batch directly into the ground when these are planted out, and another one at the beginning of August. This final crop will be picked into October.

French beans are legumes so should be part of the same rotation as other beans and peas (see page 293) and should have deeply dug and freshly composted soil. If I am sowing direct, I sow in double rows 23cm (9in) apart, with 45cm (18in) between each double row and about 10cm (4in) between each bean. If I am planting out indoor-raised seedlings, I do so in blocks with 23cm (9in) between each plant. They need plenty of water, so weed assiduously to reduce competition.

Over the years I have grown a pretty wide selection but keep coming back to the yellow and purple varieties like 'Golden Sands' and 'Annabel' – although there are others. The purple dwarf beans are better able to withstand colder weather than most other types so are good for a late sowing that will crop well into autumn.

Runner beans

Runner beans are one of the favourite vegetables for British gardeners and I have just started growing them again after forsaking them for about 20 years. Like climbing French beans, they respond directly to plenty of goodness and water, so give them an extra helping of compost and keep them well watered. They do best in mild (but not cold),

damp weather – which makes them ideal for an English summer! They are grown for the pods rather than the beans which, when eaten young and tender and cooked lightly, have a delicious green freshness to them.

My favourite varieties: 'Scarlet Emperor', 'Desiree', 'Painted Lady'

Assembling the hazel structure for the climbing beans with rods cut from our Coppice is one of my essential gardening rituals.

Peas

Thomas Jefferson, third president of the United States, author of the American Declaration of Independence, a Founding Father and one of the towering figures of western civilisation, had an obsessive interest in growing vegetables. Would that modern politicians shared this wise pursuit. At Monticello, his estate in Virginia, he grew over 250 varieties of more than 70 different species, and dutifully recorded the progress of all in his journals – but nothing excited so much horticultural passion within his presidential breast as the cultivation of peas. Some years he would raise as many as fifteen different varieties. Every year there was a race to harvest the earliest pods and he and his

Virginian neighbours would have a competition to see who could produce the first dish of peas, with the winner hosting a meal where this dish would be consumed and admired by all.

I think that this lust for early peas was partly to do with the incredible green freshness that home-grown peas have and which everyone can hanker after, in the same way that we all want new potatoes or asparagus as early in the season as possible (but not, for me at least, discordantly out of season – that spoils it). But there was also the very unmodern fact that most people ate dried peas right up until the twentieth century. Fresh peas were a luxury. Dried peas were easy to store, high in protein and would make a digestible, cheap, nutritious porridge – mushy peas. To eat them fresh, you either had to grow them yourself or be wealthy.

The freezer has changed all that. Even the most industrially produced pea does not taste bad although, to quote from *Forgotten Fruits*, Christopher Stocks' most excellent book on traditional fruits and vegetables, they are 'uniform in size and dependable in flavour but, dare one say it, a little bland'. So, if you are to grow them yourself, it makes sense to choose varieties with care and to relish and luxuriate with Jeffersonian delight in a freshness that eludes even the freezer.

For a vegetable so basic and recognisable, peas are quite fussy about how they grow. They don't like cold, wet soil and they don't like hot, dry weather. I have given up sowing mine before Christmas (the only way to get them out

Unripe peas in a pod that will be ready to harvest in a few days. Mangetout varieties are eaten pod and all.

Opposite page: The hardest thing is to resist eating too many peas as you pick them. Nigel would wait until they were ripe and then stand and munch all the pods that he could reach.

of the pod by 4 June) because they rot in the damp winter soil, sulk if they do germinate and get eaten by mice.

I like 'Alderman' for its old-fashioned extravagance of height – over 1.8m (6ft) in my rich soil – and unsurpassable flavour, which seems to have, if it is not too fanciful, a solidity and roundness that an alderman should. I also grow 'Hurst Greenshaft' and 'Carouby de Maussanne' and have often grown 'Feltham First' in pursuit of that 4 June gardening gold standard. But not this year.

There has been much debate over the years as to the best spacing and alignment of peas, ranging from single, double or even triple rows, to individual peas placed as close as 2.5cm (1in) apart or as wide as 15cm (6in). My technique is to make a double row, 23cm (9in) apart and at 5–7.5cm (2–3in) spacing with 90cm (36in) between each row. I always support them with pea sticks cut from my own hazel. This is an annual ritual I will go to great lengths to maintain – to the extent of planting a hazel coppice a decade or so ago primarily to supply bean and pea sticks.

Mangetout and sugar snap peas are eaten pods and all. The former never really develop proper peas and retain flat pods whilst the latter develop their peas slowly, which means that if you do not pick them regularly, you can harvest the maturing peas and eat them as a normal variety. Both are without the hard wall to the pod which conventional 'wrinkled' peas have. There is a lot to be said for growing sugar snap peas if you have limited space and perhaps limited patience for the bother of shelling peas. I veer between a nostalgic,

glowing pleasure at the business of shelling peas around the kitchen table, and an impatient desire for the fast-food immediacy of sugar snaps.

Purple-podded peas are worth growing if you can find them because they look absolutely lovely – although they do not taste any better than perhaps half a dozen green varieties, and the cooked peas are indistinguishable from any other.

Like all legumes, peas take nitrogen from the air into the soil via warty nodules on their roots. This makes them an essential component in the rotation of vegetables in the garden (see page 293). Traditionally they are grown in newly dug and manured ground, and are followed by brassica crops like cabbage or purple sprouting broccoli, which are put into the same plot to use the extra nitrogen the peas have left behind. The following spring the plot is then sown with root crops such as carrots or parsnips and after these are harvested in the autumn, the ground is double-dug and heavily manured before sowing with more peas.

Peas like cool (but not cold), damp weather but hate sitting in wet – hence the need for well-drained but moisture-retentive soil. Their need for coolish conditions means that you cannot really make a successful sowing after the end of May unless there is a sustained cool period. The fastest-maturing varieties (like 'Feltham First' and 'Prince Albert') take about twelve weeks to mature and the slowest maincrop varieties (like 'Hurst Greenshaft') can take a month longer – but will go on producing pods for a month.

You can easily save your peas for next year's seed. Leave the pods on the plant as long as possible, lifting the whole plant just before the pods start to split. Either hang the plant up in a dry shed or store the pods on a tray until they split open and the peas can be collected. Store them in an airtight container or paper bag in a cool, dry place.

Onions

Twenty years ago I grew onions confident of success. Some years were better than others but all years were good. This applied to all my allium crops – onions, shallots, leeks, chives and garlic alike. But then we began to be afflicted with white rot and things rapidly went downhill.

Climate change has contributed much to this as the warm, wet winters and mild, wettish summers have encouraged the fungal spores of *Sclerotium cepivorum*. The sclerotia – tiny black dots – can remain viable in the soil for at least seven years and this was the deciding factor in moving the Vegetable Garden to the far end of our plot so I could have uninfected soil to grow alliums in. For three years I did not grow any alliums at all and I now still do not grow maincrop onions but limit myself to growing garlic and shallots and a few leeks. Touch wood there has been no sign of white rot for a couple of years so we should be able to return to a full edible allium harvest very soon.

Because onions are as central a component of any vegetable garden as daffodils are of spring, they have been an integral part of the cuisine of every nation on earth for as long as recorded time. This is hardly surprising. They are easy to grow, store very well and remain juicy right to the end, taste good and do you good. In the Middle Ages onions were thought to provoke lust, notwithstanding that everyone, particularly the poor, ate them almost every day. Chaucer's summoner, for example, displayed his

Seed-sown onions grown and planted out in a clump force themselves apart and make harvesting easier.

Onions from seed store better than those grown from sets, but sets are easier, quicker and less fiddly

lechery openly through his love of 'garleek, onyons and eke lekes'. The real point is that they were considered robust, common and unrefined – all of which are precisely the honest onion's chief virtues.

It is a mistake to enrich the soil that you grow your onions in beyond a light dressing of compost, otherwise you end up with extra-lush foliage, smaller bulbs and increased fungal problems. I have learned this lesson through over-enthusiastic experience.

I used to grow a lot of onions from seed and the choice of varieties is certainly much greater if you do so, and there is some evidence that onions from seed store better than ones grown from sets. But sets are easier, quicker and – crucial for my clumsy great fingers – less fiddly. If you buy heat-treated sets they will be less prone to bolting. I start them in plugs in the greenhouse to stop the birds tugging at their emerging shoots.

Onions need a long a growing period if they are to mature into decent-sized bulbs before they go to seed. They are quick to suffer from water shortage so it is important to keep them well weeded to avoid competition and to that end, always plant them out in rows or grids to make it easy to hoe between the growing bulbs without damaging them. Sets take about 20 weeks to mature from planting and seed takes perhaps another four weeks on top of that. Once midsummer comes and the

days are getting shorter, spring-sown onions will be increasingly inclined to go to seed, at which point the bulb ceases to have much use for the plant, so it stops investing any strength in it. The time to harvest is as late as possible before the onions go to seed. So it is a good idea to plant sets as soon as the ground is ready after new year (although this might well be as late as mid-April) and to sow seed by mid-March.

It is a best to bend the leaves over two weeks before harvesting and not to water them at all in the final three weeks. Bending them over can seem a fiddle but it stops energy going into the development of flower heads. I remember filming a wonderful 76-year-old allotment holder in Nottingham who at one time single-handedly ran nine allotments, although by then was reduced to a paltry three. All were crammed with superb veg and he simply marched over his onion beds when they were fully grown with his wellies on, squashing down all the foliage as he did so. It was crude but perfectly effective. As with all bulbs do not cut off any of the leaves but let them die right back.

It is important to dig your onions out rather than pull them because the basal plate must remain undamaged if they are to store well. I dry mine on the earth for a day and then lay them out on racked staging in the greenhouse for a few weeks. It is essential that they are as dry as possible before they are stored, and the more sun that they have before harvesting, the better they will last. Their storage requirements are pretty simple but ideally the temperature should remain between 0°C (32°F) and 5°C (40°F). I always used to plait my onions and hang them in a shed but they store just as well in a wicker or wire basket in a cool, dark place.

There are over 500 hundred different varieties of onion, but here are a few that I have grown with pleasure and success.

My favourite red varieties: 'Red Baron', 'Torpedo', 'Rossa lunga di Firenze'

My favourite white varieties: 'Turbo', 'Setton', 'Sturon', 'Stuttgarter Giant', 'Rijnsburger'

Shallots

Shallots form a cluster of small bulbs from the original set rather than one big bulb. This always seems to me to be something of a miracle, a kind of cellular division on the soil's surface that happens openly but always when you are not looking. They are hardier than onions and are usually grown from sets which can be planted as early as January for a midsummer harvest. They should be put at a slightly wider spacing than onions, perhaps as much as 30cm (12in), to give the cluster room to expand. Other than that you grow them exactly as you do onions. When they are fully dried after harvest I store them in a basket in the larder and when we need some for the kitchen, just go and scoop up a handful. If they are kept cool and dark, they should reliably store well into spring.

Shallots are tenderer and tastier than many an onion, store longer and better, and are less readily available in your average supermarket. Finally they seem – on the basis of my own not-very-rigorous trials – less susceptible to white rot, so all in all a better bet for the space-strapped veg gardener.

My favourite varieties: 'Cuisse de Poulet du Poitu', 'Santé', 'Red Sun'

Carrots

You have never truly tasted a carrot until you have eaten one absolutely fresh, the soil swished off under a tap. The smell – which is such a key component of flavour – is instantly familiar and enticing, but it soon diminishes and is something that can only be experienced when growing your own. One of my favourite dishes of all is pasta primavera, made in midsummer with baby carrots, peas, broad beans, fresh garlic and good olive oil. It is the most optimistic meal of the year.

Carrots are biennial, establishing decent roots in their first growing season and – if left unpulled – producing an umbel of flowers in the second. Wild carrots have white roots and it was not until the seventeenth century that the

The carrot 'Nigel' grown in a container. These are sown then left unthinned and pulled by the handful.

Dutch bred the now ubiquitous orange carrot. Breeders have constantly worked since then on increasing its sweetness. Therefore this most distinctively 'natural' of vegetables is a man-made construct.

Carrots can be sown at any time between early spring and midsummer as long as the soil is warm, although early crops can be temperamental about germinating and be very patchy. They do best in a light, well-drained, lightly alkaline soil, which is rather different from our heavy clay – nevertheless we still get good crops.

Sow very thinly, either in shallow drills or broadcast across the surface before covering the seeds by lightly raking. I now always prefer to broadcast the seed, harvesting a clump at a time which will be made up of roots of different sizes. As well as being more convenient, this avoids the need for thinning and so reduces the attraction for carrot flies.

Carrots are in the same family as parsnips, parsley and celery, and all this group are best grown as part of a rotation (see page 293) that follows the brassicas such as cabbage and purple sprouting broccoli. The ground should be well dug but not have any manure or compost added during the previous year as this can cause splitting. Also, do not add any fertiliser to the soil as the result would be extra-vigorous growth above ground at the expense of the roots.

The earliest crops are best from Amsterdam-type cultivars that have narrow, cylindrical roots with smooth skins. Nantes types are generally bigger and can be grown both as early and maincrop.

Chantenay, Berlicum and Autumn King types are all best for maincrops that you would expect to harvest in autumn and that can have the biggest roots.

Carrot flies lay their eggs in the soil around the roots and when the larvae hatch, they eat their way into the carrots, leaving tell-tale black horizontal gouges, especially in those harvested in autumn and winter. These insects have an extraordinary sense of smell and can detect fresh carrot from up to half a mile away. Thinning the seedlings throws up the heady aroma of carrot into the air as you bruise the leaves and this is what attracts the flies. If carrot flies are a consistent problem, it is best to harvest the roots when they are still small and eat them fresh rather than leave them in the ground for long.

Beetroot

Over the past 20 years, beetroot has gained a reputation for being another (yawn) 'superfood' – mainly, I suspect, due to the proliferation of juice bars and juicers and the striking colour of juiced beetroot. Also, its earthy taste feels as though it *ought* to be doing you good. However, strip away the hype and it is both delicious and good for you.

It has always been popular with gardeners. Part of its attraction is the seed itself, a corky, fused conglomerate of seeds that is wonderfully easy to handle. Another is the versatility of the plant, as the leaves are just as important as the root. In fact, we came to the red swollen roots relatively late, not taking them up

with enthusiasm until the 1600s although the leaves had been grown and consumed for centuries before that. The Victorians loved their beetroot and certainly in the 1950s, in my early childhood, it was a staple vegetable, boiled and occasionally served hot and whole but much more commonly allowed to cool, peeled and then sliced as part of a salad, staining the white of the hard-boiled egg and salad cream that invariably accompanied it.

I have always found beetroot to be effortlessly responsive to the standard routine I use with any seed large enough to handle and small enough to be grown in a plug. Beetroot will not germinate at temperatures below 7°C (45°F) so I sow two or three seed clusters per plug (not too small) and germinate them in the greenhouse before hardening them off in a cold frame. There was a time when I always thinned beetroot conscientiously

but I now like to grow them as a little group of between two and five beets. I prepare their growing ground with a good dressing of garden compost. They respond well to plenty of richness and water, and if too dry or under-nourished, will respond by bolting, which will stop root development unless the flowering stem is cut back as soon as it is noticed.

When the seedlings have been properly hardened off – and the simplest way of doing that is to put the plug trays on the soil where they are to be grown for a week – I plant them out at 23cm (9in) spacings in each direction. This is wide enough to get a small hoe in between them and also for the groups to swell out with ease.

The ideal size for a beetroot is somewhere between a golf and a cricket ball. We harvest them by pulling the entire group of plants that grew together in each plug. Growing them in a little cluster also

Beetroot can be grown and harvested all the year round and even if the roots become inedibly woody over winter, the new leaves in spring are delicious in a salad.

Beetroot freshly lifted and washed clean.

helps stop the occasional over-enthusiastic beet from getting too big.

I find that two successional sowings are enough but that may be a measure of our consumption rather than the perfect number. I sow the first in March for planting out in May and the second in June for an August planting. This latter planting will stay in the ground all winter and although cold weather will reduce some of the roots to hollow, soggy shells, it is astonishing how new foliage can nevertheless appear in spring – and the leaves are very good either eaten raw in a salad or cooked like spinach. They have a very high vitamin A content with more iron, calcium, trace minerals and vitamin C than spinach.

I have tried many varieties but I particularly like 'Bull's Blood', 'Pronto', which is smaller than most, 'Chioggia', which is ringed pink and white, 'Carillon', which is long, and 'Burpees Golden', which has golden leaves and roots.

Finally, my two favourite ways of eating beetroot, especially as the days get colder: the first is roasted whole or halved with thyme, and the second is boiled and served with a hot cream sauce. Both are ideal with a slow-roasted shoulder of lamb and a rich glass of that miracle food that cures most of the day's troubles – red wine.

Potatoes

There are three groups of potato, first early, second early and maincrop.

First earlies mature very fast, in about 90 days from planting, tend to be exceptionally sweet but store rather badly, so they are usually left in the ground until required and are finished before the maincrop are lifted. Maincrop take another three or four weeks to mature and are less sweet but store very well and can be left in the ground until the first hard frosts. It follows that first earlies tend to be planted as soon as possible in spring for a midsummer harvest, and that maincrop varieties can wait into early summer as long as they can be lifted before winter.

As their name implies, second earlies fall between these two extremes and will serve in either capacity, although will not store for as long as maincrop so should be dug by the end of summer with the aim of eating them before Christmas. To my mind second earlies include some of the very best potatoes of all for the gardener, especially if you are limited with space – as almost all of us are.

Finding space for maincrop is becoming increasingly tricky and they are much more likely to get blight. The conditions that the fungus thrives in – it needs two consecutive days, each with a minimum of eleven hours where relative humidity is 89 per cent or more and the minimum temperature is 10°C (50°F) – are most prevalent from mid-June to late August, which is before maincrop potatoes are ready for harvesting. First and second early varieties on the other hand can usually be grown and harvested before the advent of seasonal blight.

Blight is recognisable by yellow stains on the leaves that turn pale brown, spreading in a concentric circle. As soon as you notice it you must cut off all top-growth from the variety that is blighted. This can be composted since a good compost heap will have enough heat to kill the spores. If your heap is not 'good', burn the infected haulms (the top bit of growth) on the bonfire. The potatoes can be left in the ground for at least three weeks afterwards but will not grow any further. It is best to dig them up on a dry, cool day, let them

dry and then store them in a cool, dark place. I have kept blighted potatoes which I dug in August in good condition right through to May. They had the odd blemish but tasted wonderful.

In any event, the tremendous scale of the potato growers all around us, with their vast machinery and breathtaking investment (and, in a good year, profits to match) means that blight is almost inevitable – especially if you are organic and do not wish to douse your garden with fungicides. There are some maincrop varieties that show reasonable resistance to blight, such as 'Sante', 'Sarpo Mira', 'Cara' or 'Orla', but none is immune and growing a potato just because you can rather defeats the point of the process. I want to grow potatoes – anything edible – because they are the best-tasting, healthiest option possible.

Although I enjoy eating potatoes in any and every possible manner, from roast to rosti, to my mind nothing beats really good, slightly waxy potatoes simply boiled and served with salt and pepper and perhaps a little butter or oil. If that can be combined with the sweetness of absolutely fresh new potatoes, then it is a dish fit, if not for a king, then at least for a birthday treat and I have a little ritual of not digging for any new potatoes until my birthday on 8 July. I regard it a bit like the presents under the Christmas Tree – no

Potato blight is almost inevitable, especially if you do not wish to douse your garden with fungicides

peeking, no feeling to guess the hidden object but waiting until the big day and going with the surprise.

So now, apart from a couple of short rows of 'Violetta' and 'Pink Fir Apple', I concentrate on first and second earlies. ('Violetta' and 'Pink Fir Apple' are both maincrop, with 'Violetta' a rich purple with a particularly waxy, smooth texture and taste, and 'Pink Fir Apple' famous for its knobbly, sausage shape like ginger tubers, its waxy texture and nutty flavour, but also for being very prone to blight.) 'Red Duke of York', a first early, is an old favourite of mine and 'Charlotte' is perhaps my second-best general-purpose potato, ready from late July and keeping for months. I believe the finest potato is the romantically named 'BF15', which is almost impossible to get hold of nowadays. The BF in its name derives from sports of 'Belle de Fontenay' which, in the couple of years I grew it, was almost perfect in terms of taste and texture. Mind you, the original 'Belle de Fontenay' itself is lovely too and much easier to find.

The whole point of first and second earlies is their texture, taste and, above all, sweetness. The sugars in a potato fresh from the ground are at their most intense and if you cook and eat them as soon as

These are the first early variety 'Red Duke of York' and should be eaten as soon as possible to capture their fleeting sweetness.

possible after harvesting, there really is an appreciable difference from anything that has to be lifted, packed, transported and marketed. New potatoes should be dug specifically for each meal and each harvest cooked in its entirety because leftover cold ones are almost as good as those served steaming hot.

Early (or 'new') potatoes are best planted as soon as the ground is ready in March or April. 'Ready' means workable and not cold to touch. I used to try to do this as early as possible but I have learned not to be in a hurry with them. I have planted as late as the second week of June and still got a decent crop.

People get very obsessive about how they plant potatoes, as though there was a right or wrong way. There are those that swear by holes rather than drills and others who only grow under black plastic, hay or straw. Each to their own. I use two methods. In open ground I cultivate the soil so I can draw a mattock easily through it and make V-shaped drills about 23cm (9in) deep and 90cm (36in) apart. I then place the seed potatoes along the bottom of these drills about 45cm (18in) apart. The wider they are (up to 30–60cm/12–24in), the bigger the crop from each plant and the bigger the individual potatoes. It follows that maincrop baking potatoes should be planted at a wider spacing than new potatoes grown for eating small and boiled whole. I then use the mattock to draw the soil back over the drills so that the soil forms a distinct ridge.

The other method, that I use for raised beds is simply to make holes with a trowel or dibber into which I pop the seed potatoes in a grid about 45cm (18in) apart. This is very much easier and produces just as good results – especially for first earlies.

However you plant potatoes, the top-growth is likely to appear before the last frosts and frost can blacken the leaves exactly as though a blowtorch has been at them. You can avoid this scorching by earthing them up as soon as all the leaves have appeared and the plants are about 15cm (6in) tall. This is done on open ground by drawing soil up with a draw hoe or mattock from between the rows and covering all but the very tops of the green leaves. On raised beds I use either

The whole point of first and second earlies is their texture, taste and, above all, their sweetness

a layer of compost or straw but compost is preferable because damp straw is slug heaven. Earthing up also ensures that any growing tubers remain covered from light and so stop turning green and poisonous. It also supports the haulms when they are at their floppiest. And lastly, but by no means least, the increased thickness of the soil covering works as a protective layer against blight spores being washed from the leaves down into the potatoes.

Seed potatoes, especially of early varieties, grow faster if they are 'chitted'. This means exposing them to light with most of the eyes upright so that they develop strong, knobbly buds. Chitting is really just the start of the growth of the potato – effectively like germinating and growing seedlings in a propagator before planting out.

They will take about a month if they are placed on a cool (but frost-free) windowsill. If you have them, egg boxes or trays are ideal for this but I use seed trays, which work very well.

Potatoes will grow unchitted too – in fact you cannot stop them growing – but if you chit them they have a head start once they are planted. This can be important in cold areas because potatoes are not hardy. A late frost can scorch the foliage or even kill the potatoes. Chitting is also important in areas prone to blight, as the tubers have maximum chance to develop before blight (see page 323) strikes – which is rarely before July.

Tomatoes

Tomatoes are the most popular vegetable grown by British gardeners – even though they are in fact a berry rather than a vegetable. But let us put botanical pedantry aside. Tomatoes are set foursquare in the vegetable plot.

And who cannot love a fresh tomato, still warm from the sun (keeping tomatoes in the fridge kills all taste and is an aberration)? The skin is so thin that the juice and flesh are barely contained and with that first grazing of your teeth, the juice bursts into your mouth with a warm, sweet, musty, distinct flavour, so richly redolent of sun and good living. In this country you cannot buy that but wander through any market in the Mediterranean in summer, and there will be ten, 20 varieties of tomato for sale, all at that perfect point of ripeness and all grown under a baking southern sun so their taste has a complexity and fullness the northern grower can barely aspire to. But we try.

Apparently, over 40 per cent of British gardeners grow their tomatoes outside. But for many years I gave up growing them outside the greenhouse because although they set fruit, they rarely ripened. However, in the last few years, I have planted a bed of tomatoes outside – more in hope than expectation – and have had decent harvests from them – in fact more than decent and exceeding that of the greenhouse-grown ones. However, the skins are thick and – most important of all – never have that intensity of taste that only heat can give them.

So lesson number one: grow your tomatoes, indoors or out, in as sunny and hot a spot as you can give them. But it is not just a question of daytime heat. Whereas hot midday sun helps ripen the fruits, warm nights are the secret of rapid and healthy growth.

Tomatoes always react badly to fluctuating temperatures and fruits sometimes split and develop a grey, wispy mould caused by irregular, big variations in temperature between day and night. Close the greenhouse *before* the evening cools down and keep it wide open all day. Cold nights will also cause leaves to curl up lengthways and look as though they

Whereas hot midday sun helps ripen tomatoes, warm nights are the secret of rapid and healthy growth

are about to die. Older leaves are more affected than young ones.

One way of reducing this is to plant them out a little later than you otherwise might because the real danger is from May and June nights. By midsummer the nights cool down less and by September, the main focus is not on growing healthy plants but on ripening as much fruit as possible.

The final factor for healthy, strong plants is light levels, especially early on whilst the plant is still growing strongly. A gloomy June or July is bad news regardless of the temperature, whereas a gloomy – but warm – August can make for good tomatoes.

I like to sow the seed in two or even three batches in February, March and April, scattering them thinly on the surface of peat-free compost and then very lightly covering them either with a layer of more compost or vermiculite. Water them well and put them in a warm spot to germinate. A windowsill above a radiator is ideal if you do not have a greenhouse.

When they develop their first pair of 'true' leaves – that is to say leaves, however small, that are recognisably those of a tomato rather than the ones that grow initially – you know that they have roots

Most of my tomatoes have been raised indoors because outdoor tomatoes are very prone to blight. But in recent years, probably as a result of climate change, outdoor ones have grown and cropped very successfully.

'Costoluto Fiorentino' grown outside are late-ripening but still a delicious and reliable beefsteak tomato.

and should be pricked out into better compost and individual pots or plugs. Grow them on in a warm, bright place and when they are about 10–15cm (4–6in) tall, they should be potted on again into 7.5cm (3in) pots. This may sound like a lot of work but it is important that the young, growing plant is not checked and the roots have room to grow into.

There are two basic types of tomato – cordon and bush. Cordon tomatoes will go on growing until they die and can – and do – reach 6m (20ft) or more. They are often described as 'indeterminate'. Their fruit ripens over a long period – as much as six months in certain areas – and they need supporting almost from the first, and in order to train them to grow upright in a restricted space, they have to be constantly pruned. Cordons take up far

less space and are by far the most common method of growing tomatoes.

Bush tomatoes are 'determinate', which means that when they reach their predetermined size, they stop growing. They do not need the sideshoots removing, nor need staking, although it is a good idea to prop them up to lift the fruits off the soil. The gap between the first and last fruit ripening is much shorter than in cordons – about two weeks to a month. This makes them more suitable to field and commercial production than cordons, but perhaps less useful for the gardener who wants as long a supply of ripening fruit as possible.

The process of pruning cordons is extremely simple. The most important aspect of it is to remove all sideshoots, which grow enthusiastically at 45 degrees in the angle between the stem and a leaf. This diagonal growth is very vigorous, takes a lot of space and diverts energy away from the main cordon. The easiest way to remove the sideshoots is to snap them off with a twist of finger and thumb, and is best done in the morning when the plants are turgid and the risk of tearing or damaging the main stem is much reduced. Any shoots from the base of the plant should be pulled out when removing the sideshoots.

The second form of pruning is to remove the lower leaves as the fruits mature. This allows air and light between the plants and is important for ripening and the avoidance of fungal diseases. I have two criteria for removing leaves:

- if they are directly shading a truss of fruit
- if they are yellowing (and therefore not contributing to the vitality of the plant anyway).

Another rule is to give the leaf a sharp yank. If it does not come away in your hand then it is probably too soon to remove it. By the time that all the fruit on the plant is turning red, the bottom 60–90cm (24–36in) of the plant can be completely stripped.

The young plants are ready to go out to their final growing position when they are around 23–30cm (9–12in) tall, by which time they have often developed their first flowering truss. Plant them buried right to the first leaf. This will hold them steady and encourage new roots to grow from the buried stem.

Cordons are going to get tall and heavy so they need good solid support or, when grown in the greenhouse, strong twine tied to the stem just beneath the soil and fixed to a wire or to the roof of the greenhouse so the growing plant can gradually twist round the twine.

Books have been written about the best way to grow tomatoes and the best medium to grow them in. I have tried soil, wide spacing, close spacing, big pots, small pots, terracotta and plastic pots, grow bags and ring culture. In the end I don't think it matters terribly. I have had excellent results from a cheap grow bag and very average ones from raised beds in a greenhouse filled with ideal Herefordshire loam and masses of textbook compost. What is certain is that the balance between feeding the plant enough to grow strong and well, yet restricting its food so it puts more energy into the fruit and not into the plant itself is critical, as is the watering regime.

Tomatoes are tough plants and too much kindness tends to do more harm than a little benign neglect

Tomatoes are tough plants and too much kindness tends to do more harm than a little benign neglect. In short, there is a greater danger in over-feeding and over-watering than in doing too little of either. If they are grown in a bed or large pot in a greenhouse, a good soak of the roots every two or three days is usually sufficient except in the hottest weather, when they will need daily watering.

TOMATO PESTS AND DISEASES

If you grow tomatoes in the same soil year after year – regardless of how diligently you top it up with compost – there will be a build-up of soil-borne viruses. To avoid this you need to practise crop rotation (see page 293). But obviously this is impractical when growing under cover, so instead of changing the crop, the answer is to change the soil. Every three years dig out the top 23–30cm (9–12in) of your greenhouse beds and replace with fresh soil from the garden or from a loam stack. This should make all the difference.

As well as blight (see below), tomatoes are prone to a handsome array of viruses and moulds, some of which, like tomato leaf mould, are pretty disastrous. But an unhappy-looking tomato plant can still produce delicious fruit and it is the fruits that should be the focus of attention.

As far as pests go, whitefly is the most common problem. The adult lays its eggs on the lower leaves and after a nymph stage, the new adult emerges and feeds on the leaves, sucking sap, spreading viruses and exuding honeydew on which a fungus grows. The flies overwinter on perennial plants so try not to keep plants like fuchsias overwintering in a greenhouse that is to grow tomatoes the following summer. I grow basil with my tomatoes as a deterrent (the flies dislike the strong scent of the basil), and basil and tomatoes thrive in the same regime.

The biggest potential problem for outdoor tomatoes in this garden and many parts of the country is the risk of tomato blight. This is the same fungal disease that affects potatoes (that are a close cousin to tomatoes) and will readily cross-infect the two plants. As with potatoes, it appears as pale brown blotches on the leaves that quickly radiate out, producing a spreading circle of softly collapsing and browning leaves. The fungus can then get to the fruit, making it inedible. The best means of avoiding it is to grow your tomatoes under cover and not over-water as the blight is spread mainly by rain and needs conditions of high humidity to develop. However, if you have to grow them outside, choose blight-resistant varieties like 'Crimson Crush' or 'Shirley', and give the plants maximum ventilation by spacing them as widely as you can. Once you see the first signs of blight, remove all affected leaves and fruit, and strip away all remaining foliage to expose the green fruit to

maximum light and air. By August, a tomato plant will continue to grow perfectly well with no leaves at all, so this is not, in itself, a disaster although it does look pretty dramatic. If the plant is beyond rescue, remove and burn it, although I have composted blight-affected potato and tomato foliage with no transmission via the subsequent compost.

Blossom end rot presents itself as a flattened, calloused, hard brown disc at the end of the fruit. It is caused by inadequate – or more often erratic – water supply which stops the plant from taking in enough calcium so that the cells collapse. Water regularly and, if your soil is naturally very acidic, grow only small-fruited varieties that tend to be less susceptible.

There are also a number of different viruses that afflict tomatoes but most manifest themselves in yellowing, mottled leaves, wilting and poor setting of fruit. There is not a lot that can be done once the problem has set in and often the plant will continue to provide fruit, albeit smaller and less of it. Prevention is helped by good hygiene, changing the soil that tomatoes are grown in and – as ever – by encouraging the development of healthy, unforced plants.

But consistency is the key. Erratic watering or watering too much can manifest itself with the fruit slitting or in blossom end rot (see opposite).

Feeding should be minimal and done in two stages. For most of us, indoors or out, the growing season is going to end in September or early October, whether we like it or not. If you are growing your tomatoes in soil, they will need no extra feed at all until they start to form flower trusses, and after that, a weak seaweed solution once a week is plenty. If you are using a container of any kind, a general-purpose tomato feed once a week is good or, if you have the resources, home-made comfrey feed (see page 115) works wonders.

Aubergines

I could happily eat ratatouille every day for the rest of my life, made with onions, garlic, courgettes (or squash), tomatoes and herbs, all easily grown in the garden – but ratatouille without aubergine is a pale imposter. However, I confess that most years I struggle to get a decent crop of aubergines. If they are good then we do not have enough. It becomes a case of celebrating that they have grown at all rather than the fact that they are seasonal, fresh and truly delicious – which are the standards by which all food should be judged, whether grown in the garden or served in the fanciest restaurant.

All cordon tomatoes need a vertical support and although these young 'Gardener's Delight' plants are weeks if not months away from cropping, they are tied into a strong cane at least weekly.

They only grow truly well here when we have a hot summer and are ideally grown in a bed inside the greenhouse rather than in pots. Then they reward me with scores of superb, deeply plum-coloured fruits and we are ratatouille-happy. But climate change means that our summers are – despite the gradual increase of the annual average temperature – a bit cooler, cloudier and wetter year on year, and we rarely get a truly sunny, hot, dry spell for more than a couple of consecutive weeks.

I sow the seed in March, pricking out the surprisingly modest seedlings into a 7.5cm (3in) pot and then, usually in early June when they are becoming vigorous and have a decent root system, into the 30cm (12in) pots they remain in. If I had more space I would give them double the pot size. I use the same potting mix as for cucumbers – with lots of extra garden compost but plenty of grit to create a loose enough root run. I water them daily and feed with liquid seaweed once a week.

They grow about 90cm (36in) tall and I give each a bamboo stake to stop them being bowed down by the weight of the fruits – although that is based as much on hope as on experience. The key is to pinch out new sideshoots after four or five fruits have formed, otherwise you get a bushy, luxuriant plant and no extra fruit.

Slugs and snails love the fruits and will hide up in the leaves to gouge into the flesh. The fruits can be slow to develop but should not be left too long. As soon as they are a reasonable size and shine like a guardsman's boots, then they are ready. Overripe fruits turn dull and taste impossibly bitter. Although yellowing leaves can be a sign of verticillium wilt, lower leaves will inevitably yellow and should be picked off.

Getting the balance between enough humidity and too much moisture can be tricky in a greenhouse and, as ever, the best guide is simply the appearance of the plant itself. If it is strong, with green foliage and plum-coloured stems, and is producing plenty of new flowers with fruit forming, then it is happy.

Chillies

One of my favourite breakfast dishes is an omelette made with a thinly sliced fresh chilli. I cook the omelette for a scant two minutes, fold it over and eat it with great pleasure.

Anyone who has a windowsill, let alone a garden, can grow fresh chillies and the secret of a really good chilli omelette is using chillies that are still firm and juicy and have a fruity flavour that is much more than just a sensation of heat in the mouth.

There are over 2000 different cultivars of *Capsicum annuum*, scores of which are widely available in the UK and come in a rainbow of colours and a huge variety of shapes and sizes and intensities of heat. Cayenne peppers are long and thin. They are easy to dry and store at home, either whole or ground up and kept as a chilli powder, but have a good flavour when eaten fresh. Jalapeños tend to be bigger, with firm, round flesh that often is 'corked' or traced with thin lines like scars. They tend to be less hot than most cayenne varieties. I also grow padrón chillies that we cook whilst still green and

without any heat, fried on one side and eaten as tapas as they are in Spain.

The sensation of heat from chillies is caused by a reaction to capsaicin, which is mostly in the white ribs that run down the inside of the fruits. Removing the pith and seeds from the flesh is therefore an effective way of reducing the heat. Milk in some form is the best way to provide a neutralising effect to capsaicin – which is why a hot curry is best accompanied by lassi rather than lager.

Extra heat from a windowsill or a hot sunny site in the garden, or the protection of a greenhouse will not make the fruits taste hotter but will enable them to ripen and turn red so that they have a really good fruity flavour beneath the layers of heat.

Botanically a red chilli is a berry and new flowers will continue to form whilst fruits are ripening. The plant will go on flowering well into winter if there is enough warmth. The fruits can be picked at any time, however,

when fully ripe, the chilli will have more sugars and therefore a richer, more complex taste, and will store better.

The secret of growing chillies is to sow the seed early enough – January is ideal and no later than mid-February – to give it time to germinate and grow into decent-sized plants before they start to flower in midsummer. The seedlings can be very slow to develop although as much heat and light as possible help. Once pricked out and established, a weekly feed high in nitrogen helps the young plants put on plenty of foliage and then, as the flowers start to appear in June, this should change to a weekly feed high in potash, such as liquid seaweed or a general-purpose tomato feed, to encourage flowering and fruiting over a long season from mid-July to the end of the year.

Although the plants look very handsome with their red fruits hanging like Christmas decorations, they should be

Assorted chillies growing in terracotta pots in the greenhouse. All these were picked immediately this picture was taken because leaving ripe fruit on the plant inhibits further flowering.

picked and stored – or eaten fresh – as soon as they are ripe as this will help stimulate fresh flowering and ripening of green fruits. I now store all my chillies by freezing them straight from the bush, putting them in bags by variety and taking them out individually as needed. This way they keep their lovely fruitiness and texture as well as their heat.

Courgettes

I cannot remember when courgettes came into my life. They didn't seem to be there in my childhood. Marrows were the thing. Marrows tasting of 1962 and school ties to church and the Home Service. There were always too many, a glut from the outset, that had to be waded through. Not that I dislike marrow, which can be subtle and refreshing, but marrow with a thick, floury white sauce or – much worse – the carved-out hull of a bloated marrow filled with a meaty slop that passed for mince still makes me shudder.

Marrows are, by definition, big. Courgettes are, by choice, small. Think sausage, finger or gherkin. You can eat courgettes raw and when you cook them, they have texture (but will make a satisfying mush if that is your thing). They actually taste of more than pale green water. They do not sprawl quite so louchely as your average marrow so can be accommodated in your average veg patch. They replenish themselves with vigour, and as long as you keep cutting them, dozens of small courgettes always seems like a possible solution rather than half a dozen whopping great marrows, which are always a problem.

But this difference is not horticultural or botanical. A courgette is simply a baby marrow. It is a cultural shift, learned from Italy, along with the joys of olive oil, good coffee and pizza.

Courgettes and marrows are summer squashes, the definition of which is that they have thin skins and are used fresh from the vine, as opposed to winter squashes that have thick skins and can be stored for months after harvesting. Winter squashes are encouraged to be as large as possible and are picked only once at the very end of their growing season, whereas the more that you pick a summer squash, the more fruits it will produce until the cold weather stops it. Like all the cucurbit family, summer squashes are tender although less inclined to sulk if the soil is a little cold in June, whereas most pumpkins refuse to grow at all unless the nights are warm.

There are – nowadays – dozens of different courgette varieties available for the gardener. I have grown 'Ronde de Nice', the bright yellow 'Gold Rush' and the almost-black 'Verte de Milan' – all are nutty and delicious. There are round courgettes like 'Tondo Chiaro di Nizza' or 'Tondo di Piacenza', or courgettes scalloped at the edges like little pies, such as 'Custard White'. Most of these are bred and treasured in Italy where *zucchini* are eaten in every possible permutation and vary proudly from region to region. You can also harvest the flowers, which are delicious deep-fried in a light batter or stuffed with cheese.

I sow my courgettes in 7.5cm (3in) pots in April, two seeds to a pot, and germinate them on a heated bench. A windowsill will do. As soon as both seedlings are established, I either remove one or split them and repot individually. I then grow them on in the greenhouse and cold frame until they are 15–23cm (6–9in) high before hardening them off really well.

I prepare the ground by digging a bucket-sized hole and backfilling it with garden compost. They are greedy, thirsty plants and the more nourishment they have, the better they do. I plant them into the centre of the compost, leaving a slight saucer-shaped depression so that they can be really soaked with water. They grow and fruit best with plenty of sunshine.

If the weather is warm enough and they never dry out, they will grow fast, and once they start to flower, produce dozens of fruits. They make an ideal plant for growing under or around climbing beans and sweetcorn, acting as a groundcover. This, of course, is the ancient planting combination used for millennia throughout Central and South America. I also grow them, like squashes, vertically up a frame made from strong hazel bean sticks cut from the Coppice. This works very well if you are short on space, and also means that they do not get nibbled by slugs.

Powdery mildew is a problem that seems to affect all courgettes in time and drought will make this much worse. I get round it by growing two batches, the first to cover July and August and the second, sown in June, to crop from late August into autumn. Slugs will nibble at young fruits but there are usually enough of them to go round and, truth be told, plenty left over for the compost heap too.

Cucumbers

Cucumbers are reliably easy to grow as long as you give them the conditions they love, and for us that means a greenhouse.

I have successfully grown 'ridge' types outside, such as 'Long Green Maraicher' and 'Crystal Apple' – which are small and round. These are hardier and have tougher, rougher skins but as a rule, all cucumbers need warmth and wet to thrive. Whilst this part of the world is quite good at being wet, the warmth is nearly always insufficient – and if we do have a really hot summer, it is nearly always a dry one, which is not ideal either. So I cram my cucumbers into the far end

Courgettes are all fairly easy and undemanding to grow. One of my favourite varieties is 'Goldrush' which is highly productive, looks good and tastes delicious.

I grow cucumbers in large pots filled with garden compost in the hottest, wettest part of the greenhouse.

of my greenhouse, and although there is not really enough space, they love the hot, damp, steamy conditions and reward me with dozens of fruits.

Indoors or out, I sow the seed in 7.5cm (3in) pots in late April and put them on a heated bench to germinate – a windowsill above a radiator would be fine. I let them reach about 15cm (6in) tall – big enough to have a decent root system but not so big that they are flopping about – before potting them into their final container, which should be as large as you have space for because they are big, greedy plants. I half-fill the pot with neat garden compost before adding a peat-free potting compost, which helps feed them as well as acting as a sponge to hold plenty of moisture.

I construct a bamboo tripod in the pot so they can clamber up this, and tie them

in regularly until they are established. I water them really well every day without fail and give them a liquid seaweed feed every week. This is the secret to good cucumbers – heat, food and drink, and plenty of them. If they are to be planted outside, it is best to plant them into pits or a trench and add lots of compost.

Once the fruits start to set and grow, it is important to pick them often, which will stimulate more. It is also much easier to cope with a few smaller cucumbers at a time rather than a glut of whoppers. They are delicious but can quickly become too much of a good thing, although we make tzatziki, cucumber soup and – most deliciously of all – cucumbers fried in a cream sauce and served hot. If you have a large fruit it can be cut in half whilst still on the vine and the cut end will callous over so the remainder can be harvested later.

To encourage straight growth, cucumbers need to hang cleanly from the vine and one way to ensure that is to train them up canes set at an angle – such as a wigwam or in cordons set at 45 degrees. The growing fruit will then hang vertically, unimpeded by surrounding growth.

It is likely that the Romans introduced cucumbers to Britain although they originate from the Himalayas. However, until Victorian times, they were commonly called 'cow-cumbers' and were often regarded with suspicion. This is because traditionally, cucumbers produced male and female flowers. If the male flowers pollinated the female ones, the resulting fruits were bitter so the male ones had to be pinched off on a daily basis. Today, most varieties have all-female flowers, however, if stressed – particularly by cold – the plants may still produce male flowers and these must be removed to avoid bitter-tasting fruits.

Cucumbers grown indoors are susceptible to glasshouse red spider mite, cucumber mosaic virus and powdery mildew. Red spider mite tends to build up when it is very dry so damping the floor down and watering regularly should eliminate this. Good ventilation is the best prevention for powdery mildew and cucumber mosaic virus is carried by aphids and will manifest itself by yellow and stunted leaves.

Artichokes

Artichokes are one of the few perennial vegetables and will live for many years although they are most productive in their second and third years. Like strawberries, they are best grown in a four-year cycle, with one generation of plants being added from seed or offsets each year and one thrown away.

They grow very easily from seed if sown with a little gentle heat in spring. They can then be pricked out into individual pots and planted out in midsummer. The drawback to growing from seed is that artichoke seed does not always come true – so if you sow a seed of a variety such as 'Green Globe', there is no guarantee that the mature plant will be the same variety. – However, in practice this is not a major problem as a packet of seed will provide dozens of plants, so to ditch a small proportion of them is no great tragedy. However, an alternative method of

propagation is to take offsets from existing plants. Each plant more than a year old will have young growth appearing slightly separate from the main plant. This is attached to the parent root but can be cut off with a knife or sharp spade and replanted, and although slow to establish in its first year, will grow strongly thereafter and be exactly the same as the parent.

Artichokes like a rich, well-drained soil in full sun. They need plenty of water, especially in their first year when they are developing good roots. They are not very frost-hardy and I mulch mine with a good layer of straw between November and April. If you have a wood fire and there is any ash left over after you have given some to the gooseberries, currants, onions, garlic and tomatoes – all of which get first call upon the ash in this household – then the artichokes would do well with a liberal sprinkle after you remove their protective mulch in spring. I also always mulch them well in spring with compost.

Artichokes should have any chokes produced in their first year removed to let the plants' energies go into establishing strong plants. However, the following spring, they will produce artichoke heads from the end of May onwards. In May you can fry the young, golf-ball sized ones merely split, but from June onwards, they develop large chokes the size of onions. Cut them before they get too big, boil until tender and eat with sea salt and oil or beurre blanc.
My favourite varieties: 'Green Globe', 'Violetta Precoce', 'Gros Vert De Laon'

Autumn vegetables

As the days grow shorter and the nights get colder the chicory 'Rossa di Treviso' turns a deep, dark crimson.

Autumn in this garden creeps in during September and is here with a vengeance by the end of the month. But those few weeks of changeover from summer to autumn can be amongst the most beautiful of the whole year.

It is one of my favourite times in the garden. Along with lots of good flowers and masses of ripening fruit and vegetables, this fading elegance gives the garden dignity, and the knowledge that every fine day is one of the last makes them precious.

But there is a major shift in this garden during October, going from days that feel like late summer to some of the coldest, most miserable weather that we get. The Orchard takes centre stage but there is a great deal happening in the Vegetable Garden too. However, it is never an easy time because the weather is so variable. Until the mid-1990s, all autumn work was geared towards keeping as much going as

possible until the first hard frosts – which could happen at any time from September onwards and were inevitable by the beginning of November. But increasingly, the pattern is towards very wet, mild autumns. Some years it is very wet indeed, with extensive flooding over a third of the Vegetable Garden and we cannot set foot – literally – on any bare soil. Work has to wait. Other years it can be drier and remarkably mild, so everything – including the weeds and grass – keeps growing well past any expected date.

In the Vegetable Garden, the last of the tomatoes are still being harvested and chicories, sweetcorn, leeks, squashes and pumpkins are all coming into their peak. The latter are one of the real signifiers of autumn. The fruits of the squashes have been swelling steadily since late summer although until autumn they are mostly hidden by their vast leaves. But when the leaves start to die back, they reveal the range of fruits in all their splendour, sitting amongst the decaying foliage like monstrous eggs. The French beans keep going to the first frosts, as do the late salad crops.

But always, inevitably, as the season progresses, we fast run out of light, and at the end of October the clocks go back and it is dark by 6pm. This is a bad day. From then on it is sharply downhill to the shortest day on 21 December.

Chicory

I have become very keen on chicory, both as a grower and an eater. For a few years I set out to grow every possible variety that I could lay my hands on, but back then – in the early 1990s – seeds were hard to come by and it involved a trip to the market in Venice to buy a good selection. Venice is the centre of the Veneto, which in turn is the centre of chicory growing in Italy and thus the world. They really understand chicory in that corner of Italy and celebrate the dozens of different available varieties in a hundred culinary ways.

Winter is their eating season although judicious timing can ensure a supply of some kind of chicory year round. A good head of a radicchio like 'Palla Rossa' cut in November will have been sown the previous March and been growing vigorously since May.

In October we go from late-summer days to cold and miserable weather

All chicory has two stages of growth although some make more of a performance of it than others. Stage one is to sprout green foliage. In chicories like endive or puntarelle this is very edible although many types of endive are pretty bitter unless blanched in some way. Gathering the heads up and tying them with twine is effective although makes a perfect home for slugs if the heads are damp. In practice I grow them close enough together so each plant blanches its neighbour – and in any event, the frisée varieties are pleasantly piquant rather than mouth-wrinklingly bitter.

The red chicories and varieties like 'Grumolo Verde' or 'Sugarloaf' have a first batch of leaves that are thick, tough and inedibly bitter. Their job is to feed the root that is busily establishing itself underground. But in August, as the nights start to get a little cooler, this foliage, which can be extremely profuse, slows down and sometimes shows signs of turning red. At this stage I start to remove the exterior leaves by the handful to allow light and air to circulate, otherwise chicory is very prone to becoming a slimy brown mush if it gets too wet. Gradually, through August and September, I remove all the foliage (and there is a lot – providing a generous side benefit of compost material), which is then replaced by much sweeter, more palatable leaves. In 'Grumolo Verde' they go from upright spathes to a rosette. In 'Palla Rossa' or

'Rossa di Verona' they become the tight red ball that we generically call radicchio (although in fact that term refers to all red chicories of whatever shape) and in 'Rossa di Treviso', they regrow as deep alizarin crimson fronds.

Mind you, they all have that lovely bitter tang that makes chicory so addictive. It is a grown-up taste, as far removed from the sweet pulp of fast food as fino sherry, capers or olives. It is certainly an acquired taste but once gained, is never lost and is equally good when the chicory is raw or cooked. I love a salad of a good radicchio like 'Rossa di Verona' or 'Palla Rossa' with avocado and tomato, the crunchiness of the leaves offsetting the slipperiness of the avocado and the sweetness of the tomato balancing the bitterness of the chicory. Pasta with wilted chicory, Parmesan and a little garlic is extremely good too.

I always start chicory off in plugs and transplant them when the roots are sufficiently developed so they can be lifted clear from the plug without collapsing but are not in any way rootbound. This is a fine line and in my experience there is usually about a ten-day window for this, so you have to keep checking. Over the years I realise that I can now tell from the appearance of the growing plants but if in any doubt, just gently ease a seedling from its plug and check the roots.

Chicory can be sown direct but the one year I did this, I found that I was thinning to increasingly wide spacing because of the vigour of the first flush of foliage. Better to start with plants a good 23cm (9in) apart and let them grow strong and uncluttered to make maximum root development.

The leaves of radicchio 'Palla Rossa' make a delicious bittersweet tight ball of crimson and white leaves. But you often have to remove a layer of outer green leaves that can form a slimy carapace if they get too wet.

They are very hardy and can take frost down to about -10°C (14°F) but cold and rain are a bad combination for them and that is standard winter fare here so I always cloche as many as I can simply to provide umbrellas to keep them dry.

Harvest them by cutting the top-growth back to a stub with a knife and new leaves will invariably regrow, each plant giving at least two harvests and in some years three, with new leaves reappearing in spring. However, very hot or very dry weather will cause them to send up flower stems and bolt, and unless these are removed as soon as you see them, the plant is lost for eating purposes.

Turnips

Turnips are closely related to cabbage, oilseed rape and radish, and should be grown as part of the brassica rotation in a veg plot– usually following legumes such as peas or beans (see page 293). They are prone to all the same ailments that cauliflowers, cabbages and sprouts suffer from, such as cabbage root fly (see page 361) club root and predation by the cabbage white caterpillars (see page 357). Having said that, they are very easy and quick to grow given the right conditions. They like a rich, well-drained soil that is neutral to alkaline.

The winter crop is sown from midsummer onwards and is hardy enough to take all but the coldest weather as well as relishing the wet, but I think turnips should be eaten when young and not left in the ground too long. This, for me, makes them an autumnal crop rather than a winter one.

Chicory is an acquired taste but is equally good whether the chicory is raw or cooked

Whenever you sow or eat them, they are best sown where they are to grow and carefully thinned as soon as the leaves can be handled. This is a fiddle but will encourage good root formation. The summer crop can be as close as 7.5–10cm (3–4in) apart but the maincrop ones will need up to 23cm (9in) between them.

If your soil is acidic it is a good idea to lime it a few weeks before sowing. But never add lime and manure at the same time. Best to add manure or compost at least a couple of months before liming. Turnips do best with a steady supply of moisture and it is best to grow them fast and harvest after about ten weeks, when the turnips are anything from golf- to cricket-ball size.

We tend to think of turnips as primarily white, with 'Snowball' a popular variety, but they come in all shapes, sizes and colours, from black to purple to yellow. Some, like 'Tokyo Cross' or 'Bianca Lodigiana', are flattened like hockey pucks and others, like 'Navet des Vertus Marteau', are long and slim. But all are sweet and tender when eaten young and I like them simply boiled, then glazed in butter and served whole.

Turnip leaves are very rich in calcium and are good steamed as you might cook spinach. You can cut the tops for eating and they will resprout for a second and even third harvest, and then the root can be dug and eaten as normal.

Celeriac

Although I often preach the virtue of only growing what you like to eat and eating everything that you grow, the truth is always more complex than that.

Vegetables seem to fall into two camps. There are those that any keen gardener or allotmenteer will always grow whether they are a kitchen favourite or not. I guess broad beans, lettuce, cabbages, carrots and potatoes fall into that category, along with half a dozen others, particular to all of us. Although everything gets eaten, these are vegetables driven as much by a horticultural desire to do the right thing – by yourself as much as any kind of peer pressure – as by culinary imperative. But there are other vegetables that you grow solely for their virtue on the table. For myself, these include asparagus, chicory, many different lettuces, garlic, tomatoes, rocket, Florence fennel and, most emphatically, celeriac.

Although celeriac has become surprisingly trendy over the past few years, it is never going to be the star of the show. There is no dramatic revelation when you lift it as there is with new potatoes or carrots. The swollen base is warty with root and can be, I admit, disappointing. Many flatter to deceive with a seemingly generous top of a good-sized ball lurking in the soil, which reveals itself to be the top of a flattish plate rather than the melon-sized monsters that shops sell, and when trimmed of its tentacles of root, it is whittled down to something like a squashed golf ball.

But I blame my inadequacies as a gardener for this. As a rule, celeriac demands little other than rich soil and a good supply of water, then reliably and quietly grows into a workable vegetable. I say 'workable' because its realm is the kitchen, not the garden or show bench. With the stalks, foliage and roots all lopped off and scrubbed under a cold tap with a good bristly brush to get in all the crevices, it emerges like an overgrown truffle – and in my opinion, much nicer to eat than any truffle.

I like the fact that it cannot possibly be sold as 'instant' food. You have to give it your time and attention, although this is hardly demanding. It needs peeling – but the peel can be dried and threaded on cotton and kept to flavour stocks and soups – then chopping and cooking. As well as being delicious roasted or puréed (the secret is to add *lots* of cream), celeriac adds an earthy, musky taste to soups, stews and mashed potato.

In the same way that celeriac is truculently reluctant to be fast in the kitchen, it takes its time in the garden. I sow the seeds, which, like celery, are tiny, in March, scattering them thinly on a seed tray (do not cover them) and then prick them out into plugs. These then get potted on into 7.5cm (3in) pots but if you

I like the fact that celeriac cannot possibly be sold as 'instant' food – you have to give it your time and attention

live in a milder area than here, they could go out in April and the potting on could be avoided. However, although they are quite hardy, it is a mistake to put them out too early because they will not grow in cold soil and whilst they sit, waiting like the rest of us for spring warmth, the slugs lay into them. So I wait until mid-May or even June before planting them out a generous 30cm (12in) apart in blocks or rows.

I weed and water regularly and that is it until late summer when I start to remove any foliage that is not dead upright. There is no science to this but I probably make two or three passes to get as much light and air as possible to the ground around them. This is primarily to make sure that energy is going to the root rather than into growing extravagant foliage, but also means that rainfall reaches the soil and therefore the roots rather than the canopy of leaves..

One very cold winter my celeriac had to be harvested with a pickaxe for our customary Boxing Day chestnut and celeriac soup, but they were useable when thawed. However, they should be protected from extreme cold. I vacillate between mulching them well with straw, which is good in a mild winter but encourages slugs, and lifting them and bringing them into a frost-free shed, although they very easily dry out. In my parents' day we stored celeriac, along with carrots and potatoes, in a clamp – piling them in a little mound which was covered with straw and then a layer of soil, beaten smooth. Perhaps I need to resurrect that technique.

Celery

For years I grew trench celery with a kind of evangelical zeal. This involved digging a wide trench, manuring the bottom and planting the young celery plants that I raised from seed along it. Then I would earth them up and gradually refill the soil around their growing stems until the tops of the foliage grew in green tufts from a neatly patted-down earthen ridge. This kept the light from the growing stems and thus blanched them, making them sweet and delicous when carefully extracted from their grave. It was a symbol of the 'proper' old-fashioned gardening I was brought up on and I convinced myself that the results tasted better than any alternative. Self-blanching celery was a kind of con trick, an American import that cheapened and degraded the noble art of celery growing. Yes, I was being pompous and absurd but let he who is without sin … But worse than the charade

Self-blanching celery planted in a grid so that as they grow and mature, each plant will blanch and be blanched by its neighbours.

I was playing out was that the resulting celery was nearly always pretty poor stuff.

If you have very free-draining sandy soil, then trench celery is viable but this is thick Herefordshire clay and slugs loved the damp earth-wrapped stems. Celery leaf mining fly often scorched the leaves and added a bitter tang to the stems. Carrot fly (see page 320) took the odd break from my carrots to have a munch, and fungal problems blotched the leaves though do not affect the stems.

Then in 2010 I was away for great chunks of the summer, filming gardens in Italy, and my seed tray of trench celery was left unwatered and died. Only a tray of self-blanching 'Tall Utah' happened to be ready when I was home and so got pricked out and then planted out at the right time.

Over the years I have always sown my celery seed – which is truly tiny – in a seed tray as thinly as possible and then transplanted the seedlings into plugs. It would probably make more sense to sow directly into plugs but you would have to thin out nine-tenths of the seedlings from each plug and it seems too wasteful. I then grow them on in a cold frame until they are about 10–15cm (4–6in) high, harden them off and plant them out in a grid.

I did all that in 2010, hoed them perhaps three or four times, and that was it. I did not water them, feed them or do anything beyond forking in 2.5–5cm (1–2in) of compost before planting out. But the resulting crop was better in every respect than anything I had so laboriously grown before. Since then I have stuck to self-blanching varieties and had no problems.

Celery is a hungry crop and the ground's ability to hold water will influence the success of the final harvest. As with any plant, be it edible or decorative, knowledge of its original habitat is the most useful guide as to how best to grow it. Celery occurs in Asia and Europe in marshy, boggy ground so any organic material will help replicate the plant's basic needs. If you dig the trench in March, there is time to grow a crop of 'Tom Thumb' or 'Little Gem' lettuce on the ridges made from the trench's spoil, as it will not be needed until July for the first earthing up of the celery.

Self-blanching celery is germinated and raised just like trench celery but planted out in a block, with about 30cm (12in) space in every direction. The wider the planting, the bigger the plants. The idea is that each plant shields its neighbour and only the exterior ones need blanching with brown paper or straw wrapped about the stalks. Blanching is not just cosmetic (although most people apparently find white celery more appealing than pink or green) but also reduces any bitterness. Straw, if used, has the added advantage of acting as insulation against the first mild frosts.

When people talk about celery being 'stringy', they are referring to the wisps of tough tissue that lie along the length of the stalk, that can get stuck between the teeth and are generally regarded as a disadvantage. But the strings are the pathways that carry the nutrients to and from the leaves. This means that so-called 'stringless' varieties are likely to be less robust or large than others.

A head of celery ready for harvest.

Florence fennel

Florence fennel (*Foeniculum vulgare* var. *azoricum*) or *finocchio* has evolved – with a lot of help from breeders – from the ordinary fennel herb to a vegetable. The base is swollen and forms an overlapping succession of layers like a bulb.

It is not an easy vegetable to grow but worth the effort as it is delicious, either raw or cooked, stores quite well and is, to me, an essential taste of late summer and early autumn.

The problem with growing it lies in its propensity to bolt before the bulbs swell out to any appreciable size, especially if you sow before midsummer as it is very sensitive to changing day length. The plant develops a hard core – rather like a bolting leek – leaving just the outer layers of the base edible. Ideally one should try and grow it as fast as possible. Any check at any stage in its growth seems to activate a hair trigger and set it bolting.

You can sow it direct – and I have done this with some success, sowing as late as mid-July – but I usually grow it in plugs in the greenhouse which I then plant out in late July or the beginning of August or, if space is not available, pot on into a rich compost mix in 7.5cm (3in) pots. The important thing is not to let it become remotely rootbound in the plugs as this will trigger bolting just as they get established in their vegetable bed – which might be a month later. I plant them out in rows at 23cm (9in) spacing, watering them in very thoroughly and including them in the watering regime with the celeriac and celery that get a good soak once a week. They can be left in the ground until the first hard frost rots them.

I grow 'Argo', which is fairly resistant to bolting so can be sown earlier in the summer, and 'Romanesco', which is very large and good for a later crop that will continue well into October.

Chard

Chard is one of our favourite vegetables and although it is placed here amongst the autumn vegetables, in fact we try and have some growing for most of the year. This is, luckily, not hard to do as it is very hardy both against winter cold and summer drought, and if cut regularly, will go on producing fresh leaves from what seems to be a completely wrecked stump of stem.

It is a member of the beet family and thus related to spinach and beetroot, and the wonderfully glossy leaves do look like monstrously enlarged versions of both its cousins. The stems are celery-like in texture

The trick to get Florence fennel to form a generous bulbous base to the leaves is to grow it fast and not let it dry out, get cold or rootbound – all of which will trigger it to bolt.

if not in taste, which is delicate, subtle and delicious. The leaves, which are invariably cooked having been stripped from the stems, are like a slightly coarser, more robust spinach and make a counterbalance to any meats, eggs or cheese. Swiss chard has pure white stems and great green leaves and is, to my mind, superior in taste to all other variations, but ruby chard is beautiful enough for any flower border. Rainbow chard is, as the name suggests, multi-coloured, and 'Bright Lights' has brilliant yellow stems. All are good to eat.

The great thing about chard is that it has two quite separate parts, both very good and both very different. The French value the stems over the leaves and the British the opposite, but both are tasty. There is an excellent dish of chard stems and mussels cooked in milk and we make a pasta sauce from chard stems, cheese and cream. The leaves are used like spinach, adding a slightly sharp but never acidic element to a dish, good on their own but better when either a sweet or savoury flavour is added to them. At the moment I like chard best with chilli

— but then I like almost anything with chilli. If chilli is not your thing, then try the leaves with any combination of anchovy, garlic or pine nuts. They also make a surprisingly good dessert with currants, apricots or apples. Moroccan cooking combines all this to make the stunning *pastilla* pastries filled with pigeon, currants, chard and onion wrapped in sweet filo pastry dusted with cinnamon. Writing that down makes me want to flee British wintry gloom and eat *pastilla* in Marrakech. If all that is too fancy, then try it with eggs. My wife, Sarah, makes a lovely chard frittata which somehow manages to be light and yet more substantial and more satisfying than a spinach version.

Swiss chard has nothing to do with Switzerland although the name has stuck for the past hundred years or so. The Ancient Greeks bred red chard whilst the Chinese record growing it in the seventh century, Swiss chard (although without the Swiss bit) is recorded in Britain as early as 1596 and a red-stemmed variety is mentioned in Gerard's *Herbal* from the same period.

The seeds can be sown direct but I prefer to sow them in plugs or blocks, restricting them to one seed per unit, growing them on and hardening them off before planting out at 23cm (9in) spacing. Once established, they are very drought-resistant but do best in a rich, but well-drained soil. Being biennials they will only go to seed in the first growing season if they are distressed, so the consistency of the water supply is as important as its quantity. If some do start to bolt, then I cut the central stems down to the ground and give them a soak.

Young ruby chard in midsummer. These will grow into substantial plants that will last until the following spring and provide three or more flushes of green leaves and bright red stems.

Squashes and pumpkins

All pumpkins are squashes but not all squashes are pumpkins. Pumpkins have hard skins or rinds that mean they can be stored, often for months, if dried in the sun but many squashes have thinner skins and some – the summer squashes such as courgettes – cannot be stored as they never develop a skin thick enough to prevent the ripening process from becoming putrefaction.

Squashes and pumpkins are American of course, grown initially for their seeds and the utility of their skins as bowls, although it did not take long for someone to cook the flesh and find it good. Thanksgiving celebrations on the fourth Thursday in November depend upon the two staples of the New England wild that got the Pilgrim Fathers through the first winters – turkey and squashes.

If I had to grow just one type of squash it would be acorn squash as they taste fantastic, grow well and make such beautiful objects, with their elegant, fluted shape. They come in orange, yellow, blue-black and green, and when you hold them they feel more like a stone sculpture than a vegetable. But all the Hubbards, Butternuts and varieties like 'Turk's Turban', 'Rouge Vif d'Étampes', 'Uchiki Kuri', 'Musquée de Provence' (a ravishing orange colour) are also lovely, rollicking, buxom things and given enough space, I would grow scores. I did once. It was fun, if a little crowded.

I sow my seed in 7.5cm (3in) pots, two to a pot, in early May, putting the pots onto a heated mat, although a warm windowsill or greenhouse should do fine. If both seeds germinate, I remove one seedling. If the squash is a small variety like 'Little Gem' or 'Jack be Little', then it can stay in the same pot but if it is a

I grow my squashes vertically on a frame made from chestnut stakes woven with hazel bean sticks. This takes less space and exposes the ripening fruits to more sun. These are 'Red Kuri' and are ideal for this way of growing as they do not get too big and heavy.

big'un, like 'Hundredweight' or 'Golden Hubbard', then I pot it on to a larger container so the roots can reach out.

Keep them in a warm, sheltered place – a cold frame, as ever, is ideal – before planting out at least 90cm (36in) apart – and ideally three times that. But you must do this when, and only when, the soil is warm to touch. In this garden that is usually not before mid-June and often I wait until early July. Planting them out any earlier than mid-June in my neck of the woods is asking for trouble. The risk of a cold night is too great. This stops them in their tracks and the slugs and snails tuck in, eating the stems where they touch the ground and sometimes gnawing right through them, although they only cause real harm when the plants are not actively growing – which is usually in the first few cold weeks after planting out too early.

Before planting I always dig out a hole and fill it with compost which I then cover back over with soil, using the excess to create a raised ring or saucer around the planting hole. This helps contain water and funnel it to the roots. I give each plant a good soak once a week over and above any rain we have – and we have lots of rain!

If you have a slow compost heap, then this is the ideal place to grow a pumpkin. They love it and, as long as they are watered regularly, they grow with extra enthusiasm, as well they might.

If you have plenty of space, then they will sprawl across the ground, each plant covering yards by the end of summer, but I have taken to growing my squashes up a specially built frame and this works very well. Because they are so rampant and the squashes become heavy, I use 2.5m (8ft) chestnut fencing stakes interwoven with a trellis of hazel bean sticks. I think it looks good and it means that I can grow three times as many plants in the same space – and the fruits, raised up off the ground as they are, ripen better and never get attacked by slugs or snails.

Other than slugs and snails, the only other problem that pumpkins face is powdery mildew, which is nearly always caused by the plant being too dry. It will manifest itself with a pale grey mould on the leaves which will then brown and die. Remove the affected leaves and never stint on the water.

Early frosts will reduce the foliage to blackness and if it is very wet, it is a good idea to place the fruits on a tile or some straw to raise them off the damp soil. The more sun the fruits get, the harder the skins will be and the better they will store. They should be harvested by carefully cutting the stem so that 5–7.5cm (2–3in) remain. This will stop any neck rot. I try and harvest when the forecast is good so that they can stay outside on a table for a few days to get as much sun as possible.

They need to be stored somewhere dark and dry where there is plenty of air circulation and the temperature holds between 5°C (40°F) and 10°C (50°F). Although they might feel heftily indestructible, treat them gently as they will keep much better unbruised.

My favourite varieties:
Pumpkins: 'Musquée de Provence', 'Turk's Turban', 'Jack be Little'
Squashes: 'Uchiki Kuri', 'Golden Hubbard', 'Waltham Butternut'

Sweetcorn

Like asparagus, sweetcorn taste so much better fresh than anything that you can buy. This is because as soon as they are picked from the parent plant the sugars start to convert to starch and after a few hours, that deliciously light sweet taste is replaced by a blanket mealy flavour. Still good but nothing like as good as they can be eaten fresh from the garden.

The seeds are sown in May in 7.5cm (3in) pots and planted out in July. There is no need to be earlier than this as they need hot days and warm nights to grow well. I often underplant them with courgettes and dwarf beans, which is the ancient Mayan 'Three Sisters' combination. The beans clamber up the corn stems and the courgettes (squashes can be used too) can

grow and spread before the corn becomes too big and shades them out. They must be planted in a block at about 45–60cm (18–24in) spacing in each direction, rather than in rows as they are wind-pollinated and if in a straight line, the wind can potentially blow all the pollen away from the waiting plants and you will have no cobs.

The cobs tend to be ready to pick when the tassels at their end turn dark brown but I test to see if they are ripe by carefully folding back the surrounding sheaths and squeezing the corn. If they secrete a milky juice, then they are ripe and can be picked.

I do not cut the cobs until the water in which they are to be cooked is on a rolling boil, then take them straight from garden to stove. My most recent crop was 'Doux Miner', an organic seed from France, and 'Swift' is also excellent.

A sweetcorn cob perfectly ripe and ready to eat. They say you should not pick the cobs until the water is already boiling, so as to capture their astonishing sweetness before it converts to starch.

Winter vegetables

As we go into December, the poor old garden feels bedraggled and battered into submission. Winter is not kind to it. Everything is a battle with the weather and a fight against the light. These December days can be nasty, brutish and short.

Although the Vegetable Garden in winter is much reduced, it can still provide a range of good, fresh vegetables, even in the worst weather.

But the Vegetable Garden is still important. Red cabbage, Brussels sprouts, potatoes, carrots and parsnips are all an essential part of Christmas dinner and we also enjoy chard, beetroot, cabbages, kale, rocket, mizuna, chicory and leeks fresh from the garden, as well as the summer harvests that we have stored or frozen.

However, winter here has two distinct halves. The first half, ending with the arrival of the new year, is by far the worst and has to be endured. It does not get

light until after eight in the morning and is too dark to work outside beyond half past four in the afternoon. Gradually the leaves all fall from the pleached limes surrounding the Vegetable Garden and the espaliered pears are exposed to their bare bones. Only the brick paths that we put into this area at huge expense and effort make any kind of access possible.

But Christmas is a turning point. We cut holly from the garden, make wreaths with dried stems and flowers, put up big bunches of mistletoe from the apple trees in the Orchard and fill the house with green, and as soon as the new year begins, everything gets better. The weather tends to get colder and drier, and the days lengthen. At first this happens by almost imperceptible moments, but they accumulate and by the end of February, it is light at 6.30 in the morning and stays light until after six in the evening, and however bad the weather, spring is irresistible by the beginning of March.

Winter salads

What cheers me up throughout winter is a regular supply of fresh salad leaves. In fact, the simple process of gathering material for a daily salad becomes both a reaffirmation of growth and life and a piece of counter-seasonal bloody-mindedness. I admit you can scratch around a bit but it can be done.

It certainly helps if you have cover. A greenhouse or tunnel is best but cloches, cold frames and fleece will all do to provide enough protection to cope with down to about -5°C (23°F).

But winter salads begin in mid- to late summer. The seeds must be sown by the end of August if you are to start harvesting in November, and by mid-September for plants that will be large enough to harvest in February.

The key to this is the declining light of late summer and autumn. As the days draw in, growth slows down dramatically. So anything sown much after the beginning of September will struggle to grow enough to give you a harvest before February or March – although this can be harnessed as long as the young plants are protected from slugs and cold. I have had lettuce seedlings sit dormant in plugs from late October until March which I then planted out into a greenhouse, and they grew just fine. But better to keep growth constant if you can.

I start in the first fortnight of August with slow crops like parsley, mibuna, mizuna, corn salad and endive as well as an autumn-cropping batch of quicker leaves like rocket and almost any lettuce you like to eat. In fact, these late lettuces are often amongst the best of the year, relishing the cooler night-time temperatures and warmth of the soil. But watch out for lettuce root aphids which can cause havoc in late summer if the soil is allowed to dry out at all. The top-growth will suddenly wilt and collapse and when you lift the plant, the roots will be

Christmas is a turning point with holly, wreaths made from dried stems and flowers, and bunches of mistletoe

Harvesting chard shoots in January that are on their second or even third regrowth from the original summer-grown leaves.

stunted and covered in a waxy white powder. The culprit is *Pemphigus bursarius* which sucks the goodness from the roots. It is best not grow any more lettuces on the site until next year if you do get hit.

But onwards into a leafy winter. After this first sowing – which may all get used by late autumn or Christmas – I do another in late August and another in mid-September, adding in lettuce varieties that are specifically adapted for low light levels and low temperatures, such as 'All Year Round', 'Chicon De Charentes', 'Merveille de Quatre Saisons', 'Winter Density' and 'Valdor'. Grow them strong but hard – in other words get them off to a good start so that they do not check and expose them to life in the great outdoors as soon as possible, looking to protect them from midday sun more than from night-time chill. Winter salad leaves need

less water than summer ones but they do need some, so just because it is chilly, do not forget to water them regularly.

As well as lettuce, I sow the following in late summer for eating right through October until March.

Rocket is at its best in spring but is an essential part of our autumn salads too.

Lamb's lettuce or corn salad grows very slowly and will not be properly ready to harvest for three months. I cut the whole plant in November and expect a couple more pickings in the new year and February.

Mizuna has finely serrated leaves that taste mustardy and not unlike rocket. It is a robust, large plant and I will cut this regularly throughout winter.

Mibuna has long strap-like leaves with rounded ends, and tastes similar to mizuna although is less tough. However, under the cover of the tunnel, each plant will grow into a large, 30cm (12in) diameter leafy bush.

Land cress or American land cress, looks very similar to salad rocket but is much hotter and peppery and has a distinct similarity to watercress. It loves rich soil with lots and lots of water and is very hardy, but it is very susceptible to both flea beetle (see page 301) and bolting when the weather turns warmer.

Leeks

Leeks were a staple of the medieval diet and are almost certain to have been grown in this garden for at least the last thousand years. When I was a child, leeks in white sauce were my idea of a treat. That comforting, slightly slimy, bland but distinctive texture and flavour provided my perfect comfort food. Leek or leek and potato soup used to be a mainstay of restaurants but that baby went out with the bath water. However, we still make leek soups at home, along with roasted leeks, braised leeks and leeks with Parmesan grated generously over them once they are cooked, then popped back in the oven for that to melt.

I start sowing my first leeks in February, the wispy green hairs of the new seedlings sharing garden space with last year's crop for a couple of months. I will make at least three sowings to keep a year-round supply. I used to sow in seed trays and then prick out into 7.5cm (3in) pots but nowadays I sow direct into the pots, a pinch of seed in each. By sowing in pots, the roots and young stems have a chance to develop and

do not need pricking out or disturbing until they are ready to plant out into their final position in the garden, which can be anything from June to late August. They are also one of the vegetables that grow well in an outdoor seed bed and I sometimes use this for a later crop, sowing in April and transplanting the seedlings in late May or June.

I also used to plant the seedlings out (in May – whilst the residues of last year's crop were making wonderful minaret flower heads – through to September) individually into holes made with a dibber, made, in turn, from the handle of an old spade. The leeks were nine-tenths buried with only a wisp of growth showing above ground. It was how I was taught to do it as a child. The reason for burying them is to blanch the stems so

Leeks are amongst the hardiest of vegetables and can freeze solid without damage.

that they are white and sweeter to eat. But I now plant in small clumps of between four and eight plants and use a trowel. Less ritual, less rhythm and perhaps less magic, but quicker, easier and producing leeks that are just as good, with the clumps of small to medium-sized stems ideal for each meal. Big leeks, let alone giant ones, are absurd. Keep them small and sweet for the kitchen.

Along with the white rot (see page 317) that has afflicted my onions, rust (*Puccinia allii*) has been a problem over the last few years thanks to the warm, wet climatically changed weather, and I guess will continue to be so. Wider spacing, less compost and even tougher hardening-off regimes will encourage less soft growth which will help, but not stop, the problem.

I am fickle with my loyalty to varieties, although I try and grow at least one heritage variety each year. 'Musselburgh' is the oldest British variety, 'Pandora' has a blue tinge to the leaves and is fairly rust-resistant, and 'Varna' is one of the best for mini-leeks, which, my biodynamic, market-gardener friend tells me, is the best-selling vegetable they grow.

Brussels sprouts have a bad press but are delicious, nutritious and very hardy.

Brussels sprouts

When I was a boy, my parents had a piece of land – about a quarter of an acre – where we grew potatoes and sprouts on alternate years, which were then sold in the local shop. A house and pretty garden have stood on the site for the past 40 years but the ghosts of a thousand brassicas still haunt it. You can grow a lot of sprouts on a quarter of an acre and one of my jobs over the Christmas holidays was to pick them. Picking a hundredweight of sprouts on an icy morning with frozen fingers is not much of a job for a willing adult but this reluctant child hated it with a vengeance.

The odd thing is that it never spoiled my pleasure in eating them. A properly cooked sprout, still firm to the knife or bite but giving is delicious and they are also incredibly good for you, being packed with inordinate amounts of vitamins A and C. Also, like all cabbages, they lower cholesterol and help prevent cancers.

I certainly regard Christmas dinner as incomplete without them.

Sprouts are not a natural thing. Humans bred them just as they bred cabbage heads. Although there is mention of them in Burgundian feasts of the fifteenth century, Brussels sprouts were hardly known outside France and Belgium until the nineteenth century. They reached America with French settlers and Thomas Jefferson planted them in his famous garden at Monticello in 1812, but the first-documented British recipe is from Eliza Acton in 1845 and it seems that they only became popular after World War One. So the 'tradition' of serving Brussels sprouts at Christmas with the turkey is, like many of our most cherished traditions and institutions, a relatively modern invention.

I grow Brussels sprouts in the same way and rhythm as the rest of my winter brassicas. I sow my seeds into plugs or a seed bed (depending on the weather) in March or April, potting them out into 7.5cm (3in) pots and planting them into their final position in June. Following on from broad beans is ideal but in any well-manured soil will do. If it is acidic, it is a good idea to lime it a couple of weeks before planting.

As autumn progresses, remove any leaves that start to yellow or if the plants are becoming crowded, although some leaves should be left in exposed sites as protection for the emerging sprouts. Modern F1 varieties – and most are just this, as sprouts cross-hybridise very readily – tend to ripen all at once whereas older, open-pollinated varieties such as the gloriously named 'Bedford Fillbasket' or 'Evesham Special'

will produce sprouts that gradually ripen as they progress up the stem.

Cold improves the flavour down to about -10°C (14°F), so the best pickings are likely to be after the first hard frosts – if we are lucky enough to have such a thing.

Cabbages

I sow seed of all types of cabbage or brassica in April and May into plugs, blocks or seed trays, and prick them out into individual pots or plugs. This is more labour but much easier to protect against slug damage and less wasteful on seed. The seedlings are ready for planting out by late June or whenever the peas and beans are cleared to make room for them. I have found that it makes a huge difference to their development if they can be planted out as soon as they have a reasonable root system, and a crude form of succession can be created by planting out half a dozen plants a week throughout summer so that they mature gradually during autumn and winter.

Before planting out, the soil should be trodden firm – as though preparing a lawn – and then raked over. The cabbage head makes the plant very top-heavy and the roots, which are strong enough to grow through the compaction, must be anchored as firmly as possible. If you plant out in blocks at 45cm (18in) spacing,

Brussels sprouts reached America with French settlers and Thomas Jefferson planted them at Monticello in 1812

Cabbages are sown in spring, grow in summer and can be harvested throughout autumn and winter, so although they are not a quick crop, they are invaluable in winter.

they soon cover the ground. This makes smaller cabbages but looks better and stops weeds.

Although summer cabbages such as 'Greyhound' are appreciably faster-maturing than their winter counterparts such as 'January King' or Savoys, all cabbages need quite a long growing season. This requires some planning to fit them into the garden scheme of things, but is of great value in winter as they can stand ready for eating all winter if need be.

Brassicas – the family that all types of cabbage belong to, as do cauliflowers, radishes, swedes, turnips and kohlrabi – all share the same preference for well-drained, well-manured soil in an open position. Conventional wisdom says you should grow cabbages on a piece of ground that was previously used for legumes (see page 293), which should have

been freshly manured before the legumes were sown and whose roots will have left nitrogen in the soil via their nodules. However, all brassicas are very responsive to a fresh dressing of garden compost when planted, so any well-drained, rich soil will work, regardless of what has been grown previously.

Winter cabbages come in a number of shapes and forms. Until the sixteenth century, it seems likely that all cabbages were loose-leaf, like our spring greens or what the Americans call 'collards'. The round-headed form was first described in the sixteenth century and the first mention of a red one in Britain was in 1570 – so we can reasonably assume that this was when it first arrived here – almost certainly from Germany. By the nineteenth century, breeding had become extensive and sophisticated – there were Savoys with wrinkled leaves, Brunswicks, conical cabbages and drum-head, round, red, smooth whites, green, summer, spring and autumn cabbages – the range was huge.

We do not grow anything like a comprehensive selection but I do like to have some (and there are hundreds of different varieties and hybrids available) of each of the following:

- Savoys are familiar from their crinkly, blueish leaves. They are hardy and very good to eat.
- 'January King' have a slightly purple tinge to their leaves and again are hardy and have very good flavour.
- Red cabbages are very tough with thicker leaves and are relatively untroubled by cabbage butterflies or slugs. As well as being good to eat

(especially with game), I unashamedly grow them for their decorative virtues.

Pests and diseases

The soft growth of young plants is easy meat for slugs but if they are healthy, the plants soon get too tough for them. But there are some more virulent potential disasters waiting for every cabbage, however tough. The first is likely to arrive just after planting out and comes in the pretty, shaky flutter of a cabbage white butterfly, whose caterpillars do terrible damage to brassicas. In fact there are two species of butterfly that do the damage, the large white and the small white. The large white lays its eggs on the leaves and its yellow-and-black caterpillars cover them by the hundred, stripping the young plants to a skeleton. We pick them off by hand but spraying with salt water works well.

These butterflies have the curious ability to taste the quantity of mustard in a plant, the principle being that the stronger the taste, the better the plant as a host for their eggs. The curiosity factor in this is that the plant developed the mustard taste as a defence against insects rather than as an attraction. The butterflies take on the mustard taste in their own tissues, which works effectively against predation by birds.

The caterpillars of the large white are a distinctive and very visible yellow and black whereas the small white lays deeper into the plant and its beautifully camouflaged green caterpillars do their dastardly work less conspicuously but to just as noxious effect. But plants can recover from attack. I have known cavolo nero be stripped bare

of all but the tiniest leaves. I only left them in the ground because I never got round to pulling them up but they grew back and provided meals until March.

Club root is always pronounced as the worst that can happen to a cabbage (other than being cooked at a rolling boil for 20 minutes) but I have yet to experience it. It is a fungal disease that swells and misshapes the roots and in consequence the plants limp along in a pointless fashion. The fungus stays in the soil after the affected plants are removed, so it is important never to grow cabbages on the same site in consecutive years. Like all fungi, that of club root does best in badly ventilated, badly drained conditions and is also more prevalent in acidic soil.

Red cabbages

One of the Don family's essential elements at Christmas dinner is a large pot of braised red cabbage. We have it first with the goose (or turkey – we waver between the two) and then with cold meats and even in sandwiches until it is all finished by the new year. The combination of the slowly cooking cabbage, apples, brown sugar, juniper berries, cinnamon and vinegar is as much part of our Christmas trigger as the lights on the tree.

Cabbage white butterflies are able to taste the quantity of mustard in a plant and the stronger the taste, the better the plant as a host for their eggs

Red cabbage is even hardier than green and in our household is as much part of Christmas as turkey.

But first you must grow your red cabbage. (If it is colour you are after, you can also grow red Brussels sprouts such as 'Red Bull' and 'Red Rubine', and also red kale and purple cauliflowers such as 'Graffiti' or 'Purple Sicily'.) Red cabbage seeds are sown in April along with all my other winter brassica crops such as Savoy cabbages, Brussels sprouts, kale and broccoli. This year I grew my red cabbage in an outdoor seed bed and transplanted them from there to their final growing position, but I also sow into plugs and then pot these on into 7.5cm (3in) pots ready for planting out about 45–60cm (18–24in) apart in midsummer.

Red cabbages are in fact a range of colours from purple, red and pink to blue and grey. Their colour is partly determined by the soil – acidic soil makes them redder, neutral more purple and in very alkaline soil like chalk, they tend to lose their redness and become a yellowy green. When cooked, they all turn a purplish blue – although adding vinegar to the water will stop this. Talking of vinegar, red cabbage pickles wonderfully in it and sauerkraut, for which you just need salt and water, is easy to make and has become dead trendy.

Red cabbage is better in withstanding the extremes of weather than its green cousins, which makes it very hardy indeed. It is not only hardier than green cabbage but also less attractive to the caterpillars of cabbage white butterflies (see page 357).

They are ready to plant out when the roots fill the 7.5cm (3in) pots without pressing against the sides if I am growing them under cover, or if they have made sturdy 15cm (6in) seedlings if in a seed bed. I plant them out at quite wide spacings – about 60cm (24in) – firming them in really well. Cabbages, like most leafy brassicas, will become very top-heavy, so the firmer their roots are anchored into the ground, the better they will stand when full grown. Even so, they may need staking later. But for the first month or so, there is an awful lot of bare soil between the growing cabbages so I use this to raise a catchcrop of lettuce, which will grow quickly and can be harvested and cleared before the lettuces run out of light and room from the growing cabbages.

Pigeons are the biggest pest of my cabbages over winter but, like the caterpillars, they seem to prefer green cabbages to red. All in all, red cabbage is not only a delicious addition to the Christmas table but an easy, rewarding and handsome vegetable to grow.

Kale

When I was a child, kale was only associated with the fields grown for winter fodder for the cows. It was scarcely human food. But the black Tuscan kale – cavolo nero (although also labelled as 'Nero di Toscana') – is as delicious as any cabbage. However, unlike cabbage, it has the distinctive characteristic of remaining good even when boiled for a long time. This means that it can be added to minestrone or the delicious and typically Florentine bread soup, *ribollita*. Kale also reheats very well and, mixed with garlic and cream, makes a fabulous sauce for pasta. It is versatile and delicious and high in nutrients. What's not to like?

Kale produces a sheaf of more or less upright leaves from its central stem. These leaves are tough – hence its hardiness. They need boiling for up to half an hour although a really hard frost does a lot to break down that toughness and improve the flavour. Nevertheless we eat it all the year round.

I make my first sowing in January, under cover, and plant the seedlings out just 2.5–5cm (1–2in) apart in late March. They germinate very easily and can be sown direct in a seed bed as soon as the ground

If I could only grow one brassica crop it would be cavolo nero. It is completely hardy and can be harvested all the year round as well as eaten when young as part of a salad. An essential vegetable.

warms up. My first sowing is picked very young and used as part of a mixed salad, never growing more than 7.5cm (3in) or 10cm (4in) tall, and is cleared by the middle of May. This is when the next batch, sown in mid-March, is planted into the position that it will occupy for the next twelve months. It does best with 60–90cm (24–36in) between each plant and needs staking from midsummer.

The secret of kale is to eat the leaves when they are a reasonable size but not too old – when they really are suitable only for ruminating cows. So I pick a handful of leaves from half a dozen plants at a time, working across the whole crop before returning to the first plants at the next picking – by which time they will have produced another batch of leaves. They are very satisfying to pick, yanking

them down from the central stem with an audible snap as they come away in your hand. This way each plant will provide half a dozen or more pickings between September and April.

Curly kale is much tougher to eat and harder to digest but looks magnificent. Red kale, such as the plum-coloured 'Redbor' or 'Red Russian', which has grey-green foliage with deep purple stems, is even more handsome and I grow it for its decorative value alone, although I always eat some almost as a matter of principle. But the truth is that I always return to the wonderful cavolo nero.

Cauliflowers

Cauliflower is a kind of horticultural equivalent to the place it occupies in the canon of dining. Nice enough but not special. You wouldn't want to be without it but it can easily become too much of a good thing. As it happens, I think that a good cauliflower cheese with breadcrumbs, bacon and tomato ketchup, accompanied by fresh white bread and a good salty butter is a treat. And if that isn't incentive enough to grow the best cauliflower you can, then, traveller, pass on by.

The bit that we eat is the curd, which is a flower head in an arrested stage of development. Cauliflowers came to this country in the late sixteenth century from Venice. Those early cauliflowers were small and more like white broccoli, and in fact, much of what is sold as broccoli, such as calabrese and romanesco, are really different forms of cauliflower. The white curds are only pure white if

Not all cauliflowers have white curds – they can be reddish, purple, yellow and green but all taste much the same and are grown identically.

protected from the sun, either by their natural leaf cover or by carefully tying the leaves over them as a temporary bonnet. Purple varieties like 'Purple Cape' have been around a long time and you can grow cauliflowers with curds of a green, yellow, purple or reddish hue.

Cauliflowers – and especially summer ones – need a rich soil. They make a good crop to follow potatoes although are also suitable for following on from an early legume crop like broad beans. In either case, a light dressing of garden compost worked into the surface before planting is always beneficial.

Whether grown yourself from seed (and they do well in an outdoor seed bed) or bought as young plants, cauliflowers should go into a weeded, raked and firm seed bed, spaced about 60cm (24in) apart in each direction. Whilst they are fairly drought-tolerant, give them a good soak after planting and another three weeks before harvest. As with all brassicas, the firm bed is important as any rocking of the roots will damage the health of the plant and is often a cause of small, under-developed curds.

Keep them weed-free and cover with a net to ward off pigeons and cabbage white butterflies (see page 357). The net has to be fine to stop the butterflies slipping through and laying their eggs on the plants as the eggs hatch into the familiar caterpillars that strip the leaves.

Cauliflowers are susceptible to boron deficiency, which will result in yellowing, stunted foliage and small, brown-stained curds. Boron is a micronutrient that helps control the transport of sugars in the plant, and too little in the soil will reduce or even stop fruiting and flowering.

Small curds can also be a symptom of cabbage root fly whose maggots bore into the roots and stunt them. A physical barrier is the best way to deter the flies, either using a mat as a collar around each stem or a fine mesh or fleece. The fly lays its eggs on the soil at the base of the plant, so if there is a collar, the eggs dry up and die before the grubs hatch. The mesh or fleece collar will stop the fly getting at the soil but must be properly buried into the soil to stop up any gaps.

Swedes

Although perhaps one of the least glamorous of all vegetables, I am very fond of swede, mashed and served with plenty of butter and salt and pepper. It also makes and contributes to good soup and on a cold winter's day, few things are better.

Swedes are probably a cross between the turnip and cabbage and will grow in exactly the same conditions as turnips, the only substantial difference being that swedes can sit in the ground for much longer without becoming unpalatably woody. Whilst turnips have been grown for thousands of years, swedes were first described in 1620 by a Swiss botanist, and although they originate from northern Europe, it is not certain why they should be named after Sweden specifically. Scottish swede is known as 'neeps' and what we call turnips, the Scots renamed swedes. All very confusing.

They need at least 20 weeks to mature and I sow them in June, in plugs, although

Parsnips wait for you in the ground and there is something satisfying about extracting half a dozen muddy cones

if you have a slug-free garden, it is better to sow them direct and then thin to 23cm (9in) spacing. However much you like swedes, they are large and no one family needs a huge amount. I have found that they can be intercropped with purple sprouting broccoli, which is slow to mature and needs wide spacing. By the time that the broccoli is ready for harvesting in March, the swedes have all been lifted.

Parsnips

Parsnips have been grown in this country since the Romans introduced them and were very widely eaten before the potato became the staple starchy vegetable. They are currently undervalued, perhaps because they are not quick and instant. They are a Sunday vegetable, perfect baked or roasted with a joint of meat.

They belong exclusively to winter, needing a frost to intensify the sugars in them. They will withstand any amount of foul weather and will remain unharmed in the ground until you want to eat them, unlike carrots, which need to be lifted soon after the first frosts. Parsnips wait for you in the ground and there is something reliable and immensely satisfying about digging along a row, perhaps only marked by a few wisps of leaves after a winter of rain and frost, and extracting half a dozen muddy cones tapering to a long tail.

The more you know about gardens and gardening, the more you realise how little it matters what you do or how and when you do it, as long as it more or less works out in the end. Anyway, I was told in my youth by craggy old gardeners (probably a good deal younger than I am now but they seemed ancient to me back then) that it was vital to get parsnip seed in the ground as early as possible to have any chance of the delicious sweet roots by autumn. February was triumphant, March ideal, April dodgy and May verging on the pointless.

Certainly, the flat discs of parsnip seed are slow to germinate and the seedlings do not mature fast. I would be interested to do a trial to see how much of this is influenced by soil and air temperature, but in any weather they are not to be hurried. The logic that follows from this is that if they are to be ready for harvesting after the first frost – which can be September – then they need at least five months' growing time before that.

Of course this begs all kinds of questions. How big should a parsnip be? Why the first frost? How late can you risk going before they cannot be harvested at all? Starting with the last, I know from personal experience that if you have not sown your parsnips by mid-June, then they are unlikely to grow roots large enough to be worth the fiddle of preparing and cooking. The plant will, of course, be fine.

Parsnips are, like their cousins the carrot, a native biennial. In their first season they develop a root which then provides the nourishment for the flower and seeds the following spring. For the record, these seeds fall and germinate from mid-June right through to August and produce lots of perfectly healthy plants, as anybody with the weed *Pastinaca sativa* – or the wild parsnip – will know only too well.

For the wild parsnip, the root is only a means to the all-important end of producing viable seed. For the parsnip-eater the root is everything, so the bigger it can grow, the better. At least that is the general idea, although personally I like my parsnips to be about 30cm (12in) long and 5–7.5cm (2–3in) at the top. They can easily grow to double that size but the bigger they are, the quicker they develop a woody, inedible core.

Although parsnips are perfectly edible harvested before the cold weather arrives, frost helps convert their starches into sugars and intensifies that characteristic sweetness. In fact, before sugar became widely available in the seventeenth century, the extra sweetness of the parsnip was highly valued.

Ideally they reach the preferred size before the first frosts – i.e. by October or, in colder areas and before climate change made our autumns and winters so much warmer, even early September. This is what drove the need to sow them early.

So I now sow my parsnips as part of the root rotation (see page 293) which has no compost or manure added – along with carrots, celery and parsley. I sow them as soon as the soil is ready (which is all that 'as early as possible' means), and hope that this is before the beginning of May. I always sow radishes in with them too. This helps keep the parsnip seeds apart – ideally there does not want to be any less than 2.5cm

(1in) between each seedling and twice that is fine – and it helps mark the rows as the radishes germinate very fast. Using the ground for a catchcrop works because by the time that the parsnips have slowly germinated and the seedlings are starting to jostle for space, the radishes have all been eaten or cleared to the compost heap.

Parsnips are prone to carrot fly (see page 320) although without the same disastrous consequences as afflict carrots. They also can be affected by cankers of various hues, although all have much the same effect of producing lesions in the roots. Canker is likely to be much worse in damp soil, so good drainage is the key.

If you have not sown your parsnips by mid-June, then they are unlikely to grow roots large enough to be worth the fiddle of preparing and cooking

Introducing herb growing

A herb garden can be – should be – a beautiful, self-contained place entire unto itself.

The old box ball yard transformation into a herb garden (see pages 194–197) has given me huge pleasure but it is a very functional space which we use every single day to gather herbs for the kitchen. As well as looking good it has to work well.

When planning to grow herbs there are two main considerations: the first is to grow them in a sunny part of the garden and the second is to have them as near to the kitchen as possible so that they are easy to make part of your daily meals.

Herbs are forgiving plants to grow. But even within a very small herb garden, it is important to give plants the conditions that they like, and certain herbs have very distinct preferences for where and how they grow.

Many of our favourites like rosemary, thyme and sage are perennial, potentially shrubby plants that come from the baking hills of the Mediterranean and do best in poor soil and full sun. Others, like parsley, coriander, basil and dill are annuals that grow fast and easily and can adapt to richer soil. There are also perennials such as sweet cicely or sorrel that grow best in part-shade. But as with all plants, although it is sensible to do what you can to make them feel at home, do not be inhibited or intimidated. Just grow them and see what happens!

Opposite page: The Herb Garden in midsummer is not only full of herbs for the kitchen but also full of flowers that the bees adore.

Annual and biennial herbs

Once garlic has properly dried, I take off the leaves and stems, clean up stray roots and store in a wire basket in a cool, dark place. It will keep like this for up to a year.

We grow almost all our annual and biennial herbs in the Vegetable Garden, although spare plants may be dotted into the Herb Garden if we run out of room elsewhere.

The reason for this is mainly because there is just not the space for them in the main Herb Garden and it is easier to incorporate them into the vegetable rotation (see page 293). Also, shrubby plants like sage, hyssop, rosemary and the more voracious herbaceous perennials like lovage and horseradish tend to swamp them. They need plenty of light and air to develop into vigorous plants with lots of soft growth.

It all goes back to the virtue of *quantity* in the herb garden. For most of the herbs that we use on a regular basis, we want to have a continuous supply of unlimited quantities. In practice this is difficult and involves storing many herbs in some form or another, but where fresh herbs are a possibility, I try and make them a certainty.

Of our annual and biennial herbs, three – garlic, basil and parsley – are by far the most important to us.

Garlic
(Allium sativum)

Garlic has always been powerful magic. From the ancient Egyptians and first-century Hindus to present-day herbalists, doctors have used it to keep their insides clean, cure heart disease and to ward off terrors in the night. It is an antiseptic and boosts the immune system. Whenever I feel a cold coming on, I always eat extra garlic and I try to grow enough to last until late spring, when any left in store will be sprouting.

As the Latin name suggests, garlic is a member of the onion family and does best in rich, well-drained soils. It is wrong to think of it as a Mediterranean herb – in fact it originated in central Asia. It will grow very well in the far north of Europe, although it does need as much summer sun as possible.

There are two types of garlic – hardneck and softneck. Hardneck garlics have a rigid stalk and tend to do better in very cold conditions. Although some swear by their superior flavour, all agree that they do not keep as well as softneck types. The two hardnecks I often grow are 'Sultop' and 'Sprint'. Hardnecks should be planted early as they can be rather slow to appear.

Softnecks have a flexible stalk that can be plaited, and the bulbs have white papery skin and many cloves that often form several layers around the central core. They will last much longer and tend to have a stronger flavour than the hardnecks. Almost all supermarket garlic is a softneck variety, not least because it keeps so well. There are many more softneck varieties to choose from and I have happily grown 'Cristo', 'Thermidrome', 'Printanor', 'Moraluz' and 'Germidour'. I am sure that there are others equally as good.

In order to form a head made from good-sized cloves, garlic needs at least six weeks in the ground when the temperature does not rise above 10°C (50°F) and about ten days below 4°C (40°F). October is the perfect time for planting and I usually plant hardneck varieties as early as mid-September. In practice I tend to make at least two plantings – putting out the softneck varieties and elephant garlic in October or even November. If you plant too late you will find that they grow but when you harvest, there is one small bulb that has not subdivided into cloves.

You can plant any shop- or market-bought garlic but I advise buying bulbs from an accredited supplier because garlic is prone to viruses that accumulate. Fresh bulbs grown specifically for planting rather than eating will be virus-free. (Incidentally, these viruses, which simply cause the garlic to grow less successfully, are entirely harmless to humans.) In a good year I keep my own bulbs for seed for the following year but always buy in fresh stock after that.

Break the bulb up and only plant the outer cloves. Keep the inner ones, which are smaller, for cooking. The bigger the

Garlic has always been powerful magic, from ancient Egyptians to first-century Hindus to modern herbalists

Elephant garlic fresh from the garden.

clove, the better the chance of a big, healthy bulb growing from it.

Garlic grows best in free-draining, quite rich soil with a sunny aspect. I like to plant it following legumes, not least because these have deep roots that open out my heavy soil. Rake the ground to a fine tilth (see page 85) and plant the cloves in rows – making sure you have the pointed end facing up – 2.5–5cm (1–2in) deep and about 15–23cm (6–9in) apart. I then cover the area with 2.5cm (1in) of good garden compost. This both protects the growing shoots (and effectively makes your planting a little deeper, which is never a bad thing) and enriches the soil. Keep them weed-free and make sure they are watered in spring as the foliage is growing.

This year I am growing quite a lot of elephant garlic whose delicate taste belies its large size

Garlic needs to be harvested as soon as it is ready – usually the beginning of July, the same time as the first potatoes – otherwise the bulbs start to shrivel and their storing capacity reduces. Leave them in the ground until the leaves have yellowed and then dig them up on a clear, sunny day so that they can be left on the ground to dry. Failing that, bring them in to as dry and well-ventilated a place as possible (I find the slats of the greenhouse staging ideal) and let them dry for a few weeks, leaves and all. Once they are truly dry, we cut off the leaves and roots, and strip off the very dry outer skin before storing them in a basket in our potting shed, which is very cool and dark but never freezes. This seems to suit them perfectly. I have tried using the leaves to plait them into ropes but they do not keep any better for this. The essential ingredients of storage are good airflow, dark and a constant, cool temperature.

This year I am growing quite a lot of elephant garlic. It is big, hence its name. Its taste, however, belies its size as it is more delicate than almost all 'normal' garlic. In fact its 'garlic' name belies its true family too. Elephant garlic (*Allium ampeloprasum*) is in fact a form of leek – which explains its relative mildness. It has been called 'garlic for people who don't like garlic' but that is to denigrate it. It is ideal for anything that needs a hint or touch of garlic rather than a full-throated blast. For example, we like it roasted whole and eaten with chicken or tomatoes. I am assured that you can buy elephant garlic ice cream with a flavour that is enticing rather than confrontational, although I have not tried it. However you devour it, elephant garlic is good to eat, very easy to grow and extremely healthy.

As with all garlics, it should be planted between autumn and midwinter in soil that is rich, well drained, has a pH higher than 6 and in full sun. Bury the cloves at least twice their own depth which, in practice, means dibbing a hole 15cm (6in) deep. They should be spaced at least 23cm (9in) apart or, if you have the space, 30cm (12in), which is better, in rows 30–60cm (12–24in) apart.

Keep them weed-free and well watered, especially in spring as the foliage is growing. When you sense that the garlic is full-grown (I realise that 'sensing when full-grown' means when the foliage starts to yellow and keel over, usually the beginning of July-ish), stop watering for at least two weeks.

In general, hardneck garlic should be harvested when the foliage turns yellow whilst softneck garlic can stay in the ground longer, until the top-growth all collapses and shrivels. Elephant garlic is classed in with hardneck types.

Garlic is, of course, prey to all the diseases that leeks, onions and garlic are liable to get. Rust, white rot, eelworm and onion fly will all have at it, given the chance. Rust is an increasing problem in my own garden, especially on leeks (see page 354), and I use wood ash sprinkled liberally around the growing plants as increasing potash helps protect against it. The best protection against onion fly – the emerging maggots will bore into the bulb and kill the plant – is regular hoeing in spring to disturb the eggs.

Basil
(Ocimum basilicum)

Basil is another very important herb for us, but primarily for one simple use, making pesto. No taste is more typically Italian than pesto made from fresh basil, garlic, pine nuts, olive oil and Parmesan cheese. I love it with pasta, potatoes, lettuce or just spread on bread. Delicious. We freeze it and in midwinter it tastes as fresh as the hour it was made. There is a tendency, certainly amongst the metropolitan foodie classes, to fetishise pesto and hunt out the original or perfect recipe, but it is worth remembering that pesto simply means 'paste' and all Italian pesto recipes have been created within individual families, so can vary hugely.

Planting basil into a cold frame. Basil is very tender and grows best in rich, well-watered soil with as much heat as possible.

As the individual basil plants grow, we harvest a few leaves from each one. This ensures that they become bushy and produce lots more leaves so will remain productive for months.

We make pesto with parsley and rocket as well as basil, and happily substitute walnuts for pine nuts and use whatever hard cheese is to hand. All variations can be very good indeed. But in the end it is that pungent, musky, oily taste of basil that is so good and which combines so well with the garlic, oil and the slightly burnt taste of the roasted pine nuts.

But pesto uses up large quantities of basil, so to make it – and it is incomparably good when home-made – you have to grow a lot of basil. There are many types of basil and over the years I have grown quite a few of them but we always come back to the basic sweet basil as it makes the best pesto.

The secret of good basil is to grow it fast whilst allowing the plants to become as large as possible without the leaves losing their freshness. When fully mature and ready for picking, a healthy basil plant should be 30–45cm (12–18in) tall and half that in diameter. They are lusty plants and should not be crammed into a tiny space if they are to realise a fraction of their possible flavour or abundance.

I sow my first basil seeds in March and germinate them in a heated greenhouse. A warm windowsill would do as well. As soon as they are large enough to handle I prick the seedlings out into plugs and grow them on in the greenhouse. If need be, I pot them on again into individual 7.5cm (3in) pots. The idea is to keep their growth unchecked. Above all, they like warmth, moisture and a rich but well-drained soil. As a guide, they usually do fine growing alongside tomatoes – although this year I have grown some in cold frames where the heat and humidity are greater than in the greenhouse where the tomatoes are, and the basil have loved this. I always grow some outside but unless the weather is hot for at least three weeks, the plants are smaller, yellower, tougher and not nearly as good to eat as the protected plants. Once the temperature drops below 10°C (50°F) the leaves become leathery and are the canary in the mine for the first frosts, as even if the thermometer just flickers near 0°C (32°F), the leaves are reduced to black rags overnight and the plant is killed.

I make a second sowing in May, pricking them out into individual 7.5cm (3in) pots. I use these to replace the first crop which I pull up at the beginning of August as it is tending to flower and produce more stem than leaves.

Parsley
(Petroselinum crispum 'French')

Parsley is one of the most useful all-round herbs that we grow. There are very few vegetables or meats that cannot be enhanced by the addition of some chopped parsley.

It is a fairly hardy plant, surviving quite a few degrees of frost but the cold does kill off the top-growth, so without a tunnel or greenhouse this can be tricky, although fleece and cloches do make it possible for plants to be raised outside.

Like basil, it has become commonplace for parsley to be sold fresh in pots in supermarkets. On one level, as with basil, this is a good thing because it gives millions easy access to the fresh leaves of this delicious herb. But on another, it traduces parsley's true potential. This is because each of the little wispy seedlings crammed into the pot is desperate for space. They are like battery hens, producing the goods but for a tiny period and under appalling conditions. Take a snip or two of your herb and the whole thing gives up the ghost. This means – and perhaps one might be justified in being a teeny bit cynical here – that you have to go back and buy another pot from those nice folk at the supermarket.

Grow some yourself from seed and each plant – each tiny seedling – will grow big and strong, last months and months, and give a harvest more bountiful than the biggest pot that mass production will supply.

Parsley is not a Mediterranean herb and thrives in well-drained but fertile soil, with plenty of moisture. It will also tolerate some shade. I have found that it sits much happier as part of the vegetable rotation (see page 293) than trying to fit in with the needs of the Herb Garden, which is based around Mediterranean herbs with their desire for poor soil and maximum sunshine.

It is a biennial and a member of the carrot family, and although it can be fitted in anywhere – I often use it as an edging plant, not least because it makes it easier to pick – it is fundamentally part of the carrot, parsnip and celery rotational group. Each plant will develop a long taproot – not unlike a carrot – hence the cruelty of confining it to a small pot with dozens of fellow plants packed in with it.

A healthy parsley plant between three and nine months old should be 15–30cm (6–12in) tall and bushily frondescent with edible foliage. If it gets dry then it can throw up a flowering stem which should be cut back to the base as soon as it appears. The secret is to keep it well watered and to have plenty of compost in the soil to hold

French flat-leafed parsley has, as its name suggests, a flat leaf with better flavour and texture than curled parsley. We love it and eat it daily. I grow three or four successive batches a year so we are never without a constant, generous supply.

the moisture without it becoming waterlogged. If it has the space to develop its true root system, it will regrow a new flush of leaves again and again for the first nine months of its life until its urge to develop flowers becomes overwhelming, and then it has to be dug up and added to the compost heap. When you do this you will be astonished at the size of the root.

I make two or three sowings a year, the first in January, then May and finally August. This ensures a limitless supply right through the seasons. I always used to sow parsley direct where it was to grow and then thinned it heavily, and this system still works, although it can be prey to slug attack. I now prefer to sow it in seed trays and transplant it into plugs. It needs warmth to germinate and we use a heated bench but a windowsill above a radiator works well. Once the seedlings emerge, they will not need any extra heat.

Coriander is easy to grow but is very quick to run to seed, and to keep a good supply of the pungent leaves it must not be too hot, too cold, too wet or too dry!

The January sowing is, like all midwinter seeds, slow to get going but provides plants ready to put out into the garden as soon as the soil warms up. This is the crop most likely to go to seed so should be picked hard through summer. The May sowing provides me with a supply from autumn through to early spring and the August sowing is planted out in the greenhouse after the tomatoes have been cleared, or under cloches, and tends to sit all winter a little grumpily but gives a harvest in the first half of the following year.

I principally grow flat-leafed parsley which I think has a better flavour and texture, although the curly-leafed is good and decorative, too. But the flat-leafed kind used liberally with vegetables, stews, soups, as part of salads and as a pesto is magnificent.

Coriander
(*Coriandrum sativum*)

Coriander looks just like a rather delicate parsley but its smell is distinctive and pungent, even from very tiny seedlings. It is one of the most ancient of all cultivated herbs and has been used both to aid digestion and also as an accompaniment to many dishes. The seeds are ground up and used in curries and chutneys but we only use the fresh leaves. I grow it in exactly the same way as parsley, in plugs which are then transplanted to their growing place. I make the first sowing in January and grow these on in the greenhouse. By the middle of May, they will be bolting uncontrollably and I pull them up and replace them with tomatoes.

The second sowing is made in April and the seedlings are planted out in a shady corner of the Vegetable Garden.

The problem with raising coriander is delaying its going to seed, or bolting. When it does this, the leaves grow rapidly and change from the useful, widely splayed ones to become very finely cut, like fennel. You can, of course, make a virtue of this and harvest the seeds, but for me the plant ceases to have a function at that point. I just try and keep it well watered and cool   which of course gets increasingly difficult after May. The plain *Coriandrum sativum* is the least likely to bolt, whereas *C.s.* 'Moroccan' is best for seed.

Dill
(Anethum graveolens)

Dill is certainly worth growing in any garden for aesthetic pleasure alone. It is an exceptionally beautiful herb with feathery fronds for leaves and a wonderful lemon-yellow starburst flower head.

We also grow dill partly for the way that it can enhance the flavours of fish or lamb and partly because it is a good umbellifer that attracts hoverflies to the Vegetable Garden, and the nymphs of these will eat aphids.

It is best to sow it in plugs or soil blocks rather than seed trays, as it resents being transplanted, which can trigger early bolting. Whenever you read that a plant dislikes being moved or transplanted, what is meant is that the roots are very sensitive to any movement and will usually react by going into emergency survival mode. For most annuals, this means

Dill grows very well from seed and has very beautiful feathery foliage as well as yellow umbels of flower that attracts hoverflies.

setting seed as soon as possible. The great advantage of sowing in plugs or blocks is that the young plant can be moved without the roots being unduly disturbed.

Dill is a tender plant and I plant the seedlings out as soon as there is no risk of frost. It grows best on very well-drained poor soil with as much sun as possible, so is a good bedfellow with thyme, rosemary or any of the other Mediterranean herbs. It has a tendency to blow over, so if the plants are in a row, support them as you would broad beans, with string staked at the corners.

Dill is a good umbellifer that attracts hoverflies to the Vegetable Garden, and the nymphs of these will eat aphids

Top: Borage is a wonderful plant for attracting pollinators as well as providing the essential blue flowers for Pimms!

Bottom: Angelica is a biennial that self-seeds prolifically and has done so in our Jewel Garden for the past 25 years – all from one original plant.

Borage
(Borago officionalis)

No plant is easier to grow than borage as once you have planted one in your garden, it seeds itself with the promiscuity of forget-me-nots. It will flower from midsummer until the first frosts, although occasionally it will behave like a biennial and start flowering in April.

In general it likes hot sun and poor, well-drained soil, to the extent that it will grow in every cranny of a stone path, but it is not fussy and will make itself at home in a well-dug bed alongside any herbaceous plant. The leaves are rich in mineral salts and are good with any savoury dairy food.

Much nonsense is written about the efficacy of its non-flatulent role as a cucumber substitute but it exists in its own right as an essential ingredient in a glass of Pimms. No other qualification is necessary. It does have, as a great bonus, beautiful blue flowers, and as long as it is kept under control by extensive weeding and thinning, it is a really welcome addition to our Walled Garden.

One word of warning – the adult plant is covered in very fine hairs which are extremely abrasive. If you are handling borage plants (as opposed to merely collecting leaves to eat) wear gloves and resist any temptation to rub your eyes.

Angelica
(Angelica archangelica)

Angelica is such a prolific self-seeder that once you have an established plant, you are likely to have some angelica forever. But the seed does not spread far so the clumps remain in the same place, giving the impression that it is the same perennial plant that returns each year, whereas in fact it is a biennial. The seed falls in July and August and immediately germinates, establishing small plants that overwinter beneath the shade of their parent before growing strongly the following spring when the parent plant has died. And strongly it does grow, too, a healthy plant producing wonderful giant umbels of flower as big as footballs on strong stems.

It loves our heavy, damp soil and is best when in some shade. As a rule of thumb it is unlikely ever to grow well wherever Mediterranean herbs like rosemary or thyme are thriving, and vice versa.

An essential in any garden for its appearance, angelica was traditionally used as a confectionery, the stems being candied, but it is also good added to stewed rhubarb.

An essential in any garden for its appearance, angelica was traditionally used as a confectionery

Perennial Mediterranean herbs

Ours are a climate and location that are not ideal for growing any of the Mediterranean herbs. It is cold and wet in winter and cool and wet in summer. The soil is as rich and fat as best butter. Drainage is generally poor.

But this neither deters us from growing these herbs nor the plants from making the best of the conditions we offer them.

The thing to bear in mind about all the Mediterranean herbs is that they like a bit of rough. It is always salutary to go and see plants growing in their natural habitat and with so-called 'Mediterranean' plants there are two things that invariably strike me. The first is just how extreme the conditions are. A dry, sun-baked hillside is a desperately harsh place. Our holiday-centred experiences tend to lock us into coastal countryside softened by human pampering, but take a walk in July across the hills of inland Provence or the Atlas mountains, and you are soon way out of your holiday comfort zone.

The second thing is that plants that we are accustomed to knowing in our gardens are always twice the size of the 'wild' originals. These have adapted to survive and multiply, and in order that the multiplication takes place successfully, the plant wastes little energy on surplus growth. Its only job is to set seed and set seed fast, bypassing the niceties of form and foliage if necessary.

But the gardener has to strike a balance. We cannot construct a Mediterranean hillside for the occasional Mediterranean herb. If we are growing herbs to look good and to provide an abundant supply for the kitchen, we don't want the plant to replicate its natural behaviour. We want an unnatural lushness that only comes from unnaturally mild conditions.

But it is terribly easy to err on the side of softness with all the Mediterranean herbs. Given our absence of Mediterranean heat and drought, you really cannot overdo the coarsening of ground for rosemary and its ilk. This does not mean planting into heavy subsoil, more a case of diluting the topsoil as much as possible with grit (ideal) or sharp sand (pretty good), but not with any kind of organic material (too nutritious). If you have a deep, water-retentive soil it is a good idea to barrow some of it away and replace it with hardcore, leaving your thinned-down topsoil as a layer no deeper than 15cm (6in) over this. If these seem absurdly hostile growing conditions, then you will have got it just right.

This is where those gardeners with a thin layer of soil over solid chalk the colour of a cup of tea – such as I grew up with – have a running start. All the

Opposite page: A rosemary hedge flanks the path through the Herb Garden from the Cottage Garden. The variety is 'Miss Jessopp's Upright' which, as the name suggests, has especially vertical growth.

Mediterranean herbs love chalk. Both lavender and rosemary will grow very well in a pot as long as they have enough space for a root run, in other words, just because they like poor soil and dry conditions, don't fall into the trap of letting them get potbound. Any plant that has evolved to live in drought will have roots that want to range freely to seek out moisture.

Rosemary
(*Rosmarinus officinalis*)

Rosemary is essential for lamb and very good with potatoes but I would grow it even if I never ate it at all. Every time I pass a rosemary bush – which is at least half a dozen times a day – I dabble my hands in the leaves as I go and they release a breath of sunshine. The leaves – simultaneously dry and sticky – reek exotically of southern sun.

But I must have lost two dozen good rosemary bushes over the past ten years solely through poor drainage coupled with winter wet. They absolutely hate sitting in wet ground and show their displeasure by dying back, first one branch turning brown and black-tipped, and then always inexorably followed by the whole damn thing. Young plants seem to be more prone to this than older ones, but this could just be because they have smaller root systems.

You can – and should – make the drainage around the roots as free as possible, and I plant any new rosemary bushes into a bucketful of pure grit, but beware of creating a sump into which all the surrounding water drains. The only

Rosemary grows very easily from cuttings taken in late summer. Strip off the lower leaves from new, straight shoots and insert into a very free-draining compost around the edges of the pot. They will be ready to pot on or plant out next spring.

long-term solution is to create an area that is exceptionally well drained and keep your rosemary limited to it.

I have seen rosemary grown as a climber and espaliered in rather stringy layers, and the upright form, 'Miss Jessopp's Upright', is very popular because it fits into smaller gardens. We have it growing as a hedge flanking the path from the Herb Garden to the Cottage Garden and it responds well to quite fierce trimming in spring to keep it tight and compact. However, I like rosemary bushes that sprawl and buckle under the weight of their own gnarled branches and we have another rosemary hedge in the Paradise Garden that I let sprawl untrimmed and – so far – it seems very happy. But again, we added a mass of grit to the soil to help drainage.

Given sunshine, shelter and drainage, a rosemary bush can live for a generation, although it will lose its youthful vigour after about five years. Occasionally I prune one of the two whopping bushes we have and chuck the prunings on the fire to fill the room in midwinter with fabulously evocative scent – a whole southern hillside breathing into our Herefordshire house.

Thyme
(Thymus vulgaris)

For years we had problems growing thyme. I would plant it in the same beds as the rosemary, with good drainage and lots of sunshine, and it would start out well and grow strongly. But by midsummer it would start to get bare-stemmed and the leaves would blacken and die off, and by autumn all that would be left were a few sad leaves at the end of lanky, woody branches. Not good. After a while (too long a while) I worked out that it could not tolerate shade of any kind and that it was not suited to the hurly burly of the Herb Garden. Since then I have grown it in the Vegetable Garden and the thyme has never looked back.

There are dozens of different kinds of thyme but we only grow two sorts, common thyme (*Thymus vulgaris*) and lemon thyme (*T.* x *citriodorus*), which is especially good for cooking. I grow the common thyme from seed, broadcasting it onto a seed tray and pricking out the tiny seedlings into plugs or at a wider spacing in another tray once they are large enough to handle. They grow slowly but are big enough to plant out by midsummer, although I sometimes leave them to overwinter in a frame and plant them out the following spring.

All thymes can be grown from cuttings, which take very easily from new soft growth any time between May and July. I take a few dozen, each 5–7.5cm (2–3in) long, and stick them at 2.5cm (1in) spacing around the edge of a pot. They take a few weeks to root and then they can be planted out into a very sunny spot (at very wide spacing so that they do not become shaded) or potted up and grown on before planting out in late summer. For cooking purposes it is much easier to keep a supply of young, tightly cropped plants, so I replace the plants completely every two years and harvest them by cutting a whole plant right down to the ground whilst all the stems are still very soft. This avoids all the twiggy bits and the bother of stripping the leaves.

Sage
(Salvia officinalis)

I grow sage in three colours: green (*Salvia officinalis*), purple (*S. o.* 'Purpurascens') and variegated (*S. o.* 'Tricolor'). As well as the normal broad-leafed sage, I have the narrow-leafed version (*S. lavandulifolia*) which is really much the better for culinary use and grows just as easily, which is to say that once planted, you can hardly stop it performing year after year. If there was only room for one sage in my garden, this is the one that I would grow. At the end of a cold winter it could look like a straggly refugee but cut back hard in March, it soon sprouts new leaves of exuberant freshness. Then come the flowers, a mass of violet and purple spikes sprouting a typically salvian lowered bottom petal with a raised hood arched above it. Even if you cannot abide the taste or smell of the plant, the flowers make its place in the garden essential. But I love the taste and instantly

Below left: *Salvia lavandulifolia*.
Below centre: *S. officinalis* 'Purpurascens'.
Below right: *S. o.* 'Tricolor'.

distinctive scent. Just the words make me hungry. Sage has very powerful healing and antiseptic properties and was also used to preserve meat.

Purple sage grows slower and smaller than its green cousin and seems to like the non-Mediterranean winters less, but as long as the drainage is kept good, it always restores itself by mid-spring.

It is important to prune sage hard as it can become very lank and bow down under the weight of its branches, thus shading all the interior and lower leaves. I always used to prune it in early spring but now do it after flowering in late summer so that we get the best possible show from the flowers and yet there is time for the new shoots to harden off before the winter frosts come. But perhaps this is a sign of the encroachment of global warming, because we now seldom seem to get real frosts much before mid-November, whereas they used to be a threat from September onwards.

Sage takes easily from cuttings and we refresh our plants every few years, growing perhaps a dozen plants from cuttings every year. It is also easy to raise from seed. We pot up the young plants, whether from cutting or seed, trim them back to make them bushy, and then keep them in a cold frame all winter before planting out in spring. They quickly become strong plants.

Lavender labels and defines a colour even though, on inspection, it comes in lots of colours

Lavender
(Lavandula angustifolia)

Few plants evoke so many things so powerfully. Lavender labels and defines a colour even though, on inspection, it comes in lots of shades from dark purple to white. It colours a whole mood or atmosphere of gentle if not genteel refinement and prettiness and, above all, the scent of it released by crumbling a few of the tiny flowers in your careless fingers will trigger a chain of evocations that can be provoked by nothing else.

It is a healing plant 'of especial use', as one Tudor writer noted, 'for all the griefes and pains of the head and heart'. Lavender water is supposed to be one of the most ancient of all manufactured perfumes, mentioned in twelfth-century literature, and we know that the Romans added it to their baths, giving it the name *lavandula* which comes from *lavare*, to wash. Certainly, a few drops of lavender oil added to your bath seem to induce an extra restfulness and ease.

It is curious how this most Mediterranean of plants has become so English, so perfectly suited to tea on an Edwardian lawn and a hazy patrician charm. Some of this is simply the glaucal shimmer of its tiny leaves matched with the fuzz of flowers hovering on their spikes that associates well with any pastel colours. It is also a robust and very tolerant plant. It likes full sun, plenty of air around it, alkaline soil and good drainage, but lavender will struggle on where the more temperamental rosemary will give up the ghost, even though both

plants have the same origins. The important point is winter drainage. Lavender, like rosemary, hates sitting dormant in cold water. In summer it will respond to some watering and I have lost plants in pots through under-watering.

They also live for ages, their flowers becoming sparser and sparser in proportion to the woody growth. The secret of keeping a lavender bush in good shape is to clip it in spring, but try to avoid cutting into the old wood as plants will not always regenerate. If you crop the entire plant back to old wood it can mean big trouble. Lavender is evergreen, which means that it keeps – and needs – its leaves all winter. If you cut into the old

wood, which does not have any leaves, and new leaves do not grow, then it will not survive. After it has flowered, cut back to the leaves with perhaps a third trim in October. With this treatment it will hold a tight pebble shape well.

We used to only grow it in terracotta pots – and still do grow some like that, especially the more tender French lavender (*Lavandula stoechas*) – but a few years ago I planted a hedge of *L. angustifolia* 'Hidcote' on the Mound, adding mountains of grit to the soil. Since then, it has coped with some of the wettest winters in memory and is growing well.

There are many different types, varieties and colours of lavender to

The lavender hedge on the Mound is planted behind a wall and has a large amount of grit added to the soil to ensure it has sharp drainage. Although it is hardy, like many Mediterranean herbs, lavender is easily killed by the combination of cold and wet.

choose or confuse. Here are just a few. *L. angustifolia* is common or English lavender. It has the familiar mauve spikes of flower and will grow to a height and spread of about 90cm (36in). The two most common varieties are *L. a.* 'Munstead' and *L. a.* 'Hidcote'. 'Hidcote' is a deeper mauve and a bit more vigorous than the paler, bluer, faster-growing 'Munstead'. Both make good hedging plants, where hedge and edge combine to make a gentle demarcation line. There is a white form, *L. angustifolia* 'Alba', which does not grow quite so tall, and *L. a.* 'Nana Alba' which, like all plants with 'nana' and 'alba' in their name, is white and small. *L. a.* 'Rosea' has pink flowers as does *L. a.* 'Jean Davis'. But pink lavender is like white chocolate, perfectly nice but somehow not perfectly right.

Lavandula lanata makes a dome of soft woolly leaves, which then throws up long spikes twice as high again, topped with purple flowers. *L. stoechas* has unusual mauve bracts on top of the flower spikes and very narrow leaves that grow distinctively up the stems. It will grow well in acidic soil, unlike all other lavenders. *L. dentata* var. *dentata* has leaves that are prettily ribbed or crimped and the flowers are also topped with bracts, although of a paler blue colour. It is not entirely hardy so needs protecting in a cold winter or bringing indoors.

Lavender will grow from seed as well as take easily from cuttings. Seed should be sown in autumn and the seedlings overwintered before pricking out in spring and planting in early summer. They grow on fast.

Cuttings are best taken either from non-flowering stems as softwood cuttings in May or as semi-hardwood cuttings in late summer from new growth. Overwinter the rooted cuttings under cover and plant out the following spring.

Lavender is prone to cuckoo spit, which is the white frothy liquid caused by the immature nymph stage of froghoppers. It is unsightly but does little harm and the best way to get rid of it is to spray with water.

Marjoram
(*Origanum vulgare and O. majorana*)

It is easy to get confused between oregano and marjoram because there is nothing in practice between them, but for the record, *Origanum vulgare* in Britain is known as wild marjoram and in the Mediterranean, the same plant is known as oregano. Pot marjoram is *O. onites*, and *O. majorana* is sweet marjoram, which comes from North Africa and has perhaps the best flavour.

It grows into low mounds and by cutting boldly into these as you need the herb, it stops it becoming straggly and woody. If it is growing quicker than you can use it – which it invariably seems to do – be brutal and give it a hard prune. The new growth will return very quickly.

We mostly use golden marjoram (*O. v.* 'Aureum') and the variegated *O. v.* 'Gold Tip' for cooking because in our damp, mild climate they have a better flavour than the Greek oregano – although in its natural Mediterranean home, the Greek version is stronger and more aromatic. I would not dream of making a tomato sauce without marjoram, although between December and February I am scratching around for enough good leaves to make it worthwhile collecting. I also suspect that we stick with the yellow and variegated marjoram because both grow strongly and the yellow adds a good touch of colour to both garden and plate.

Although marjoram grows easily from seed, it often does not come true and I take cuttings to propagate the stock. I treat these exactly as I do thyme, putting perhaps half a dozen around the edge of a pot of compost with extra grit or perlite, and placing them under the mist propagator where they root very easily. I then pot them on and plant them out the following spring

Hyssop
(Hyssopus officinalis)

I tried growing a hedge of hyssop in our Walled Garden when it was still the Herb Garden. This failed dismally because – like all edging hedges here – it became suffocated by the plants that it was supposed to be bounding. The moral of the story is to give hyssop – as with all the Mediterranean plants – plenty of space, light and air. To be honest I never grow hyssop well – it seems to need exceptionally dry, sunny conditions and because it is rather a marginal herb for us, it tends not to get pride of Mediterranean place.

But *Hyssopus officinalis* is a beautiful shrub with intense violet blue flowers. You can also find white hyssop (*H. o.* 'Alba') and pink-flowering hyssop (*H. o.* 'Roseus').

It grows very well from seed, even from direct sowing where it is to grow and – given the right conditions – does make an excellent edging hedge for a herb garden. It also attracts butterflies and bees and in researching this book I found out that hyssop is good for diverting cabbage white butterflies (see page 357), which is something I wish that I had known years ago.

I trim it back lightly in autumn and then again hard in spring after the worst of the weather has passed. It is important to keep it trimmed if the plant is not to become a very woody bush.

The leaves are an aid to digestion, particularly of fatty foods like sausages, and are traditionally used with game.

Hyssop flowers have a lovely intense blue. When the flowering has finished, I trim the whole plant back by half.

Bay
(Laurus nobilis)

Fresh bay leaves are really useful for adding a distinctive, rich, aromatic flavour to soups and stews, and it is an important plant for any herb garden, but it is a problem for us. In ten years in this garden we have never managed to overwinter a bay without at least a third of it being killed off by cold weather. They are not designed for cold, wet winters, are evergreen, which makes them prone to desiccation in very cold winter winds, and are shallow-rooted, which makes them more susceptible to hard ground frosts. All in all, you might think that bay contradicted my basic rule of never forcing a plant to grow wherever or whenever it is made to behave unnaturally.

But they are tough trees and usually recover from what might seem a hopeless situation (and, given that the bay is most definitely a tree, bear in mind the principle that you should not declare a tree dead until it has been dead for a full twelve months). If it does die back I cut it back to green growth – which might be the base – and it usually regrows. For the same reasons that we cannot grow rosemary without losses, we have long given up trying to grow bay planted in the ground. The combination of winter wet, icy winds and air temperatures below -12°C (10°F) is too much for them. So we grow small plants in pots and bring them into the greenhouse in November until March. But well into May I keep some horticultural fleece near each outdoor plant to drape over it if it is a cold night. Hence the reason for keeping the plants small!

Other than its hatred of cold, wet winters, the bay is remarkably tough and easy to grow. It hardly ever needs watering and you should never feed it. I change its potting compost every two or three years, moving it into a slightly larger pot each time (but only slightly – it is a mistake to greatly increase the pot size of anything in one jump), and make sure that the compost has a lot of extra grit or perlite added to it.

I find that cuttings – taken in September – have about a 40 per cent chance of taking. But without a mist propagator they are much more tricky.

Occasionally bay will get attacked by scale insects, especially if grown indoors alongside citrus plants, but these are easily tackled with soap and water or by wiping each leaf with white spirit. However, the latter does little to improve the flavour of the leaves.

Fennel
(Foeniculum officinale)

Wherever it can bask in full sunshine in our garden, fennel grows like a weed, loving our rich soil and yet able to grow in seemingly soilless cracks in paving or even walls. We love it, both to eat but especially to look at, so we only pull up those plants that are spoiling the desired aesthetic effect. We use the feathery foliage with fish and the fresh seeds are a wonderful addition to roast pork. We pound up fennel seeds, garlic, olive oil and salt in a mortar and spread the resulting paste over the meat, which sits on a deep bed of chopped Florence fennel. This is then roasted slowly for three hours or so and the result is incredibly tender meat cut through with the flavour of the fennel. Munching fennel seeds is a very good way of settling a dodgy stomach and I often grab a handful as I pass the plant between August and October.

Given a good soil that it can get its deep roots into, fennel will make a really substantial and handsome plant, and we grow it in the Walled Garden for its foliage and the bronze version (*Foeniculum vulgare* 'Purpureum') in the Jewel Garden. Bronze fennel is less robust than its green cousin, both in size and resistance to the cold and wet, although it is seldom actually killed by bad weather. It just looks thoroughly defeated.

Fennel is very easy to grow from seed and mature plants can be lifted and divided in autumn or early spring. I find it best to either transplant self-sown seedlings in spring or to lift a mature plant, take off young sections of root and throw away the older core, as the plant does not do very well after three or four years of growth.

Tarragon
(*Artemisia dracunculus*)

Tarragon did not enter the English herb garden until the Tudor period and still seems distinctly foreign, even exotic. Part of this is down to its excellence as a herb, particularly with chicken and eggs, and partly because it can be tricky to grow. In fact it is as at home in my garden as any of the other Mediterranean herbs, which is to say, not entirely.

There are two kinds of tarragon, French (*Artemisia dracunculus*) and Russian (*A. dracunculoides*), and unfortunately the French, which is by far superior for culinary purposes, is more difficult to grow in this garden. It hates the cold and the wet, whereas Russian tarragon is able to put its roots down in any soil or conditions but is not really worth its space in the garden. So there is no easy solution, but I maintain a supply of tarragon by replacing the plants every few years with new stock taken from softwood cuttings, which root fairly well under the mist propagator. This is not a bad idea however suitable your garden, because the leaves of young plants have the best flavour.

Fennel does not just grow in the Herb Garden but self-seeds itself all over the rest of the garden and we encourage this as it is a wonderfully statuesque plant in all its phases from spring to late winter.

We tend to associate herbs with the few very familiar Mediterranean ones like rosemary and thyme, but there is a wide range that grow best in cooler, northern conditions.

Perennial non-Mediterranean herbs

The very word 'herbs' has come to evoke heat, sunshine and the oily, resinous aromas of the Mediterranean. But the variety of herbs that will grow happily in a more northern, temperate climate is very large.

Nowadays we tend to only grow and use a very limited range of herbs and nearly all for the kitchen, and we in this household are as guilty of that as anyone. However, throughout the thousand years that there has been a house on this site, herbs would have been the household's pharmacy. The old lady that we bought the house from in 1991 had lived here all her life and she told us that her mother's chemist was 'the hedge', meaning that she gathered wild herbs and plants for all her needs, including, amongst many others, elderflowers for shampoo and soap, nettles for purifying the blood, dandelions for kidney disorders and comfrey for bruises and sprains. A small supply of essential

herbs growing in the garden was considered as sensible as the modern first-aid kit. But whether for health or to improve the taste of our food, the following herbs are easy to grow and an invaluable part of any herb garden.

Mint
(Mentha spp.)

The quality of the plant resides in the aromatic oils that have been used since ancient times both for culinary and medicinal purposes. It is a great aid to digestion, a mouth freshener and an antiseptic. It is also used to ward off flies and is, of course, delicious, whether eaten with dozens of different foods or simply drunk as a tea.

Bees and other pollinating insects love mint whereas many 'bad' insects are deterred by the menthol. Peppermint, planted as a companion plant with brassicas, repels cabbage white butterflies (see page 357), aphids and flea beetles (see page 301). In a greenhouse, mint will also deter ants which can burrow into pots, disturbing the roots and consequentially damaging plants (although it is worth stressing that ants do not feed off plants in any way).

One of the great attractions of growing mint for the inexperienced herb grower is that its greatest problem is its greatest strength. Mint, in all its forms, is famously invasive, its rhizomatous roots spreading voraciously and quickly becoming a weed. A delicious and wonderfully aromatic weed but a weed for all that. This means that the best way to grow it is in a container. That container can be anything from a small pot on a kitchen windowsill to the old cattle trough I have outside my back door. It even pays to grow mint in a container in a border. An old bucket with holes in the bottom is ideal as this will allow the roots to grow down as far as they like but restrict their lateral spread.

One of the reasons that mint spreads so easily is that it is a very adaptable plant, growing in sun or shade and in dry or wet soil. But the best-quality mint is grown in well-drained, rich soil in plenty of sunshine and you should try and mimic those conditions.

There are many different mints, including eau-de-cologne mint, ginger mint and pineapple mint, but the best

three to grow for the kitchen are spearmint (*Mentha spicata*), peppermint (*Mentha* x *piperita*) and apple mint (*M. suaveolens*). Peppermint makes the best mint tea although spearmint is also used in teas and is a good all-round culinary mint. Apple mint, which has large downy leaves, has a more delicate taste and is the best for new potatoes.

Water mint (*M. aquatica*), grows in boggy, damp places and is too harshly strong for cooking but makes a deliciously aromatic bunch to place in a small vase. Corsican mint (*M. requienii*) has tiny leaves and minute purple flowers. It makes an excellent groundcover plant to grow between the cracks in paving and will release its minty fragrance as you crush the foliage underfoot.

Once the mints start to flower, the leaves become faded and coarse, and it is best to cut them right back to the ground. Clearly, if you do this to all the mints at the same time, it will result in a period of mintlessness, so I do half at a time, waiting until new leaves are growing strongly before cutting the remaining half.

It is a good idea to take a section of root of any these mints at the end of summer, pot it into good compost and keep it in the greenhouse or on a windowsill. It will grow throughout winter, not producing a vast amount of leaves but at least providing a fresh taste when needed. At the end of autumn the plant will become straggly and the leaves reduced to tatters. Cut it back hard. In spring I clean out the containers, get rid of straggly growth and top up the compost to give the new shoots a boost.

Mint can be grown from seed but it takes so easily from root cuttings that it is

Top: Apple mint has furry, apple-green leaves that are perfect for accompanying new potatoes.

Bottom: If you only grow one kind of mint, then spearmint is the best all-rounder – although like all mints, it is very invasive so should be grown in a container.

hardly worth the bother. Dig up some root and cut this into sections, each with a visible node or shoot. Place each in a pot or seed tray of compost and put in a sheltered place. They will almost inevitably produce shoots that can be planted out after four weeks or so.

There are very few problems growing mint if it has sufficient water. However, some mints can be prone to mint rust, which is the fungus *Puccinia menthae* causing orange pustules on the stems and leaves. These may be followed by dusty yellow or black pustules which cause leaves to die but rarely kill the entire plant. Remove the plants from the container and start again with new ones and new soil or compost.

Chives
(*Allium schoenoprasum*)

I now grow chives in the shadiest part of the Herb Garden and in modest quantities but there was a time when I used it as hedging for the carrot bed so that their scent would deter carrot fly (see page 320). It did mean that we had unlimited chives to eat as well as delivering barrowloads to the compost heap two or three times a year.

Chives are very easy to grow from seed so you can afford to be profligate with them but remember that each tiny wisp of seedling will make a substantial plant. But once you have successfully propagated a few plants from seed, it is much easier to divide existing plants in future years. When I move mine each year, I divide them as I go, throwing away old plants that are getting tired and creating new from the divisions.

Chives look good with their grassy tubes of leaf but look even better in flower, their purple bobbles balancing on stalks indistinguishable from the leaves. Unlike many herbs, they taste as good in flower as before and the flowers are delicious in salads. Bees also like them. Before they start to set seed, I cut the whole lot to the ground, filling a barrow with the rank tang of onion, and they regrow anew. In a good year this can be repeated four or five times.

Comfrey
(*Symphytum officinale*)

You can buy many different types of comfrey. The stuff I grow is the wild, self-sown *Symphytum officinale* that you find fringing rivers and all damp ground. It is a beautiful plant with pink and mauve bell-like flowers. *S. asperum* has bright blue flowers and the flowers of *S. grandiflorum* are creamy red. All prefer deep, rich soil and like plenty of moisture. It seeds itself easily and can become an intrusive, if not invasive, weed in the wetter parts of the garden. But we only pull it up where it is actively interfering with the desired aesthetic effect because it is handsome in full fig, up to 1.8m (6ft) tall and carrying pink- and purple-tinged white flowers. One of the problems of growing comfrey in amongst other plants is that it is very prone to falling over in wind or heavy rain and swamping plants beneath it. It is best to treat it rather like broad beans and to either stake each plant well or grow it in rows, supported by string and canes.

Comfrey is easy to divide into sections in autumn or spring to make new plants or it can be grown from root cuttings – which is

The flower heads of chives are good to eat along with the leaves, and look very pretty sprinkled on a salad.

a fancy way of saying that any piece of comfrey root popped into the ground will develop into a plant.

Comfrey is perhaps the most effective of all British plants at taking up nutrients from the soil. Its deep roots – 3m (10ft) or more – absorb all available goodness and store it in the large, hairy leaves. When cut, these leaves break down very fast and so transfer the nutrients back into the soil. You can simply lay comfrey leaves around the base of plants such as tomatoes as a mulch, and they will feed the soil as they rot down. And you can use it make a liquid feed (see page 115).

It is known as 'knitbone' and was considered an essential part of the physic garden because a poultice made of the mashed-up roots has long been used to speed up the healing of broken or cracked bones or damaged joints, although I have yet to prove the efficacy of this on myself.

Lovage
(Levisticum officinale)

Lovage grows very happily in rich, damp soil and seems to be wholly unaffected by the worst of British winter weather. It originates from the Middle East and was brought to Britain by the Romans, becoming an essential element in monastic herb gardens. Its main uses are as an aid to digestion (as so many herbs are!) but it was also valued as an aphrodisiac (perhaps simply on the basis that one was likely to be a lover if one didn't have belly ache) and as a deodorant and antiseptic. In the kitchen lovage makes a very useful addition to sauces, soups, stews or anything that needs a celery flavour with an added hint of aniseed.

We grow it extensively for its value as a foliage plant as the slightly chalky leaves are the perfect foil for any flowers with softer colours – and especially roses. It will grow from seed but I find that the best method of propagation is by division. Dig up the very fleshy root in autumn or spring (I always do this in spring) and chop it with a spade. As long as each section of root has a visible bud, it can be replanted to make a separate plant. By its second year it will have become very established and after three or four years, very substantial indeed, growing to 1.8m (6ft) on rich soil.

The real secret of growing lovage is to be ruthless with cutting it down. Let the umbels of tiny, almost green flowers develop for their beauty and the way that they attract hoverflies (and perhaps for their seeds), and then cut the whole plant right down to the ground. It will regrow vigorously and the young leaves are much nicer to eat than the old, faded ones. In rich soil, each plant can take two or even three such prunings a year.

Horseradish
(Armoracia rusticana)

Horseradish is another of our favoured weeds. I am very fond of it but for a while it was the bane of the garden, appearing in borders and beds despite continuous weeding. This is no easy business as it has an enormously long and robust taproot – which supplies the material for horseradish sauce. The only way to control it is by digging out every scrap of root anywhere other than your desired horseradish area.

Horseradish grows vigorous leaves all summer but the roots are best – and strongest – when the foliage has completely died down in winter.

It is therefore not a plant for the herb garden and we grow ours in the weedy verge of what is now the car park. Like mint, it needs its own separate area but unlike mint, the length of its root makes it unsuitable for all but the largest container. It is said to help potatoes resist disease but as I rotate my potatoes, and horseradish needs a permanent bed, their association and its benefits must perforce be temporary and occasional.

The best way to propagate it is to take a piece of root with a crown attached and simply plant it where you want it to grow. Nothing will stop it. But any piece of fresh root will 'take' and can either be planted in a hole in situ or in a pot and then transplanted.

Fresh horseradish is a treat and the perfect accompaniment to beef and smoked salmon. I have also eaten a hot horseradish sauce with a pike – bony but good – caught in the river at the bottom of the garden. A very eastern European Christmas dish. You can apparently eat the young leaves, but I have not tried them.

The root becomes stronger and stronger in flavour as the year progresses, with spring roots almost subtle but Christmas roots blisteringly powerful. One sniff of them can reduce grown men to tears. I speak from sobbing experience.

Sweet cicely
(*Myrrhis odorata*)

The sweet-scented, white, frothy flowers of sweet cicely appear in April when few other herbs are showing much sign of life. The foliage is soft and finely cut – and has a distinct aniseed fragrance when crushed – initially creating mounds of ferny leaf before growing tall umbels of flower that last for months. The leaves were used as a natural sweetener for stewed fruit when nearly all fruit was eaten cooked. If left uncut, the flowers become seedheads filled with long, pointed black seeds that can be eaten and are good sprinkled on a salad. However, I cut them back as soon as the flowers have finished and the foliage soon grows back fresh at a time when much of the Herb Garden is beginning to fade. It is a plant of woodland edge, so likes cool, dampish shade and is very happy under our east-facing wall. It grows well from seed although the plants take a year to become large enough to plant out.

Lemon balm
(*Melissa officinalis*)

This is one of the more thuggish of all herbs, edging its way sideways with brutal determination. But it has many saving graces, being bright of leaf, easy to grow and deliciously lemony when eaten raw in salads, with cheese or as a herbal tea. But it is horrid when cooked.

We grow two types, the standard green-leafed *Melissa officinalis* and the variegated *M. o.* 'Aurea'. Both will grow almost anywhere, the roots spreading into otherwise inhospitable corners, but they really thrive in a deep, rich soil. Like ours. I have found that the only way to control its invasive instincts is to chop out at least half every year and throw away (or replant elsewhere) the innermost section, leaving the healthier outside part.

The flowers are very popular with bees so are useful to have on that account alone, however they grow on long stems that can look rather dry and the whole plant loses its zest, so once the novelty of the flowers has worn off (after about three days), I leave a few plants for the bees and cut the whole of the rest right back. They quickly regrow with fresh leaves.

Lemon verbena
(Lippia citriodora)

Lemon verbena is one of the best plants of all to grow for the fragrance of its leaves, which have the freshest, cleanest lemon scent possible and make a deliciously lemony herbal tea. It is a tender, deciduous shrub with lance-shaped bright green leaves and rather small flowers borne in delicate panicles in summer. Unless you live in a very sheltered, warm location, it is best to grow it in a pot so you can enjoy the lemon-zest scent every time you pass and it can be brought in under cover to spend the winter in a frost-free place.

Let it become almost completely dry over winter and start watering again in spring. Cut back the seemingly dead, bare branches in early April and new growth will sprout from the bare wood, creating a plant dense with those intensely fragrant leaves. If given suitable protection it will reach 3m (10ft) and grows very well as a standard.

Because it is not hardy, we grow our lemon verbena in pots that we take into the greenhouse over winter and bring out again after the last frost in May.

Introducing fruit growing

Until the nineteenth century fruit was regarded as the ultimate prize for anyone who had a garden.

Medieval orchards were carefully protected – as well as being the prime setting for romance – whilst seventeenth- and eighteenth-century gardens saw the development of new varieties and novel exotic fruits such as oranges, melons and pineapples introduced from newly conquered colonial territories.

But growing fruit now plays second fiddle to vegetables, an optional extra that gardeners indulge in as a fancy rather than a necessary joy. I suspect that the main reason for this is the development of cold storage. Even in my lifetime, fruits such as oranges – which I remember as a Christmas and New Year treat – have become ubiquitous.

Historically, fruit was a succession of such seasonal treats and would involve a parade of cherries, strawberries, gooseberries, currants, raspberries, apricots, peaches, apples, pears, grapes, quinces, medlars, mulberries, crab apples, plums and damsons, all in their season. Now you can shuffle into any supermarket and have all of these all the time. The price of this constant availability is a familiarity that has bred if not contempt, then a lack of respect and delight.

Growing fruit is fundamentally easy and fun, and the various ways it can be shaped and trained make it ideal for smaller gardens. But the best reason for growing your own fruit is that it chimes with the deep rhythms of the season and provides harvests that taste better and fruitier than any out-of-season 24/7 fruit that money can buy.

Opposite page: The only drawback to growing large standard apples is that the biggest, brightest and ripest apples are invariably at the top of the tree.

Above: 'Ribston Pippin' apples ready for picking. The best way to test ripeness is by gently lifting the fruit and if it does not come away in your hand, it is not ready.

Above right: We store hundreds of apples to eat throughout winter and spring using metal trays in a shed, which keeps them cool and humid and fresh for months.

Top fruit

Top fruit is the term used to describe all fruit that grows on trees, from the familiar apples and pears to apricots, oranges, quinces and medlars.

These trees can be any size or shape and can be trained to form espaliers, cordons, step-overs and fans, or allowed to grow into great magisterial specimens. They are all top fruit.

The hardier fruits are all very easy to grow. Apples, plums, damsons, quinces, crab apples – these are all fruits that more or less look after themselves. Even some of the more particular top fruits like oranges or peaches are not difficult at all.

Fruit looks good too. An apple or pear tree smothered with blossom in spring is a floral extravaganza and then, when hung with ripe fruit, is as decorative as anything you will find in the garden. Fruit trees also make superb specimens and will live hundreds of years.

But the the main advantage of growing your own top fruit, be it on a step-over apple just 30–60cm (12–24in) high or in an orchard filled with mature standards 9m (30ft) tall, is that seasonal ripeness which can be fine-tuned down to a single day or even hour. Your own apples, tested day after day for ripeness, then picked so that the stem snaps gently from the tree and then placed carefully into a basket are more to be treasured than a casual, waxy, vaguely appley wet crunch in the mouth.

Damsons are another favourite. They can easily be made into damson cheese – that thick, almost solid, jam that is so good with cheese or meat and so hard to buy. Damson crumble, damson fool, damson pie – all to be had from one small, scruffy tree, and all damson trees are small and scruffy.

In an age when all fruit is sold in supermarkets wrapped and uniform in size, weight and often tastelessness, the appreciation of variety within a particular type of fruit is both novel and interesting. We proudly enjoy different roses or rhododendrons but tend to lump pears or strawberries together as one homogenous fruity experience when in reality there are hundreds of variations and tastes to discover and enjoy.

When you grow your own fruit you immediately escape the tyranny of idealised size, shape and colour. Two apples of different sizes can taste as good as each other and you can make delicious apple pie from a windfall just by cutting the bruised section out. It also brings a sense of responsibility in not wasting anything – we all know how much fruit (and veg) is wasted because it is not the right shape or size, whereas when you grow your own, everything can be used in some form or another.

I have morello cherries trained as fans and growing against an east wall, and I harvest them in mid-July to make jam. Plums like 'Victoria' and 'Czar' grow better against a cool, shady wall so a

lack of full sun need not be a deterrent to growing top fruit.

Greengages and plums will ripen between early August and mid-September, whilst September and October belong to apples and pears. At last count I had over 40 different varieties of apple and seven different pears, and I treasure them all.

Our final harvest of top fruit, usually deep into October, comes from the three quince trees planted around the pond in the Damp Garden. Each quince will be treasured and used to add fragrance to apple dishes, to stuff chickens for a deliciously medieval mixture of meat and sweet, or to make thick *membrillo* (quince paste) and the thin, translucent quince jelly that is the most delicate and exquisite of all teatime treats.

These morello cherries are destined to be made into jam. Morellos are one of the few fruits that do best grown against a shady wall.

Apples

I love apple trees, their blossom, even love the smell of the wood on a fire. And I love to eat apples in every conceivable way. But some apples are very much better than others. An apple should have an identity. Its taste, texture, shape, colour and aroma must be distinctive. But whatever your choice of variety, any apple is best left on the tree until ripe, then stored carefully – two things that commercial production cannot cater for as that is driven by considerations of longevity of storage, ability to withstand handling and appearance over and above taste.

A basket of 'Ribston Pippin' eating apples ready for storing.

So bland, indistinctive apples are the unfortunate supermarket norm.

When it comes to choosing the varieties of apple, it is rather like planning a wine cellar. You are laying down fruit for the future. Some will take a while to mature whilst others will provide plenty of fruit after just a few years. Some varieties grow into sizeable trees whilst others, regardless of rootstock, never attain more than a scruffy maturity. A good apple tree should last for at least a hundred years and should have apples of a distinct character. That character as well as the tree must be of the locality.

Herefordshire is such a richly appley place that I wanted some varieties that had local meaning as well as merely providing good fruit. Of the 39 different apple varieties I planted in 1997 and 1998, 'Herefordshire Beefing', 'William Crump', 'Doctor Hare's', 'Worcester Pearmain', 'Tydeman's Early Worcester', 'Stoke Edith Pippin', 'Tillington Court', 'Madresfield Court' and 'Crimson Queening' all originated from within 32km (20 miles) of this garden. They are of this soil. The other 30 ranged from the very widespread, such as 'Bramley's Seedling' and 'James Grieve', to the interesting but not particularly local, such as 'Tom Putt' and 'Norfolk Beefing'. (Beefing apples, by the way, were those used for drying. The fruits of beefing apples are particularly low in moisture and were dried in a slow oven and compressed into puck-like tablets before being packed for transportation so British familes could have apples from British orchards whilst ruling the outer reaches of Empire.)

In fact, apples are able to adapt to an amazing breadth and variety of growing environments. If you chuck an apple core from your car into a hedgerow and if its seeds germinate, the 'wilding' apple tree that results will not produce the same apple that you so nonchalantly threw aside. This is because they do not grow true from seed. Every apple contains the genetic material in its seeds for a brand new apple variety that would, amazingly, bear very little resemblance to either parent tree. This heterozygosity accounts for the apple's ability to grow in such a range of locations around the world. Given the permutations of 'appleness' that each tree can potentially produce, sooner or later one crops up that will be adapted to almost any environment that it finds itself in. So varieties have evolved and died out throughout recorded history.

As most apples are extremely bitter and only good for making into cider (which until the nineteenth century was by far the most common way of consuming apples), those that are sweet enough to eat have been jealously preserved – and the only way to do this was by grafting. Apples, like roses, are now always grown on a rootstock (see page 402) as vegetative reproduction is always true. So they are grafted onto the roots of another compatible tree, which is always a type of crab apple. (Pears, on the other hand, are always grafted onto quince rootstock.)

I wanted to have as wide a cross-section of apples as possible, both in eating quality and characteristics, and covering as long a season as possible. In this last respect I don't think that I succeeded very well and

were I to plant another orchard, I would have fewer early varieties, which keep very badly, and would have more later-ripening cultivars chosen for their keeping qualities to provide us with apples in early spring. A few apples go a long way in August and September, and even in October.

My dessert apple varieties:
'Chivers Delight', 'Crimson Queening', 'Jupiter', 'Laxton's Fortune', 'Madresfield Court', 'Mondial Gala', 'Ribston Pippin', 'Rosemary Russet', 'Spartan', 'Stoke Edith Pippin', 'Strawberry Pippin', 'Tydeman's Early Worcester', 'Worcester Pearmain', 'William Crump'

We put crates under every tree and collect the windfalls daily. These cannot be kept but are perfectly good for making juice or eating straightaway, and supply all our apples well into November.

POLLINATION

The first apples, like the cooker 'Arthur Turner' or the eater 'Tydeman's Early Worcester', can be ripe in August, whereas 'Norfolk Beefing' will not be properly ripe until the middle of November. However, if you want to have a spread of ripening times you will also have a spread of blossom, and as no apple is reliably self-fertile, each tree will need a pollinator. Apples are categorised in seven groups according to their flowering times, with Group 1 the earliest and the few very late ones in Group 7.

It is best to make sure that every tree is accompanied by another apple from the same group so that they can cross-pollinate each other. What this means in practice is that an 'Egremont Russet' (Group 2) is unlikely to cross-pollinate with 'King of the Pippins' (Group 5). But 'Ribston Pippin', 'Reverend W. Wilks', 'George Cave' and 'Lord Lambourne', amongst others, will all do fine in conjunction with it. Likewise the 'King of the Pippins' will pollinate happily with 'Newton Wonder', 'William Crump' or 'Mother'.

Adjoining groups largely overlap in flowering so reliably pollinate each other, and a good rule of thumb is that if there is another apple tree within 30m (100ft) in flower the same time as yours for at least three days, then you should get fruit.

A cooker will happily pollinate a dessert apple and in practice, most highly desirable apples come from Groups 2, 3 and 4.

Some apples such as 'Bramley's Seedling' , 'Blenheim Orange' and 'Ribston Pippin' are triploid, which means that they can produce good fruit but poor pollen, so need two other varieties for pollination – one to pollinate them and another to provide pollen to pollinate the first pollinator.

My culinary apple varieties:
'Arthur Turner', 'Blenheim Orange',
'Bramley's Seedling', 'Devonshire
Buckland', 'Glory Of England',
'Hambledon Deux Ans', 'Herefordshire
Beefing', 'Newton Wonder', 'Norfolk
Beefing', 'Reverend W. Wilks',
'Tillington Court'

Pruning

There are two types of pruning. One
is to keep the tree and fruit healthy,
maximise production and curtail
awkward or intrusive growth, and the
other is to train a tree into a particular
shape or size. This latter applies
particularly to fruit trees grown as
espaliers, cordons or fan shapes.

Pruning when the tree is dormant
the lack of leaves is a good guide for this
but in the UK dormancy tends to happen
any time between early December and the
end of February – will stimulate growth
the ensuing spring and summer, and is the
best time to work on fruit grown as trees
or bushes. The exceptions are plums
and cherries which have a nasty tendency
to bleed sap if pruned in winter, so it is
best to only prune them in midsummer
and then only when absolutely
necessary. But for apples, pears and
quinces, the winter months are a good
time to maximise both the health of your
fruit trees and their productivity.

With winter pruning the first reason for
it is to remove any damaged wood or any
that is growing in the wrong place – and
by that I mean across a path or causing
too much shade or starting to damage
another perfectly good branch.

The second reason is to let light and air
into what can otherwise become a very
crowded, dense tangle of branches. For
best fruit production and ease of
harvesting, as well as to create an
attractive garden tree, it best to train trees
to an open structure like a basket or wine
glass, with the trunk as the stem.

Start by dealing with any obvious
damage. Cut back to healthy wood just
above a side branch or bud. If two
branches are crossing and rubbing against
each other, one or both of them will
inevitably develop an open wound that is
a likely entry point for bacterial or fungal
disease, so one of the crossing branches
should be cut back. Before cutting always
try and stand back and assess what the
resulting shape and structure of the tree
will be like after the cut.

Winter pruning will inevitably result in
lots of new shoots, some of which you can
then leave to become future structural
branches but none of which will bear any
fruit for a few years.

Most apple trees are spur-forming.
This means that the fruit is made on the
knobbly side shoots or spurs that grow
laterally from the branches. These take three
or even four years to develop so should not
be cut off. In fact you can usually tell which
ones are ready to bear fruit because they will
have a slight swelling at their base. To aid
their development, anything that you can
prune with secateurs or loppers should
always be cut back to a side bud rather than
flush with the stem of another branch. This
bud will then develop into a fruiting spur.

However, there are tip-bearing varieties
which produce most of their fruit from

Most apples form
their fruit on woody
spurs so unwanted
growth should be
pruned back to just
above these
thickened growths.

the terminal fruit buds of shoots made the previous summer. Cut these off and you will have no fruit next summer! In a tree more than three or four years old, the spurs will be very obvious but some varieties are both tip- and spur-bearers, which is confusing. If in doubt, simply do not prune except to remove crossing or diseased wood. The lists below are by no means inclusive.

Tip-bearers: 'Irish Peach', 'Lady Sudeley', 'Worcester Pearmain'

Tip- and spur-bearers: 'Discovery', 'Gladstone', 'Laxton's Early Crimson', 'Tydeman's Early Worcester', 'Blenheim Orange', 'Bramley's Seedling', 'Hambledon Deux Ans'

Pruning in summer – ideally between the first growth flush and the second, which for me is some time in July – reduces vigour so is useful for curtailing over-long shoots or indeed the overall size of a tree or bush. It is when most trained fruit should be pruned. Sometimes you harness both these growth patterns on the same plant. Espalier fruit are the perfect example. In winter they should be pruned to encourage new shoots in the appropriate places and the harder you cut them back, the stronger and therefore better the growth will be the following summer – albeit growth that is structural rather than fruiting. In July, however, you reduce all upright new growth and any other growth that goes outside the limitations of the parallel rows. In other words, the summer pruning is serving to restrict and fine-tune growth and shape, and the winter pruning promotes growth that can then be organised more exactly in summer.

As you prune, keep standing back to assess the shape of the tree, aiming at creating a permanent structure like an open bowl or goblet.

BASIC RULES OF PRUNING

• Always cut back to something – ideally a side branch or shoot.

• Make your larger cuts at an angle so that water runs off the wound.

• Never paint or cover wounds as this will only seal in possible disease – let the wounds heal naturally.

• Always use sharp tools. This is better for the tree as it makes a cleaner cut and is safer for you as it is much more controllable. A good pair of secateurs and a small sharp saw should cover most eventualities.

• Remember that winter pruning stimulates lots of regrowth but summer pruning curtails it.

Protecting against fungal problems

Ventilation is the best prevention against fungal problems such as powdery mildew, rust or scab (caused by the *Venturia pirina* fungus) that affect both apples and pears. Scab causes brown areas on the fruits and leaves that are typically accompanied by deep cracks and fissures. In a good year this looks unsightly but does not seriously damage the fruit other than reducing its keeping quality but in a bad year, the leaves can fall and the fruits drop prematurely, which exposes the tree to other fungal infections. It improves matters to prune your apples, so thin the branches so that plenty of light and air can get in and through the tree. With smaller trees I start by cutting back everything growing inwards so that the centre is completely open. With larger standards or semi-standards the open spaces between branches can be more localised, but a good rule of thumb is to imagine a bird flying through from one side of the tree to the other without having to break its stride, so to speak.

Canker is another problem affecting both apples and pears. It is caused by the fungus *Neonectria ditissima* syn. *Neonectria galligena* which circles a stem, causing it to crack and die back. You are supposed to cut out all signs of it, going well back into healthy wood and burning all prunings, but my experience is that it invariably comes back, despite the tree regrowing vigorously. The difficulty lies as much in cultivation as anything else. This garden is a low-lying, fundamentally damp site so fungal problems associated with dampness are always a potential.

Training fruit trees

Apples and pears lend themselves very readily to being pruned and trained to grow productively in limited spaces. You can train them as arches over a path, as espaliers to line a path or against a wall (great for improving the ripening of pears), as step-overs along the edge of a bed, with just a single horizontal branch 60–90cm (24–36in) off the ground, and as cordons, which can be upright but are usually trained at 45 degrees against a permanent wire support or against a fence.

The fact that this training is decorative means that training top fruit is doubly attractive to anyone with limited space – and that means just about everyone. It also maximises productivity because it exposes every fruit and bud to as much light as possible and means that the tree puts most of its energy into producing fruit rather than new wood or foliage.

We have cordon apples and pears around the soft-fruit area, step-over apples in the veg garden and espalier pears both on the Mound and in the Cottage Garden. But the truth is that I love the full-blown standards in the Orchard. The very notion of an orchard is a rural luxury but one I am delighted to indulge in. And even in an average garden, one full-size apple or pear will be smothered in blossom in spring, give shade and structure in summer and, provided there is a pollinator nearby, will provide hundreds of fruits in autumn. In every sense of the word it is garden-worthy.

Harvesting and storing

However you grow your apples, whether in an orchard big enough to house chickens, pigs and dozens of varieties, or as a line of step-overs along the edge of a path, the fruit should be properly treasured. Early varieties can and must be eaten more or less as they ripen whilst any that ripen from late September can easily be stored in a cool, dark place. People are out of the habit of storing food because everything is so available all the time – everything that is, except the real thing. Out-of-season fruit never tastes as good as properly ripe fruit in its time because in

If apples are to be stored they must always be picked from the tree and must be handled very carefully to avoid any damage.

order to travel and store well, it is picked unripe. Also, these commercial varieties are chosen not for taste but for their ability to continue looking good and storing well. So do not just grow your own but store your own.

Never be tempted to store even slightly damaged apples, so pick them very carefully, holding the apple in the palm of your hand and twisting gently so that it comes free. Then place rather than throw it into a basket. If it does not come away from the tree easily, then leave it – whatever it looks like.

I do not wrap mine individually before storing although undoubtedly were you to do so – my father always used squares of newspaper – they would keep better. We now store ours in large metal drawers with perforated bottoms (originally used for keeping day-old chicks in a battery farm), which is ideal as the metal stays cold and retains humidity but the drawers are well ventilated. But this was serendipity and for years we stored them on wooden racks which are much easier to source or make. The important thing is to keep them cool, dark and humid but frost-free. Then, right through to next blossom time, you can regularly withdraw them from their lovely cidery vaults to cook them or eat fresh. Every one is a treat.

Rootstocks

The starting point of any apple tree is the right rootstock. This will determine the size, vigour and characteristics of the tree although will not affect the fruit. In other words you can have exactly the same apple fruiting on trees of very different

size, shape or vigour. This means that depending on your soil, location and how you wish to train the tree, the choice of rootstock is really significant.

The top part, the graft, determines the fruit and leaves, and the bottom bit, the rootstock, will determine the size and vigour of the tree. So an M27 rootstock will never produce a tree much bigger than 1.8m (6ft) tall even if it lived to be a hundred years old. Likewise, exactly the same variety on an M25 rootstock is unsuitable for a small space and will always be trying to become a big tree however much you prune it.
The following are the characteristics of the common rootstocks.

• **M27** (very dwarfing). Ideal for containers, but needs rich soil. Good for very vigorous cultivars, especially triploids. Needs support throughout its life.

• **M9** (dwarfing). Makes for a small tree, 1.8 2.5m (6 8ft) tall. The fruit tends to be large and ripens earlier than identical varieties on bigger trees. Good for cordons and containers but needs rich soil.

• **M26** (semi-dwarfing). Will tolerate poorer soil than M9 but is a slow starter. Needs permanent staking. Can be used for espalier and cordons on good soils.

• **MM106** (semi-dwarfing). Medium-sized tree that grows and crops well on most soils. Suitable for half-standards (with a clear trunk of 1.2m/4ft) or large bush-shaped trees. Crops heavily. Best for espalier or cordon trees in poorish soils.

• **MM111** (vigorous). Ideal for smaller standard or half-standard trees, can resist potash deficiency in the soil and is notably drought-resistant.

• **M25** (very vigorous). Best for large standards, especially if grown in grass.

Planting fruit trees

The best way to ensure a good start and long life for the tree is to dig a square hole that is at least 1m (3ft) wide but no more than one spade, or 23cm (9in), deep. Break up the bottom of the hole, and the sides too if they are compacted, but do not add any manure or compost. Plant the tree in the centre of the hole so that the roots are just below the surface but covered and the soil firmed very well around them. Then stake it diagonally so that the support is facing the prevailing wind. This stake should be removed after three years.

Finally, water very well and then mulch thickly with manure or compost. Keep the planting hole weed-free and mulched for at least three years and preferably longer.

We store our apples in metal trays in a shed. This keeps them cool but frost-free and retains humidity so they do not shrivel. We check them regularly to remove any that are bad but on the whole they last well into spring.

Pears

Apples have become homogenised to the point where they are largely ubiquitous, seasonless symbols of the 'real' home-grown thing. But pears, so easily coupled with apples as a kind of sibling fruit, resist this kind of treatment. That is not to say that you cannot get a bland, tasteless fruit masquerading as a pear, but it is always evidently a sham. No good pear is anything less than spectacular. A ripe pear is so explicit, so unfakeable, that everything else has to be set aside to savour the moment.

The pleasure from devouring a properly ripe pear is not just a culinary experience but sensual in every possible way. You have to cast aside inhibitions and thoughtless consumption, and dedicate yourself to the very physical moment. A ripe pear has slippery, silky flesh whose honeyed juices coat your fingers and dribble down your chin. Fingers should be licked. Lips smacked. The remnants of flesh on the peeled skin (and a good pear should always be peeled) should be nibbled of their last traces. The sweetness is intense but not cloying and the irreducible pearness of it deeply and lastingly satisfying.

The chances of buying this experience are fetchingly remote, in this country at least. By far the best place to go for it is your garden.

A standard pear tree is hugely impressive, as big as a large ash or beech, but can also easily be trained to grow as an espalier, cordon, fan or a small bush. Pears can be fantastically long-lived and hardy, especially if grown on their own

Opposite page:
Espalier pears provide fruity fences to both terraces of the Mound.

A pair of 'Concorde' pears – fully grown but not yet ripe.

POLLINATION

The principles of pollination are the same for both apples and pears. They are placed in groups according to their period of flowering. Obviously only two trees that are simultaneously in flower can perform successfully – although 'Conference' is, to a degree, self-pollinating but will always fruit better if it has another pollinator. So 'Conference' and 'Williams' Bon Chrétien' are both in Group 3 and 'Beth' and 'Doyenné du Comice' are in Group 4. So you need another tree from the same or an adjacent group that will flower at the same time. In fact there are only four groups of pear, with an overlap from one to another, so any two from adjacent groups will pollinate each other and the chances of accidental pollination from another pear in the vicinity are quite high.

The best way to ripen a small number of pears is to place them on a sunny windowsill where they will ripen in a matter of days.

roots, although modern trees are invariably grown on a quince rootstock. This produces a smaller, earlier-fruiting tree, with Quince 'A' moderately vigorous and Quince 'C' more dwarfing.

I have a – now huge – perry pear growing in the Orchard, that produces thousands of tiny, rock-hard fruits that are inedible but which make very good cider. I also have two groups of espalier pears. There is the double row of 'Doyenné du Comice' espaliers in what is now the Cottage Garden. They were amongst the first things to be planted in the garden back in the spring of 1993 but are now chronically afflicted by canker and bear very little fruit. I should remove them really but their structure is so much part of the garden that I can forgive their lack of productivity.

Then there are the other espaliers on the Mound – 'Doyenné du Comice', 'Williams' Bon Chrétien', 'Concorde', 'Conference' and 'Beth' planted on both terraces – which are much more productive. There is also a large 'Concorde' in the Paradise Garden which is now about 20 years old and bears a lot of fruit but which suffers badly from brown rot (see opposite). Finally, I have a 'Concorde' growing in the traditional manner, trained against the south-facing wall of the house.

Due to scab, my espaliered 'Doyenné du Comice' are as shrivelled and gnarled as a sunbathing Miami matron

Pruning

The pruning regime for pears is very similar to apples. I give my espalier pears a summer prune sometime in July, removing at least two-thirds of all new growth. This stops the tree – and especially one that is trained – from putting all its energy into getting bigger at the expense of fruit bearing. Pears are produced on spurs (see page 399) and these need to be thinned so that they do not overlap or crowd each other. I do this any time between Christmas and March as well as cutting back weak shoots that I wish to become branches, which encourages renewed vigour.

Protecting against fungal problems

Pears have been having a bad time of it over the past run of our cool, wet summers that climate change is making the norm. Although they are tough trees – hardier than apples in most cases – the fruit needs sun to ripen. And all my trees – and I have about 30 – are afflicted to some degree with brown rot, scab and canker.

Brown rot is a fungus called *Monilinia laxa* that manifests itself with unbroken chocolate-brown areas on the skin. The pear is then irretrievable. It needs an entry point into the fruit caused by a crack, a bird or an insect and as it will not afflict unblemished fruits, you can remove any that have signs of it to reduce the spread.

Scab is caused by the *Venturia pirina* fungus (see page 401) and canker by the fungus *Neonectria ditissima* syn. *Neonectria galligena* (see page 401). 'Concorde' seems to be more resistant, as is 'Conference',

whereas my espaliered row of 'Doyenné du Comice' are as shrivelled and gnarled as a sunbathing Miami matron.

Assuming the fruit come through these various maladies, autumn is their season. The first to ripen here are 'Williams' Bon Chrétien' which I pick in mid-September, and the last is 'Conference' which is rarely ready before we reach October.

Harvesting and storing

Always harvest pears by carefully lifting the fruit until it is horizontal. Don't prod or poke it. Just cup its curves in your hand and gently lift. If it does not come away in your hand, then it is not ready. The harvested pears are not yet ripe so should be stored in a cool, dark, preferably rather moist place to ripen.

They should be checked by carefully pressing at the flesh around the stalk. It is no use prodding and pushing a pear to test ripeness because all you will do is bruise the flesh, leaving a mushy wound beneath the skin. Pears ripen from the inside out so that the flesh immediately beneath the skin is the last to be ready. You must be gentle. If I press my thumb at the base of the pear there will be a slight yielding. You want to eat it as soon as there is any softness to it at all. And never bite into it like an apple. That is barbaric. Sit. Get a clean plate and if possible a beautiful knife. Consider and admire the pear before you. Cut it into quarters, always peel it (not for the sake of your health but because the tough skin detracts from the perfect texture), slither the core away and eat the firm juiciness whilst surrendering completely to the moment and revelling in its unexpurgated sensuality.

Harvesting pears is a delicate business. Gently lift the fruit to the horizontal and if it comes away cleanly then it is ready. Pears bruise very easily so handle them like eggs, and store them somewhere cool.

Damsons and plums

When we came here there were damson and plum trees growing in the shelter of the curved wall in amongst the building rubble of what was to become the Walled Garden. The southern boundary of this piece of garden was made up of a hedge of damsons and, other than the large hazel growing beyond the back door, these were the only indicators of 'gardening' that survived the last occupant. However, I found out that the Walled Garden was the vegetable patch for the farm and obviously damsons, and to a certain extent plums, were nurtured carefully.

There is some debate as to whether these 'Shropshire Prune' damsons are true damsons or plums, or a hybrid of both. Either way, they are delicious.

Damsons, greengages, bullaces and myrobalans are really just forms of plum, although they tend to be treated separately. All members of the plum family like our rich, heavy soil, although only damsons, which are by far the toughest of them, really relish our strong winds and very cold snaps of winter weather.

The damson is one of the first fruit trees to come into blossom, following on just after the blackthorn in late March. The leaves turn an amazing yellow in September but are the first to fall.

Damsons are not difficult to grow. They will come true from a stone (thus a stone from a 'Bradley's King' will produce a 'Bradley's King' tree) and will bear fruit within fifteen years. Alternatively, one can buy a tree grafted onto a rootstock that will control the amount of growth. Unlike apples, whose rootstocks are named with bureaucratic anonymity, these all have names. 'Pixy' is a dwarfing rootstock, so is suitable for growing a damson in a container. 'St Julien A' is a larger rootstock, making a tree up to 3.5m (12ft) and is also used for peaches and apricots. 'Brompton' is a vigorous rootstock and used for standards and half-standards.

All my damsons are on 'Brompton' rootstocks as I want the biggest trees possible – although no damson ever grows very large. I planted 'Shropshire Prune' – which is a very plum-like damson – in the Orchard and it is a fine example of the damson's ability to crop extremely well every year with almost total neglect. It is a variety known since the sixteenth century and is perhaps the nearest taste we can have to the fruit of the Tudor dining table.

Damson jam is the richest and best, and damson cheese is very good with lamb or game as well as with bread and butter and, ironically, is also delicious with a strong cheese. We collect the fruit from our trees primarily to make damson cheese. For the uninitiated, this has nothing to do with any dairy product but is a very thick, very intense conserve. Damsons also work well in pies and crumbles and are also delicious on their own, stewed. They are one of the few fruits better preserved in a Kilner jar than frozen – the rich red fruits swimming in crimson liqueur are an ornament.

The plums burst into blossom just after the damson, overlapping by a few days, the baton passing from hedgerow to orchard. Plum blossom sits on the trees thinly, measured as much by the sky between the flowers as by the massing of the blooms themselves, and a spring sky never looks so pure a blue as it does when seen between the flowers of plum blossom.

For many years the 'Oullins Gage' I planted in the Walled Garden grew healthily but bore no fruit, but about three years ago – 20 years after planting – it suddenly delivered a fine harvest and has done so since, giving delicious golden-fleshed plums with green skins in July. As a rule greengages do best in well-drained, fertile soil, with plenty of warmth and water, and are more picky about their growing conditions than your average plum. But we can over-fuss about these things. Soil and aspect are rarely reasons not to grow something as long as it is reasonably hardy. Pruning greengages is the same as any plum. Best not to unless you have to and then only in summer. However,

they do train perfectly well against a wall, either as fans or in a herringbone pattern.

We know this green-skinned plum as the greengage not through any connection with its appearance but because in 1724, an English Catholic priest called John Gage, who was studying in Paris, sent some young trees to his brother Sir William Gage, who lived at Hengrave Hall just outside Bury St Edmunds. However, the trees lost their labels in transit so the gardener planted them and labelled them 'Green Gages' after his master. The name stuck (the *Oxford English Dictionary* dates its usage to 1759) and has endured to this day.

Plums are all liable to a handful of annoying – but not serious – diseases and attacks, like silver leaf, brown rot (see page 406), the plum leaf-curling aphid and the plum moth. Damsons simply take no notice whilst the plums look out of sorts but produce fruit every year. The only rule that is worth observing is to prune during the growing season to avoid the cuts being infected with silver leaf or canker (see page 401), and to prune only to thin or correct a tangled growth. If in doubt, they are best left well alone.

Although good raw, we use most of our damsons to make damson cheese, which is like the Spanish *membrillo* in consistency and is superb with meat or cheese.

Figs

Figs are a member of the mulberry family and we have four trees that regularly crop well. They are all 'Brown Turkey' – which is the hardiest variety – and the fruit, which starts to ripen at the beginning of August and carries on into October, is uniformly delicious. By mid- to late summer a fig tree will be carrying three separate crops. There will be large figs that, in the case of my 'Brown Turkey' variety will have chocolate-coloured skins and deep scarlet within, and will be teardrop-shaped and the size of a large plum. In a normal year there will also be rather smaller fruits that will be rock-hard, still green and very unripe even at the end of a long summer. Finally, for the third crop, look closely at the end of the shoots and you will also see tiny little fruitlets the size of a pinhead to a small pea. These will spend the winter on the tree before growing ready for harvesting twelve months later.

The smaller, unripe green figs, although looking promising, are destined to ripen in January or February and any that are not edible by early October should be removed from the tree and composted. This might seem like an appalling waste but not only will they never ripen and become edible, but their presence and continued growth take energy away from next year's minute fruits that will ripen.

If I had more south-facing walls I would be tempted to cast my fig net a bit wider and grow 'White Marseilles' or even 'Rouge de Bordeaux', although I fear our weather would be too harsh for it even with a south-facing wall. They need sunshine for the fruit to ripen but fig trees are tougher than you might think and can take all but the harshest cold – I lost a couple in 2010 when the temperature dropped to -18°C (0°F), but by and large they are very resilient.

Figs can happily be hard-pruned to grow in a pot or against a wall or fence. The best time to do this is in April and the only thing to bear in mind is that they produce their fruit on the previous year's growth, so any material you cut off will be replaced by shoots that will not carry fruit until the following year.

They do need good drainage and a certain amount of restriction or impoverished soil will improve fruiting. However, although everyone knows about restricting the roots of figs to make them fruit more, most people underestimate their need for water. If your figs are dropping off prematurely it is nearly always because they are too dry, so give them a good soak once a week and a generous mulch each spring. Prune off overhanging leaves shading the fruit and with a decent wind behind you – and some sunshine – you should have a lovely figgy harvest.

Our quince trees (along with the 'Tai Haiku' cherry) line the back of the pond in the Damp Garden. Quinces do better in damp conditions than most other fruit trees.

Quinces

I have three mature quinces – 'Leskovac', 'Portugal' and 'Vranja' – growing around the pond. In fact they started life in what are the now the Grass Borders but I moved them and the positioning of the pond was determined by them – I didn't want to move them again, let alone lose them. Quinces are magisterial fruits with a gloriously intense floral aroma. Training them in any way is hopeless – they like to grow as a squiggle of branches – but they can be pruned both to give them air and to make the most of the artistic expression of their inevitable contortions. 'Portugal' is the smallest of mine but was the quickest to grow and produce fruit. 'Vranja' and 'Champion' are both tall and 'Leskovac' is the most reliable cropper.

They will cope with extreme heat and a surprising degree of damp – certainly tolerating much wetter roots than apples or pears would. They are one of the last blossoms to appear in spring (but can be early and get caught at the end of April) and one of the last fruits to harvest, often continuing into November.

All quinces are completely hardy – in fact they must have a period of cold in order to flower and therefore fruit properly – and all are self-fertile, so you can grow a solitary tree and still get a crop of fruit every year, although cropping will always be more reliable if you have two trees.

As they are members of the rose family (along with apples, pears, medlars, rowans and hawthorns) they can get fireblight but this is very uncommon in this country although far more prevalent in America. However, there is a quince blight, which been prized so highly throughout history. Until the nineteenth century all raw fruit was regarded with suspicion and it was considered much healthier to cook it before eating. This meant that a quince was no more trouble to prepare and eat than an apple and it had equal billing with apples in any well-stocked orchard from Roman times right up to the eighteenth century. Once cooked, quinces impart their fabulous scent to any dish. The Persians, for example, have used them with vegetable and meat dishes for thousands of years. Simply add one quince to a dish of stewed apple or an apple pie to see how it transforms it into something really special.

Quinces look like a handsome hybrid between an apple and a pear but are rock-hard when ready to pick and, in the northern hemisphere at least, are only eaten cooked.

can make the leaves flop and blotch brown, and makes the tree look very unhappy, but it will not kill it and the tree can completely recover for the following year.

Their blossom, which is a delicious pink emerging from a tight-pointed bud and opening into a simple-petalled perfect flower, is the best of any fruit. The fruit vary in shape and size according to variety, but all start out life greeny yellow, with some ripening to gold and others becoming an intense lemon colour. All look like a hybrid between an apple and a pear with some, like 'Vranja' or 'Champion', distinctly pear-shaped whilst others like 'Leskovac' are almost round. Unlike apples and pears, all – in this country at least – are rock-hard when ripe and cannot be eaten raw.

This need to cook them accounts both for their fall from popularity in modern times and also for the way that they have

Cherries

All cherries like well-drained soils and do well on limestone and chalk. In principle they will grow wherever you have a healthy pear tree, as they like the same conditions. They will need watering when young but cast a pretty dry, heavy shade when mature, with very greedy, shallow roots that will vein any lawn with wooden lumps, so not much will thrive under them unless you have very rich soil.

My two wild cherries – *Prunus avium*, or gean – in the Coppice produce a mass of small fruits but all are eaten by the birds and the trees have now become large, with a squirrel's dray in one and owls roosting in the other.

I have recently planted two morello cherries against an east-facing wall and they are one of the few fruits ('Victoria' plums are another) that will successfully ripen on

Morello cherries grow happily on a shady north- or east-facing wall and make wonderful jam or tarts. Unfortunately the birds love them as much as we do so they must be netted or else every one will be eaten overnight.

a shady wall. They have a delicate, pure white flower that studs the fan-trained branches like little floral rosettes.

The morello is one of the oldest of all cherries. It originated from the wild *Prunus cerasus* which comes from the area around the Caspian and Black Seas. Cerasus was a settlement on the Black Sea coast, which is now the modern Turkish town of Giresun. Morello cherries are sour so used for cooking and preserving rather than eating raw, although a hybrid between sour morello cherries and sweet cherries was made in the mid-seventeenth century to create 'Dukes' which were very popular.

Unlike most sweet cherries, morellos are self-fertile so will reliably crop, and the fruit for the following year is borne on the current year's growth, so it should be hard-pruned around the time that the fruits are harvested in mid- to late summer. However, a word of warning – like all fruiting cherries, they are

irresistible to birds so need netting as soon as they start to turn red otherwise there will be nothing to harvest by the time that they ripen.

Mulberries

I added a black mulberry (*Morus nigra*) to the Orchard a few years ago. Mulberries live to a grand old age and I have a vision of its spreading branches dropping fruit onto the grass below a couple of hundred years from now. The mulberry has been very slow to get growing and can take up to ten years before producing a single fruit, but once established will grow fast and make a lovely gnarled tree full of character within 20 years.

They are easy to grow and also bear a harvest of delicious mulberries that are rarely available in shops. These are good raw, stewed and made into jam. Their only downside is that their juice stains almost indelibly. The trees are very tough and almost invariably recover when cut right back or blown over, the branches rooting where they fall into the soil. They are also one of the last of all trees to lose their leaves in autumn.

The fruits are best harvested by letting them fall onto grass that has been mown short and then collecting them up, which is why I planted my mulberry in the Orchard rather than in a border. But they are thirsty, hungry trees so don't grow grass right up to the trunk for at least the first ten years so they can get established. Leave a metre radius of bare soil that should be generously mulched every autumn and not allowed to dry out.

The leaves of the white mulberry (*M. alba*) are the preferred food of the silkworm and it has thus been an important tree wherever silk is spun and woven. However, the British climate is better suited to the black mulberry, which the silkworms shun. This led to a disastrous planting of nearly a million 'wrong' mulberries by James I (in fact, Buckingham Palace was the site of one of the first mulberry orchards in the country) but left thousands of these marvellous trees in the gardens of Jacobean houses.

Medlars

At the same time as planting the mulberry in the Orchard I planted a couple of medlars in the Cottage Garden – where I already have four dessert apple trees and four crab apples growing in the borders. This is my second go at growing medlars.

I had a pair of trees in the Walled Garden but they suffered badly from fireblight and I removed them. Hopefully these two will have better ventilation and they seem quite happy, if yet to produce any of their brown, unattractive-looking yet rather delicious fruit.

A hundred years ago you might well have rounded off a good autumnal dinner with a glass of port and a few bletted medlars, although now they are thoroughly out of fashion. ('Bletting' is an odd word, only used, as far as I am aware, in association with medlars. It is lifted straight from the French *blettir*, meaning to make soft.)

The truth is that medlars are an acquired taste. If you really cannot bring yourself to eat them raw, try medlar jelly, which is delicious. It is hard to set and the addition of pectin robs it of its idiosyncratic flavour, but lemon juice should do the trick. There is no need to blet them to make the jelly – collecting them from the ground when they are still hard works fine.

The trees are rather like quince in that they are smallish and gnarled, growing in an unruly tangle. 'Royal' has small fruits as does 'Nottingham' and both are supposed to be the most tasty. Despite these cultivated varieties, medlars are ancient and can still be found growing wild in hedgerows and woodland, with their large white flowers as fine as any fruit blossom in spring.

And if that does not convince you, medlars have excellent autumn colour and never get too big, so they make good ornamental trees for small gardens.

Top: Mulberries ripen to a deep burgundy.

Bottom: Medlars have a leathery skin and are traditionally eaten 'bletted', or slightly rotten. Sounds bad, but tastes good.

Soft fruit

I had to go through old photos to remind myself where the soft fruit was grown 20 years ago because since then it has moved at least three times, although now we have a dedicated soft fruit garden in the Orchard.

I suspect that this shuffling of locations has been as much to do with our general attitude to soft fruit as to horticultural necessity. Many of us have a tendency to relegate it behind top fruits like apples and pears, let alone vegetables and herbs. It is too often treated as an optional extra rather than a mainstay of the garden, and I suspect I have been as guilty of that as anyone.

But I love raspberries, gooseberries, blackcurrants, redcurrants and blueberries, whilst a good strawberry – although much rarer and almost impossible to buy – is delicious. To have really good soft fruit, eaten in season and perfectly ripe, with varieties chosen for their taste rather than their ability to travel and look alluring, you must grow them yourself. As it happens, this is very easy to do. They are generally very robust, forgiving plants.

The last port of call for our soft fruit was as part of the Cottage Garden, since currant and gooseberry bushes work in well with flowers of all kinds. But in 2017, as part of the general development of the Orchard Beds, we made a brand-new area – digging into the virgin grassland where an apple tree had blown down and left a space – dedicated to soft fruit. The idea was to combine all the different fruitiness together in one place rather than keep shunting it off to odd corners of the garden.

This new(ish) area has a row each of summer- and autumn-fruiting raspberries, a row of blackcurrants along with redcurrant and whitecurrant bushes, and some freestanding blackberry bushes. We have blueberries growing in pots filled with ericaceous compost (made from composted bracken) and around the outside we have a fence made up of cordon gooseberries as well as cordon apples and pears. For the first time since we began the garden back in 1992, it feels as though the soft fruit has found its true home.

I used to have a fruit cage. This was a hugely expensive affair, the framework made from aluminium over which the net was draped. But, against advice, I left the net up in winter and there was a light snowfall that froze hard. The result was that some of the aluminium frame buckled irreparably under the weight of the frozen netting. It was an expensive lesson.

Since then, we have netted fruits as needed rather than use a general, permanent set-up. In fact, we have found that although blackbirds do take raspberries, they always leave enough for us so we don't bother to net those at all. Blackcurrants and

Opposite page: Tying in the new canes of summer-fruiting raspberries for next year's harvest. This is a job done in late summer, immediately after the fruit have finished and just as the autumn-fruiting varieties start cropping.

redcurrants will all be pillaged when ripe, so I construct a very basic framework from canes and drape a net over those, whilst strawberries also need protection as they ripen. Then, when the fruit has been harvested, all the protection comes off.

Strawberries

When I was a child at boarding school, my parents used to bring strawberries for my birthday, at the end of the first week of July. This was always a high-quality treat – but the quantity was very variable. Some years the crop was almost over and others barely begun – but if my birthday and the season combined to hit the sweet spot, then my parents brought trays of them and I became the most popular boy in the school when they were shared out at teatime.

Home-grown strawberries eaten perfectly ripe taste better than any you can ever buy.

But back then – in the 1960s – strawberries were always an archetypal treat because they were so seasonal and that season was so short. Nowadays we are saturated with strawberries. Every day of the year you can eat fruits that look like strawberries and smell just like them but taste – well, mostly of a mushy nothing. No other soft fruit varies so dramatically in quality from the divine to the disappointing, so if you want to eat strawberries that taste as good as folk and marketing lore are extolling, you must grow your own, wait until June for your harvest and eat them as they should be eaten, still warm from the sun. Certainly a strawberry should never venture into the chilly depths of a fridge if it is not be ruined forever.

But none of this is the fault of the strawberry. A really good, fresh strawberry accompanied by single cream or with a sprinkling of pepper is still a wonderful treat.

The maincrop strawberry starts to fruit in June and is all done by the end of July or earlier. It is essential to choose your varieties with care and avoid at all costs the commercial types like 'Elsanta' that are chosen for their robustness for handling, for storage and for aroma – which promises a lot but invariably fails to deliver. This year I am growing the French Provençal variety 'Gariguette' which is classed as 'mid-season'. The point about a strawberry like 'Gariguette' is that you are unlikely to buy it because it does not keep or travel well. The fruits are only at their best for about a day or two. This is also true of another superb old variety, 'Cambridge Favourite'. But this is all the more reason to grow them because you hardly ever come across them in a shop or even restaurant.

Perpetual or remontant strawberries ripen between July and October, taking over when the conventional summer crops have finished. I grow 'Aromel' and 'Mara des Bois' both of which crop well and have a lovely flavour.

The small but delicious alpine strawberry (*Fragaria vesca alpina*) fruits constantly from June right through to October in a good year. This is easily grown from seed and makes a good decorative edging, although it can be a bit invasive – we now let it run freely along the bottom of our hedges and it has become a deliciously tasting weed. I have some 'Mignonette' plants which grow strongly for an alpine and produce some of the most fragrant fruit of all, and 'Four Seasons' is also easy to grow from seed.

Although alpine strawberries can only be propagated from seed, it is easier to propagate maincrop varieties by taking runners. You simply peg down the tendril either side of the immature plant and about a month later, cut the stem either side of the pegs and lift the rooted plantlet, which can either be grown in a pot or planted out into a new bed. To avoid transferring disease or viruses, it is best to take runners from one-year-old plants, after their first harvest.

Strawberries grow best on rich soil but whatever soil you have, the addition of garden compost or manure will improve both the quality and quantity of the harvest. The best point at which to put in first-time plants is late summer, which will give them time to establish so that they

will produce a crop the following June. The young plants should be put in at 45–60cm (18–24in) spacing to allow them to develop fully, in rows or blocks with the base of the central crowns at soil level.

Strawberry plants are at their peak in their second and third years and the chance of them developing viruses increases as they age, so it is best to ditch plants after their third harvest and put them onto the compost heap. Hence the need to take runners. To avoid soil-borne viruses you should always plant into a fresh site that has not grown strawberries for at least four years.

The fruits should be kept off the ground to avoid slugs and rotting, so tuck straw or a cardboard or felt mat around each plant. Blackbirds love strawberries and are drawn to them like magnets as soon as they begin to ripen, so a net is essential once any of the green fruits start to turn red. But the netting can be a temporary affair, held in place by canes and upturned plant pots, and can be easily rolled back for picking.

Once the last strawberries have been collected, cut the foliage off to within about 7.5cm (3in) above the crown. New foliage will appear before autumn but most energy will go into the roots ready for next spring's regrowth. A mulch of garden compost after this annual cut-back is the only feeding that strawberries need.

Growing your own strawberries means you can have delicious varieties that you rarely see in the shops

Raspberries

A good raspberry is my favourite of all the fruits in my garden. I love the dollops of juiciness beneath the taut skin and its just-enough toughness that survives careful picking but easily explodes inside the mouth. I would not want to eat them every day and indeed probably only do so a couple of dozen times a year. But each of those times, even when idly standing between the rows of canes, gently pulling the pink fruits off their bleached cone of stalk before popping them into my mouth whilst reaching instantly for another, holds firm in the memory with the intensity of a wonderful meal. Like all soft fruit, raspberries must be eaten perfectly ripe to be appreciated for what they are, and they are only in this state for a day or so at the most, so are worth any amount of time, space and effort to grow them at home.

There are two kinds of raspberry – summer- and autumn-fruiting. Summer raspberries fruit between the end of June and August, and autumn ones overlap for a week or so in August and then, depending on the weather, can be picked well into October. For summer I grow 'Malling Jewel', an old-fashioned variety with large fruits and more modest growth, 'Glen Moy', which is an abundant early cropper and has no prickles on the canes, and 'Glen Ample', which also is prickle-free and crops in mid-season with large fruits. My autumn raspberries are 'Autumn Bliss', which are delicious and 'All Gold', which is a yellow sport of 'Autumn Bliss'.

Although they like moist air and plenty of rainfall, raspberries hate sitting in cold, wet soil, so in our heavy, wet ground, I dig a good trench mixed with plenty of organic material, backfill it and plant the raspberries on the surface, mounding the soil over them rather than burying them. This will improve drainage and avoid the risk of the plants standing over winter in a puddle of water.

Summer-fruiting raspberries need permanent support. This could be a trellis or fence and in New Zealand I saw them supported by espalier apples, but the simplest and best way to hold them up is to drive a couple of 2.5m (8ft) posts in the ground, repeating the posts every 1.8m (6ft) and stretching three strands of thick wire between them, spaced about 60cm (24in) apart which new growth can be tied into after pruning the old canes in late summer. The support should be erected after the ground has been prepared but before planting to avoid any risk of damaging the plants.

New plants should be set in the ground vertically at their 60cm (24in) spacing. As soon as healthy new growth appears the following spring, the original canes should be pruned to ground level. This means that there will be no fruit in the first year from summer raspberries, which carry next year's berries on this year's new canes, but it will ensure vigorous growth of a number of fresh new canes over the summer, which will then bear the following season's fruit.

From their second year, summer raspberries need to have a particular pruning regime. It is a job to do in stages. First, as soon as there are no more berries being produced – usually mid- to late

August in this garden – the brown canes that bore that summer's fruit can be cut down to the ground, leaving the fresh new green canes standing. These will carry next summer's crop. Then reduce the canes from each plant to a maximum of five strong, straight growths, cutting any others to ground level.

Finally, the canes that remain need tying in to the support to hold them secure for the coming year. The end result will look beautifully neat and trained and – together with the autumn-fruiting varieties – they need no more attention other than a generous mulch in the spring.

Autumn-fruiting raspberries are planted in exactly the same manner but a little further apart as they make bushes rather than upright canes and bear their berries on the current year's growth. This means that their pruning regime is different. Once they have lost the last of their leaves – around Christmas – everything above ground can be cut back to the ground ready for the new, fruit-bearing growth the following spring.

Both types hate very dry weather so a really thick mulch each spring will keep the shallow roots cool and moist. This mulch should not be mushroom compost as raspberries much prefer slightly acidic conditions and mushroom compost is made with added lime, so inclines to be alkaline. We find that a really thick layer of shredded garden prunings works very well.

As with strawberries, picking a few fresh raspberries to eat whilst still warm from the sun with lashings of cool cream is one of life's great luxuries.

Gooseberries

Raw, stewed, in a pie, crumble, fool or ice cream, gooseberries are one of the least appreciated and best of all fruits. I adore them. So when I first planted my batch of assorted gooseberry bushes – 'Invicta', 'Langley Gage' and 'Whitesmith', with a couple of the red-fruited 'Whinham's Industry' – I treated them with reverence and respect. Their planting holes were lavished with manure and compost, they were sheltered from the nasty bit of wind that tears through that corner of the garden, and each March, after I had carefully pruned them, I mulched them with liberal amounts of compost. In short, they were loved.

All this care was repaid with mildew and sawfly on a pestilential scale. They grew vigorously and produced lots of fruit but not a single bush escaped fungal or insect attack. This went on for a few years whilst I responded by lavishing even more care on them – which was the worst thing possible.

I wrote about this problem in a Sunday newspaper and received a letter from an old lady who said that her father's gooseberries were his pride and joy. Not only did they eat enormous gooseberry pies every year, but he regularly won first prize for them at the local show. His secret was neglect. The bushes were in a shady corner near the back door. Once a year her mother emptied a bucket of wood ash over the bush and her father pruned it with shears, but it never had any other attention. Her letter closed with the advice, 'Remember, they like it tough.'

So I moved my ailing bushes to a new site that was exposed to that wind which howls across the fields. I converted a dozen of the prickliest bushes to cordons, so the air could get up and round them and they would be easier to pick. I added nothing to the soil they were planted in and gave them a mulch of ash from the fire in spring.

Things improved from the first year. Sawfly hate wind so on a windy site, the adults will move on to a sheltered spot to lay their eggs. Likewise a cordon, pruned back hard to spurs just 5 7.5cm (2–3in) long each spring, offers no shelter for them.

I now am growing my gooseberries as bushes in a corner of the Cottage Garden and as cordons around the shadier perimeter of the New Soft Fruit Garden, within the Orchard. These are new plants, just a couple of years old, and yet are very happy and very productive.

The mould that all gooseberries are prone to is American mildew (*Podosphaera mors-uvae*), which thrives on moist, stagnant air and manifests itself as a grey powder on the leaves and fruit. There is little one

Opposite page and left: Cordon gooseberries take up very little space and are pruned to a single stem that is tied at an angle to a permanent support of canes and wires.

Prune gooseberries so they have a central stem – this allows air to get underneath, thus avoiding mould

can do about the moisture, but wind helps more than anything else to keep it at bay. I have pruned all my bushes to have a central stem or 'leg' about 30cm (12in) high, which allows the air to get under the bush. I also prune all inward-growing growth just as new leaves start to show, which maximises light and air into the centre to both aid ripening of the fruit and inhibit sawfly activity. It is also much easier to pick from an open, goblet-pruned bush or from a cordon.

Once all the fruit has been picked, I prune the bushes lightly, reducing fresh new growth by about a third and ensuring the plants remain open to the wind.

Gooseberries take well from hardwood cuttings taken in autumn from straight, new growth, so if you plan to take cuttings, leave the strongest new shoots unpruned.

Sawfly

Sawfly are an ever-present liability with gooseberries and redcurrants. There are three species – the common gooseberry sawfly (*Nematus ribesii*), the lesser gooseberry sawfly (*Nematus leucotrochus*) and the pale gooseberry sawfly (*Pristiphora pallipes*). All lay their eggs at the base of the bush, as near to the centre as possible. The overwintering pupae hatch in April and lay eggs on the young leaves, placing them in rows parallel to the main vein. When the small, caterpillar-like larvae hatch, they proceed to eat as many of the leaves as possible, stripping them back to the midribs so that ghostly tatters are all that remain. As they munch – with astonishing hunger, stripping a good-sized bush in 24 hours from the inside out – the first signs of them are usually after they have reached the outer parts of the bush and most of the damage has already been done.

There are usually about three cycles in a summer. The larvae can be knocked or shaken off the bushes but prevention is the best cure and exposure to wind, and pruning or training so that there is a good airflow within and around the gooseberry bush is the best prevention.

Blackcurrants

Blackcurrants (*Ribes nigrum*) were introduced to Britain in the seventeenth century by John Tradescant the same time as the 'Red Dutch' redcurrant. However, they were restricted almost entirely to medicinal uses, to treat gallstones, coughs and chest infections, and had none of the redcurrant's culinary popularity. The Victorians did try and breed bigger berries and there was apparently one variety that had currants as big as gooseberries – although it certainly does not exist today. But it seems that the sole aim was to increase the volume of health-giving juice rather than to develop the flavour.

Few plants have a higher level of vitamin C and in World War Two every British schoolchild was issued with a free ration of blackcurrant juice. Even today, 90 per cent of this delicious fruit is used to make the juice, with my home county, Herefordshire, the place that the vast majority of all British blackcurrants are grown. There are few other places in the world where it is grown at all widely. In 1911, black- and redcurrants were prohibited in the USA because it was thought that they spread a virus that damaged pine trees. In New York state this ban was only lifted as recently as 2003.

Blackcurrants' growth and fruiting behaviour and requirements are very different to redcurrants and if grown side by side, one will almost certainly prosper and the other struggle. Whereas redcurrants adapt to shade and poor soil, blackcurrants need lots of sunshine for the new wood and fruit to ripen, so should have the sunniest, best spot you can give them and need a rich, moisture-retentive (but not waterlogged) soil. They should also have a generous mulch of manure or garden compost every spring as much to feed as to preserve moisture and keep down weeds. They are very hungry plants. However, they crop best with exposure to cold weather in winter, and global warming and warm winters may severely limit their cropping.

Birds love all these currants so they must be netted from the time the berries start to ripen to the last picking – about mid-June until mid-August – or else the entire crop can be stripped overnight. A net loosely draped over canes will do, although a more permanent fruit cage is worth it if you have more than a few bushes.

Unlike redcurrants, blackcurrants produce their fruit on new growth. In the first year they produce some fruit, lots in the second year, and the crop begins to fall

Blackcurrants are produced on young wood so, unlike redcurrants, do not need a permanent framework of branches.

off thereafter. So the pruning regime is to remove the oldest third of each bush right down to the ground every year immediately after harvest and certainly no later than September. I often harvest them by pruning whole stems back to the ground, the cut wood deliciously fragrant of fresh berries, and carry a pungent armful of wood loaded with currants into the kitchen where they can be stripped from the stems.

Blackcurrants take easily from hardwood cuttings from pruned material and should be left for a year before transplanting. Keep any buds on the cuttings to encourage bushy growth.

'Ben Sarek' is a compact variety and good for a pot or small space although you will get a bigger harvest from 'Ben Lomond', 'Boskoop Giant' or 'Ben More'.

Blueberries need acidic soil, so I raise them in containers, using a peat-free ericaceous compost, and they grow well like this, giving me lots of delicious berries.

Blueberries

Certain foods belong to certain meals and there is no crossing those divides. So I have marmalade on my breakfast toast but never dream of eating it at any other time of day. Likewise porridge is for breakfast and breakfast only. As it happens, I don't think that I have ever eaten a blueberry save at breakfast time either, but they are delicious, and as I grow them myself and as I grow wild in my old age, I could contemplate blueberries brightening any time of day.

Blueberries have come to us from America and belong to the Vaccinium family that also includes cranberries and our native bilberries. Although cranberries have crossed the Atlantic in the shape of jelly, none of the other berries has become so popular or available as blueberries. Just down the road from where I am writing this are fields and fields of pot-grown blueberries, all probably destined for a supermarket near you.

But you could just as easily grow your own at home. Blueberries need acidic soil, so unless you live in an area that favours rhododendrons, azaleas, heathers, camellias, pieris and most magnolias, they will need growing in a container. This means that any garden, anywhere, can accommodate a bush or two. And, as if the fruit were not incentive enough, they are very decorative plants, with stunning autumn colour ranging from brilliant red through orange and gold.

You will need to buy a peat-free ericaceous potting compost. This is usually made from composted bracken or pine bark. Improve the drainage by mixing in a generous amount of perlite or horticultural grit and if you have leafmould, add about 25 per cent in volume. This will provide the good, loose root run that blueberries like. The pot needs to be generous but no more than twice the size of the container that the plants were sold in, otherwise water and air movement around the roots becomes stagnant and will damage the growing plant. It can always be potted on as and when it outgrows its container. Water plants well and keep them watered, especially in spring and summer when the buds and fruits are forming. But only ever use rainwater as tap water is almost always too alkaline for them.

Position the bushes in a sunny spot or with sun for at least half the day. This will not only help ripen the fruit but also the new wood, which will carry the next season's crop. The better this wood ripens, the better the fruit next year.

The fruit is harvested almost daily as it ripens rather than in one big harvest. Unfortunately, birds like blueberries as much as humans, so they do need netting to protect them or, if the pots are small enough to carry, do as I do and keep them in the greenhouse once the fruit is ripe. They can then be brought outside in autumn.

Pruning is based upon a balance between having enough new stems to provide next year's crop and leaving enough of last year's growth for this season's harvest. The best time to prune is between Christmas and the end of February. Remove all dead or very spindly growth and cut back last year's fruiting stems. Different varieties have different growth patterns but 'Bluecrop' typically produces very vigorous upright growth that must be thinned back to the base, leaving no more than about ten stems per plant.

Rhubarb

One of my March breakfast treats is freshly picked rhubarb eaten with home-made yoghurt. No combination has a cleaner, sharper, more hauntingly sweet taste (although the previous night's cold rhubarb crumble with fresh single cream pushes it hard). It is guaranteed to brighten the sleepiest head and clear your palate and brain for the rigours of the day ahead.

But that sharpness is only made palatable by the presence of some sugar or honey and until sugar became cheap and accessible in the mid-nineteenth century, rhubarb was hardly ever ingested other than for medicinal reasons, and even then, it was the powdered root that was taken as a purgative.

Rhubarb also contains a lot of oxalic acid, which gives it that slightly metallic (and to my mind, attractive) aftertaste, and the foliage has a much higher concentration still, so should never be eaten. However, if you put it onto the compost heap, it will not affect the safety of the resulting compost.

I grow a number of different varieties that provide a staggered harvest from the first fragile shoots that we pick to eat at Christmas to the last harvest at the beginning of July. It is important to stop harvesting around midsummer to give the plant a chance to recharge its roots via the great floppy leaves that the stems carry ready for next year's crop. If you pick everything edible right through into

autumn, you will find that the returns rapidly diminish and the plant will need replacing in a year or two.

When you harvest your rhubarb, never cut the stalks but pull them instead, holding each one low down near its base and giving it a twist as you pull, so that it tears off. Cutting lets in crown rot, which will manifest itself via spindly stems and damaged buds.

Commercial growers look for a very short but very productive life from their rhubarb plants. I remember visiting a rhubarb farm near Wakefield in Yorkshire where the pale stems grew from great lumps of root sitting in rows on concrete. The whole place was kept pitch black so as to reduce the foliage to mere candle flames of leaf – and in fact, the picking back then was still done by candlelight. After the roots were exhausted, the plants were dumped. I brought back a sack of those discarded 'Timperley Early' roots

A terracotta rhubarb forcer excludes light so the stems grow pale, extra early and extra sweet and, unlike those plants growing in full light, with tiny leaves.

and planted them in my garden, and after a bit of horticultural TLC, they are still providing superb rhubarb 25 years later.

'Timperley Early' is, as the name suggests, an early forcing variety but if you do force rhubarb by blocking all light with an old chimney pot or, if you are fortunate to find one, with a proper terracotta rhubarb forcer with a lid, the later growth will be much weaker so I rotate the plants yearly for forcing duty.

Rhubarb should be lifted and divided every few years, like any other herbaceous perennial. Divide the root into a number of sections, each with a visible bud, and put the old, central section on the compost heap. Replant the new pieces with plenty of manure or compost and keep them well watered. Do not pick any stalks from these new sections for the first year and cut the flowers off as they appear. By the second year you should have a good crop and a really good one two years after planting. Then the process can be repeated. If you have more than one plant, then it makes sense to do this to one or two plants at a time so you always have a supply even while the replanted sections are getting going.

Rhubarb likes a deep, rich soil although the crowns can rot if they sit in the wet. It is completely hardy and in fact needs a spell of cold weather to trigger it into stem production.

A few years ago I added three more varieties – 'Victoria', a nineteenth-century favourite, 'Hawke's Champagne', which is supposedly the sweetest of all rhubarbs and a good modern variety, 'Stockbridge Arrow'. All are doing well and add subtle variety to my breakfasts.

Grapes

Climate change is not all bad news. It certainly means that more and more parts of Britain are becoming conducive to growing grapes. We all know that in the last warm period of our modern history – from Roman times until the early Tudor period – there were vineyards all over the country. Most monasteries grew grapes and if you have a south-facing spot, preferably with protection from or absence of late or early frosts in spring and autumn, you can grow good grapes for wine. A bottle of wine takes roughly 1kg (2 ¼lb) of grapes, which is about five clusters or bunches. A healthy vine should produce around 40 clusters a season or up to ten bottles of wine. So plant a dozen vines and you could have a harvest of ten cases of your very own vintage every year.

However, most gardeners treat grapes as soft fruit and grow them with the protection of a greenhouse. If you visit Hampton Court Palace then you will see the great vine, a 'Black Hamburg' variety, planted there in 1768 by Capability Brown. It has a huge root system, which is the engine that produces over 270kg (600lb) of grapes from that one vine every year.

When we built the wooden greenhouse in spring 2013, we left a hole at the base of the south side of the brick wall so that we could plant a 'Black Hamburg' grape in the border outside and train the vine through the hole into the warmth and protection of the greenhouse. This means that whilst the fruit and foliage are growing within the frost-free and sun-baked protection of the greenhouse, the roots stay nice and cool and can grow as wide and deep as they like in our Herefordshire soil.

It is an old-fashioned way to go about things but an ideal solution to the need for rich, deep soil and plenty of moisture at the base of the plant, and as much sunshine as possible for the fruit. I mulch the roots very well each spring and in fact the problem I now have is that the vine has grown so well that I am seriously thinking of doubling the size of the greenhouse to accommodate it. A case of the tail wagging the dog …

You can grow grapes in containers but it is always a compromise and it is better to plant them into the ground if you can. Vines will grow in most soils as long as the drainage is good. The roots go down very deep – up to 9m (30ft) or more – which enables them to withstand drought but means that they are prone to drowning if there is a hard pan below the surface, so prepare the ground by digging deeply. Plant the vine with the point where the rootstock is grafted to the stem clear of the soil. Do not add any compost to the planting hole as this will create a waterlogged sump. Just refill the soil around the roots and firm well.

Vines are greedy and respond directly to feeding, so water well and then mulch very generously with garden compost or well-rotted manure. Top this mulch up

Bunches of 'Black Hamburg' grapes hanging from the vine inside the greenhouse and almost ripe and ready to pick.

every spring, leaving as large an area as you can free from weeds around the base of the vine.

Early in the new year is the best time both to plant a vine and to prune it if you are already growing one. The first year of any vine is really just to establish a healthy root system, so all top-growth should be pruned back by two-thirds, leaving brown, ripened wood. In the second year you should remove any flower trusses unless the vine is very vigorous and healthy, in which case you should restrict them to just two token bunches. In fact, one of the common problems with home-grown vines is that they have far too many grapes, both in number of bunches and per bunch. This results in small fruit of low quality, and letting too much fruit form will also restrict formative growth and put a strain on the roots. Be patient.

There is a great deal of confusion about and instruction on the pruning and training of vines, but in practice this can be kept pretty simple as long as the basic principles of a vine's growth and fruiting are understood.

Grapes form on new wood so the vine needs to be pruned back every year to a permanent framework. Another way of putting this is that the branches that are left when the leaves have fallen will not produce any grapes, so pruning should remove all those, leaving just the basic structure.

Pruning excess foliage in midsummer so the bunches of grapes can have maximum sunshine in order to ripen.

Conventional advice is that vines should be pruned in December or January whilst they are still dormant to avoid bleeding. But when I visited Sunnybank Vine Nursery on the Welsh border where they have the National Collection and over 450 varieties of vine, Sarah Bell – who does all the pruning – said that she will sometimes not prune until April, and that any time between the New Year and as they start into growth is fine.

Above all, do not be frightened to cut hard – vines grow very strongly and always fruit on new growth so will 'repair' any seemingly disastrous cuts extremely quickly. You can do little harm by pruning the entire vine back to a stub with three healthy buds each winter.

My indoor vine has two permanent shoots breaking from one single stem that grows into the greenhouse from the exterior roots. These two shoots are trained along the full length of the greenhouse at head height. Sideshoots break vertically from these two horizontal shoots all along their length. These are trained as permanent cordons, or rods, tied to parallel wires running the length of both sides of the greenhouse, so they make a strong and fixed framework. When freshly pruned in January, it looks like a row of widely spaced railings about 1.5m (5ft) long and 90cm (36in) apart. Although this seems extremely wide spacing, it ensures better grapes and better ventilation. These vertical cordons in turn sprout the sideshoots that will produce the bunches of grapes.

When you first plant a vine it is tremendously exciting to see all the new growth and the bunches of grapes that are

Do not be frightened to cut vines hard as they fruit on new growth and will quickly recover

created on it. But if, like me, you are growing dessert grapes, then all the focus should be on quality rather than quantity. Far better to have ten bunches of fabulous fruit than a hundred of small grapes of inferior quality.

So, as the new sideshoots appear from the vertical cordons, I reduce them to no more than one every 30cm (12in) and cut them right back every year to no more than two buds – mere stubs. Any fresh sideshoots that subsequently appear during the growing season are removed. In midsummer I cut back excess growth again to make sure that the grapes get as much ventilation as possible to avoid fungal problems.

Then, in time, I reduce the grapes to no more than two bunches for each of the sideshoots – which means taking off over half those produced, so that each of the upright cordons carries a maximum of about ten bunches. Even this drastic reduction results in over a hundred bunches from one vine in our fairly small greenhouse, and this is probably too much. Finally, to ensure nice, big individual grapes you should ideally thin each bunch by at least half, cutting out young fruits so that none is touching. This is, however, a counsel of perfection and only for those who enjoy an extremely fiddly job or who have a great deal of time and patience.

Index

Page numbers in *italic* refer
to illustrations.

SECOND EDITION
Senior Designer Barbara Zuniga
Senior Editor Alastair Laing
Project Editor Hilary Mandleberg
Designers Amy Child, Vanessa Hamilton
Editorial Assistant Kiron Gill
Managing Editor Dawn Henderson
Managing Art Editor Marianne Markham
Production Editor Tony Phipps
Production Controller Luca Bazzoli
Jacket Designer Amy Cox
Jacket Editor Lucy Philpott
Art Director Maxine Pedliham
Publishing Director Katie Cowan

Photography Marsha Arnold
Illustration Daniel Crisp

FIRST EDITION
Project Manager Bella Pringle
Designer Anne-Marie Bulat
Senior Managing Editor Anna Kruger
Senior Managing Art Editor Lee Griffiths

This edition published in 2021
First published in Great Britain in 2003 by
Dorling Kindersley Limited
DK, One Embassy Gardens, 8 Viaduct Gardens,
London, SW11 7BW

The authorised representative in the EEA is
Dorling Kindersley Verlag GmbH. Arnulfstr.
124, 80636 Munich, Germany

A CIP catalogue record for this book
is available from the British Library.
ISBN: 978-0-2414-2430-8

Printed and bound in China.

For the curious
www.dk.com

MIX
Paper from
responsible sources
FSC™ C018179

This book was made with Forest Stewardship
Council ™ certified paper – one small step in DK's
commitment to a sustainable future. For more
information go to www.dk.com/our-green-pledge

Acknowledgements

Author's acknowledgements

Normally a book of this kind is a collaboration that is often face to face, with photoshoots involving the design team as well as the photographer, with numerous editorial and design meetings, and with a physical to and for that I have always largely taken for granted. But thanks to Covid-19, almost all this interaction – although real enough – has been remote and the connection has been digital.

The one exception to this has been the connection with Marsha Arnold, who photographed the garden at least once a month for over a year, and working with her – albeit always at a socially distanced two metres – was a joy. I should also like to thank Derry Moore for his superb cover photograph.

My agent Alexandra Henderson supported and encouraged me throughout, and my assistant Polly James did much to create the time and space that allowed me to focus despite rather a lot of other things going on.

At Dorling Kindersley I would particularly like to thank Mary-Clare Jerram for her enthusiasm in setting this new edition up, Barbara Zuniga and Amy Child, who did a superb job designing the book under very difficult circumstances, and my editor, Hilary Mandleberg, who held the whole project together and meticulously steered me through every stage without ever losing her good humour or calm wisdom.

But my greatest thanks is to my wife Sarah, not just for the practicalities of running absolutely everything, but also for making the garden with me over the past quarter of a century. Without her there would have been none of this. None of it at all.

Publisher's acknowledgements

DK would like to thank the following people for help in preparing this book: Tom Morse, Rajdeep Singh, and Sunil Sharma for colour work, Anne Newman for proofreading, and Marie Lorimer for indexing.

Picture credits

The publisher would like to thank the following for their kind permission to reproduce their photographs:
(Key: a-above; b-below/bottom; c-centre; f-far; l-left; r-right; t-top)
Cover photographs: Derry Moore (front), Marsha Arnold (back). 10 Monty Don: (tl, tr, cl, bl, br, cr). 11 Monty Don: (t, cl, cr, bl, br). 260 Dorling Kindersley: Mark Winwood / RHS Wisley. 330 Dorling Kindersley: Alan Buckingham. 335 Marsha Arnold. 353 Marsha Arnold. 379 Dorling Kindersley: Mark Winwood / RHS Wisley (bc, br). 382 Dorling Kindersley: Mark Winwood / Hampton Court Flower Show 2014. 387 Dorling Kindersley: Peter Anderson / RHS Hampton Court Flower Show 2010 (tr); Mark Winwood / RHS Wisley (cr). 388 Getty Images: Reggie Casagrande / Photodisc. 413 Dorling Kindersley: Alan Buckingham. 425 Dorling Kindersley: Alan Buckingham / Hampton Court Flower Show 2009. 427 Marsha Arnold

All other images © Dorling Kindersley
For further information see: **www.dkimages.com**